CONTENTS

INTRODUCTION TO ACCOUNTING

SECOND EDITION

J. R. Edwards and H. J. Mellett

P·C·P
Paul Chapman
Publishing Ltd

Paul Chapman Publishing Ltd
144 Liverpool Road
London
N1 1LA

British Library Cataloguing in Publication Data

Edwards, J. R.
  Introduction to Accounting. – 2Rev.ed. –
  (PCP Accounting & Finance Series)
  I. Title   II. Mellett , H. J.   III. Series 657

  ISBN 1–85396–278–3

Typeset by Anneset, Weston-super-Mare, Avon
Printed and bound by The Cromwell Press, Wiltshire

C D E F G H   9 8 7

SERIES EDITOR'S PREFACE

The second edition of *Introduction to Accounting* has been thoroughly revised to reflect recent developments in both the theory and practice of accounting. It has retained, however, the highly readable style which made the first edition so popular.

Each chapter of the second edition now begins with a statement of the learning objectives. This provides a clear and concise summary of the concepts and techniques to be covered in the chapter. Students are then able to use the questions at the end of each chapter, many of which have suggested solutions at the end of the book, to assess their progress towards achieving these learning objectives.

The requirement that companies publish cash flow statements in addition to a profit and loss account and balance sheet, is now recognised by the inclusion of a separate, new chapter devoted to the subject. The authors provide a detailed description of the cash flow statement and how it is derived from the other primary financial statements. In addition, and very innovatively, they demonstrate how the cash flow statement can be used as a technique alongside ratio analysis to interpret and explain a company's financial performance during the year.

The main emphasis of the second edition, as with the first, is on financial accounting, including the preparation and interpretation of the principal financial statements to be found in the accounts of sole traders, partnerships and companies. However, the authors recognise the increasing importance of accounting for management decisions within the organisation. In addition to a revised chapter on the use of accounting information for decision making, the authors have included a completely new chapter on standard costing and budgetary control.

Throughout the book the authors have used illustrations from the published accounts of actual companies to make the subject come alive. The authors also have an ability to describe the concepts and techniques of accounting in a style which will appeal both to students on specialist accountancy courses and to students taking accounting as an option in a business studies or management course. This book has already stood the test of time, and the second edition will ensure that it will remain one of the best introductory textbooks on accounting.

Michael Sherer
Colchester, 1995

PREFACE

Recent years have seen an increasing interest in the study of accounting both as a subject in its own right and as an adjunct to other disciplines, such as engineering and medicine. This trend reflects recognition of the fact that the financial aspects of human enterprise cannot be ignored; the activities of almost any undertaking have financial consequences which should be measured and controlled, and this requires the involvement of someone versed in the appropriate techniques. However, it must be remembered that the operation of an accounting system is itself neutral, and the financial information produced has to be interpreted and its relevance weighed, alongside other considerations, before decisions are made. This process requires that the users of accounting information understand what lies behind it and the extent of its uses and limitations.

The authors have produced this book to provide an introduction to accounting which embraces both the basic techniques and the underlying theoretical concepts and shows how these are applied in various circumstances. It is designed to meet the needs of both the non-specialist and those intending to qualify, in due course, as accountants. To meet these objectives the text is fully illustrated with worked examples and, for reinforcement, the text contains chapter-end questions of varying complexity. The solutions to approximately half of these questions are given in the Appendix at the end of the book. The remaining solutions are included in a tutor's manual.

Questions in the book and companion manual have been taken from the papers of the following examining bodies: Royal Society of Arts; Association of Accounting Technicians; London Chamber of Commerce and Industry; The Chartered Association of Certified Accountants; The Institute of Chartered Secretaries and Administrators; and The Associated Examining Board. We gratefully acknowledge permission granted by the examining bodies to reproduce questions contained in these texts; the contents of the solutions are entirely our responsibility. The particular examinations of these bodies for which this book is appropriate are set out in the 'Matrix of subjects covered and examining bodies' immediately following the preface.

The book has been designed to be read in chapter order, and readers are advised to follow this. The first three chapters introduce the subject, the balance sheet, and the calculation of profit as an increase in the value of an enterprise. Chapter 4 examines one of the most basic records, that of cash received and paid, and shows how its contents are converted into a comprehensive set of accounting statements. Chapters 5 to 7 cover the accounting process based on the double entry system of book-keeping from the initial record of each transaction through to the production of a final report. By this stage the reader should have grasped the underlying techniques, and Chapter 8 discusses the more subjective areas of asset valuation and profit measurement. Chapters 9 and 10 consider the application of accounting theory and techniques to specific forms of enterprise, namely partnerships and limited companies, while Chapter 11 covers the use of techniques in certain specialized areas.

Chapters 12 and 13 deal with the role of the cash flow statement and ratio analysis in the interpretation of financial information. Chapters 14 and 15 focus on aspects of costing relevant to an introductory text on accounting; specifically, the calculation of total cost, the use of costs as the basis for decision-making and the operation of systems of standard costing and budgetary control.

The second edition naturally includes numerous minor changes to bring it up to date. The major differences compared with the first edition are as follows:

- The inclusion of a statement of learning objectives at the beginning of each chapter.
- The revision of Chapter 10 to incorporate recent developments in the regulation of company accounts, including the establishment of the Financial Reporting Council and the Accounting Standards Board.
- The amendment of Chapter 10 to provide students with an appreciation of the nature and purpose of group accounts.
- Chapter 12 on the statement of source and application of funds has been replaced by a chapter on the cash flow statement to reflect the replacement of SSAP 10 by FRS 1.
- Chapter 14 on decision-making has been expanded to incorporate material on total costing and overhead recovery rates including reference to the place of activity-based costing in this process.
- A new chapter has been added to provide students with an understanding of the nature and operation of systems of standard costing and budgetary control.
- The chapter on computers and accountancy contained in the first edition has been removed. Reference is made at various points in the text to the relevance of computers for matters discussed, but the technical procedures are left to the specialist texts which have developed in large numbers since the date of the first edition.

We are grateful to the Chartered Institute of Bankers for permission to include extracts from *Introduction to Accountancy for Banking Students* written by the same authors and published by the institute.

MATRIX OF SUBJECTS COVERED AND EXAMINING BODIES

AEB Accounting 0600 and 0978; AAT Accounting paper 5; RSA Accounting Stage II (QP 201); LCCI Book-Keeping and Accounts, 2nd level (2006); ACCA Foundation Stage; ICSA Introduction to Accounting

	AEB	AAT	RSA	LCCI	ACCA	ICSA
CHAPTER 1						
The accounting process	X	X	X	X	X	X
Suppliers of accounting information	X	X	X	X	X	X
Financial/management accounting compared	X	X	X	X	X	X
External users	X	X	X	X	X	X
Principal statements	X	X	X	X	X	X
CHAPTER 2						
The entity concept	X	X	X	X	X	X
Reporting capital	X	X	X	X	X	X
Raising further finance	X	X	X	X	X	X
Investment decision	X	X	X	X	X	X
Business development	X	X	X	X	X	X
Trading cycle	X	X	X	X	X	X
Changes in capital	X	X	X	X	X	X
A = C + L	X	X	X	X	X	X
Assets and sources of finance	X	X	X	X	X	X
Valuation of assets	X	X	X	X	X	X
CHAPTER 3						
Profitable activity	X	X	X	X	X	X
Profit and gross assets	X	X	X	X	X	X
Vertical format	X	X	X	X	X	X
Profits and losses	X	X	X	X	X	X
Profit = Capital change	X	X	X	X	X	X
Capital injections and withdrawals	X	X	X	X	X	X
CHAPTER 4						
Accounting systems	X	X	X	X	X	X
Matching concept	X	X	X	X	X	X
Gross and net profit	X	X	X	X	X	X
Periodic profit	X	X	X	X	X	X
Realization concept	X	X	X	X	X	X
Matching	X	X	X	X	X	X
Accounts from cash records	X	X	X	X	X	X
Clubs and societies	X	X	X	X	X	

	AEB	AAT	RSA	LCCI	ACCA	ICSA
CHAPTER 5						
Cash flows	X	X	X	X	X	X
Flows of goods and services	X	X	X	X	X	X
CHAPTER 6						
Interlocking effect	X	X	X	X	X	X
Ledger accounts	X	X	X	X	X	X
Books of prime entry	X	X	X	X	X	X
Control accounts	X	X	X	X	X	X
Trial balance	X	X	X	X	X	X
Computerization	X				X	
Double entry	X	X	X	X	X	X
CHAPTER 7						
Periodic accounts	X	X	X	X	X	X
Adjustments	X	X	X	X	X	X
Stocks	X	X	X	X	X	X
Depreciation	X	X	X	X	X	X
Fixed asset disposal	X	X	X	X	X	X
Prepayments and accruals	X	X	X	X	X	X
Bad debts	X	X	X	X	X	X
Adjusted TB	X	X	X	X	X	X
CHAPTER 8						
Asset valuation	X	X	X		X	X
Tangible fixed assets	X	X	X		X	X
Reducing balance	X	X	X		X	X
Intangible fixed assets	X	X	X		X	X
Stock valuation	X	X	X		X	X
Concepts	X	X	X		X	X
CHAPTER 9						
Partnership agreement	X	X	X	X	X	
Creation	X	X	X	X		X
Profit division	X	X	X	X	X	
Capital and current accounts	X	X	X	X		X
Membership changes	X		X	X	X	
Profit ratio	X		X	X		X
Dissolution				X	X	
CHAPTER 10						
Formation	X	X		X	X	X
Annual report	X	X		X	X	X
Other sources of information	X	X		X	X	X
Share capital	X	X	X	X	X	X
Share premium	X	X	X	X	X	X
Share forfeiture	X	X		X	X	X
Rights issue	X	X		X	X	X
Loan capital and debentures	X	X	X	X	X	X

	AEB	AAT	RSA	LCCI	ACCA	ICSA
Appropriation account	X	X	X	X	X	X
Revaluation reserve	X	X		X	X	X
Debenture redemption	X	X		X	X	X
Bonus issue	X	X		X	X	X
Limitations of accounts	X	X		X	X	X
CHAPTER 11						
Manufacturing account		X	X	X		
Departmental accounts						
Branch accounts	X			X		
Instalment credit	X					
Business transfer						
VAT		X				
Stock and cash losses			X			
CHAPTER 12						
Cash flow format			X		X	X
Construction			X		X	X
Complexities			X		X	X
Interpretation			X		X	X
CHAPTER 13						
Profit and cash	X	X	X	X	X	X
ROCE	X	X	X	X	X	X
Profit ratios	X	X	X	X	X	X
Solvency ratios	X	X	X	X	X	X
Asset turnover ratios	X	X	X	X	X	X
Gearing	X	X	X		X	X
Cash flow			X		X	X
Limitations	X	X			X	X
Cash flow ratios			X		X	X
CHAPTER 14						
Cost behaviour	X		X			X
Total costing	X					X
Investment appraisal	X					
Forecast results						
CHAPTER 15						
Budgetary control	X					X
Budget preparation	X					X
Standard costing	X					
Variances	X					

1
THE FRAMEWORK OF ACCOUNTING

The objectives of this chapter are to

- explain the accounting and decision-making process;
- identify the main entities involved in the supply of accounting information;
- distinguish between financial accounting and management accounting;
- identify the external users of accounting information; and
- outline the nature and content of the principal accounting statements.

THE ACCOUNTING PROCESS

Accounting is a data-processing system that has been vividly described as the 'language of business'. It may be defined as a system for recording and reporting business transactions, in financial terms, to interested parties who use this information as the basis for performance assessment, decision-making and control.

The various stages in the accounting and decision-making process are presented diagrammatically in Figure 1.1. It can be seen that the accounting process contains two basic elements, namely recording business transactions (stages 1–5) and reporting financial information to enable decisions to be taken (stages 6–10). These are inter-related since accounting records form the basis for accounting reports.

The accounting process begins with an economic event, such as the receipt of goods from a supplier. An originating document or voucher is then made out to record the movement of goods, services or cash into, within or out of a business. It is important that the document is made out immediately, since any delay increases the risk of an error that can undermine the entire accounting process. The term 'garbage in, garbage out' has been coined to describe the effect, on the information system, of starting with incorrect data.

Documents and vouchers quite naturally originate in many different departments of a company, but copies of all of them are sent to the accounts department where they are summarized, analysed and then entered in the books of account. Periodically, at least once a year but probably more often, the balances are extracted from the ledger accounts and assembled in a 'trial balance'. This is used as the basis for preparing the final accounts, which consists of a profit and loss account and a balance sheet. These accounting

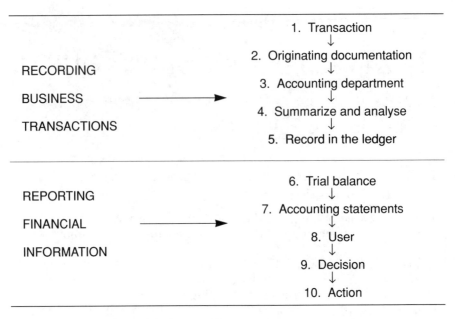

Figure 1.1 Accounting and decision-making process

statements are then made available to both management and a variety of 'external' users (see later in this chapter) to help them reach better informed decisions than would otherwise have been possible – for example, the financial statements prepared for a well-known company, such as The Boots Company plc, may indicate that good progress has been made over the last year. On this basis, an individual might decide to purchase some of the company's shares. That individual will use financial statements subsequently published by Boots to judge whether the performance has come up to expectations and whether to retain the shareholding, add to it or sell the shares.

The profit and loss account and balance sheets of Boots for 1993 are given in Figure 1.2.

SUPPLIERS OF ACCOUNTING INFORMATION

Suppliers of accounting information include the following business units operating in the *private* sector of the economy. They are listed in no particular order of priority:

1. *Sole traders* These are businesses that have a single owner who also takes all the major managerial decisions. Operations are usually on a small scale, and typical examples are an electrician, the local newsagent and the milkman. The main reason why accounts are prepared for the sole trader is to help establish the amount of income tax due to the Inland Revenue. He or she makes little use of accounting statements for business decisions that he or she instead bases on knowledge obtained as a result of direct

Group Profit and Loss Account for the year ended 31st March 1993

	Notes	1993 £m	1992 £m
Turnover from continuing operations	2	3,962.1	3,660.3
Cost of sales		(2,129.4)	(1,995.7)
Gross profit		1,832.7	1,664.6
Operating costs less other income	3	(1,411.0)	(1,265.0)
Operating profit from continuing operations	3	421.7	399.6
Provision for loss on discontinued operations sold in prior years	4	—	(15.8)
Profit on ordinary activities before interest		421.7	383.8
Net interest	5	(16.5)	(43.1)
Profit on ordinary activities before taxation	2	405.2	340.7
Taxation on profit on ordinary activities	6	(124.4)	(109.7)
Profit on ordinary activities after taxation		280.8	231.0
Minority interests		(1.7)	(1.5)
Profit for the financial year attributable to shareholders	7	279.1	229.5
Dividends	8	(139.0)	(126.4)
Profit retained		140.1	103.1

Balance Sheets, 31st March 1993

	Notes	Group 1993 £m	Group 1992 £m	Parent 1993 £m	Parent 1992 £m
Fixed assets					
Intangible assets	10	52.1	58.1	9.0	10.3
Tangible assets	11	1,397.7	1,568.2	213.8	190.2
Investments	12	70.8	57.5	912.1	951.5
		1,520.6	1,683.8	1,134.9	1,152.0
Current assets					
Stocks	13	553.0	519.6	186.2	147.5
Debtors (see note below)	14	346.9	287.1	560.0	633.6
Investments	15	364.1	187.6	184.4	51.2
Cash at bank and in hand		10.9	10.3	.2	.1
		1,274.9	1,004.6	930.8	832.4
Creditors: Amounts falling due within one year	16	(897.4)	(986.2)	(645.3)	(790.0)
Net current assets		377.5	18.4	285.5	42.4
Total assets less current liabilities		1,898.1	1,702.2	1,420.4	1,194.4

Creditors: Amounts falling due after more than one year	17	**(385.0)**	(230.6)	**(541.7)**	(358.9)
Provisions for liabilities and charges	19	**(27.9)**	(34.6)	**(4.8)**	(6.6)
Net assets		**1,485.2**	1,437.0	**873.9**	828.9
Capital and reserves					
Called up share capital	20	**259.5**	250.1	**259.5**	250.1
Share premium account	21	**196.0**	80.9	**196.0**	80.9
Revaluation reserve	21	**292.2**	528.3	—	—
Profit and loss account	21	**730.9**	572.6	**418.4**	497.9
Shareholders' funds		**1,478.6**	1,431.9	**873.9**	828.9
Minority interests		**6.6**	5.1	—	—
		1,485.2	1,437.0	**873.9**	828.9

Figure 1.2 Profit and loss account and balance sheets of The Boots Company plc,

contact with all aspects of business activity.

2. *Partnerships* These exist where two or more individuals join together to undertake some form of business activity. The partners share between them ownership of the business and the obligation to manage its operations. Professional people, such as accountants, solicitors and doctors, commonly organize their business activities in the form of partnerships. Accounting statements are required as a basis for allocating profits between the partners and, again, for agreeing tax liabilities with the Inland Revenue.

3. *Clubs and societies* There are, in Britain, many thousands of clubs and societies organized for recreational, educational, religious, charitable and other purposes. Members invariably pay an annual subscription and management powers are delegated to a committee elected by the members. The final accounts prepared for (usually large) societies, formed by registering with the Registrar of Friendly Societies, are often controlled by statute. For the local club or society, the form of the accounts is either laid down in the internal rules and regulations or decided at the whim of the treasurer. Conventional accounting procedures are sometimes ignored in a small organization. Reasons for this are lack of expertise, the meagre quantity of assets belonging to the organization and the fact that the accounts are of interest only to the members.

4. *Limited companies* A limited company is formed by registering, under the Companies Act, with the Registrar of Companies and complying with certain formalities. The company may be private, indicated by the letters Ltd at the end of its name, or public, in which case the designatory letters are plc. The main significance of the distinction is that only the latter can make an issue of shares to the general public. In the case of public companies there is the further distinction between quoted companies, whose shares are traded on the stock exchange, and unquoted companies. In general, public companies are larger than private companies and quoted companies larger than unquoted.

The directors of all limited companies are under a legal obligation to prepare and publish accounts, at least once in every year, which comply with the requirements of the Companies Act. (It should be noted that there are also in existence a small number of unlimited companies – for example, this method of incorporation is sometimes used by professional firms who are not allowed to have limited liability but want the tax advantages of being a company.)

A limited company may, alternatively, be formed by means of either a private Act of Parliament or a royal charter. These are called statutory and chartered companies respectively. The form of their accounts may be regulated by the charter or statute. In addition, it is normal practice to comply with the general requirements of the Companies Acts.

Reporting units in the *public* sector include local authorities, nationalized industries, state colleges and the health service. These are outside the scope of this book, although many of the accounting techniques they employ are exactly the same as those used by organizations in the private sector.

FINANCIAL ACCOUNTING AND MANAGEMENT ACCOUNTING COMPARED

A conventional division of accounting is into financial accounting and management accounting. The former is concerned with the provision of accounting information for external user groups while the latter concentrates on the provision of information for management. The principal accounting statements – the balance sheet and the profit and loss account – are of interest to internal and external users but, when presented to the latter, they will normally be in a condensed form. It will be noticed that the final accounts of Boots (Figure 1.2) summarize on a single sheet the financial effect of millions of individual transactions. For example, the balance sheet reports total assets of £2,795.5 million (fixed assets £1,520.6 million + current assets £1,274.9 million) divided into just seven categories: intangible assets, £52.1 million; tangible assets, £1,397.7 million; investments held long term, £70.8 million; stocks, £553 million; debtors, £346.9 million; investments held on a temporary basis, £364.1 million; and cash, £10.9 million.

The main factor affecting the amount of detail contained in the accounts is the requirements of the user group. In general, external users wish to assess the overall performance of the entity and an enormous amount of detail is inappropriate both because it is of little interest and because it is likely to obscure the important trends. It is mainly for this reason that information is presented in a highly summarized form in published accounts. A further reason is that the disclosure of too much detail might be used by competitors to analyse the company's strengths and weaknesses.

Financial statements prepared for management contain much more detail. The explanation for this difference may be found in the types of decision to be taken. Shareholders base their decision to sell shares, retain their investment or buy more shares mainly on the level of reported profit and dividends declared. Management, in contrast, is keenly interested in the costs and revenues that make up the profit figure. This is because they are responsible for taking the following kinds of decisions which influence *individual items* of revenue and expenditure: whether to expand or contract production; whether to substitute one material for another, or one type of worker for another; whether to replace labour-intensive production methods by machinery; whether to acquire property instead of renting it; and which type of power supply to use. In many instances reports must be specially prepared to help reach these decisions, and appraisal techniques have been developed to help the management process. After the decisions have been made, the outcome is monitored to see the extent to which expectations have been fulfilled.

This book introduces accounting techniques that form the basis for both branches of accounting – financial and management – although individual chapters or sections of chapters focus on specialist aspects of each. Chapters 2–8 deal, in detail, with the calculation of profit, the valuation of assets and the preparation of the profit and loss account and balance sheet. As has already been explained, these documents are widely used by both internal and external consumers of accounting information. Chapters 9–11 cover the application of certain specialized accounting techniques and identify the distinctive features of final accounts prepared for partnerships and limited companies. Chapters 12 and 13 explain how the information contained in the accounts may be analysed and interpreted to help both internal and external users decide how to commit resources at their disposal. Chapters 14 and 15 contain an introduction to some of the important accounting techniques used by management for the purposes of planning business activity, allocating resources and monitoring progress made.

EXTERNAL USERS OF ACCOUNTING INFORMATION

In 1975 the accounting profession published a discussion document, called *The Corporate Report*, in an attempt to stimulate interest in the scope and aims of financial reports in the light of modern needs and conditions. The following seven user groups were identified as having a reasonable claim to corporate financial information:

1. The equity investor group made up of existing and potential shareholders.
2. The loan creditor group made up of present and potential holders of debentures and loan stock, and providers of short-term loans and finance.
3. The employee group made up of existing, potential and past employees.
4. The adviser group made up of financial analysts and journalists, economists, statisticians, researchers, trade unions, stockbrokers and credit-rating agencies.
5. The business contact group made up of customers, suppliers, competitors, business rivals, and those interested in mergers, amalgamations and takeovers.
6. The government, particularly the tax authorities, departments and agencies concerned with the supervision of commerce and industry, and local authorities.
7. The public, including taxpayers, ratepayers, consumers and other

community and special interest groups such as political parties, consumer and environmental protection societies and regional pressure groups.

Each of the above groups has a common interest in company accounts, but they use financial information as the basis for quite different decisions. For instance, shareholders require assistance to help reach share-trading decisions, i.e. whether to retain their present investment, increase it or sell. Employees require financial information to help assess employment prospects and also for the purpose of collective bargaining. Suppliers require accounting information to decide whether to advance credit to a potential customer. Loan creditors, such as the bank, need accounting information to help decide whether to make an initial advance, and to monitor progress and the ability of the customer to repay the amount due at the end of the loan period. A marked deterioration in the company's financial position might well cause the bank to call in the loan before the financial position deteriorates even further.

There are significant variations in the quantity of financial information made available to each of these groups. This results from differential legal requirements, voluntary decisions by management to make financial information available to particular users and the ability of certain individuals to insist on additional disclosures.

PRINCIPAL ACCOUNTING STATEMENTS

The two main accounting statements, the profit and loss account and the balance sheet, are now introduced in a little more detail.

The profit and loss account
Revenues are generated and costs are incurred as the result of undertaking business activity. These revenues and costs are summarized in the profit and loss account, which may be prepared to cover a week, a month, a year or any other chosen interval. Provided total revenue exceeds total expenditure a profit is earned; in the converse situation a loss is suffered.

The published profit and loss account of Boots (Figure 1.2) covers the twelve months to 31 March 1993. The account starts with turnover and, from this figure, is deducted cost of sales to arrive at the figure for gross profit and, from this figure, are deducted operating costs to produce the figure for operating profit. Interest payable (net of interest receivable) to providers of loan finance is then deducted to give the figure for profit before tax. Taxation is then deducted and, next, the amount due to the minority interest (the latter item appears only in accounts prepared for 'groups' of companies – see Chapter 10). Finally, dividends payable to shareholders are deducted to leave the balance of profit retained and reinvested in the business. Full details of each of these items is given in notes 2–8 to the accounts (not reproduced).

The advantages of the profit and loss account are that it sets out the following information: whether a profit has been earned; how much profit has been earned; how the profit figure has been arrived at; and how the profit is appropriated between taxation, dividends and the amount retained for reinvestment.

The balance sheet

This sets out the financial position of the business at a chosen point in time. It is the date to which the profit and loss account is made up. The most common accounting dates are the calendar-year end (31 December) and the tax-year end (31 March).

An obvious difference between the profit and loss account and balance sheet is that, whereas the former reports inflows and outflows of resources over a period of time, the latter sets out the assets and liabilities at a particular point in time. It is for this reason that the balance sheet has been likened to a financial photograph of a business. Like all photographs, the position just before or just afterwards may be entirely different. This provides scope for management to undertake cosmetic exercises that present the company's position in the best possible light. For example, it might borrow money just before the year end in order to inflate the cash balance and make repayment on the first day of the next accounting period. Such devices are called 'window dressing' and it is part of the auditor's job to ensure that decision-makers are not misled by the adoption of such procedures.

The balance sheet of Boots shows fixed assets of £1,520.6 million and current assets of £1,274.9 million. Moving down the balance sheet a range of liabilities are then deducted made up of creditors due for payment within one year and creditors and provisions due for payment in more than one year's time. The 'net asset' figure is £1,485.2 million. The remainder of the statement shows how these assets have been financed by shareholders in the form of capital and reserves.

The aim of a business is to make a profit and, if this objective is achieved, the financial position of the business improves and the assets increase. Certainly this is happening at Boots where the shareholders' interest at the end of March 1993 amounts to £1,478.6 million compared with £1,431.9 million a year earlier.

The preparation of the balance sheet is examined in Chapters 2 and 3, and readers are introduced to the profit and loss account in Chapter 4.

2
THE BALANCE SHEET

The objectives of this chapter are to

- explain the nature and purpose of the 'entity' concept;
- outline the relationship between 'assets' and 'sources of finance' as disclosed in the balance sheet;
- explain the impact of individual transactions on both sides of the balance sheet;
- demonstrate the impact of profit on assets and on the owner's capital;
- show how assets and sources of finance are presented in the balance sheet, distinguishing between 'fixed assets' and 'current assets' on the one hand and 'capital', 'current liabilities' and 'non-current liabilities' on the other;
- outline different possible ways of valuing assets; and
- explain why historical cost is widely used for reporting purposes.

THE ENTITY CONCEPT

In Chapter 1 we saw that there are three main forms of trading organization (clubs and societies don't usually trade) within the private sector of the economy – the sole trader, the partnership and the limited company. There are two important differences between sole traders and partnerships (sometimes referred to as 'firms') on the one hand and limited companies on the other:

1. *The relationship between ownership and management* In the case of firms, the owner or owners also run the business, whereas in the case of the limited company there may well be a significant separation between the ownership and managerial functions. This is particularly likely in the case of the public limited company where the bulk of the finance is provided by the general public.
2. *The owner's liability for business debts* Sole traders and partners normally have unlimited liability for the debts of their firm, whereas the shareholders of limited companies are not required to contribute beyond the amount originally paid for shares issued by the company.

The latter distinction is significant when a business runs into financial difficulties. In the case of firms, the creditors claim first against the business assets but, if these are insufficient to satisfy the amounts due, creditors can then claim against the owner's personal wealth. In an extreme situation, the owner of a bankrupt firm could be forced to sell his or her home and all other personal belongings to meet demands from the firm's creditors. (It is to avoid this outcome that a person in business sometimes transfers the ownership of personal assets to his or her spouse.) This contrasts with the relative position of investors and creditors of a limited company, where any deficiency of business assets compared with liabilities at the date of liquidation is borne by the creditors.

Company law, therefore, regards a limited company as a separate legal entity. The creditor contracts with the company and can claim only against its assets. No such legal distinction is recognized where the business is carried on by a sole trader or by partners. *The position in accountancy is quite different*. It is always assumed, for accounting purposes, that the business entity has an existence separate and distinct from owners, managers or any other individuals with whom it comes into contact during the course of its trading activities. The assumption of a separate existence, usually referred to as the *entity concept*, requires a careful distinction to be drawn between business affairs and personal transactions. One of the reasons for requiring this distinction to be made is that it facilitates performance assessment. A sole trader forms a business in the hope that it will earn him or her a satisfactory profit and, to discover whether this objective has been achieved, profit must be calculated only on the basis of business transactions.

Illustration 2.1

On 1 January 19X1 Mr Old was made redundant and received £30,000 in compensation. He used the cash as follows:
(a)   Purchased a sports car – £19,500.
(b)   Arranged the redecoration of his house – £1,000.
(c)   Paid off his personal overdraft – £3,500.
(d)   Decided to form a business called Old Ventures and, as a first step, opened a business bank account and paid in £6,000.

To comply with the entity concept it is necessary to distinguish between Mr Old's personal transactions and the business transactions of Old Ventures. An examination of the above information shows (a), (b) and (c) to be personal transactions and (d) to be a business transaction.

Readers should now work Question 2.1 at the end of the chapter. In all cases readers should work the question *and only then compare their answer with the solution provided in the appendix at the end of the book*. (Only the odd-numbered solutions are given in the appendix – as are solutions 6.2 and 6.4–6.6; all other even-numbered solutions are to be found in the *Solutions Manual*.)

REPORTING CAPITAL IN THE BALANCE SHEET

Because the business is regarded as a separate accounting entity, all business transactions must be recorded *twice*: *first*, to show the effect of the transaction on the assets belonging to the business; and *second*, to show the effect of the transaction on the relationship between the business, on the one hand, and providers of finance on the other.

Applying this rule to transaction (d) in Illustration 2.1 we find that its effect is as follows:

Effect on business assets:	Assets increase from zero to £6,000 as the result of the injection of cash.
Effect on relationship with providers of finance:	The business now owes Mr Old £6,000.

The financial effect of this transaction may be presented in a balance sheet in the following manner:

Illustration 2.2

Balance Sheet of Old Ventures at 1 January 19X1

Assets	£	Sources of finance	£
Cash at bank	6,000	Capital: Mr Old	6,000

The left side of the balance sheet shows that the assets belonging to the business consist of cash amounting to £6,000. The right side of the balance sheet shows that Mr Old is owed £6,000. Put another way, the right-hand side shows that Mr Old has made an investment of £6,000 in the business. This is called his capital. Readers should note that there is numerical equality between the two sides of the balance sheet. This must always be the case. Assets belonging to the business are not conjured out of 'thin air' and must have been financed in some way or another. The corresponding finance is shown on the right side of the balance sheet and the following fundamental equation continues throughout the life of the business:

Assets = Sources of finance

We may therefore describe the balance sheet as a financial statement that shows on the one side the assets belonging to the business and on the other the way in which those assets have been financed.

Two obvious differences should be noted between the above balance sheet and that given for Boots in Chapter 1, Figure 1.2:

1. The balance sheet of Boots contains much more information. This is because it has been in business for many years, and the balance sheet reports the accumulated financial effect of literally millions of transactions undertaken between the date of formation and 31 March 1993. Old Ventures, by way of contrast, has only just been formed and has undertaken a single transaction.
2. The balance sheet of Boots is presented in vertical format with the assets listed *above* the sources of finance. The balance sheet of Old Ventures is presented in horizontal format with assets on the left and sources of finance on the right. Either presentation is perfectly legal.

RAISING FURTHER FINANCE

Before a business commences operations, sufficient finance should be raised to support the planned level of activity. Too many businesses begin their lives with insufficient cash resources and most of them fail before they get off the ground. At best, the early years of the firm's life are marked by a continuous shortage of cash and much of management's time is taken up coping with cash flow problems rather than being directed towards the development of profitable trading activities.

Mr Old has made a personal investment of £6,000 in Old Ventures (see Illustration 2.2), and we will assume that he has estimated that a total initial investment of £10,000 is required to finance the planned level of business operations. He is £4,000 short and is likely to explore a number of avenues in the endeavour to obtain this sum and to place the business on a sound financial footing. One possibility is to borrow from family, friends or the bank; another is to seek government aid; and a third might involve acquiring some of the business assets on hire purchase. We will assume that Mr Old convinces his bank manager that there are sound prospects for Old Ventures and on 2 January the bank lends his business £4,000. The effect of the transaction is as follows:

Effect on business assets: Cash increases by £4,000.

Effect on relationship   Indebtedness to bank
with providers of finance: increases from zero to
                                          £4,000.

Illustration 2.3

The revised balance sheet becomes as follows.

Balance Sheet of Old Ventures at 2 January 19X1

Assets	£	Sources of finance	£
Cash at bank	10,000	Capital	6,000
		Loan from bank	4,000
	10,000		10,000

The equality between assets and sources of finance is retained with the increase in business assets financed by the bank loan. There are now, however, two different types of finance. The amount advanced by Mr Old, his capital, is a permanent investment that will not usually be withdrawn until the business is wound up, whereas the amount advanced by the bank is a liability that must be repaid in due course. The relationship Assets = Sources of finance, therefore, needs to be extended as follows, by dividing the sources of finance into its two component parts:

$$\text{Assets} = \text{Capital} + \text{Liabilities}$$

This may be abbreviated to

$$A = C + L$$

Readers should test their understanding of this relationship by working Question 2.2 at the end of this chapter.

THE INVESTMENT DECISION

It is the job of management to employ profitably the resources that have been placed at its disposal, and to carry out this function many decisions have to be made. These result in a continuous flow of cash and other assets into, through and out of the business. Accounting statements, among which the balance sheet is one of the most important, are prepared at regular intervals to enable management to monitor the results of their decisions and to gauge the extent to which they are achieving the objective of profit maximization. In the case of Old Ventures, Mr Old, when performing his managerial role, must decide how to employ the cash available to the business, i.e. he must make an *investment decision*. Mr Old decides to go into business as an antique dealer and purchases a small warehouse for cash, £7,000, on 10 January 19X1. On the same day he acquired various relics, second-hand goods and memorabilia (this is called his *stock-in-trade*) for cash, £2,500. The effect of these transactions is as follows:

Effect on business assets:	Premises increase by £7,000.
	Stock-in-trade increases by £2,500.
	Cash at bank reduces by £9,500.
Effect on relationship with outsiders:	Zero.

Illustration 2.4

Balance Sheet of Old Ventures at 10 January 19X1

Assets	£	Sources of finance	£
Premises	7,000	Capital	6,000
Stocks*	2,500	Loan from bank	4,000
Cash at bank	500		
	10,000		10,000

Note
* This is the commonly used abbreviation for stock-in-trade.

Illustration 2.4 sets out the revised financial position of Old Ventures at 10 January. No additional sources of finance have been raised and the right-hand side of the balance sheet remains unchanged. The effect of the investment decision is merely to cause a reallocation of resources between business assets.

Before Old Ventures is ready to commence trading, Mr Old must make sure that his display of antiques is sufficiently extensive to attract customers into his warehouse. Let us assume that a further consignment of furniture, costing £2,000, is required for this purpose. The above balance sheet shows that the company has insufficient cash available for this purpose and an additional source of finance must be obtained. In practice, very few businesses operate entirely on the cash basis. Instead, a proportion – often a high proportion – of purchases and sales are made on credit, i.e. a period of time elapses between the dates that goods are supplied and paid for. Normally businesses take the maximum period of credit allowed because, during this time, stock is financed by suppliers rather than by the firm itself. The period of credit allowed by suppliers varies a great deal but thirty days is most common.

Old Ventures takes delivery of furniture costing £2,000 on 11 January 19X1. The supplier allows thirty days credit. The effect of the transaction is as follows:

Effect on business assets: Stock-in-trade increases by £2,000.

Effect on relationship with outsiders: Trade creditors increase by £2,000.

Illustration 2.5

Balance Sheet of Old Ventures at 11 January 19X1

Assets	£	Sources of finance	£
Premises	7,000	Capital	6,000
Stocks	4,500	Loan from bank	4,000
Cash at bank	500	Trade creditors	2,000
	12,000		12,000

The above balance sheet shows that the firm now owns assets totalling £12,000 made up of premises, stocks and cash at bank. The finance has been obtained from three sources: ownership, the bank and suppliers who are described as trade creditors for balance sheet purposes. The investment made by the owners is normally permanent, while the loan is likely to be the subject of a formal agreement that covers such matters as the repayment date and the rate of interest payable. Trade creditors expect to be repaid in accordance with the normal practice of the particular trade, in this case thirty days. An important feature of trade credit is that it is a renewable source of finance in the sense that, provided the firm pays money currently owed, it will be able to acquire further supplies on credit, thereby maintaining a constant level of indebtedness.

Readers should now work Question 2.3 at the end of the chapter.

BUSINESS DEVELOPMENT

Old Ventures is now ready to start trading. Mr Old established the business in the expectation that it would earn profits, and stocks must therefore be sold for sums sufficiently in excess of cost to convince Mr Old that his capital is efficiently employed and would not yield a larger return if invested elsewhere.

On 12 January Old Ventures sells antiques costing £2,000 to Rustic Relics (a nearby antique shop) for £3,500, payment to be made by the end of the month. Ignoring interest charges and other operating costs, a profit of *£1,500* (sales price £3,500 minus cost £2,000) has been earned that accrues to Mr Old and is added to his capital to show that the value of his investment in the business has increased. The effect of the transaction is as follows:

Effect on business assets: Stock-in-trade decreases by £2,000.
                                      Trade debtors increase by £3,500.

Effect on relationship with outsiders: Capital increases by £1,500.

Illustration 2.6

Balance Sheet of Old Ventures at 12 January 19X1

Assets	£	Sources of finance	£
Premises	7,000	Capital	6,000
Stocks	2,500	Add: Profit	1,500
Trade debtors	3,500		
Cash at bank	500		7,500
		Loan from bank	4,000
		Trade creditors	2,000
	13,500		13,500

The total assets of Old Ventures (an alternative description is *gross assets*) have increased from £12,000 in Illustration 2.5, to £13,500 in Illustration 2.6. This is because one asset (stock) costing £2,000 has been replaced by a new asset (trade debtors) worth £3,500. A similar increase occurs in the sources of finance as the result of adding the profit earned to Mr Old's initial capital investment. It should be noticed that profit is recognized despite the fact that the price paid by the customer has not yet been received in cash. This brings us to a second assumption made by accountants when preparing accounting statements, namely, the *realization concept* (considered further in Chapter 4). This concept assumes that profit is earned or realized *when the sale takes place*, and the justification for this treatment is that Old Ventures now possesses a more valuable asset, since the £3,500 is a legally enforceable debt. The trading cycle is completed by Old Ventures collecting £3,500 from Rustic Relics on 31 January 19X1 and paying £2,000 to its supplier on 8 February 19X1, thirty days after the goods were supplied. The effects of these transactions are as follows:

Effect on business assets: Trade debtors decrease by £3,500.
Cash increases by £3,500.
Cash decreases by £2,000.

Effect on relationship with outsiders: Trade creditors decrease by £2,000.

Illustration 2.7

Balance Sheet of Old Ventures at 8 February 19X1

Assets	£	Sources of finance	£
Premises	7,000	Capital	6,000
Stocks	2,500	Add: Profit	1,500
Cash at bank	2,000		
			7,500
		Loan from bank	4,000
	11,500		11,500

Readers should now work Question 2.4 at the end of this chapter.

THE TRADING CYCLE

The single trading cycle for Old Ventures, examined above, is now complete, and can be expressed in the form of a diagram as in Figure 2.1.

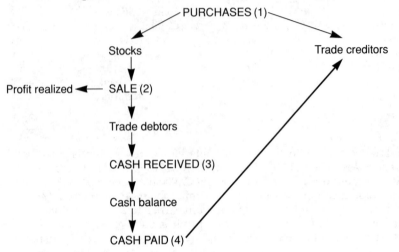

Figure 2.1   The trading cycle

The cycle consists of the following four stages:

Stage 1   The purchase of goods on credit that gives rise to balance sheet entries for trade creditors and stock.

Stage 2   The sale of stock on credit results in a profit being realized or a loss incurred. At this stage some of the stock is replaced by trade debtors in the balance sheet.

Stage 3   The collection of trade debts. This produces a change in the composition of the firm's assets, from debtors to cash.

Stage 4   The payment of the amounts due to suppliers. This causes a reduction in cash and the removal of trade creditors from the balance sheet.

A comparison of the position before (Illustration 2.4) and after (Illustration 2.7) completion of the trading cycle shows just two differences: cash has risen by £1,500 and the owner's capital investment has increased by a similar amount to reflect profit earned.

The trading cycle examined above is obviously a simplified version of what happens in practice. A company does not complete one cycle before commencing another but is involved in a continuous series of overlapping business transactions. The purchases cycle consists of ordering goods, receiving them into stock as an asset and paying for them by means of a cash outflow, while the sales cycle consists of making a sale, parting with the stocks sold as an asset outflow and collecting the money due from the customer to produce a cash inflow. Therefore even before one creditor is paid another is created and debtors are turned over in a similar manner. It is the responsibility of management to ensure that all these flows are adequately controlled and recorded. Thus no payment should be made without ensuring that the related goods or services have in fact been received, and no goods should be allowed to leave the firm except in exchange for cash or by the creation of a debt. In the latter case there must be adequate follow-up to ensure that the cash is subsequently collected.

A simplified version of the trading cycle occurs when purchases and/or sales are made for cash. There are just two stages: stage 1, the purchase of goods, involves the exchange of cash for stocks; stage 2, the sale of goods, involves the exchange of stock for cash of a greater or lesser value, with the amount of the difference recorded as a profit or a loss.

REPORTING CHANGES IN OWNER'S CAPITAL

The capital section of the balance sheet records the indebtedness of the business to its owner. This indebtedness is initially created by ownership advancing money to the business, but the amount changes over time – for example, a profit increases the indebtedness whereas a loss reduces the value of the owner's capital investment. The capital section also reports all other transactions between the business and its owner – for instance, it reports any additional capital investment made by the owner during the life of the business, and also the regular withdrawals of cash and goods made for personal use. The manner in which these matters are reported is shown in Illustration 2.8. Because we are only interested in changes in capital, the remainder of the balance sheet is omitted.

Illustration 2.8

C. Newman started in business on 1 January 19X1 and paid £2,000 into his business bank account. On 30 June he transferred to the business his car valued at £1,400. Each week he withdrew £60 from the business in cash. The accounts prepared for 19X1 showed that his business had earned a profit of £4,100 during the year.

Extracts from Balance Sheet at 31 December 19X1

	£
Opening capital, 1 January 19X1	2,000
Add: Additional capital investment	1,400
Profit for 19X1	4,100
	7,500
Less: Drawings (£60 × 52)	3,120
Closing capital, 31 December 19X1	4,380*

Note
*The closing capital for 19X1 is the opening capital for 19X2.

The owner does not normally wait until profit is calculated before making withdrawals. He or she is often dependent on the business for his or her livelihood and profits are withdrawn, for personal use, as they are earned during the year. Where profits exceed drawings, as is the case in Illustration

2.8, the surplus of £980 (profit £4,100 minus drawings £3,120) is retained in the business and increases the owner's capital by an equivalent amount. These extra resources may be used to finance an expansion in the level of business operations. Illustration 2.8 also demonstrates the fact that capital may be introduced in the form of assets other than cash. The motor vehicle, transferred to the business by Newman, appears as an asset in the balance sheet and is matched by a corresponding increase in the value of his capital investment. Similarly, drawings may be made in a non-cash form (e.g. the family of a farmer is likely to consume some of the farm produce) though this has not happened in the above illustration.

Readers should now work Question 2.5 at the end of the chapter.

ASSETS = CAPITAL + LIABILITIES: A Further Illustration

In the case of Old Ventures we saw that the equality between sources of finance and assets was maintained throughout the trading cycle and, because all assets must be financed in some manner or other, we can be confident that this equality will continue throughout the firm's life. In this context there are four basic categories of business transaction:

1. Where an increase in an asset is matched by a corresponding increase in a source of finance – for example, cash increases as the result of extra capital being invested by the owner.
2. Where an increase in a source of finance is matched by a decrease in a different source of finance – for example, a loan raised from the bank to enable trade creditors to be paid the amount due to them.
3. Where a reduction in an asset is matched by a reduction in a source of finance – for example, cash is used to pay trade creditors.
4. Where an increase in an asset is matched by a reduction in a different asset – for example, a new motor vehicle purchased for cash.

A complication occurs in the case of a transaction involving the sale of goods, since this gives rise to a profit or a loss that must also be recorded. For example, assume an item of stock that cost £80 is sold on credit for £100. In the balance sheet stock is replaced by debtors, i.e. a category 4 transaction takes place. In addition a category 1 transaction occurs, because the higher value of debtors, £20, gives rise to a profit that must be added to the owner's capital.

Example 2.1   Examine separately the effect of each of the following transactions on the relationship A = C + L:

1. The owner of a business received a legacy of £2,000 and paid it into his business bank account.
2. Machinery costing £3,000 is purchased for cash.
3. Stock-in-trade is purchased on credit for £800.
4. A business computer is purchased for £5,000 and is financed by a loan from a friend.
5. Trade debts amounting to £750 are collected from customers.

6. Stock-in-trade costing £1,000 is sold for £1,400.
7. A supplier is paid £220 due to him.
8. Stock-in-trade is purchased for cash, £350.
9. A filing cabinet is purchased for £60 by increasing an existing bank overdraft.
10. The owner of a business drew a cheque for £100 on his business bank account to meet private expenses.

You should present your answer in the following form:

Transaction	Assets £	=	Capital £	+	Liabilities £
1	+2,000	=	+2,000		0
2	+3,000 −3,000	=	0		0

Note
In transaction 2, the machinery acquired increases assets by £3,000 but the payment reduces assets by the same amount. The net effect is zero.

Transaction	Assets £	=	Capital £	+	Liabilities £	**Solution**
1	+2,000	=	+2,000		0	
2	+3,000 −3,000	=	0		0	
3	+800	=	0		+800	
4	+5,000	=	0		+5,000	
5	−750 +750	=	0		0	
6	−1,000 +1,400	=	+400		0	
7	−220	=	0		−220	
8	+350 −350	=	0		0	
9	+60	=	0		+60	
10	−100	=	−100		0	

Readers should now work Question 2.6 at the end of this chapter.

CLASSIFICATION OF ASSETS AND SOURCES OF FINANCE

Assets

Business assets may be defined as resources owned by an entity that have the potential for providing it with future economic benefits in the sense that they help to generate future cash inflows or reduce future cash outflows. The fact that a business asset exists, however, does not necessarily mean that it will be reported in the balance sheet. For this to be done, the asset must satisfy the further requirement that the benefit it provides can be measured or quantified, in money terms, with a reasonable degree of precision. This rule is called the *money measurement concept*. For example, stock-in-trade is reported as a business asset because it is owned by the firm, it has an identifiable monetary value (its cost) and it is expected to produce an at least equivalent cash benefit to the firm when it is sold. Expenditure incurred on training staff, on the other hand, presents a more difficult problem. While it is possible to identify the amount of the expenditure, it is not possible to forecast with a high degree of certainty whether the firm will benefit from the expenditure. Employees may be poorly motivated and fail to improve their competence as the result of attending training courses. In addition, they may leave the firm and take their new expertise elsewhere. Because of this uncertainty concerning the likely extent of any future benefit, such expenditure is not reported as a business asset but is instead written off against profit as it is incurred.

Assets reported in the balance sheet are divided into two categories:

1. *Current assets* These are defined as assets that are held for resale, conversion into cash or are cash itself. There are three main types of current assets: stock-in-trade, trade debtors and cash. A *temporary* investment of funds in the shares of a quoted company or government securities should also be classified as a current asset. A characteristic of current assets is that the balances are constantly changing as the result of business operations and, in earlier times, the evocative term 'circulating assets' was used to describe these items.
2. *Fixed assets* These are assets a firm purchases and retains to help carry on the business. It is not intended to sell fixed assets in the ordinary course of business and it is expected that the bulk of their value will be used up as the result of contributing to trading activities. Examples of fixed assets are premises, plant, machinery, furniture and motor vehicles. A characteristic of fixed assets is that they usually remain in the business for long periods of time and will only be sold or scrapped when they are of no further use.

It is important for readers to realize that it is possible to classify an asset as current or fixed only by examining the reason why it was purchased, i.e. was it purchased for resale or retention? Assets purchased by one company for resale may be purchased by another for retention. For example, a garage purchases motor vehicles for resale while a manufacturing concern acquires them as fixed assets to be used by sales representatives.

Assets are reported in the balance sheet in the order of increasing liquidity, i.e. the list starts with the items least likely to be turned into cash and ends with the items expected to be converted into cash in the near future. A typical balance sheet presentation of assets is given in the left-hand column of Figure 2.2.

Sources of finance

We have seen that sources of finance are divided into the capital invested by the owners and the liabilities due to non-ownership groups. These liabilities may be further classified into current liabilities, defined as amounts repayable within twelve months of the balance sheet date, and non-current liabilities. Typical examples of current liabilities are a bank overdraft, amounts owing to suppliers of stock-in-trade and creditors for miscellaneous services. Any loans repayable within the following year are also listed under current liabilities. The only loan outstanding in the case of Nut and Bolt Engineering (Figure 2.2) is not repayable for another seven years (in 19X8) and is therefore classified as a non-current liability and positioned between the capital section and current liabilities in the balance sheet.

	£	£		£	£
Fixed assets			Capital		179,000
Land and buldings	75,000				
Plant and machinery	49,000		*Non-current liabilities*		
Motor vehicles	21,500		Loan repayable 19X8		
50,000					
		145,500			
Current assets			*Current liabilities*		
Stock-in-trade	145,700		Trade creditors	170,000	
Trade debtors	143,700		Expense creditors	1,900	
Investments	2,600		Bank overdraft	36,700	208,600
Cash in hand	100	292,100			
		437,600			437,600

Figure 2.2 Balance Sheet of the Nut and Bolt Engineering Company at 31 December 19X1

We can see from Figure 2.2 that sources of finance are arranged in order of permanence, with the most permanent sources at the top and amounts repayable (or potentially repayable) in the near future at the bottom of the balance sheet. Most sources of finance are easily classified into one or other of the three categories, but certain items cause a little more difficulty. For example, the terms of a bank loan may provide for an advance of £100,000 repayable by five equal annual instalments of £20,000. In these circumstances the liability must be divided into two parts, with the next instalment repayable, of £20,000, shown as a current liability and the balance reported as a non-current liability. Therefore at the end of the first year, £20,000 is reported as a current liability and £80,000 as a non-current liability.

As accounting is a device for communicating relevant financial information to interested parties, it is important that the information reported should not only be technically accurate but also be presented in an orderly fashion so that it can be readily understood by owners, managers and others who wish to assess progress. The balance sheet of the Nut and Bolt Engineering Company is drafted in a manner that helps to achieve this objective. It is divided into five sections and, for each of these, an appropriate description is given and subheading provided. Users of accounting statements are therefore able to see, at a glance, the amount of finance provided by the owners, the volume of long-term loans and the quantity of short-term finance. The statement also shows how the total finance has been allocated between fixed and current assets. If a firm is to be financially stable, it is normally important for long-term investments in fixed assets to be financed substantially by the owners and for current assets to be sufficient to meet current liabilities falling due over the next twelve months. A well prepared balance sheet enables these and other forms of financial analysis, examined in Chapters 12 and 13, to be efficiently carried out.

Readers should now work Questions 2.7–2.9 at the end of this chapter.

VALUATION OF ASSETS

The balance sheet contains a list of assets belonging to the company and, for each category, a value is given. For example, a freehold property may be shown in the balance sheet at £50,000. What does this value represent? If a lay person was asked this question, it is quite likely that he or she would say: 'It is what the asset is worth.' This seems reasonable on the face of it, but it leads to further questions, such as: 'Worth to whom, when, and for what purpose?'

There are four possible methods for valuing assets, although we will see that only one of these normally finds favour with the accountant. The four methods are as follows:

1. *Historical cost* The asset is valued at its original purchase price.
2. *Replacement cost* The asset is valued at the amount it would cost the business to buy the asset at the balance sheet date.
3. *Realizable value* This is the price at which the asset could be sold at the balance-sheet date. It differs from replacement cost as anyone who has ever attempted to sell, say, a second-hand motor vehicle will know.
4. *Present value* This is a little more complicated and is the present value of cash expected to be generated, in the future, as a result of owning a particular asset. These estimated cash flows are then discounted, at a rate of interest, to take account of the fact that £1 receivable, say, in one year's time is worth rather less than £1 receivable immediately.

The appropriate method of valuation depends on the purpose for which it is required. If the company is contemplating the acquisition of an asset, purchase price is most relevant. The replacement cost of an asset is likely to be of interest if the existing asset is worn out. Realizable value is relevant if there is an intention to sell the asset in the near future, while the present value calculation should be made if the asset is to continue in use for some time generating a stream of cash flows stretching into the future.

In general, assets are shown in company accounts at their historical cost less, in the case of fixed assets, a reduction to reflect wear and tear (depreciation) that has occurred since the acquisition took place. At first glance this is a little surprising. The analysis in the preceding paragraph shows that, although historical cost is of interest at the date of the initial purchase, it is the other valuation methods, particularly market price and present value, that are likely to be more relevant when a balance sheet is prepared at some subsequent date. Why is historical cost so popular? Perhaps the main reason is because this figure is readily available. Most assets are purchased on credit and are entered in the books at their historical cost so as to provide a record of the amount to be paid to the supplier at some future date. Once the figure is in the books it is simply convenient to use it for the purpose of preparing the balance sheet.

Many people believe that this is not a sufficient justification for continuing to use historical cost. For example, it seems quite ridiculous to report a share investment in the balance sheet at £7,000 – the price paid ten years ago – if the shares could today be sold for, say, £25,000. But this is what is done. A further reason for this, apparently, curious choice is the difficulty of obtaining a more relevant estimate of value. If the shares are quoted on the stock exchange it would be relatively easy to obtain their current market price from the *Stock Exchange Daily Official List*. However, this figure is only relevant if there is an intention to sell the securities at once. If the asset is to be retained indefinitely, the more relevant figure is present value. As indicated earlier this must be calculated on the basis of future cash flows – dividends and sales proceeds – which it is, of course, impossible to forecast with any degree of accuracy. In the case of most business assets – for example, land, buildings, plant, machinery and unquoted shares – it is even very difficult to get an accurate figure for current market price.

It is therefore clear that historical cost is used, not so much because it is relevant but because the data is readily available. This limitation should be borne in mind when assessing the usefulness of information appearing in the accounts.

Example 2.1

Lexington owns a fleet of cars that are rented to customers. One of the cars, H634 HAB, was purchased a couple of years ago for £7,000. The company has discovered that it could purchase a car in similar condition, today, for £5,000 from the local distributor. Cars no longer needed by Lexington are usually sold to employees or their families. It is estimated that H634 HAB would now sell for £3,800.

The company's intention is to retain the vehicle as part of its fleet for one year. It will be rented to a single customer for an annual rental of £2,000, payable in arrears. The car will then be immediately sold for £3,000.

Assume the rental arises at the end of the year and that future cash flows have to be discounted at 10 per cent in order to convert them into an equivalent present value.

Required

Valuations of the car on the following bases:

(a) historical cost;
(b) replacement cost;
(c) realizable value; and
(d) present value.

Solution

(a) *Historical cost £7,000*, less a deduction for wear and tear or depreciation suffered since the date of purchase.
(b) *Replacement cost £5,000.*
(c) *Realizable value £3,800.*
(d) *Present value*

$$\text{Rentals, £2,000} \quad \times \frac{1^*}{1.1} = \quad 1,818$$

$$\text{Sales proceeds, £3,000} \quad \times \frac{1^*}{1.1} = \quad \underline{2,727}$$

$$\underline{4,545}$$

*The effect of this fraction is to discount the future cash flows to an equivalent present value using an interest rate of 10 per cent. Looked at another way, £4,545 invested at 10 per cent for one year increases to £5,000 (£4,545 × 1.1), which is the cash expected to be received if the asset is retained for use within the business.

2.1 Indicate which of the following transactions relate to Clive's business as a newsagent and which are his personal transactions:

1. £50 win on premium bonds owned by Clive.
2. £100 paid for the following advertisement on a hoarding at the local football ground: 'Clive's for all the up-to-date news'.
3. Payment to the newspaper wholesaler, £1,260.
4. Sale of unsold newspapers to a local fish-and-chip shop.
5. Purchase of a new car for family use, although it will be used each morning to collect papers from suppliers.

2.2 John decides to start up in business on 1 April 19X2, and pays £4,000 from his private bank account into a newly opened business bank account. On 2 April 19X2 John's father loans the firm £600 to help with the new venture, and this amount is paid immediately into the business bank account. On 4 April the firm borrows £150 from John's friend, Peter. This amount is kept in the form of 'ready cash' to meet small business expenses.

Required
Balance sheets for John's business after the transactions on:

(a) 1 April,
(b) 2 April,
(c) 4 April.

2.3 Roger starts up in business on 1 September with a capital of £1,200 which he pays into his business bank account on that day. The bank agrees to provide him with a business overdraft facility of £1,500 for the first three months. The following business transactions take place:

2 September	A machine is bought, on three months credit, from Plant Suppliers Ltd for £750. £1,000 is borrowed from the Endridge Local Authority, which is keen to encourage this type of enterprise.
3 September	£1,820 is paid for a second-hand machine. Stock is purchased, for cash, £420.
4 September	Stock is purchased, on credit, for £215.

Required
Balance sheets for Roger's business following the transactions on:

(a) 1 September,
(b) 2 September,
(c) 3 September,
(d) 4 September.

2.4 The following balance sheet was prepared for Jeff's business at 1 October 19X5. The firm has an overdraft facility of £700.

Balance Sheet

	£		£
Machinery	2,200	Capital	5,300
Stocks	2,870		
Debtors	800	Trade creditors	690
Cash at bank	120		
	5,990		5,990

Jeff enters into the following transactions:

2 October	Sells goods that cost £120 for £200, cash. Sells goods that cost £240 for £315, on credit.
3 October	Collects £150 from customers. Purchases stock for £190, on credit.
4 October	Pays trade creditors £75. Purchases a machine for £600, cash.

Required

Balance sheets for Jeff's business following the transactions on:

(a) 2 October,
(b) 3 October,
(c) 4 October.

2.5 (a) Prepare the balance sheet of Daley from the following list of assets and liabilities at 31 December 19X1:

	£
Cash	1,750
Stock	5,250
Owed by customers	3,340
Owed to suppliers	2,890
Business premises	9,000
Loan from Weakly	3,000

(b) Prepare the balance sheet of Daley's business at the end of each of the first seven days of January taking account of the following transactions:

January 19X2
1. Purchased, on credit, a typewriter for office use, £500.
2. Received £190 from a customer.
3. Paid a supplier £670.
4. Purchased stock, on credit, £260.
5. Sold goods that had cost £350 for £530 cash.
6. Repaid Weakly £1,000 of the balance due to him (ignore interest).
7. Withdrew stock costing £100 for private use.

2.6 Prepare balance sheets to determine the amount missing from each of the following lists of balances at 31 December 19X1:

	A	B	C	D	E	F
	£	£	£	£	£	£
Capital at 1 January 19X1	2,500	2,000	3,000	4,000	3,800	?
Profit for 19X1	1,000	3,200	?	5,700	2,300	7,000
Drawings during 19X1	800	3,000	1,000	4,900	?	4,500
Current liabilities	750	?	600	1,300	1,700	2,100
Fixed assets	1,800	1,750	2,800	?	3,700	8,500
Current assets	?	850	1,200	1,900	1,600	3,500

2.7 Review your understanding of the following concepts and terms discussed in this chapter by writing a short explanation of each of them:

1. Accountancy.
2. Entity concept.
3. Balance sheet.
4. Realization concept.
5. Trade credit.
6. Trading cycle, credit transactions.
7. A=C+L.
8. Owner's capital.
9. Money measurement concept.
10. Fixed assets.
11. Current assets.
12. Current liabilities.
13. Gross assets.

2.8 For a fish-and-chip shop, indicate which of the following items are current liabilities, which are current assets and which are fixed assets:

1. Microwave oven.
2. 2,000 kilos of King Edward potatoes.
3. Cash register.
4. Amount owing to the Fat Fishy Company Ltd.
5. Capital investment of Mr V. Greasy, owner.
6. Mrs Greasy's pearl necklace and gold wrist-watch.
7. 250 mackerel.
8. Loan from V. Greasy's father, repayable in two years' time.
9. Last instalment due, in one month's time, on the microwave oven acquired on hire purchase.
10. Shop rented from a property company.

For items not classified as current liabilities or current assets or fixed assets, describe how they would be reported in the balance sheet, if at all.

2.9 The following list of balances relate to the business of C. Forest at 31 December 19X3:

	£
Plant and machinery	26,500
Stock-in-trade	14,200
Loan repayable June 19X4	2,500
Capital of C. Forest at 1 January 19X3	52,380
Trade creditors	10,600
Trade debtors	14,100
Cash-in-hand	270
Bank overdraft	3,940
Profit for 19X3	12,600
Owner's drawings during 19X3	10,950
Loan repayable 19X9	9,000
Leasehold premises	25,000

Required

The balance sheet of C. Forest's business at 31 December 19X3 *presented in good style*.

3
PROFIT CALCULATED AS THE INCREASE IN CAPITAL

The objectives of this chapter are to

- explain the importance of profit and outline the way in which it may be appropriated;
- outline the procedure involved in preparing a balance sheet in accordance with the horizontal format;
- show how capital can be calculated as the difference between assets and liabilities;
- explain the relationship between profit and changes in the owner's capital; and
- demonstrate how profit can be calculated as the increase in capital after making allowance for any capital introduced or profit withdrawn during the year.

PROFITABLE ACTIVITY

The maximization of profit has been traditionally regarded as the principal factor motivating the individual to invest in a business venture. However, business organizations, particularly the very large ones, have responsibilities which are wider than the obligation to produce an adequate return for their investors. A list of the responsibilities acknowledged by business people can be obtained by examining the corporate objectives declared by company chair persons in their annual reports to shareholders. These include such matters as an increase in the market share, the improvement of product quality, a contented workforce, pollution-free production processes, the maximization of exports and survival.

It is difficult to say whether these aims are each of equal importance, but probably they are not. One view is that profit maximization is the main objective, and other stated goals have as their central purpose to contribute, either directly or indirectly, to the long-run achievement of that principal aim. This view may attach rather too much significance to profit, but widespread agreement that profit is an essential product of business activity in Great Britain can safely be assumed.

There are basically two competing claims on the profits generated by business activity:

1. *Withdrawals* The owner requires a satisfactory return on his or her investment in the form of drawings or dividends. An inadequate return

will cause him or her to close down the business and invest his or her money elsewhere.

2. *Reinvestment* The second claim on profit arises from the fact that retained profits are a major source of finance for business expansion. For example, the balance sheet of Unilever plc at 31 December 1993 shows share capital as £145 million, whereas retained profits amount to £2,665 million, i.e. over eighteen times more. The retention of profits increases the value of the owner's investment in the business, of course, and should produce higher profits and dividends in the future.

When trading conditions are difficult there may be insufficient profits to finance expansion or even to pay a return on the owner's investment. In these circumstances management must look elsewhere for the finance required for a continuation of business activity. This is not a situation that can persist indefinitely; just as consistent profitability generates the resources necessary for a healthy business, equally a succession of losses gradually deprives a company of the finance needed to support a continuation of business activity. Failure to achieve an adequate level of profitability eventually results in the cessation of business activities. It is part of the accounting function to help management guard against such an outcome by enabling it to monitor progress and ensure that resources are efficiently employed.

PROFIT AND CHANGES IN GROSS ASSETS

In Chapter 2 attention was drawn to the fact that, where management organizes business activity in an efficient manner and a profit is earned, gross assets increase by a similar amount. This relationship was illustrated by means of a series of balance sheets setting out the financial development of a firm called Old Ventures. Readers should now revise their understanding of the link between profit and the level of business assets by working the following example.

Balance Sheet of Larch at 31 December 19X1   *Example 3.1*

Assets	£	£	Sources of finance	£
Fixed assets			Capital	2,000
Plant and machinery		1,600	Current liabilities	
Current assets			Trade creditors	700
Stocks	600			
Trade debtors	300			
Cash	200	1,100		
		2,700		2,700

On 1 January 19X2 Larch sold stock (cost price £140) on credit for £220.

The balance sheet of Larch following the transaction on 1 January 19X2.   **Required**

Solution   **Balance Sheet of Larch at 1 January 19X2**

Assets	£	£	Sources of finance	£
Fixed assets			Capital	2,000
Plant and machinery		1,600	Add: Net profit (220 – 140)	80
Current assets				2,080
Stocks(600 – 140)	460			
Trade debtors (300 + 220)	520		Current liabilities	
Cash	200	1,180	Trade creditors	700
		2,780		2,780

A comparison of the two balance sheets shows that the financial effects of the single trading transaction undertaken by Larch are as follows:

1. Gross assets have increased from £2,700 to £2,780 as the result of stock costing £140 being replaced by a debt due from a customer of £220.
2. Total sources of finance have increased by the same amount as the result of adding the profit realized, of £80, to Larch's opening capital.

BALANCE SHEET PRESENTATION: VERTICAL FORMAT

The balance sheets used, so far, have usually been presented in what is conventionally described as the horizontal format, with assets on the left and sources of finance on the right. Since the early 1960s industry has gradually discarded the horizontal format in favour of the vertical format, e.g. the accounts of Boots reproduced in Chapter 1, Figure 1.2. The vertical presentation is further illustrated (Example 3.2) by rearranging the information taken from Larch's balance sheets in Example 3.1.

The main advantage of the vertical presentation is that it is easier to compare the position of a business at a series of accounting dates. The above illustration gives the position at just two dates, but a columnar presentation dealing with five or even ten accounting dates poses no particular difficulty. It is then a relatively easy matter to glance across the series of figures to discover relevant changes and overall trends. Such an analysis might show that large amounts of money are being spent each year on fixed assets, suggesting a policy of rapid expansion. By way of contrast, a continuous decline in the balance of cash, perhaps converting into a substantial overdraft, suggests that the company is suffering from increasing cash difficulties.

A second advantage of the vertical presentation is that it contains an item of useful information that does not appear in the horizontal balance sheet, namely working capital. This is the balancing figure obtained by deducting current liabilities from current assets. A financially stable business is one that is able to meet its debts as they fall due for payment, and an adequate balance of working capital is an essential requirement if this desirable state of

Vertical presentation of the balance sheets of Larch: *Example 7.5*

	1 Jan. 19X2		31 Dec. 19X1	
	£	£	£	£
Fixed assets				
Plant and machinery		1,600		1,600
Current assets				
Stocks	460		600	
Trade debtors	520		300	
Cash	200		200	
	1,180		1,100	
Less: Current liabilities				
Trade creditors	700		700	
Working capital	——	480	——	400
		2,080		2,000
Financed by:				
Capital				
Opening capital		2,000		
Add: Net profit		80		
Closing capital		2,080		2,000

affairs is to exist. It is not possible to specify a figure for working capital that all firms should try to maintain. Much will depend on individual circumstances, such as the size of the firm, the speed with which creditors are paid, stocks are sold and cash is collected from customers. Nevertheless managers, shareholders, creditors and other users of accounting statements normally hold firm views concerning what can be regarded as an acceptable balance for a particular business. Working capital is examined further in Chapter 13.

PROFITS, LOSSES AND CHANGES IN NET ASSETS

The vertical balance sheet contains the same basic financial information as does the horizontal balance sheet, since the facts are in no way altered by adopting a different method of presentation. Similarly, the overall financial relationship between sources of finance and assets, expressed in the formula $A = C + L$ (Assets = Capital + Liabilities) remains unchanged. The revised presentation does, however, focus attention on different aspects of the relationship between the three magnitudes, since it emphasizes the fact that capital is equal to gross assets minus liabilities, i.e:

$$A - L = C$$

In practice, the term 'gross assets minus liabilities' is normally shortened to 'net assets'. We can therefore say that capital equals net assets. Indeed these are two descriptions of the same financial total; the only difference is the way in which the figure is calculated. Capital is computed by taking the owner's opening investment, adding profit earned and deducting withdrawals for private use to give his or her closing investment at a particular date. Net assets, on the other hand, are computed by adding together the values of the various assets owned at the balance sheet date, and then deducting the amount of finance obtained from suppliers and other creditors. Since assets are, by definition, financed either from capital or from liabilities, the balance that remains must necessarily be equal, in value, to the owner's investment.

Example 3.1 reminded us that profit produces an equivalent increase in the gross assets of a firm; the profit of £80 resulted in gross assets increasing from £2,700 to £2,780. The presentation of the same data in the form of a vertical balance sheet (see Example 3.2) draws attention to the fact that profit also results in an equivalent increase in *net* assets; these are up from £2,000 to £2,080. Where a firm suffers a loss, net assets and, therefore, the owner's capital, are reduced by the amount of the loss. These circumstances are illustrated in Example 3.3.

Example 3.3 The following balance sheet is prepared in respect of Elm at 31 December 19X1:

Balance Sheet of Elm at 31 December 19X1

Assets	£	£	Sources of finance	£
Fixed assets			Capital	7,600
Plant and machinery		4,000	Current liabilities	
Current assets			Trade creditors	1,200
Stocks	1,900			
Trade debtors	2,200			
Cash	700	4,800		
		8,800		8,800

On 1 January 19X2 Elm sold, on credit for £480, goods that cost £600 some weeks ago.

Required (a) Calculations of:

    (i)   Elm's net assets at 31 December 19X1;
    (ii) the profit or loss arising on the 1 January sale;
    (iii) Elm's capital investment on 1 January after the above transaction; and
    (iv) Elm's net assets on 1 January after the above transaction.

(b) Elm's balance sheet at 1 January 19X2, presented in vertical format.

Solution (a) (i)

	£
Assets	8,800
Less: Liabilities	1,200
Net assets	7,600

(ii)	*Cost of stock*	600
	Less: Sales proceeds	480
	Loss	120
(iii)	*Capital at 31 December*	7,600
	Less: Loss	120
	Capital at 1 January	7,480
(iv)	*Assets*	
	Plant and machinery	4,000
	Stock (£1,900 – £600)	1,300
	Trade debtors (£2,200 + £480)	2,680
	Cash	700
		8,680
	Liabilities	
	Trade creditors	1,200
	Net Assets	7,480

(b) Balance Sheet of Elm at 1 January 19X2

	£	£
Fixed assets		
Plant and machinery		4,000
Current assets		
Stocks	1,300	
Trade debtors	2,680	
Cash	700	
	4,680	
Less: Current liabilities		
Trade creditors	1,200	
Working capital		3,480
		7,480
Capital		
Opening capital		7,600
Less: Net loss (£600 – £480)		120
Closing capital		7,480

We can therefore conclude from the above examples that

Profit = Increase in net assets (or capital)
Loss = Decrease in net assets (or capital).

An awareness of the relationship between profits, losses and changes in net assets is fundamental to a sound understanding of the financial effects of business activity. The relevant connections between the various financial magnitudes can be expressed diagrammatically as shown in Figure 3.1.

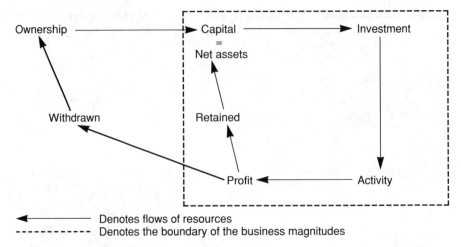

Figure 3.1   Connections between financial magnitudes

The ownership group invests capital that is used to acquire business assets. These assets form the basis for business activity subsequently undertaken in order to generate profit. Some of the profit is likely to be withdrawn by the owners (sole traders and partnerships) or paid out to them as dividends (limited companies). The remainder is retained and this results in an increased volume of net assets to be used for trading purposes during the following accounting period. The reinvestment takes place in the expectation that the greater volume of net assets will enable a higher profit to be earned.

Readers should now work Question 3.1 at the end of this chapter.

PROFIT MEASURED BY CAPITAL CHANGES

It sometimes happens that the accountant is faced with the task of measuring profit despite the fact that no record exists of business transactions undertaken during the accounting period under review, for example because the records have been lost or destroyed by fire. In these circumstances it is *not* possible to calculate profit by comparing the cost of goods sold with their selling price, as in the previous examples worked. Instead the calculation must be based on the fundamental fact, established earlier in this chapter, that profit produces an equivalent increase in net assets or owner's capital, i.e.

Net profit* = Closing capital – Opening capital; or
Net profit* = Increase in capital

Note
* If opening capital exceeds closing capital, the result of the calculation is a negative figure and this means that a loss has been suffered.

The accountant, when faced with the job of calculating profit based on capital changes, must first take steps to establish the proprietor's investment at the beginning and end of the period. This process usually involves a significant element of estimation and judgement, particularly in relation to assets owned at the earlier of the two accounting dates. The existence of fixed assets can usually be established by physical verification but the valuation of these items may prove more difficult. Evidence of the price paid may well be available in view of the large sums often involved; otherwise it is necessary to use information that can be obtained from suppliers of the relevant items or, alternatively, to arrange for a professional valuation.

Reliable figures for stocks are difficult to obtain unless steps were taken to arrange for them to be physically counted and valued at each of the balance sheet dates. If this task has not been undertaken then an estimate of the likely values must be made by the proprietor of the business. Figures for trade debtors and trade creditors can be constructed if the sales and purchase invoices are retained and, where the company deals in products subject to value added tax (see Chapter 11), the likelihood of this information being readily available is much increased. The amount of money due to or from the bank can be established by an examination of the relevant bank statements. The measurement of profit by capital changes is illustrated in Example 3.4.

The following information is provided relating to the affairs of James who trades in fashionable garments from rented property:

Example 3.4

Assets and liabilities	31 Dec. 19X1 £	31 Dec. 19X2 £
Motor vehicles	1,800	1,350
Fixtures and fittings	450	820
Stocks	1,060	1,610
Trade creditors	730	810
Trade debtors	240	300
Bank overdraft	920	760
Cash-in-hand	40	50

(a) Calculations of James's capital investment in the business at the end of 19X1 and 19X2.

Required

(b) A calculation of the profit earned by James during 19X2.

(c) The balance sheet of James's business at 31 December 19X2, presented in horizontal format.

(a) Capital is calculated at each date by deducting liabilities from assets.

Solution

Statements of assets, liabilities and capital at 31 December

		19X1		19X2
Assets	£	£	£	£
Motor vehicles		1,800		1,350
Fixtures and fittings		450		820
Stocks		1,060		1,610
Trade debtors		240		300
Cash-in-hand		40		50
		3,590		4,130
Less: Liabilities				
Trade creditors	730		810	
Bank overdraft	920	1,650	760	1,570
Capital		1,940		2,560

(b) Profit is calculated based on the increase in capital.

	£
Closing capital	2,560
Less: Opening capital	1,940
Profit	620

(c) **Balance Sheet at 31 December 19X2**

	£	£		£	£
Fixed assets			*Opening capital*		1,940
Motor vehicles		1,350	Add: Net profit		620
Fixtures and fittings		820			
			Closing capital		2,560
		2,170			
Current assets			*Current liabilities*		
Stocks	1,610		Trade creditors	810	
Trade debtors	300		Bank overdraft	760	1,570
Cash-in-hand	50	1,960			
		4,130			4,130

Readers should now work Question 3.2 at the end of the chapter.

CAPITAL INJECTIONS AND WITHDRAWALS

There are two categories of business transaction which cause capital to increase or decrease during an accounting period:

1. Transactions which produce a profit or a loss.
2. Transactions involving the injection of capital or withdrawals by the owners.

The previous section of this chapter demonstrated the measurement of profit by capital changes assuming that there are no capital injections or withdrawals. This assumption is now dropped. Where capital injections or withdrawals occur, their financial effects must be isolated if profit is to be measured accurately. This is because, although an investment or withdrawal of funds causes capital and, therefore, net assets to increase or decrease, these changes have not come about as the result of trading activity and therefore give rise to neither a profit nor a loss. The following adjustments must therefore be made:

1. *Drawings* These reduce closing capital but, because they are not a business expense, they must be *added back* to the increase in capital arrived at by deducting opening capital from closing capital.
2. *Capital injections* These increase closing capital but they are not business profits and so their effect must be eliminated by *deducting* the amount of the additional investment from the increase in capital arrived at by deducting opening capital from closing capital.

The calculation of profit therefore becomes:

Profit = Increase in capital + Drawings − Capital introduced

Assume the same assets and liabilities as are given in Example 3.4. In addition you discover that James withdrew cash totalling £1,000 to meet living expenses during 19X2, while on 1 August he paid into his business bank account the first prize of £200 won in his golf club's raffle.

Example 3.5

(a) A calculation of the corrected profit earned by James during 19X2.
(b) The capital section of James's balance sheet at 31 December 19X2.

Required

(a) Profit is calculated, based on the increase in capital, as follows:

Solution

	£
Closing capital	2,560
Less: Opening capital	1,940
Increase in capital	620
Add: Drawings	1,000
Less: Capital introduced	(200)
Profit	1,420

Note
The assets and liabilities remain the same as in Example 3.4, and so the increase in capital is unchanged at £620 (£2,560 − £1,940). However, account must be taken of the two 'non-trading' transactions that have affected the value of closing capital and caused a net reduction of £800 (cash withdrawals of £1,000 partly compensated by a capital injection of £200). This amount must be added back to the observed increase in capital to produce a 'true' profit figure of £1,420.

(b) **Balance Sheet extract 31 December 19X2**

Capital section	£
Opening capital	1,940
Add: Capital introduced	200
Net profit	1,420
	3,560
Less: Drawings	1,000
	2,560

Note:
The balance sheet now contains a full and accurate statement of transactions affecting the owner's capital during the year. It shows that James made an additional capital investment of £200, that he made personal withdrawals of £1,000 and that a profit figure of £1,420 (not £620) should be used as the basis for assessing the firm's performance and as a starting point for computing tax payable.

An injection of additional capital by the owner is an unusual event and is normally quite easy to identify. Sources of extra capital might include a legacy or gambling winnings or the sale of a non-business asset belonging to the proprietor. Drawings are usually more difficult to calculate as they may well vary from week to week and comprise both cash and stock-in-trade, the latter being particularly likely in the case of a retail business. In the absence of a reliable record of withdrawals, a careful estimate is required from the proprietor. The various matters discussed in this chapter are incorporated into Example 3.6.

Example 3.6 The following information is provided relating to the affairs of John, who owns a tobacconist, confectionery and newspaper kiosk:

Assets and liabilities	1 Jan. 19X3	31 Dec. 19X3
	£	£
Kiosk	2,000	2,000
Stocks of tobacco and confectionery	450	600
Trade creditors	250	320
Bank balance	160	940
Cash-in-hand	20	30

During 19X3 John received a legacy of £800 that was paid into his business bank account. Cash drawings are estimated at £200 per week and, in addition, John took from the business goods worth £150 for his own use during the year.

Required
(a) A calculation of the profit earned by John during 19X3.
(b) The balance sheet of John's business at 31 December 19X3, presented in vertical format.

Solution
(a) (i) Calculation of capital by deducting liabilities from assets:

Statement of assets, liabilities and capital at:

	1 Jan. 19X3	31 Dec. 19X3
Assets	£	£
Kiosk	2,000	2,000
Stocks	450	600
Bank balance	160	940
Cash-in-hand	20	30
	2,630	3,570
Liabilities		
Trade creditors	250	320
Capital	2,380	3,250

(ii) Calculation of profit on the basis of the increase in capital:

	£
Closing capital	3,250
Less: Opening capital	2,380
Increase in capital	870
Add: Drawings	10,550 W1
Less: Capital introduced	(800)
Net profit	10,620
W1 drawings: Cash, £200 × 52 =	£10,400
Goods	150
	10,550

(b) Balance Sheet at 31 December 19X3

Assets	£	£
Fixed assets		
Kiosk		2,000
Current assets		
Stocks	600	
Bank balance	940	
Cash-in-hand	30	
	1,570	
Less: Current liabilities		
Trade creditors	320	
Working capital		1,250
		3,250
Capital		
Opening capital		2,380
Add: Capital introduced		800
Profit		10,620
		13,800
Less: Drawings – cash	10,400	
– goods	150	10,550
		3,250

The procedure for calculating profit, described above, is also used by the Inland Revenue where existing business records are unreliable but profit needs to be estimated because the taxpayer is believed to have understated his or her income in his or her tax return. In such cases, the major area of dispute is usually the level of drawings that have been made. The taxpayer will attempt to argue that they have been fairly modest, whereas the Inland Revenue will endeavour to demonstrate that much larger drawings *must* have been made to support the taxpayer's observed lifestyle. When the amount of the profit understatement has been computed, tax due will be calculated and penalties and interest added. The level of the penalty will depend, a great deal, on the co-operation received from the taxpayer since the initial discovery of the deception.

Readers should now work Questions 3.3 and 3.4 at the end of this chapter.

Questions

3.1 The following balance sheet relates to the affairs of Columbus who works for the government and also buys, repairs and sells second-hand cars. The balance sheet of his second-hand car business is as follows:

Balance Sheet at 31 December 19X1

	£	£		£
Fixed assets		2,000	Capital	6,500
Current assets			Current liabilities	
Stock of cars	2,700		Trade creditors	200
Debtors	1,000			
Bank	1,000	4,700		
		6,700		6,700

Transactions undertaken in January 19X2:

1. Columbus collects the £1,000 owing in respect of the second-hand car sold in December 19X1.
2. Columbus wins £500 on the football pools and pays the proceeds into his business bank account.
3. Columbus sells for £1,200 a car that was in stock on 31 December 19X1 at a value of £1,300.
4. Columbus withdraws £50 for private use.
5. Columbus purchases a friend's car for £150, and promises to pay him in February.
6. Columbus purchases a new machine for £700 and pays in cash.

Required

(a) Give the totals for gross assets, net assets and working capital based on the figures in the above balance sheet.
(b) Taking each of the transactions listed above separately, give their effect (increase or decrease) on:

   (i)   profit,
   (ii)   net assets,
   (iii)   gross assets, and
   (iv)   working capital.

3.2 The balance sheet of Paul at 30 June 19X3 is as follows:

Balance Sheet at 30 June 19X3

	£	£		£	£
Fixed assets		7,500	Capital		10,330
Current assets			Current liabilities		
Stock	3,280		Trade creditors	1,220	
Debtors	1,750	5,030	Bank overdraft	980	2,200
		12,530			12,530

During the year to 30 June 19X3, Paul received a loan of £3,000 from a friend. The loan is interest free and repayable at the end of 19X6. On 1 December 19X3 Paul purchased fixed assets costing £2,350. At 30 June 19X4, trade creditors amounted to £1,890, stock was valued at £4,270 and debtors amounted to £1,450. In addition Paul had £570 in his bank account and cash in hand of £30.

Required

(a) A calculation of Paul's capital investment in the business at 30 June 19X4.
(b) A calculation of the profit earned by Paul's business during the year to 30

June 19X4.

(c) The balance sheet of Paul's business at 30 June 19X4, presented in vertical format.

3.3 The following information is obtained in connection with the business of G. Haze, a trader:

	31 December	
	19X3	19X4
	£	£
Fixed assets at book value	9,000	see below
Stocks	2,650	3,710
Trade debtors	5,200	5,600
Trade creditors	1,710	1,210
Bank balance (overdraft)	(360)	50

During 19X4 motor vehicles were purchased at a cost of £3,144, part of which was met by G. Haze trading in his private motor car at an agreed valuation of £600. Cash drawings made by G. Haze amounted to £150 per week and, in addition, stocks valued at £300 were taken during the year for personal use.

Required

(a) A calculation of the profit earned by G. Haze's business during 19X4.
(b) The balance sheet of the firm at 31 December 19X4 presented in the horizontal format.

3.4 The following table shows the cumulative effects of a succession of separate transactions on the assets and liabilities of a business. Each letter identifies the assets and liabilities *after each single transaction*.

Transaction		A	B	C	D	E	F	G	H	I	J
	£000	£000	£000	£000	£000	£000	£000	£000	£000	£000	£000
Assets:											
Buildings, at cost/valuation	200	200	200	200	200	200	200	250	250	250	250
Equipment, at cost	100	100	100	100	125	125	125	125	125	125	125
Stocks, at cost	35	35	46	32	32	22	22	22	22	22	22
Trade debtors	48	43	43	43	43	43	43	43	40	40	40
Prepaid expenses	5	5	5	5	5	5	5	5	5	5	3
Bank	0	0	0	15	15	15	15	15	15	10	10
Cash	3	3	3	3	3	3	1	1	1	1	3
	391	**386**	**397**	**398**	**423**	**413**	**411**	**461**	**458**	**453**	**453**
Liabilities:											
Capital	235	235	235	241	241	231	230	280	277	278	278
Loan	80	80	80	80	105	105	105	105	105	105	105
Trade creditors	55	55	66	66	66	66	66	66	66	60	60
Accrued expenses	11	11	11	11	11	11	10	10	10	10	10
Bank overdraft	10	5	5	0	0	0	0	0	0	0	0
	391	**386**	**397**	**398**	**423**	**413**	**411**	**461**	**458**	**453**	**453**

Required

Identify clearly as fully as you can what transaction has taken place in each case. Use the reference letters from the table to identify each transaction. There is no need to copy out the table.

(20 Marks)

(AAT, Basic Accounting, June 1990)

4

THE PREPARATION OF ACCOUNTS FROM CASH RECORDS

The objectives of this chapter are to

- illustrate the presentation of a summarized statement of receipts and payments;
- explain how profit is measured by matching revenue with expenditure;
- demonstrate the difference between gross profit and net profit;
- explain the significance of the realization concept for the identification of revenue and the benefit principle for the measurement of expenditure;
- demonstrate the preparation of accounts from cash records; and
- outline the special rules relating to the preparation of accounts for clubs and societies.

ACCOUNTING SYSTEMS AND INFORMATION REQUIREMENTS

For the unincorporated enterprise, the complexity of the accounting system for recording and reporting business transactions depends mainly on the size of the organization. (The position is different in the case of a limited company which, irrespective of its size, is legally required to keep formal accounting records.) The large number of transactions undertaken each day, in the case of a substantial business concern, requires a sophisticated accounting system for the dual purposes of *control* and *assessment*. In the small firm the accounting system is usually far more rudimentary, since effective protection of valuable resources is achieved through the owner's close personal contact with all aspects of the firm's business activities. Control is enhanced if the firm's most vulnerable assets, e.g. the cash balance and the bank account, are under the direct control of the owner. Other resources, e.g. stocks, which may be in the custody of trusted personnel, nevertheless remain under the close scrutiny of the proprietor.

Neither is it necessary, in the small firm, to employ formal reporting procedures as a basis for performance assessment. Trade creditors and customers are likely to be relatively small, in number, and any difficulties associated with the supply of or demand for the firm's products should come quickly to the attention of a diligent proprietor. Similarly, in the absence of a significant level of capital expenditure, changes in the bank balance are likely to provide a fairly reliable indication of progress; the function of accounting reports, in these circumstances, is simply to provide a basis for agreeing tax liabilities with the Inland Revenue and, where there are a number of proprietors, as a means of allocating profit between the partners. Although an increase in the scale of a firm's activities implies the need for a more formal system of accounting, it does not necessarily follow that transactions will be recorded daily in accordance with the system of double entry described in Chapter 6. It is essential that accounting systems be judged in terms of their usefulness, and a decision to invest the time and money required to operate a complex system must be justified in terms of the benefits it produces.

There is a certain minimum range of financial information that must be made available, however, to enable the accountant to prepare both a trading and profit and loss account, which gives a detailed list of business revenues and expenditures arising during the year (see p. 46 of this chapter), and a balance sheet. The information required consists of

1. assets at the beginning and at the end of the year;
2. liabilities at the beginning and at the end of the year; and
3   cash receipts and payments during the year.

The steps that must be taken to obtain details of assets and liabilities are discussed in Chapter 3. This information is used to compile the closing balance sheet and also the opening balance sheet unless this statement was prepared at the end of the previous year. Details of cash transactions are required as the starting point for preparing the trading and profit and loss. The business bank statements fulfil an essential role in this context, since they contain a wide range of reliable information concerning cash transactions undertaken during the year. There is, of course, usually a large number of bank statements and the analysis of these documents is a lengthy process, particularly because the statements provide few details. For example, the only information usually given in respect of cheque payments is the amount and the cheque number, while in the case of receipts only a brief description, indicating the source of the lodgement, is provided. It is, therefore, important for cheque books and paying-in books to be retained so that an accurate description of the various items appearing on the bank statements can be constructed. Details must also be obtained of any cash transactions that have *not* gone through the bank. This information may be recorded in a 'petty' cash book (see Chapter 5); alternatively, it may be possible to build up the relevant figures from files of cash receipts and payments. In examination questions the analysis work has generally been done, and figures for receipts and payments are given in a summary form similar to that given in Figure 4.1. The receipts side of the summary shows cash from customers of £23,750 that, when added to the sum available at the start, £510, means that cash totalling £24,260 came available to the business at some stage during 19X1. From this total, cash payments of £21,775 must be deducted, leaving a cash balance at the year end of £2,485.

Provided the rudimentary financial facts referred to in this section can be

Cash transactions, year to 31 December 19X1

Receipts	£	Payments	£
Opening balance of cash	510	Payments to suppliers	17,380
Sale of goods	23,750	Wages	2,560
		Rent and rates	840
		Lighting and heating	620
		General expenses	375
			21,775
		Closing balance of cash	2,485
	24,260		24,260

Figure 4.1   Summary of figures for receipts and payments

assembled, it is possible to prepare a full set of final accounts. The process, described as the preparation of accounts from cash records, is examined in this chapter.

THE MATCHING CONCEPT: Profit = Revenue – Expenditure

Chapter 3 demonstrated how profit can be measured in the absence of detailed information concerning trading transactions undertaken during a particular accounting period, i.e. it is computed by identifying the change in capital between the beginning and the end of the year. Where there exists an adequate accounting record of transactions undertaken, *during the year*, profit is instead computed in accordance with the *matching concept*, i.e. the accountant measures profit by comparing or 'matching' the total cost of the many trading transactions undertaken during an accounting period with the total revenues arising therefrom.

Mex Cars Ltd is a motor vehicle distributor that prepares its accounts on the calendar-year basis. Ten cars are purchased during 19X1 for £4,500 each and sold for £6,000 each.   ***Example 4.1***

Calculate profit by matching revenues with expenditures.   **Required**

	£	**Solution**
Revenue:		
Proceeds from sale of cars (£6,000 × 10)	60,000	
Less: Expenditure:		
Cost of cars sold (£4,500 × 10)	45,000	
Profit	15,000	

GROSS PROFIT AND NET PROFIT

The balance of profit, which is arrived at by matching sales proceeds with the actual costs of goods sold, is called *gross profit*. In practice many other costs are also incurred, such as salaries paid to employees, commissions paid to salespeople, rent and rates for the showroom and office accommodation, and the numerous incidental expenses such as telephone costs, stationery, etc. Since these outlays are incurred to help generate sales revenue, they must also be deducted to leave a final balance called *net profit*. Revenues and expenditures are matched against one another in the *trading account and the profit and loss account* (usually abbreviated to trading and profit and loss account), and a common method of presenting this accounting statement is given in Figure 4.2.

The gross profit is calculated in the trading account and the remaining expenses are deducted in the profit and loss account. It might occur to readers that the calculation of profit on the basis of changes in capital is a rather more straightforward process than by comparing revenue with expenditure. The accumulation of figures for sales revenue and the many items of expenditure incurred during the year is a far more laborious and time-consuming task than the identification of figures for capital at just two dates: the beginning and end of the accounting period. Part of the justification for the extra work is that trading transactions entered into during an accounting period are recorded not only to enable profit to be measured but also to facilitate effective control over inflows and outflows of cash and goods, e.g. to ensure that cash is collected from customers and that employees are paid the amounts due to them.

Detailed accounting records also enable management to make a more useful calculation of profit because, although the end result is the same, the

Trading and Profit and Loss Account, Mex Cars Ltd, year to 31 December 19X1

Expenditure	£	Revenue	£
Cost of cars sold	45,000	Sales	60,000
Gross profit	15,000		
	60,000		60,000
Salaries	6,200	Gross profit	15,000
Commissions	600		
Rent and rates	1,400		
Lighting and heating	250		
Telephone	150		
Postage and stationery	220		
Advertising	370		
General expenses	500		
	9,690		
Net profit	5,310		
	15,000		15,000

Figure 4.2   Trading account and profit and loss account

preparation of a trading and profit and loss account produces the following advantages. First, it contains a comprehensive statement of *how* the net profit balance has been achieved. Second, it is a valuable means for assessing performance, e.g. by comparing this year's gross profit and expenses with results achieved last year, and for reaching decisions concerning the future allocation of resources.

THE PROBLEM OF PERIODIC PROFIT CALCULATION

The frequency with which the profit and loss account and balance sheet are prepared varies depending on the circumstances of the particular business. As a minimum, however, accounts must be prepared once a year – limited companies are legally required to prepare annual accounts for publication, while sole traders and partnerships are obliged to prepare annual accounts for tax purposes. To provide the information needed to take day-to-day decisions designed to achieve the most effective use of available resources, management requires more frequent calculations of profit, and the preparation of quarterly or even monthly management accounts is a common feature within commerce and industry today.

The calculation of periodic profit causes difficulties because business activity is continuous. For example, a business may last for ten years but, for accounting purposes, it must be split into at least ten accounting periods, each lasting one year. Many transactions cause no difficulty because they can be easily identified with a particular accounting period. For example, assuming accounts are prepared on the calendar-year basis, an item of stock purchased and paid for in January 19X1 and sold for cash in February 19X1 must clearly be taken into account in computing the profit for 19X1. Problems arise with transactions that *overlap* the end of one accounting period and the beginning of another. Consider the following facts assuming a 31 December accounting date:

1. Stocks delivered to a customer in December 19X1 but not paid for until January 19X2.
2. Stocks purchased and paid for in November 19X1 but not sold until March 19X2.
3. Rates paid on 1 October 19X1 for the six months to 31 March 19X2.
4. Machinery purchased and paid for in 19X1, which is expected to last for eight years.

The problem of deciding whether these transactions give rise to revenues and expenditures in 19X1 or 19X2 or another accounting period is solved by the accountant making certain assumptions and applying a range of accounting conventions to the factual information generated by the accounting system. These procedures are examined in the following sections.

THE IDENTIFICATION OF REVENUE: THE REALIZATION CONCEPT

Revenue is obtained from the sale of goods purchased in the case of a trading organization, from the sale of goods manufactured in the case of an industrial concern and from the supply of services in the case of a service industry. For accounting purposes, revenue is assumed to arise at the point of sale. In the case of a cash sale this is when the goods or services are supplied in exchange for cash; in the case of a credit sale, it occurs when the goods or services have been supplied and the sales invoice delivered to the customer. The assumption that revenue, and therefore profit, arises when the sale takes place is called the *realization concept* and it is a good illustration of how accounting procedures are based on generally agreed conventions rather than indisputable facts.

For example, consider the case of a manufacturer of motor vehicles where demand exceeds supply. A great deal of work goes into building the car and, when completed, little more needs to be done to earn the profit. Demand exceeds supply and so delivery to a motor vehicle distributor is likely to take place fairly soon to satisfy consumer requirements. No profit is recognized during production, however, and the motor vehicle remains in the books at cost until the sale takes place. This procedure demonstrates the rather cautious approach towards profit measurement the accountant generally adopts.

It might be argued that, during the course of the production process, profit is gradually being earned that should be recognized in the accounts, but the accountant prefers to wait until the expected profit is validated by a sale. This view is taken partly because it would be difficult to decide how much extra value to recognize at any interim stage and partly because it is considered imprudent to anticipate sales that may not occur. At the other extreme it might be argued that, in the case of a credit sale, it would be even safer to wait until the cash is actually collected before recognizing a profit. But although the accountant rightly has the reputation of being cautious, he or she is not that cautious. The goods have been supplied and, in exchange, the business has a legally enforceable debt against the customer. The collection of cash will in most cases be a mere formality and no further delay in the recognition of revenue is thought to be justified (the complication of bad debts is examined in Chapter 7).

Example 4.2   On 1 January 19X1 Jubilee Ltd received an order for an 'indestructible' aluminium pallet. The pallet was priced in the company's catalogue at £5,000. The pallet was manufactured during the week ended 6 January and production costs totalling £2,000 were incurred. At close of business, on 6 January, the pallet was transferred to the company's warehouse and held in stock until 15 January when it was dispatched to the customer. Cash, £5,000, was collected from the customer on 12 February 19X1.

Required   Calculate (a) the value recognized in the accounts, and (b) the profit recognized in the accounts at each of the following stages of the transaction:

(i)   receipt of order;
(ii) production of pallet;
(iii) transfer of pallet to stock;
(iv) dispatch of pallet to customer; and
(v)   collection of cash.

Stage	Value recognized £	Profit recognized £
(i) Receipt of order	—	—
(ii) Production of pallet	2,000	—
(iii) Pallet to stock	2,000	—
(iv) Dispatch (sale)	5,000	3,000
(v) Collection of cash	5,000	—

Note
Profit is recognized when the pallet is dispatched to the customer. No additional profit is
recognized when cash is collected. The only amendment to the accounts made at this
date is that a debtor of £5,000 is replaced by cash of a similar amount.

.

Calculating sales from records of cash receipts

The sales figure is calculated by taking the figure for cash received from
customers during the year, deducting opening debtors and adding closing
debtors. The purpose of the calculation is to convert the figure for cash received into the figure for goods or services supplied.

During 19X1, John received £17,500 from customers in respect of credit   **Example 4.3**
sales. At 1 January 19X1, his trade debtors amounted to £3,600 and at 31
December 19X1 they were £4,720.

The calculation of sales for 19X1.   **Required**

Calculation of sales: £   **Solution**
   Cash received in respect of credit sales   17,500
   Less: Opening trade debtors   3,600

                                                                 13,900
   Add: Closing trade debtors   4,720

Sales   18,620

Of the £17,500 received during the year, £3,600 was collected from customers
to whom goods were sold in 19X0 and that would have been reported as
revenue in the trading account for that year. The balance, £13,900, represents
cash received in respect of sales actually made *during* 19X1. To this must be
added closing debtors for goods sold during 19X1, but not yet paid for, to

produce the sales figure of £18,620.

The rule to remember is therefore

$$\text{Sales} = \text{Cash received from customers} - \text{Opening debtors} + \text{Closing debtors}$$

MATCHING EXPENDITURE WITH REVENUE: THE BENEFIT PRINCIPLE

The first step in the calculation of profit for the year is to compute revenue; the second step involves identifying the expenditures that must be matched against revenue. The basic test is, 'Which accounting period benefits from the expenditure?' If the answer is the current accounting period then the expenditure is charged against revenue for the current year. If the answer is a future accounting period, then the expenditure must be carried forward as an asset in the balance sheet and charged against the revenue of the future accounting period that benefits. If the answer is both the current period and one or more future periods, an apportionment must be made. This process, which bases the charge on *benefits received* during the year, rather than payments made during the year, is called the *accruals concept*. The application of this concept to specific business facts is examined next.

Accounting for stock

The calculation of the figure for cost of goods sold, to be matched with sales revenue for the purpose of computing gross profit, involves two steps:

1. *Calculate purchases* The procedure is analogous to that followed when computing sales, and may be summarized using the following formula:

$$\text{Purchases} = \text{Cash paid to suppliers} - \text{Opening creditors} + \text{Closing creditors}$$

2. *Calculate cost of goods sold* It is unusual for all the goods purchased during the year to be sold by the end of the year. The items that remain in stock, at the year end, should be deducted from purchases and carried forward, in the balance sheet, to the following accounting period that will benefit from their sale. In a similar manner, stocks brought forward from the previous year and sold during the current accounting period must be added to purchases and matched with the current year's sales proceeds. The calculation that must be memorized in this case is

$$\text{Cost of goods sold} = \text{Opening stock} + \text{Purchases} - \text{Closing stock}$$

Example 4.4 James made payments by cheque to suppliers of goods on credit amounting to £27,300 during 19X2. In addition, he made cash purchases of £1,600. Trade creditors at 1 January 19X2 and 31 December 19X2 amounted respectively to £4,750 and £6,100. Opening stocks were £10,250, while closing stocks amounted to £9,640.

Calculate (a) purchases and (b) cost of goods sold for 19X2. **Required**

Solution

(a) Calculation of purchases:

	£
Cash paid to suppliers:	
Credit purchases	27,300
Cash purchases	1,600
	28,900
Less: Opening creditors	4,750
	24,150
Add: Closing creditors	6,100
Purchases	30,250

(b) Calculation of cost of goods sold:

	£
Opening stock	10,250
Add: Purchases	30,250
	40,500
Less: Closing stock	9,640
Cost of goods sold	30,860

The calculations discussed and illustrated above are central to the measurement of profit by matching revenue with expenditure. Readers should test their understanding of these calculations by working Example 4.5.

The following information is provided relating to Peter's business for 19X3: *Example 4.5*

Cash collected from customers in respect of	£
Credit sales	41,750
Cash sales	12,350
Payments to suppliers	36,590

Balances at	1 January £	31 December £
Trade debtors	12,650	11,780
Trade creditors	6,540	8,270
Stock	9,150	9,730

(a) Calculations for 19X3 of **Required**

    (i) receipts from customers,
    (ii) sales,
    (iii) purchases, and
    (iv) cost of goods sold.

(b) The trading account of Peter's business for 19X3.

Solution   (a) (i)   Cash collected in respect of: £
                         Credit sales   41,750
                         Cash sales   12,350

                         Receipts from customers   54,100

           (ii)   Receipts from customers   54,100
                  Less: Opening debtors   (12,650)
                  Add: Closing debtors   11,780

                  Sales: 53,230

           (iii) Payments to suppliers   36,590
                  Less: Opening creditors   (6,540)
                  Add: Closing creditors   8,270

                  Purchases   38,320

           (iv)   Opening stock   9,150
                  Add: Purchases   38,320
                  Less: Closing stock   (9,730)

                  Cost of goods sold   37,740

       (b)

Trading Account for 19X3

	£	Sales	£
Opening stock	9,150	Sales	53,230
Add: Purchases	38,320		
Less: Closing stock	(9,730)		
Cost of goods sold	37,740		
Gross profit	15,490		
	53,230		53,230

Note
Readers should note that it is conventional practice to show the calculation of cost of
goods sold on the face of the trading account, but not the calculations of purchases and
sales.

Accounting for services: accruals and prepayments

When preparing accounts from cash records, it is also necessary to adjust
cash payments for services rendered to the company, so that the amount
charged in the profit and loss account reflects the cost of benefits actually
consumed during the year.

For certain services, payments are made before the associated benefits are
received, i.e. the payment is made *in advance*. In the case of rent and rates,

advance payments are made for the right to occupy the property for a fixed future period of time. Where the period of occupation covers the end of one accounting year and the beginning of another, an arithmetic apportionment of the amount paid must be made between the two consecutive accounting periods. For example, if a rental of £600 is paid on 1 April 19X1 for the forthcoming twelve months, and the accounts are made up on the calendar-year basis, nine months (or three-quarters) of the total benefit is received during 19X1 and three months (or one-quarter) of the benefit is received during 19X2. Therefore, ¾ × £600 = £450 is charged against revenue arising during 19X1 and ¼ × £600 = £150 is carried forward in the balance sheet as an asset; it is called 'prepaid expense' and is charged against revenue arising during 19X2.

The majority of expenses are, however, paid *in arrears*, mainly because the amount charged depends on the extent to which the service has been utilized. Examples are electricity charges, telephone charges (except the rental) and the wage bill. In these cases it is necessary to raise an 'accrual', at the end of the accounting period, representing the value of the benefit received but not yet paid for. The amount of the accrual may be estimated on the basis of past experience. Alternatively, where the bill is received by the time the accounts are prepared, an apportionment may be made in the manner described in the previous paragraph. This does not necessarily produce strictly accurate results because the service will not have been utilized at an even rate throughout the period under consideration. However, the error is unlikely to be significant, and the extra work and cost involved in obtaining a more precise apportionment would not be justified. The amount accrued is charged against revenue in the profit and loss account and carried forward in the balance sheet as a current liability under the heading 'accrued expense'.

The following information is provided relating to Mark's business for 19X4:			**Example 4.6**

Payments during the year for	£
Rates	500
Telephone	375

Balances at	*1 Jan.*	*31 Dec.*
	£	£
Rates paid in advance	100	125
Telephone charges outstanding	50	62

Calculations of the amount to be charged against revenue for 19X4 in respect of (a) rates (b) telephone. **Required**

(a) Rates:	£	**Solution**
Payments during 19X4	500	
Add: Amount prepaid at 1 January 19X4	100*	
	600	
Less: Amount paid at 31 December 19X4	125	
Charge for the year	475	

Note
* This amount was paid in 19X3, but relates to the occupation of the premises during 19X4 and must be carried forward and charged against revenue arising during 19X4.

(b) Telephone:

Payments 19X4	375
Less: Amount accrued at 1 January 19X4	50†
	325
Add: Amount accrued at 31 December 19X4	62
	387

Note
† This amount was paid in 19X4, but relates to services received during 19X3; therefore it will have been charged against revenue arising during 19X3.

Accounting for depreciation of fixed assets

Fixed assets are usually paid for at the date of acquisition, or soon afterwards, but they are expected to *benefit* the firm for many years. For example, a motor vehicle might last five years, a machine ten years and a building fifty years or more. It would therefore be unreasonable to burden revenue arising during the year that the asset is acquired with its entire cost. At the same time, most fixed assets have a limited useful life, and it would be equally wrong to keep these items indefinitely in the books at cost.

The term accountants use to describe the fall in the value of a fixed asset between the date it is acquired and the date it is sold or scrapped is 'depreciation'. It may be defined as the fall in the value of a fixed asset due to the passage of time, usage or obsolescence. This reduction in value is acknowledged, in the accounts, by making an annual charge designed to spread the loss over the periods that are expected to benefit from using the asset. There are many different methods of charging depreciation, and we will concentrate here on the one that is most common and easy to apply for illustration purposes, namely the straight-line method (sometimes called the equal instalment method). This method assumes that each accounting period receives the same amount of benefit from using the asset and the total decline in its value is therefore spread equally over the period of ownership. The formula used to calculate the depreciation charge for one year is as follows:

$$\text{Straight-line depreciation} = \frac{\text{Original cost} - \text{Estimated disposal value}}{\text{Estimated life}}$$

Paul purchased a machine for £130,000 on 1 January 19X1. It is estimated that the machine will have a useful life of six years and then be sold for £10,000.

Example 4.7

(a) Calculate the straight-line depreciation charge for each of the years 19X1–X6, for inclusion in the profit and loss account; and

Required

(b) calculate the book value of the machine at the end of each of the years 19X1–X6, to be reported in the balance sheet.

(a) Depreciation charge = $\dfrac{£130,000 - £10,000}{6}$ = £20,000 per annum

Solution

(b)

Balance Sheet extracts, 31 December

	19X1 £000	19X2 £000	19X3 £000	19X4 £000	19X5 £000	19X6 £000
Fixed assets						
Machine at cost	130	130	130	130	130	130
Less: Accumulated depreciation	20	40	60	80	100	120
	110	90	70	50	30	10

The effect of charging depreciation is that the balance sheet value of the machine is gradually reduced to its disposal value. If everything works out as planned, on 31 December 19X6 the written-down value of the machine, £10,000, will be removed from the balance sheet and replaced by cash of an equal value. Events may not progress quite so smoothly, and it may turn out that the estimates on which the calculation was based prove to be wrong, i.e. the machine might not last for six years or sell for £10,000 at the end of its useful life. These complications are considered in Chapters 7 and 8.

THE PREPARATION OF ACCOUNTS FROM CASH RECORDS: A WORKED EXAMPLE

The preparation of accounts from cash records involves the following four steps:

Step 1 Prepare an opening balance sheet, sometimes called the 'statement of affairs'. This shows the proprietor's opening capital, which is needed when preparing the year-end balance sheet.

Step 2 Calculate revenues and expenditures for inclusion in the trading and profit and loss account.

Step 3 Prepare the trading and profit and loss account.

Step 4 Prepare the closing balance sheet.

Example 4.8   William is a trader who has carried on business for a number of years. In the past a friend has prepared accounts that were sufficient to enable William to agree his tax liabilities. William's friend has now left the country and is therefore unable to help. William maintains separate files of invoices received from suppliers and issued to customers.

The following summary has been prepared from William's paying-in books, cheque books and bank statements for 19X2:

Bank Summary

	£		£
Cash sales	39,640	Opening balance	3,520
Proceeds from credit sales	18,500	Payments to suppliers	31,910
Sale of furniture	250	Rates	2,800
		Personal drawings	6,500
		Wages for part-time staff	5,930
		General expenses	3,180
		Vehicle	4,000
		Closing balance	550
	58,390		58,390

The following additional information has been obtained from the files of invoices and other books and records of William:

1. William has paid all sales proceeds into his bank except for £200 that was used to pay additional part-time staff over the busy Christmas period.
2. Assets and liabilities at 31 December, based on an analysis of the invoice files, and from discussions with William, were as follows:

	19X1	19X2
	£	£
Premises at cost	6,600	6,600
Furniture at book value	3,000	Note 3
Stocks	4,250	5,760
Trade creditors	4,630	4,920
Trade debtors	2,140	2,320
Rates paid in advance	180	200
General expenses accrued	320	290

3. During the year furniture with a book value of £300, on 1 January 19X2, was sold for £250.
4. William charges depreciation at 10 per cent on the book value of furniture owned at the end of the year.
5. The vehicle was purchased on 1 July 19X2 and is to be written off over five years assuming a resale value of £1,000 at the end of that period. Ignore depreciation of premises.

Required   The trading and profit and loss account of William's business for the year ended 31 December 19X2 and the balance sheet at that date.

Solution   This question is answered by following the four steps outlined at the beginning of this section.

Step 1
Balance Sheet at 1 January 19X2

	£	£
Fixed assets		
Premises		6,600
Furniture		3,000
		9,600
Current assets		
Stocks	4 250	
Trade debtors	2,140	
Prepaid expenses	180	
	6,570	
Less: Current liabilities		
Trade creditors	4,630	
Accrued expenses	320	
Bank overdraft	3,520	
	8,470	
Working capital		(1,900)
Capital		7,700

Step 2

Workings

		£
W1	Sales:	
	Paid into bank:	
	Cash sales	39,640
	Credit sales	18,500
	Proceeds not paid in	200
	Total cash received	58,340
	Less: Opening debtors	(2,140)
	Add: Closing debtors	2,320
		58,520
W2	Purchases:	
	Payments to suppliers	31,910
	Less: Opening creditors	(4,630)
	Add: Closing creditors	4,920
		32,200

W3 Rates:
    Paid during year   2,800
    Add: Opening advance payment   180
    Less: Closing advance payment   (200)
                                               ─────
                                               2,780

W4 General expenses:
    Paid during year   3,180
    Less: Opening accrual   (320)
    Add: Closing accrual   290
                                               ─────
                                               3,150

W5 Wages:
    Paid by cheque   5,930
    Paid in cash   200
                                               ─────
                                               6,130

W6 Loss on furniture sale:
    Book value   300
    Sales proceeds   250
                                               ─────
                                                  50

W7 Depreciation of furniture:
    $(£3,000 - £300) \times 10\% = £270$
W8 Depreciation of vehicle:
    $(£4,000 - £1,000) \div 5\frac{1}{2} \times {}^* = £300$

Note
* The vehicle has only been owned for six months.

Step 3

Trading and Profit and Loss Account for 19X2

	£			£	
Purchases	32,200	W2	Sales	58,520	W1
Add: Opening stock	4,250				
Less: Closing stock	(5,760)				
Cost of goods sold	30,690				
Gross profit	27,830				
	58,520			58,520	
Rates	2,780	W3	Gross profit	27,830	
General expenses	3,150	W4			
Wages	6,130	W5			
Loss on sale of furniture	50	W6			

Depreciation:		
furniture	270	W7
vehicle	300	W8
	12,680	
Net profit	15,150	
	27,830	

27,830

Step 4

Balance Sheet at 31 December 19X2

	£	£		£	£
Fixed assets			Opening capital		7,700
Premises at cost		6,600	Add: Net profit		15,150
Furniture	2,700		Less: Drawings		(6,500)
Less: Depreciation	270	2,430			16,350
Vehicle at cost	4,000		*Current liabilities*		
Less: Depreciation	300	3,700	Trade creditors	4,920	
		12,730	General expenses	290	5,210
Current assets					
Stocks	5,760				
Trade debtors	2,320				
Prepaid rates	200				
Bank	550	8,830			
		21,560			21,560

Trading and profit and loss account presented in vertical format

Chapter 3 drew attention to the fact that today the balance sheet is usually presented in the vertical format rather than the horizontal format. The same is the case with the trading and profit and loss account. The reasons are similar: the layout is thought to be more easily comprehended by the non-accountant; it is possible to present a number of years' results on a single sheet; and comparison of results between years is made much easier. The trading and profit and loss account of William is now reproduced in Figure 4.3 in vertical format for the purpose of illustration. In exam questions, instructions to use either the horizontal format or vertical format must be complied with but, where no instruction is given, either presentation may be followed.

Readers should now work Questions 4.1, 4.2, 4.3 and 4.4 at the end of this chapter.

	£	£
Sales		58,520
Less: Purchases	32,200	
Add: Opening stock	4,250	
Less: Closing stock	(5,760)	
Cost of goods sold		30,690
Gross profit		27,830
Less: Rates	2,780	
General expenses	3,150	
Wages	6,130	
Loss on sale of furniture	50	
Depreciation:		
furniture	270	
vehicle	300	12,680
Net profit		15,150

Figure 4.3   Trading and profit and loss account of Williams for 19X2

CLUBS AND SOCIETIES

Clubs and societies are a common feature of most local communities. Such organizations are often formed as the result of a group of individuals, possessing a common interest, voluntarily joining together with the objective of providing a social facility otherwise not available. For instance, most towns have their own tennis club, parent–teachers' association and children's play-group. Such clubs and societies are usually described as *non-profit-making organizations* whose objectives are to further recreational, educational or religious activities. This description is a little misleading. Many clubs and societies expect to generate an excess of income over expenditure but, unlike commercial concerns, this is not their principal objective. Furthermore, any profit that does arise is not distributed to members but is instead viewed as a source of finance for facilities required to extend their activities. These facts should be clearly spelt out in the rules governing the activities of the club or society. Provided this is done, the organization is exempted from taxation.

The scale of the activities undertaken by many, though by no means all, clubs and societies is relatively small. The officers of these organizations, namely the chairperson, secretary, treasurer, etc., are unpaid volunteers. For these reasons a comprehensive accounting system is unlikely to exist. Indeed, in the majority of clubs and societies, the accounting system is unlikely to consist of more than a record of receipts and payments during the year. At the year end, a decision must be taken concerning the form the final accounts should take. Perhaps because of the absence of necessary expertise, and also perhaps because there is little demand for accounting information from the members, the treasurer may simply prepare a 'receipts and payments account' for the year. This is an analysed list of total cash coming into and going out of the club during the year; no attempt is made to take account of debts and liabilities outstanding at the balance sheet date and no balance sheet is prepared. This form of account may be satisfactory for the very small club or society, but is totally inadequate for the larger organization where there exist valuable assets or substantial outstanding liabilities (perhaps because a bank loan has been raised to build a new squash court) of which the members should be made aware. For the larger organizations, the accounts must be prepared in accordance with the *accruals concept,* and the procedure then followed is almost exactly the same as that described for industrial and commercial concerns earlier in this chapter.

Accounting terms used by clubs and societies

The only distinction, of any significance, between properly prepared final accounts of clubs and societies, on the one hand, and those of industrial and commercial concerns, on the other, is that different terms are used to describe certain essentially similar financial magnitudes. The main differences are as shown in Table 4.1.

Table 4.1 Differences in terms used by clubs and societies

Industrial and commercial concerns	Club/society	Comment
Profit and loss account	Income and expenditure account	These differences reflect the fact that clubs and societies are not profit orientated. When computing income and expenditure, however, the accruals concept is usually applied in exactly the same way as when calculating figures for inclusion in the profit and loss account
Net profit/net loss	Surplus/ deficit	
Capital	Accumulated fund	The term capital denotes a proprietorial interest that does not exist in clubs and societies, e.g. if a member resigns he or she has no right to reclaim his or her joining fee

Readers should now work Question 4.5 at the end of this chapter.

Subscriptions and entry fees

A main source of revenue for clubs and societies is the subscriptions received from members, but it is often considered inappropriate to apply the full force of the accruals concept to this item. At the end of an accounting period, there are usually subscriptions that remain unpaid for that year and subscriptions received in advance for the following year. Strict application of the accruals concept requires subscriptions outstanding to be credited to income and treated as a debt due to the club. This treatment is rarely followed in practice, although there may be no doubt that an individual has made use of the club's facilities during the year. The fact that his or her subscription remains unpaid at the year end is a fairly clear indication that it will never be collected. The former member has probably now left the club and the amount outstanding would be insufficient to justify the costs of any legal ac tion needed to achieve its recovery. In accordance with the accruals concept, however, subscriptions received in advance should be shown as a liability in the balance sheet and treated as income of the following accounting period.

Example 4.9

At the end of 19X2 subscriptions outstanding amounted to £300 and subscriptions received in advance for 19X3 amounted to £90. During 19X3 subscriptions received amounted to £5,400. This included the £300 outstanding at the end of 19X2 and £120 in advance for 19X4. Subscriptions outstanding at the end of 19X3 amounted to £500.

Required

Calculate the amount to be credited to the income and expenditure account for 19X3 assuming that subscriptions are accounted for on (a) the cash basis, (b), the accruals basis and (c) the prudent basis.

Solution

		£
(a)	Cash basis	5,400

(b)	Accruals basis:	
	Cash received in 19X3	5,400
	Add: Received in 19X2 for 19X3	90
	Outstanding at end of 19X3	500
		5,990
	Less: Outstanding at end of 19X2	(300)
	Received in 19X3 for 19X4	(120)
		5,570

(c)	Prudent basis (subscriptions outstanding ignored):	£
	Cash received in 19X3	5,400
	Add: Received in 19X2 for 19X3	90
		5,490
	Less: Received in 19X3 for 19X4	(120)
		5,370

Many clubs charge new members an entry fee. These receipts may be credited either to income or direct to the accumulated fund. Either treatment is acceptable, but the method chosen should be applied consistently from year to year with the amount involved clearly disclosed. Life membership fees may also be accounted for in a variety of ways. There are three main alternatives:

1. Credit to the accumulated fund.
2. Credit in full to the income and expenditure account in the year received.
3. Credit initially to a life membership account, and transfer the fee to the income and expenditure account, in instalments, over an agreed number of years.

The third alternative is theoretically superior, since it attempts to relate income to the periods when the member uses the club's facilities, but it is also the most time-consuming accounting treatment.

Identifying the results of separate activities

It is always important, when deciding what form the annual accounts should take, to consider carefully the information that is likely to be of interest to the recipients of these reports. For this reason the accounts should be designed to reflect the particular nature of the organization's activities. It is quite usual for clubs and societies to have a number of spheres of interest. For instance, a recreation club may provide facilities for lawn tennis, squash, table tennis, bowls, rugby and cricket. It is usually considered useful to identify the contribution of each section, whether positive or negative, to the overall finances of the club. This information is not, however, necessarily required as a basis for deciding to extend or discontinue particular facilities. It must be remembered that it is the aim of clubs to provide recreational facilities, not to make a profit.

However, the extent to which the profitable sections can subsidize the unprofitable is not unlimited and, if a succession of poor results reflects a decline in the demand for a particular sport, the facility may have to be withdrawn in the interests of the club members as a whole. More likely, significant deficits in certain areas will be interpreted as evidence of the need to revise subscriptions upwards. For these reasons a separate income and expenditure account should be prepared for each section, and the balances transferred to a general income and expenditure account where they will be combined with any unallocated items of income and expenditure arising from the club's activities.

Many clubs provide bar facilities at which drinks and perhaps tobacco and refreshments are sold and, where this occurs, the relevant items of income and expenditure are collected together in the bar trading account. The balance of this account, whether a profit or a loss, is also transferred to the general income and expenditure account.

In the case of industrial and commercial organizations, separate identification of the results of different product lines in order to show whether they are operating at a profit or a loss is a principal basis for management decisions on whether to expand or close down an area of activity. The information made available for the purpose of this type of management decision is examined in Chapter 9. Readers should now attempt Questions 4.6 and 4.7 at the end of this chapter.

Questions

The preparation of accounts from incomplete records involves fundamental accounting procedures that must be mastered before readers can expect to make progress in their accounting studies. It is for this reason that questions testing students' understanding of these procedures are extremely common in examinations. Such questions often follow a pattern similar to William (Example 4.8 in this chapter), and solutions should consist of the same four steps recommended for answering that question. Questions 4.1, 4.5, 4.6 and 4.7 are of this type. Some variation is of course possible, and the remaining questions in this section include certain innovations. The opening balance sheet is provided in Question 4.2 so that only steps 2, 3 and 4 need to be processed. Question 4.3 is a revision question that deals with matters covered in Chapter 3 as well as the present chapter. Question 4.4 is a new business and so only steps 2, 3 and 4 apply.

4.1 Stoll, a trader, pays all his business takings into his bank account. All business payments are made by cheque. The following is a summary of his bank account for the year 19X5:

Bank Summary

	£		£
Balance 1 January 19X5	480	Trade creditors	24,800
Received from debtors	31,560	General expenses	2,524
		Rent	300
		Drawings	3,600
		Balance 31 December 19X5	816
	32,040		32,040

The following information is obtained from the available records:

	31 Dec. 19X4	31 Dec. 19X5
	£	£
Debtors for goods sold	1,900	2,344
Trade creditors	1,630	1,930
Stock	2,040	1,848
Furniture and fittings:		
at cost less depreciation	400	360

Required

(a) Calculate the balance of Stoll's capital at 31 December 19X4.
(b) Prepare the trading and profit and loss account for the year 19X5 and the balance sheet at 31 December 19X5. Present these accounting statements in vertical format.

4.2 Bennett commenced business as a retail trader at the beginning of 19X0. He maintains no formal system of ledger accounts for recording business transactions. An accountant was called in during 19X2 to prepare accounts for 19X1, in order to enable tax liabilities to be agreed. The following balance sheet was prepared as at 1 January 19X1:

Balance Sheet, 1 January 19X1

	£		£
Motor vehicles at cost	10,000	Capital	8,720
Less: Accumulated		Loan at 15%	2,000
depreciation	2,000	Creditors	850
	———	Accrued expenses	260
	8,000	Bank overdraft	2,030
Stock	3,750		
Debtors	1,060		
Prepaid expenses	400		
Bank deposit account	650		
	———		———
	13,860		13,860

The following information is provided regarding 19X1:

1. An analysis of the business bank accounts provided the following information:

Receipts	£	Payments	£
Cash sales	32,100	Paid to suppliers	20,850
Proceeds from credit sales	7,560	General expenses	7,560
Legacy from relative	2,650	Drawings	12,500
Bank interest received	50	Motor vehicle	4,000
	———		———
	42,360		44,910

2. During the year, a new motor vehicle was purchased for £4,000; Bennett depreciates vehicles at the rate of 20 per cent on cost.
3. Debtors outstanding at the end of 19X1 amounted to £1,840, none of which was considered to be bad or doubtful.
4. Amounts due to suppliers at the end of 19X1 totalled £1,140 and stock was valued at £4,600.
5. Accruals and prepayments of general expenses, at the end of 19X1, amounted to £310 and £520 respectively.

Required

The trading and profit and loss account of Bennett's business for 19X1 and the balance sheet at 31 December 19X1.

4.3 The following is the balance sheet of Stondon, a trader, at 31 December 19X2:

Balance Sheet

	£		£
Furniture and fittings	800	Capital	7,940
Stock	5,384		
Trade debtors	4,162	Trade creditors	3,294
Balance at bank	888		
	———		———
	11,234		11,234

In January 19X3 Stondon sold certain private investments for £4,200; he purchased a motor van for business use for £3,000 and paid the balance of the proceeds into his business bank account.

At 31 December 19X3, trade debtors amounted to £4,124, stock-in-trade was valued at £6,891 and trade creditors amounted to £3,586. Stondon's business bank account was overdrawn by £782. His drawings during 19X3 were £12,840.

The total of running expenses charged to the profit and loss account for the year 19X3 amounted to £14,420. This total included £500 for depreciation of the motor van.

Stondon's gross profit is at the rate of 25 per cent of selling price for all goods sold during 19X3.

Required

(a) Prepare Stondon's balance sheet at 31 December 19X3.
(b) Calculate Stondon's net profit for 19X3 on the basis of changes in capital.
(c) Reconstruct the trading and profit and loss account of Stondon's business for the year 19X3.

Note
Ignore depreciation of furniture and fittings.

4.4 Nigel Appleby had lived abroad for six years before returning during April 1992. He had saved enough money to enable him to think carefully about his future. After several weeks research, Appleby decided to start his own business, retailing office furniture.

Appleby started his business by depositing £62,500 of his savings into a business bank account on 1 October 1992. In addition, he negotiated a bank loan of £40,000. Suitable premises had been identified and were purchased for £95,400. Shop fittings and other equipment were acquired at a cost of £8,800.

By 8 October, stocks of office furniture, costing £31,900, had been purchased and Appleby commenced trading at this time. Initially, sales were slow but as time went by sales improved.

On 1 October 1993, Appleby reflected on his first year of business. He felt that the year had gone well until he received his bank statement which showed an overdraft at 30 September 1993. A summary of the business bank account for the financial year is shown below:

Receipts	£	Payments	£
Appleby	62,500	Premises	95,400
Loan	40,000	Fittings & equipment	8,800
Customers	233,660	Trade suppliers	180,790
Interest	100	Business rates	6,000
Shop fittings	1,150	Heat & light	680
Balance c/f	2,090	Wages	21,920
		Deposit account	5,000
		Loan interest	4,400
		Bank loan	4,000
		Miscellaneous expenses	12,510
	339,500		339,500

Other information available:

On 30 June 1993, Appleby sold some of the shop fittings he had bought previously. These had cost £2,500 on 2 October 1992 but he only managed to sell them for £1,150. He had originally planned to keep all shop fittings for three years.

Appleby did not bank £12,420 of his takings from customers. He retained this amount for personal use.

One he became reasonably well established, his suppliers allowed him cash discount if their accounts were settled by the end of the month following the date of supply. The total value of discount received by Appleby was £570.

On 1 April 1993, Appleby invested £5,000 in a special deposit account which carries an interest rate of 8 per cent per annum. The interest is normally credited at three monthly intervals.

At 30 September, Appleby estimated the value of the shop fittings and equipment as £4,200. He thought that the value of the premises remained intact. He calculated that customers owed him £48,610 and that he owed trade suppliers £16,960. His records showed unsold office furniture in stock at cost of £32,500. In addition, he had an electricity bill for £140 in respect of quarter ended 30 September 1993, unpaid and he owed wages of £230.

The business rates payment made during his financial year covered the eighteen-month period commencing 1 October 1992.

Required

(a) Prepare Appleby's trading and profit and loss accounts in respect of the year ended 30 September 1993, and a balance sheet at that date.

(18 marks)

(b) Note four ways in which Appleby might clear his bank overdraft.

(4 marks)

(Total: 22 marks)

(ICSA, Introduction to Accounting, December 1993)

4.5 The following details are extracted from the books of the Fellowship Club:

Balances at	31 Dec. 19X7	31 Dec. 19X8
	£	£
Bar stock	8,200	11,936
Creditors for bar supplies	4,080	4,568
Creditors for expenses	160	248

Summary of Bank Account for 19X8

	£		£
Balance 1 January 19X8	13,280	Bar purchases	80,760
Subscriptions received	12,400	Salaries	16,840
Bar sales	107,600	Rent of club premises	2,800
Interest on investments	4,160	Rates	2,000
		General expenses	5,360
		Cost of new investments	26,000
		Balance 31 December 19X8	3,680
	137,440		137,440

On 1 January 19X8 the club held temporary investments it had purchased for £49,200, and the furniture in use was valued at £30,400. The club is building up its investments to enable it to purchase its own clubhouse in due course. Depreciation should be charged on the furniture at the rate of 10 per cent per annum on the opening value.

Required

(a) A bar trading account for 19X8.
(b) A general income and expenditure account for 19X8.
(c) A balance sheet as at 31 December 19X8.

4.6 The Ridlingham Recreation Club consists of a tennis section and a rugby section. The following information has been obtained relating to the position of the club on 1 January 19X1:

	£
Clubhouse at cost	38,000
Creditors for bar purchases	3,720
Creditors for general expenses	500
Tennis courts at cost (£40,000), less depreciation to date	24,000
Furniture and equipment at book value	5,000
Bar stocks	4.400
Bank balance	1,500

The club's bank statements for 19X1 have been analysed and the following summary prepared:

Bank Account, 19X1

	£		£
Balance 1 January	1,500	New tennis court	16,000
Ten-year membership	12,000	Repairs to tennis courts	2,520
Other subscriptions: Tennis	6,400	Prizes for tennis tournaments	140
Rugby	1,300	Rugby kit	900
Tennis tournament		Rental of rugby pitch	400
entry fees	240	Rates on clubhouse	1,100
Bar sales	69,660	Payments for bar supplies	48,400
Collections at rugby		Wages of bar steward	7,800
matches	180	General expenses	17,300
Tennis court fees	5,700	Balance 31 December	2,420
	96,980		96,980

You discover that all cash received is paid into the club bank account and all payments are made by cheque.

During the year a new tennis court was built that was first used on 1 July 19X1. In order to help pay for the new court, ten-year memberships were offered for sale, at the beginning of the first year, at £400 each.

At 31 December 19X1 creditors for bar purchases and general expenses amount to £4,300 and £640 respectively. Bar stocks are valued at £5,280. It is the club's policy to write off the cost of the tennis courts over a ten-year period. Furniture is depreciated at 10 per cent on the balance at the year end. For the purpose of the accounts the rugby kit is considered to possess a nil value.

Required

(a) The bar trading account and a general income and expenditure account for 19X1. The general income and expenditure account should show the net surplus or deficit arising separately from the tennis section and the rugby section.

(b) The balance sheet at 31 December 19X1.

4.7 The Baylandsea Sailing Club is an association for sailing enthusiasts and it provides members with a number of activities:

(i)   a clubhouse with a bar for drinks and other social functions;
(ii) yacht racing competitions;
(iii) hire of boats for members. Non-members are charged an extra 20 per cent for boat hire;
(iv) a sailing training school for all age groups.

1.   The following financial information is available as at 1 June 1992:

	£	
Paint and trim shop	50,000	all at net
Freehold premises	400,000	book
Boatyard and launch facilities	80,000	value
Fixtures and fittings	30,000	
Club-owned boats and yachts	350,000	
Members' subscriptions:		
in arrears	4,000	
in advance	5,600	
Balance at bank	110,700	
Bar stocks	31,000	
Bar creditors	5,000	

2.   The following financial information is available for the year ended 31 May 1993:

Receipts	£	Payments	£
Receipts from training school	20,500	Purchase of 2 new club yachts	50,000
Boat hire charges:		Repairs to yachts and boats	19,200
For members	9,000	Purchase of bar stocks	50,100
For non-members	19,600	Bar and social functions' wages	12,600
Members' subscriptions	200,900	Outgoings on yacht racing	
Bar and social functions'		competitions	18,700
takings	80,000	Wages for training school staff	
Fees and charges from yacht		and boat hire	15,000
racing competitions	30,800	General expenses	22,000
Salvage receipt from sunk boat	2,000		

Additional information:

(i)   At 31 May 1993 there were members' subscriptions in arrears of £3,500 and members' subscriptions in advance for 1993–94 of £7,900.

(ii) During the year a club boat was involved in a collision whilst at sea. The boat was sunk and is recoverable only as salvage. Net book value of the boat was £20,000.

(iii) The club depreciates its fixed assets as follows:

Freehold premises
Boatyard and launch facilities   } 5% per annum of
Club boats and yachts   } net book value

Fixtures and fittings   } 10% per annum of
Paint and trim shop   } net book value

(iv) As at 31 May 1993 there were outstanding creditors for the following:

	£
Bar purchases	6,100
Bar wages	350
Repairs to yachts and boats	3,200

(v)   The bar's stock valuation was £28,500 at cost on 31 May 1993.
(vi) The retired club member had recently died and in his will left the club two boats. The boats were valued at £30,000 and were formally acquired on 1 May 1993.
(vii) Of the 20 per cent extra charge on the annual receipts from boat hire to non-members, 25 per cent of the charge was donated to a local charity. This donation has not yet been paid.

Required

(a) An income and expenditure account for the year ended 31 May 1993, showing profits/losses on relevant activities.   *(26 marks)*
(b) A balance sheet as at 31 May 1993.   *(18 marks)*
(c) Comment on the club's liquidity.   *(6 marks)*

(AEB, Accounting, June 1993)

5

THE DOUBLE ENTRY SYSTEM I: THE INITIAL RECORD OF TRANSACTIONS

The objectives of this chapter are to

- show how the record of cash flows is created in the cash book;
- demonstrate the preparation of the bank reconciliation statement and outline its uses;
- explain how to record petty cash transactions;
- explain how cash flows are analysed in the cash book; and
- show how initial records of the flows of goods and services are made using day books.

INTRODUCTION

Accounting reports are based on summarized information, and are accurate only if the initial record of the individual transactions is correct. The operation of a company results in numerous individual transactions taking place; in the case of large companies there is likely to be a massive volume of these. Inflows and outflows of goods, services and cash occur, and it is the responsibility of management to ensure that there is an efficient system of accounting. This system must be designed both to record and control individual transactions and to enable the production of summarized results in the form of accounting reports. For example, a retail shop that makes a large number of relatively small sales must have controls to ensure that all items that leave the shop are paid for and that all cash received is recorded; summaries showing the total value of sales, possibly analysed by product, are then produced for management so that the shop's progress can be monitored. This chapter covers the detailed recording of the separate items in such a way as to provide an adequate foundation for the rest of the accounting process.

CASH FLOWS

Control of cash receipts and payments is obviously of particular importance to the company as resources that are in the form of cash are vulnerable to misappropriation; the cash book, in which all receipts and payments are recorded, is the central element of this control. The objective is to ensure that all cash due to the company is received and retained until its subsequent, properly authorized, disbursement takes place. A simple way to establish this control is to ensure that

1. all cash receipts are recorded as they are received;
2. all cash receipts are paid with little delay into the company's bank account; and
3. only senior personnel are permitted to authorize the bank to make payments from the bank.

One result of using a bank account is to create an additional source of information on cash flows since all the entries in the cash book have a corresponding entry in the statement of account, which is provided periodically by the bank. (The importance of this is discussed later in this chapter.) The initial record of cash receipts is usually in the form of a memorandum list that should be prepared at the point and time of receipt. The necessary documentation is completed as each sale is made when the goods are exchanged directly for cash, as is the case with a retail shop, or at some other point where goods are sold on credit and the cash received some time after the sale. For example, if it is usual for cheques to be received in the post, a reliable employee should be made responsible for opening all letters, removing and listing the cheques enclosed and passing them to the cashier for prompt payment into the bank. The inclusion of a number of different people in this line of control reduces the possibility of undetected theft since the list produced by the person responsible for opening the post is independent of, and can be checked with, the sum accounted for by the cashier. On the payments side, it must be ensured that only a limited number of senior people are authorized to sign documents, such as cheques and standing order mandates, which are accepted by the bank as instructions to pay sums of money out of the account. The official signing the document – for example, the cheque – should require evidence to warrant its completion, such as a valid invoice received from a supplier. In this example, the invoice should be referenced to the cash payment and retained so that the transaction's validity can, if required, be subsequently verified. This involves a system of cross-referencing, with the payment recorded in the cash book cross-referenced to a supplier's account in which the liability has been recorded on the previous receipt of a valid invoice.

The cash account

The cash account is used to record the inflows and outflows of cash and is kept in an accounting record called the cash book. The account consists of two lists of figures, one of which gives details of cash receipts and the other cash payments; in accordance with the rules of double entry book-keeping (explained in detail in Chapter 6), the receipts are known as 'debits' and are placed on the left-hand page of the cash book, while payments are recorded on the right-hand page and are termed 'credits'. (The terms debit and credit are often abbreviated to 'dr.' and 'cr.' respectively.) A period of time, such as a week or a month, is covered by the lists and, as well as the cash flows that take place during the period, the opening cash position is included so that the closing balance of cash can be determined. If the company starts the period with cash-in-hand, the amount is entered at the top of the cash received (debit) column, while an overdraft is entered at the top of the payments (credit) column.

To find the closing balance of cash, the account is 'balanced'. This is done by finding the difference between the total values of debits and credits. The closing balance of one period, known as the 'balance carried down', is the opening balance for the following period, when it is termed the 'balance brought down'; this balance appears in the company's balance sheet.

Example 5.1

Wire Ltd balances its cash book each week, and at the end of week 8 of 19X7 held cash of £782. During week 9 the following receipts and payments took place:

		£
Receipts:	Sales	5,769
	Loan from Newbank plc	2,000
Payments:	Purchase of goods for resale	3,150
	Wages	790
	Rent	126
	Advertising	75
	Delivery van	3,500

Required

Prepare the cash account for week 9 of Wire Ltd as it would appear in the company's cash book and show the balance carried forward to week 10.

Solution

Cash Account

Cash in = Receipts (Debit)		£	*Cash out = Payments* (Credit)		£
Week 9	Balance brought down	782	Week 9	Purchases	3,150
	Sales	5,769		Wages	790
	Loan	2,000		Rent	126
				Advertising	75
				Van	3,500
					7,641
				Balance carried down	910
		8,551			8,551
Week 10	Balance brought down	910			

Notes

1. Although the £910 is a debit balance, i.e. the debit items exceed credit items by this amount, it is conventionally added to the list of credits so that the two columns add up to £8,551. The surplus is then brought down as the opening balance for week 10. As, in this case, the balance brought down is on the debit side of the account, it is a debit balance; credit balances are those brought down on the credit side of the account.

2. The terms 'balance carried down' and 'balance brought down' are often abbreviated to 'balance b/d' and 'balance c/d' respectively.

Readers should now work Question 5.1 at the end of this chapter to test their understanding of the preparation of the cash account.

The bank reconciliation

A company's cash account should contain exactly the same receipts and payments as pass through its bank account. A valuable check on the accuracy of the cash account is provided by the routine preparation of the bank reconciliation statement that agrees the cash account's balance with the bank statement. To provide additional control, the reconciliation should ideally be prepared or checked by an official of the company who is otherwise independent of the control and recording of the flows of cash.

The bank reconciliation statement is prepared by comparing items in the cash account with those in the bank statement. Entries that appear in both during the period under examination are checked off, but usually these records, although covering the same period of time, do not correspond exactly. This is the result of some or all of the following:

1. *Payments in the cash account not on the bank statement* These mainly result from the fact that there is a delay between the issue of a cheque, at which time it is entered in the cash account, and its clearance by the bank, when it appears on the bank statement.

2. *Receipts in the cash account not on the bank statement* A company may enter the cash received each day in the cash account, but pay it into the bank the following day, or even allow it to accumulate for a short period of time. This causes a lapse of time between the cash account record and the bank statement entry. For security reasons, the delay should be kept to a minimum.

3. *Payments on the statements not in the cash account* Some payments, such as those for bank charges, are generated by the bank. The company may know that they have been paid only when a statement has been received, and they would not have been previously entered in the cash book. Other items that fall into this category are payments made by standing order and direct debits.

4. *Receipts on the statement not in the cash book* It is common nowadays for sums to be paid directly into the recipient's bank account, and sometimes they are identifiable only when the statement is received.

Items 1 and 2 above are merely timing differences and, although appearing in the bank reconciliation, require no further entry in the cash account. Items 3 and 4, however, are additional items that, if valid, should be entered in the cash account when the statement is received.

The procedure for preparing a bank reconciliation statement is to take the entries in the cash account for a certain period of time and mark off in both records those that also appear on the bank statement for the same period. Any items left unmarked must be examined and classified into types 1, 2, 3 and 4. Items of types 3 and 4 are entered in the cash account from which the balance is then extracted. This balance will still differ from that shown on the bank statement if there are any items of types 1 and 2, and so a memorandum statement is drawn up that adjusts the balance on the statement for these items, after which it should agree with that shown on the cash account.

The following information relates to Check Ltd for the month of March: **Example 5.2**

Cash Account

Receipts (debit)		£	Payments (credit)		£
March			March		
1	Balance b/d	1,000		Cheques issued:	
9	Receipts paid into bank	350	4	No. 11	150
16	Receipts paid into bank	200	9	No. 12	225
23	Receipts paid into bank	475	15	No. 13	75
30	Receipts paid into bank	150	22	No. 14	445
			30	No. 15	160
			31	No. 16	330
			31	Balance c/d	790
		2,175			2,175

Bank statement

		Debit £	Credit £	Balance £
March				
1	Balance brought forward			1,000 Cr.
6	Cheque No. 11	150		850
11	Lodgement		350	1,200
	Cheque No. 12	225		975
17	Cheque No. 13	75		900
18	Lodgement		200	1,100
24	Cheque No. 14	445		655
25	Lodgement		475	1,130
	Standing order	60		1,070
26	Direct credit		50	1,120
31	Bank charges	100		1,020
	Balance carried forward			1,020 Cr.

Note
As the bank statement is prepared from the point of view of the bank, payments made by the company are shown as debits and deposits with the bank as credits, i.e. the terms are the opposite way round compared with the cash account in the company's books.

(a) Make the necessary adjustments to the cash account for the month of March.   **Required**

(b) Prepare the bank reconciliation statement at the end of March.

When the entries in the cash account are checked with those on the statement, the following differences are found: **Solution**

1. Payments in the cash account not on the bank statement:
   Cheque No. 15 £160
   Cheque No. 16 £330
2. Receipts in the cash account not on the bank statement:
   Lodgement £150
3. Payments on the bank statement not in the cash account:
   Standing order £60
   Bank charges £100

4. Receipts on the bank statement not in the cash account:
   Direct credit £50

Items 3 and 4 are used to complete the cash account, and items 1 and 2 appear in the bank reconciliation statement.

(a) Completion of the Cash Account for March

Receipts (debit)		£	Payments (credit)		£
March			March		
31	Balance b/d	790	31	Standing order	60
31	Direct credit	50	31	Bank charges	100
			31	Balance c/d	680
		840			840

(b) Bank Reconciliation Statement at 31 March

	£	£
Balance per bank statement		1,020
Less: Outstanding cheques:		
No. 15	160	
No. 16	330	
		490
		530
Plus: Outstanding lodgement		150
Balance as per cash account		680

Notes
1. Subsequent bank statements should be checked to ensure that all outstanding items are cleared without undue delay.
2. It is possible for banks to make mistakes. Any unexplained entry on the bank statement should be queried as it may have been entered in the company's account in error. Until a satisfactory explanation is obtained, such items should be shown as part of the reconciliation statement and not entered in the cash book.

Readers should now attempt Question 5.2 at the end of this chapter to test their understanding of the preparation of the bank reconciliation statement.

The double column cash book

It was stated above that all cash receipts should be paid into the firm's bank account without delay, and that all disbursements should be made from the bank account. Although this is a very good rule to observe in practice, there are occasions when it is not applied, especially in the case of small businesses. In these circumstances it is particularly important to ensure that all cash flows are recorded so that none is overlooked – for example, a trader may make sales of £100 for cash and out of the proceeds pay wages of £30 and motor expenses of £5 before banking the residual £65. It is incorrect merely to record in the books of the firm the lodgement of £65 in respect of sales, since this ignores the receipt of the additional £35, which was paid out on wages and motor expenses. The effect of the omission would be to under-state sales, wages and motor expenses.

Where sums are paid out of cash takings before they are banked, it is nec-essary to maintain two cash accounts, one to deal with the flows of cash that take place through the bank account, called the 'cash-at-bank account', and one to deal with other cash flows, called the 'cash-in-hand account'. Trans-fers between the two accounts are made in the usual way, so that, for exam-ple, when cash is banked a payment is entered in the cash-in-hand account and a receipt recorded in the cash-at-bank account. Although it is possible to maintain two completely separate accounts, it is usual in these circumstances to modify the traditional cash book format and use what is known as a dou-ble column cash book.

Glue Ltd undertook the following transactions between 1 and 10 June: **Example 5.3**

Date	Details	£
June		
1	Cash balance in hand	50
1	Balance at bank	200
3	Received from cash sales	1,275
4	Cash paid into bank	1,000
7	Pay wages in cash	100
8	Make cash purchases	200
9	Draw cash from bank	300
10	Pay for purchases by cheque	150
10	Pay rent in cash	175

Prepare the double column cash book to record the above transactions, carrying down the balances on 10 June. **Required**

Double column cash book **Solution**

	Receipts (debits)				Payments (credits)		
Date	Detail	Cash-in-hand £	Cash at bank £	Date	Detail	Cash-in-hand £	Cash at bank £
June				June			
1	Balance b/d	50	200	4	Cash to bank	1,000	
3	Sales	1,275		7	Wages	100	
4	Cash paid in		1,000	8	Purchases	200	
9	Cash from bank	300		9	Cash withdrawn		300
				10	Purchases		150
				10	Rent	175	
				10	Balances c/d	150	750
		1,625	1,200			1,625	1,200
10	Balances b/d	150	750				

Note that the accounts shown above comply with the usual convention that debits are recorded on the left and credits on the right, but it differs from the usual format as there are two columns on each side, one to record the flows of cash into the business and the manner of its disposition, while the other contains details of the cash flows that take place through the bank account. The opening balances are respectively cash-in-hand and at the bank on 1 June, and the first transaction increases cash held by £1,275, which is debited in the cash column to represent a cash receipt. Of this cash, £1,000 is paid into the bank on June 4. Cash-in-hand is credited with this amount to show that the payment was made out of cash, while the bank is debited to show the corresponding receipt. Conversely, when cash is drawn from the bank to be used for cash payments, cash at bank is credited and the cash-in-hand column debited.

Readers should now work Question 5.3 at the end of this chapter.

The analysed cash book

To enable accounting reports to be prepared it is necessary to ascertain why particular cash flows have taken place. For example, cash from sales and the receipt of a loan are both recorded as cash inflows, but the former is an element in the calculation of profit while the latter is entered in the balance sheet as a liability. A simple way to break down cash flows into their constituent parts is to maintain an analysed cash book. This has columns not

Example 5.4   The following cash transactions were undertaken by Thorn & Co.:

Day	Receipts	£	Payments	£
1	Sales	250	Purchases of stock	125
2	Sales	300	Wages	76
3	Sales	270	Purchases of stock	150
4	Sales	315	Wages	79
4	Loan	150	Rent	50
4			Purchase of fixed assets	200

Required   Prepare the company's analysed cash book to record the above transactions.

Solution   **Cash Account**

		Receipts side (debit)		
Day	Detail	Total £	Sales £	Sundry £
1	Sales	250	250	
2	Sales	300	300	
3	Sales	270	270	
4	Sales	315	315	
	Loan	150		150
		1,285	1,135	150

Payments side (credit)						
Day	Detail	Total	Purchases of stock	Wages	Rent	Sundry
		£	£	£	£	£
1	Purchases of stock	125	125			
2	Wages	76		76		
3	Purchases of stock	150	150			
4	Wages	79		79		
	Rent	50			50	
	Purchase of fixed assets	200				200
		680	275	155	50	200

only for cash inflows and outflows but also further columns for different types of flows. When a type of receipt or payment occurs on a regular basis, such as payments for goods or wages, a separate column is devoted to this category of transaction; infrequent transactions are entered in a sundry, or ledger, column. An advantage of the use of an analysed cash book is that the nature of each item must be ascertained at the time it is recorded; errors are more likely to occur if there is delay in this process, due, for example, to lapse of memory.

The fact that the aggregate of the totals in the analysis columns is equal to the total of the 'Total' column provides a useful check of arithmetical accuracy.

Readers should now work Question 5.4 at the end of this chapter.

The petty cash account

All businesses have to meet small incidental expenses in the course of operating and, as it is often inconvenient to pay these by cheque, it is usual to maintain a petty cash float. The normal procedure is to adopt the 'Imprest' system, which uses a fixed sum as a float from which money is paid in return for a properly authorized petty cash voucher. The size of the float should be sufficient to cover the normal level of disbursements during the length of time between replenishments. At regular intervals the petty cashier exchanges the petty cash vouchers for a cheque equal to their total value, which is then used to restore the fund to its designated amount. An advantage of using this system is that at any time the cash-in-hand plus that represented by vouchers should total the amount of the initial float. This facilities spot checks by an appropriate official.

Although petty cash expenditure, by definition, covers only relatively small amounts, it is still necessary to ensure that it is properly controlled and accounted for. The use of the Imprest system gives control, and to ensure that a proper record exists it is usual to maintain a petty cash book, in which the details of the receipts and payments of petty cash are entered. The petty cash book also acts as the petty cash account. Example 5.5 shows entries in a petty cash account recording the transactions of an Imprest petty cash fund of £50.

Example 5.5   **Petty Cash Account**

Receipts (debit)		Payments (credit)					
Date	£	Date	Voucher no.	Total	Postage	Travel	Cleaning
				£	£	£	£
June		June					
1 Balance b/d	12	4	11	10		10	
3 Bank	38	11	12	7			7
		18	13	5	5		
		24	14	8		8	
		29	15	4	4		
				—	—	—	—
				34	9	18	7
		30	Balance c/d	16	—	—	—
	—			—			
	50			50			
	—			—			
July							
1 Balance b/d	16						
2 Bank	34						

The opening balance of £12 shows that expenditure of £38 has been made
in the previous period and should be represented by vouchers to support
the amount of cash drawn from the bank. The debit entry in the petty cash
account of £38 shows the receipt of cash and will correspond with a credit
in the cash-at-bank account from which the payment is made. The fund
stands at £50 immediately after reimbursement. Withdrawals of cash are
entered as payments on the credit side of the book in the cash column and
this has the effect of reducing the petty cash balance. Analysis columns
are used to provide a summary of the amount spent for each purpose.
Vouchers 11 to 15 account for £34, and this sum is drawn from the bank to
replenish the fund at the beginning of July.

Question 5.5 at the end of this chapter should now be worked.

FLOWS OF GOODS AND SERVICES

Accounts are designed to reflect the economic activity that takes place during a period of time, and this is not accurately shown by simply reporting
cash movements. This is because it is usual for sales and purchases to be
made on credit and, in these circumstances, the movement of goods is not
immediately accompanied by equivalent transfers of cash. Companies must,
therefore, keep records of inflows and outflows of goods and services as well
as for flows of cash. For example, the fact that goods have been purchased on
credit must be reported, even if they have not been paid for.

One reason for making a record of flows of goods and services is because
control is needed to ensure that cash is subsequently collected from credit
customers and that suppliers are paid on time. This section deals with the
initial record of economic events – the control of debtors and creditors is
dealt with in Chapter 6.

Day books

In its simplest form a day book is a list of sales or purchases that have taken place on credit with the name of the customer or supplier entered next to each item. The total of each list gives the value of purchases or sales that have taken place during a period of time.

To make certain that all sales are recorded, steps should be taken to ensure that a sales invoice is made out each time goods are supplied. A number of copies of the sales invoice are normally required, one of which goes to the customer and another to the accounts section as the basis for entering the transaction in the sales day book. A final control, such as prenumbering, should be used to ensure that copies of all invoices are entered in the day book; any missing numbers should be investigated.

The purchases day book is written up on the basis of invoices received from suppliers. To ensure that payment is made only for goods received, a record should be kept of goods delivered to the company against which the invoice can be checked. The record of goods received is cancelled after checking the invoice to prevent the possibility of paying twice for one delivery. The invoice should also be matched with its originating order to make sure that goods delivered are actually required by the company. An invoice not supported by both evidence of receipt of the goods and a purchase order should be investigated and not passed for entry in the books until there is sufficient proof that it relates to a valid transaction. Invoices for services, such as cleaning, should be supported by an order or contract and passed for payment only by an authorized official.

To produce final accounts and provide management with relevant information, the inflows and outflows of goods and services must be broken down, and this is achieved by adding analysis columns to the day books, as was done in the case of the cash book. The analysis headings are determined on the basis of which aspects of the organization are to be monitored. Excessive detail impairs comprehension and so too many headings should not be used. On the other hand, significant matters may be masked if the headings are too broad. Management needs to identify areas of strength and weakness, and this is achieved if, for example, sales and purchases are analysed by type of product, and the department or branch in which they originate.

House Ltd owns a shop that consists of two distinct departments, one selling bricks and the other mortar. All purchases are made on credit and management requires reports that show the individual results of each department.

Example 5.6

Prepare from the following details the purchases day book in a manner that provides the information needed by management:

Required

Purchases: 1 March from Builder Ltd – bricks £100; mortar £75 (supplied on one invoice)
2 March from Cement Ltd – mortar £50
3 March from Jerry Ltd – bricks £65

Solution   **Purchases Day Book**

Date	Supplier	Total	Bricks	Mortar
March		£	£	£
1	Builder Ltd	175	100	75
2	Cement Ltd	50		50
3	Jerry Ltd	65	65	
		290	165	125

The use of day books is not restricted to purchases and sales – they can be used for any routine transactions, such as the return of goods from customers or to suppliers. In all cases appropriate controls must be established to ensure that only valid entries are made in the records.

Readers should now work Question 5.6 at the end of this chapter to test their understanding of the preparation of day books.

Questions

5.1 Mr Wall decided to set up in business as a sole trader on 1 January 19X1. He opened a business bank account into which he pays all the takings and from which he pays all business costs. His transactions for January 19X1 were as follows:

(a) Pay £5,000 into the bank as capital on 1 January.
(b) Buy for cash a second-hand delivery van for £4,000 on 2 January.
(c) Pay one month's rent on premises £100 on 3 January.
(d) Sell goods for £2,250 cash during the month.
(e) Collect £450 from debtors and pay £2,500 to creditors during the month.
(f) Withdraw £110 on 15 January.
(g) Pay insurance for one year, from 1 January 19X1 of £120 on the 30 January.

Required
Write up the cash account for January 19X1.

5.2 At the close of business on 31 May 1985, the bank statement of Amos Jones, a sole trader, showed that his balance with the bank amounted to £1,960. This does not agree with the bank balance according to his cash book, and the following transactions account for the difference:

(a) On 31 May the bank allowed Jones interest amounting to £76, but this had not yet been entered in the cash book.
(b) During May 1985 the bank had paid on behalf of Jones, under a banker's standing order, the rent of his business premises amounting to £110. This had not been entered in the cash book.
(c) On 31 May, William Smith, a *debtor* of Jones, paid direct to Jones's account with his bankers the sum of £89, but this had not yet appeared in the cash book.
(d) During May, Jones had drawn several cheques but, at the close of business on 31 May 1985, the following three cheques had not yet been presented for payment: £21, £44 and £39.

Required

Commencing with the bank statement balance of £1,960, prepare the bank reconciliation statement of Amos Jones as at 31 May 1985, ending with the correct bank balance as shown in his cash book.

(LCC, Book-Keeping, summer, 1985)

5.3 Ray Gunne set up in business on 1 January 19X3. The firm's transactions for the first week of January 19X3 were as follows:

(a) Pay capital of £10,000 into the bank.
(b) Buy premises for £8,000 and equipment for £2,750 – both paid by cheque.
(c) Borrow £5,000 from Gunne's brother. He provided this sum in cash of which £4,000 was used to buy a delivery van and £750 was paid into the bank.
(d) Buy trading stock: £3,000 by cheque and £1,000 for cash.
(e) Make cash sales of £5,500.
(f) Pay wages of £100 in cash.
(g) Take cash drawings of £150.
(h) Pay rates by cheque of £250.
(i) Pay £4,250 of cash into the bank.

Required

Prepare the double column cash book of Gunne's business for the first week of January 19X3 and carry down the balances at the end of the week.

5.4 At the start of a trading week the cash account of Laser Ltd showed that the company was £6,510 overdrawn. During the week the company undertook the following cash transactions:

Day	Receipts		£	Payments	£
1	Sales		1,790	Purchases	2,250
2	Sales		2,190	Wages	380
3	Sales		1,250		
3	Sale of fixed asset		1,000		
4	Sales		3,720	Interest on loan	400
5	Sales		1,540	Purchases	3,140
6	Sales		2,710	Wages	450

Required

Prepare the analysed cash book of Laser Ltd to record the above information and carry down the balance at the end of the week.

5.5 James Walton is a sole trader who keeps his petty cash on the Imprest System – the Imprest amount being £50. At the start of business on 1 October 1985, the petty cash in hand was £3.75.

Walton's petty cash transactions for the month of October 1985 were as follows:

1 October	Petty cash restored to Imprest amount
4 October	Wages paid – £11.60
5 October	Stamps purchased – £3.94
8 October	Stationery purchased – £4.09
11 October	Stamps purchased – £2
18 October	Wages paid – £12.93
21 October	Paid to F. Smith, a creditor – £3.42
24 October	Stationery purchased – £4.66
28 October	Stamps purchased – £3.80

Required

Draw up Walton's petty cash book for the month of October 1985, carry down the balance on 31 October 1985, and restore the petty cash to the Imprest amount on 1 November 1985.

Note
Your analysis columns should be Wages, Postage, Stationery and Ledger.

(LCC, Book-Keeping, autumn, 1985)

5.6 Office Ltd owns a shop that sells typewriters and also repairs office equipment. The following credit sales took place:

Day 1   Sold a typewriter for £300 and stationery for £75 to Gum Ltd.
         Repaired Glue Ltd's typewriter for £100.
Day 2   Sold stationery to Stick Ltd for £70.
Day 3   Sold a typewriter to Fast Ltd for £450.
         Repaired Stick Ltd's typewriter for £50.

Required

Prepare an analysed sales day book for Office Ltd to record the above transactions. The results of each separate activity are to be ascertained.

5.7 On 2 April 1993 Mostar Motors Ltd received their monthly bank statement which showed that there was a bank overdraft of £2,129. This balance was not in agreement with the balance shown in the bank column of the company's cash book. The chief cashier carried out a reconciliation which revealed the following:

1. Bank charges for the quarter ended 31 March 1993 amounting to £48 had been omitted from the cash book.
2. A page in the cash book of debit entries had been undercast by £600 and the incorrect total carried forward to the next page.
3. A dividend cheque received for £340 had been entered twice in the cash book.
4. The company's agent in Southshore had paid into a local bank a sum of £1,550 but this was not shown on the bank statement.
5. A standing order of £110 to a trade association had been duly paid by the bank but there was no entry in the cash book.
6. Cheques totalling £4,920 had been delivered to suppliers on 30 March 1993 but none of these had as yet been presented to the bank.
7. A cheque for £154 had been received from a customer on 25 March 1993 but had been entered in the cash book at £145.
8. A hire-purchase agreement for equipment had been entered into by the company. This required £120 to be paid every month for two years. The first payment was due on 20 January 1993. These amounts were correctly entered by the company but the bank had inadvertently debited another company.
9. The bank statement revealed a credit transfer receivable for £291 but after inquiries it was discovered that this related to another company.
10. The bank statement recorded that a cheque for £185 paid into the bank had been subsequently dishonoured. The company was unaware of this.

After taking appropriate action to update the cash book, the bank reconciliation statement was prepared.

Required

(a) A corrected cash book and bank reconciliation statement as at 31 March 1993.   *(32 marks)*
(b) Explain why it is necessary to prepare bank reconciliation statements.
                                                                          (12 marks)

(AEB, A-level paper 1, June 1993)

6
THE DOUBLE ENTRY SYSTEM II: LEDGER ACCOUNTS AND THE TRIAL BALANCE

The objectives of this chapter are to

- Introduce the concept of double entry book-keeping using ledger accounts;
- show how the double entry system is used to record transactions;
- demonstrate how transactions recorded in the books of prime entry, including the journal, are transferred to ledger accounts;
- explain the use of control accounts for debtors and creditors;
- show how the trial balance is extracted from the ledger accounts; and
- outline the operation of computerized accounting systems.

INTRODUCTION

The previous chapter explained the manner in which the primary records of flows of goods, services and cash are compiled. This chapter examines how the information on inflows and outflows is recorded by means of the system of double entry book-keeping, thereby enabling control to be exercised and the conversion of prime data into accounting reports.

THE INTERLOCKING EFFECT OF TRANSACTIONS

In Chapter 2 the impact on the balance sheet of a number of transactions was examined. Assets remained equal in value to sources of finance after each transaction, and the relationship

$$A(assets) = C(capital) + L(liabilities)$$

remains true in all circumstances. The interlocking effect of transactions is fundamental to the system of double entry book-keeping, and is now given further consideration.

To maintain the relationship $A = C + L$, each transaction must have two equal, but opposite effects. The alternatives are shown in Figure 6.1. A single transaction can affect any of the items listed as *Effect 1* and be paired with

Effect 1 (debit)	*Effect 2 (credit)*
Increase asset	Decrease asset
or	or
Decrease liability	Increase liability
or	or
Decrease capital	Increase capital

Figure 6.1   Alternative effects on relationships A = C + L

any item from the *Effect 2* list. The interlocking effect means that the total value of either of the two impacts must be the same as that of the other.

Figure 6.1 covers changes in assets, liabilities and capital; it can be extended to include revenues and expenses. Items of revenue and expense are recorded separately – the impact of an expense is to decrease capital, and so it is recorded as an effect 1, while revenue increases capital and so is an effect 2. The effects of revenues and expenses are compared to calculate the firm's net profit or loss. A net profit is then added to capital and any net loss is deducted from it. Figure 6.2 extends Figure 6.1 to include revenues and expenses. A practical application of the interlocking effect is given in Illustration 6.1.

Effect 1 (debit)	*Effect 2 (credit)*
Increase asset	Decrease asset
or	or
Decrease liability	Increase liability
or	or
Decrease capital	Increase capital
or	or
Increase expense	Decrease expense
or	or
Decrease revenue	Increase revenue

Figure 6.2   Figure 6.1 extended to include revenues and expenses

Illustration 6.1

The following transactions were undertaken by Bernard Egin, a sole trader, when starting his business:

Transaction number	Description	Value £
1	Introduce cash as capital	1,000
2	Raise a loan for cash	500
3	Buy plant for cash	1,000
4	Buy stock for cash	250
5	Buy stock on credit	350
6a	Sell stock on credit	550
6b	Cost of stock sold	350
7	Collect cash from debtors	550
8	Pay cash to creditors	350
9	Pay cash for general expenses	80

The twofold effect of each of these transactions is as follows:

Transaction number	Value £	Effect 1 (debit)	Effect 2 (credit)
1	1,000	+ Asset (cash)	+ Capital
2	500	+ Asset (cash)	+ Loan
3	1,000	+ Asset (plant)	– Asset (cash)
4	250	+ Asset (stock)	– Asset (cash)
5	350	+ Asset (stock)	+ Liability
6a*	550	+ Asset (debtor)	+ Revenue
6b*	350	+ Expense	– Asset (stock)
7	550	+ Asset (cash)	– Asset (debtor)
8	350	– Liability	– Asset (cash)
9	80	+ General expenses	– Asset (cash)

Note
* Trading transactions 6a and 6b have the combined effect of producing a gross profit of £200 from which general expenses of £80 (item 9) are deducted to leave a net profit of £120. The net profit is added to capital when the balance sheet is prepared.

Both effect 1 and effect 2 have the same value and so their combined impact on the relationship C + L = A is to leave it in balance. For example, transaction 1 adds £1,000 to each side, while transaction 3 both adds and subtracts £1,000 from the same side; the asset cash is exchanged for the asset plant. Readers should now revise their understanding of the relationship A = C + L by preparing the balance sheet of Egin as it appears after each individual transaction has been completed.

The dual effect of each transaction has given rise to the system of *double entry book-keeping*, under which each transaction is recorded twice: its effect 1 is recorded as a debit and its effect 2 is a credit. The equality between debits and credits holds true even if more than two elements are affected by a single deal. For example, a customer buys and takes away goods for £250. The price is settled by an immediate cash payment of £100, and an agreement to pay the remaining £150 in one month's time. The facts to be recorded at the time of sale together with their impact are as follows:

	Value £	Effect 1	Effect 2
Sales	250		250 + Revenue (sales)
Cash received	100	100 + Asset (cash)	
Creation of debtor	150	150 + Asset (debtor)	
		250	250

There is a credit of £250 and total debits of £250; equality has been sustained.

LEDGER ACCOUNTS

The practical operation of a set of double entry books to record transactions involves the use of a separate record for each type of revenue, expenditure, asset and liability. Each record is named according to the item to which it relates, and is known as an 'account', for example, each company maintains a cash account, as described in Chapter 5, in which all inflows and outflows of cash are recorded. The guiding principle that must be followed when designing a system of accounts is that it must provide the information needed to prepare the accounting statements, which comprise at least a trading and profit and loss account and a balance sheet. The complete set of accounts kept by a firm is called its 'ledger', and this term is also used to refer to particular groups of the accounts, such as the 'debtors' ledger' and the 'nominal ledger'.

'T' accounts
The ledger accounts in which business transactions are recorded are known as 'T' accounts, a name derived from each account's appearance, as is apparent from the following examples. The T account represents an open ledger and has two sides – the left is used to record debits and the right credits. An example, containing no accounting entries, is shown in Figure 6.3.

Debit	£	Credit	£

Figure 6.3   A 'T' account

We can now return to the transactions of Bernard Egin given in Illustration 6.1. The first was the introduction into his firm of capital in the form of cash of £1,000. The two accounts needed to record this transaction are 'cash' and 'capital'; cash, an asset, is increased by an inflow of £1,000 and so is debited with this sum, while capital, the liability to ownership, is increased by £1,000 and the account is credited. The accounts appear as follows when the transaction has been entered:

Cash Account

Debit		Credit	
	£		£
Capital	1,000		

Capital Account

Debit		Credit	
	£		£
		Cash	1,000

Note that a system of cross-reference is used whereby, in each account, the location of the corresponding entry is named. Thus, for this transaction, the credit entry corresponding to the debit entry in the cash account can easily be traced to the capital account. This referencing is necessary as the separate accounts would not necessarily be adjacent to each other in the ledger.

The transactions undertaken by B. Egin, given in Illustration 6.1, are reproduced for ease of reference:

Example 6.1

Transaction number	Description	Value £
1	Introduce cash as capital	1,000
2	Raise a loan for cash	500
3	Buy plant for cash	1,000
4	Buy stock for cash	250
5	Buy stock on credit	350
6a	Sell stock on credit	550
6b	Cost of stock sold	350
7	Collect cash from debtors	550
8	Pay cash to creditors	350
9	Pay general expenses in cash	80

Record the transactions of B. Egin in a set of T accounts. Insert the transaction number before each item. (The impact of each item is given in Illustration 6.1 above.)

Required

Cash Account

Solution

	Debit				Credit	
		£				£
1	Capital	1,000	3	Plant		1,000
2	Loan	500	4	Stock		250
7	Debtor	550	8	Creditor		350
			9	General expenses		80

Capital Account

	Debit				Credit	
		£				£
			1	Cash		1,000

Loan Account

	Debit				Credit	
		£				£
			2	Cash		500

Plant Account

	Debit	£		Credit	£
3	Cash	1,000			

Stock Account

	Debit	£			Credit	£
4	Cash	250	6b	Cost of goods sold		350
5	Creditors	350				

Creditors Account

	Debit	£			Credit	£
8	Cash	350	5	Stock		350

Debtors Account

	Debit	£			Credit	£
6a	Sales	550	7	Cash		550

Sales Account

	Debit	£			Credit	£
			6a	Debtor		550

Cost of goods sold*

	Debit	£		Credit	£
6b	Stock	350			

General expenses Account

	Debit	£		Credit	£
9	Cash	80			

Note
*In this example, the asset 'stock' is converted to the expense 'cost of goods sold' at the time of sale. In practice, the cost of goods sold is found by preparing a trading account in which purchases are adjusted for opening and closing stocks. See Chapter 7 for the explanation of how to achieve this using double entry techniques.

At the end of the accounting period, the accountant prepares the profit and loss account and balance sheet and, at this stage, it is necessary first to balance each of the accounts in the manner described in Chapter 5. The balances on the accounts that relate to items of revenue and expense are then transferred to the trading and profit and loss accounts where the net result of trading is calculated; the balances remaining, together with the net result of trading, are then used to compile the balance sheet.

(a) List the balances from the ledger accounts in Example 6.1 in two columns, one for debit balances and one for credit balances.

(b) Prepare B. Egin's trading and profit and loss accounts and balance sheet from the balances listed in answer to part (a).

Example 6.2
Required

(a)

Solution

	Debit £	Credit £
Cash	370	
Capital		1,000
Loan		500
Plant	1,000	
Stock	250	
Sales		550
Cost of goods sold	350	
General expenses	80	
	2,050	2,050

Notes
1. There are no debtors or creditors as, in this instance, their inflows and outflows are exactly equal in value and so cancel each other out.
2. The debit balances are equal in value to the credit balances; this provides a check of accuracy, the importance of which is discussed later in this chapter.

(b) **Trading and Profit and Loss Account**

	£
Sales	550
Less: Cost of goods sold	350
Gross profit	200
Less: General expenses	80
Net profit	120

Balance Sheet of Bernard Egin

	£	£		£
Fixed assets			*Capital*	
Plant		1,000	At start of period	0
Current assets			Introduced	1,000
Stock	250		Profit for period	120
Cash	370			1,120
Loan		620		500
		1,620		1,620

The balances carried forward in the sales, cost of goods sold and general expenses accounts are zero. The transactions that were entered in them relate to a period of time; at the end of the period the accounts are cleared to the trading and profit and loss account and appear as follows:

Sales Account

	£		£
Transfer to trading account	550	Balance b/d	550

Cost of Goods Sold Account

	£		£
Balance b/d	350	Transfer to trading account	350

General Expenses Account

	£		£
Balance b/d	80	Transfer to profit and loss account	80

Once the balances on all the accounts cleared to the trading and profit and loss account have reverted to zero, these accounts are ready to accumulate information for the next period. The assets and liabilities shown in the balance sheet are carried forward to the next accounting period in their individual accounts where they are adjusted for any changes which then occur.

Alternative formats for ledger accounts

The advent of machine and, more recently, computer-based systems of accounting have resulted in a move away from the T-account format, although all of the rules of double entry are still complied with. There are a number of possible alternatives, for example, there may be separate columns for debits and credits or the transactions in an account may be listed with credits identified by an asterisk. One rule that must be observed is that, irrespective of the method used to distinguish debits from credits, it must be consistently applied. Figure 6.4 lists three ways for recording the same information in a mechanized or computerized cash account.

	1		2	3		
	Debit £	Credit £	£	Debit £	Credit £	Balance £
Opening balance	500		500DR			500DR
Cash from sales	1,250		1,250DR	1,250		
Cash for purchases		1,000	1,000CR		1,000	
Closing balance	750		750DR			750DR

Figure 6.4 Three ways of recording in a mechanical or computerized cash account

The ledger in practice

Accounts can be classified into the types shown in Figure 6.5. Personal accounts are those that record the relationship between the entity and outsiders, such as debtors, creditors and investors. There should be a separate account for each individual who owes money to or is owed money by the company so that it can be established how much to demand or pay respectively.

Figure 6.5   Classification of accounts

Impersonal accounts are either nominal accounts or real accounts:

Nominal accounts contain all of the items that are transferred to the trading and profit and loss account and so include such items as sales, purchases, wages and expenses.
Real accounts are used for the non-personal assets of the company, such as cash, stock and fixed assets.

Personal accounts should be first classified according to general type such as trade debtors, trade creditors, debenture holders and capital. Normally total, or control, accounts are maintained in the main ledger for each of these classes, and subsidiary, or memorandum, ledgers kept for individual details (see later in this chapter). Some of the real accounts can be treated in the same way, so that while the main ledger contains such general accounts as plant and machinery and stock, they are backed up by a register of plant and machinery or stock records to show the detail that comprises their total value.

The decision as to which nominal accounts to use should be based on a compromise between providing information that is of little use, because it is too general, or alternatively giving too much detail. The exact selection is based on the type of activity the business undertakes and the items management wishes to monitor and control, but in general the rule applies that accounts should be opened in respect of all items that are likely to be material (see Chapter 8). For example, it would not be deemed important in normal circumstances to identify individually the costs of petrol and motor insurance since they are both consequent upon running a vehicle and are reported under the heading 'motor expenses'. The income derived from sales made in the normal course of trade, however, should be distinguished from the proceeds of the sale of fixed assets. A failure to distinguish between them would mask the sources of revenue and would be seriously misleading if, for example, a large amount had been derived from the sale of a surplus piece of land that had been held as a fixed asset.

BOOKS OF PRIME ENTRY

It is unwieldy to attempt to enter each individual flow of cash, goods or services in the accounts ledger. To overcome this problem each transaction is entered, in the first instance, in a 'book of prime entry'. The initial record of transactions is made in either a day book, the cash book or the journal; each of these is now considered in turn.

Day books

The sales and purchases day books were described in Chapter 5. It is also advisable to use day books for any type of transaction that occurs frequently, such as the return of goods sold from customers who decide not to keep them (returns inwards) and the return of goods purchased to suppliers (returns outwards). Day books are used to summarize the flows of goods and services into and out of the company in order to generate entries for the appropriate ledger accounts. The sales day book must produce

1. the value of debtors created from sales to be debited to the debtors account; and
2. the value of credit sales to be credited in the sales account, possibly analysed according to type of sale.

The purchases day book creates

1. the total to be credited to the creditors account; and
2. the values to be debited to the various expense and asset accounts.

For example, the following are the totals from a purchases day book:

Total	Goods for resale	Stationery	Motor van (fixed asset)
£	£	£	£
18,450	11,500	500	6,450

The totals of the analysis columns add up to the total value, and are entered in the following ledger accounts:

	Debit	Credit
	£	£
Goods for resale (increase asset)	11,500	
Stationery (expense)	500	
Motor van (increase asset)	6,450	
Creditors (increase liability)		18,450
	———	———
	18,450	18,450

There should be clear cross-referencing between the books of prime entry and the accounts so that the trail can be retraced if necessary. A note should be made in the day book of the account, and its location, to which the figures are posted. The entry in the accounts should refer to the source of the figure, preferably also stating the page in the book of prime entry on which it can be found.

The cash book and discounts

The cash book, unlike the day books, is itself a ledger account; it is therefore necessary only to complete the corresponding double entry for the transactions it contains. At the end of the accounting period the cash book is balanced and the result entered in the balance sheet. Again, only the analysis totals need to be posted and not each separate transaction. For example, the following are the totals from an analysed cash book:

Cash Book

Receipts			Payments			
Total	Debtors	Cash sale	Total	Wages	Creditors	Rent
£	£	£	£	£	£	£
5,000	3,500	1,500	4,000	1,000	2,500	500

The total of cash received, £5,000, is already debited in the ledger as the result of including it in the total column of the cash book, and so the double entry is completed by making the following credit entries:

	£	
Sales (revenue)	1,500	(credit)
Debtors (reduce asset)	3,500	(credit)

The entries to complete the record of the effect of cash payments are:

	£	
Wages (expense)	1,000	(debit)
Creditors (reduce liability)	2,500	(debit)
Rent (expense)	500	(debit)

The cash balance of £1,000 (£5,000 debit – £4,000 credit) is entered in the balance sheet as a current asset.

The petty cash book (see Chapter 5) is also part of the double entry accounts, and is operated in the same way as the main cash book. The totals of its analysis columns are posted to the ledger accounts, and its balance is entered in the balance sheet.

The full value of each sale made on credit is entered in the debtors account, and in some cases this may be cleared by the receipt of cash together with the grant of a discount for prompt payment, that is, the cash received is less than the value of the debt. To remove the full amount of indebtedness shown in the debtors account it is necessary to credit the account with the value of the discount; the corresponding debit is to the 'discounts allowed account' in which all such discounts are accumulated. The balance on this account is transferred to the profit and loss account when the periodic accounting reports are prepared. If, alternatively, the company takes a discount offered by a supplier, the creditors account is debited and the 'discounts received account' is credited; the balance on the latter account is income and is credited to the profit and loss account. Where, as is the case with discounts given for purchasing large quantities, the discount is received as a reduction in price, that is, a trade discount, no entry in the discount column is needed as the amount invoiced is reduced by the discount. The procedure for recording discounts for prompt payment is illustrated in Example 6.3.

Example 6.3   Seller sells goods on credit to Buyer for £500. A discount of 4 per cent may be taken if the debt is settled within ten days.

Required   On the assumption that the discount is taken, prepare

(a) the debtor and discount accounts in Seller's books; and
(b) the creditor and discount accounts in Buyer's books.

Solution   (a) The books of Seller:

Debtor Account

	£		£
Sales	500	Cash	480
		Discounts allowed	20
	500		500

Discounts Allowed Account

	£		£
Debtor	20		

(b) The books of Buyer:

Creditor Account

	£		£
Cash	480	Purchases	500
Discounts received	20		
	500		500

Discounts Received Account

	£		£
		Creditor	20

It is quite likely that a large number of discounts will be received and allowed during an accounting period. To save time, each transaction is not recorded separately; instead, discounts allowed and received are accumulated in the cash book and transferred to the ledger at the end of the period. Example 6.4 shows how this method is operated. It should be noted that the cash book record of discounts is purely memorandum.

Disco owes £400 to Dancer and £760 to Tapper. He is owed £540 by Jumper **Example 6.4**
and £880 by Runner. Prepare the cash book for Disco on the assumption
that all of the above debts are settled subject to a 5 per cent prompt payment discount.

Cash Book – Disco   **Solution**

	Discount allowed	Cash		Discount received	Cash
	£	£		£	£
Jumper – debtor	27	513	Dancer – creditor	20	380
Runner – debtor	44	836	Tapper – creditor	38	722
	——	——		——	——
	71	1,349		58	1,102

The cash received of £1,349 is credited to the debtors account and
the £1,102 cash paid is debited to the creditors account; this completes the
double entry in both cases. Since the columns in which the discounts are
recorded are only memorandum, it is necessary to make both debit and
credit entries in respect of their contents. The total of discounts allowed, £71,
is debited to the discounts allowed account and credited to the debtors
account while the £58 of discounts received is debited to the creditors
account and credited to discounts received. In all cases the value of the discount plus the amount of cash flow is equal to the total amount of indebtedness.

It is useful to keep the discounts received and discounts allowed in separate accounts, rather than to net them, so that the cost of granting discounts
and the benefit of taking them can be easily identified and their impact
assessed. If discounts allowed rise in value, the question should be asked
whether the terms are too generous, and the benefits of taking discounts
must be weighed against the alternative advantages of retaining the cash in
the business for a longer period of time.

The three column cash book
Chapter 5 covered the operation of a double or two column cash book in
which separate columns are used to record the flows of cash-in-hand and
cash at bank. It is possible to add an extra column to create a three column
cash book; the additional column is used to record discounts allowed and
received in the manner explained above. The use of a three column cash
book is shown in Example 6.5.

Henry York is a sole trader who keeps records of his cash and bank trans- **Example 6.5**
actions in a three column cash book. His transactions for the month of
March 1986 were as follows:

March
1 Cash-in-hand £100. Cash at bank £5,672.

4 York received from W. Abbot a cheque for £246 that was paid directly into the bank.
6 Paid wages in cash £39.
8 Sold goods for cash £152.
10 Received cheque from G. Smart for £315, in full settlement of a debt of £344; this was paid directly into the bank.
11 Paid sundry expenses in cash £73.
14 Purchased goods by cheque £406.
18 Paid J. Sanders a cheque of £185 in full settlement of a debt of £201.
23 Withdrew £100 from the bank for office purposes.
24 Paid wages in cash £39.
26 Sold goods for cash £94.
28 Paid salaries by cheque £230.
31 Retained in office cash amounting to £150 and paid the remainder into the bank.

Required

(a) Enter the above transactions in the three column cash book of Henry York.
(b) Balance the cash book at 31 March 1986 and bring down the balances.

(LCCI, Book-Keeping, summer, 1986)

(See p. 99 for solution.)

The journal

There are a few transactions not entered in the cash or day books, and these are instead initially entered in the 'journal'. The use of a journal ensures that every entry in the ledger first passes through a book of prime entry, which fully explains the nature of the transaction. Each entry in the journal should be authorized to ensure that no unsanctioned changes are made in the ledger. Journal entries are likely to be relatively small in number, and include such items as the following:

1. *Transfers* These occur when it is necessary to transfer value from one account to another, for example, to correct a mistake made in the original posting that placed the entry in the wrong account.
2. *Adjustments* The original entry may be made in the correct account in the light of prevailing knowledge, but circumstances may change and require a further entry. For example, a debtor is created when a credit sale is made but if, at a later date, it becomes apparent that the money will not be collected, the debt must be written off by transfer to the bad debts account, since it no longer represents an asset. (Bad debts are considered further in Chapter 7.)
3. *Closing entries* Adjusting entries must be made at the accounting date to enable the periodic accounts to be drawn up. (These are dealt with in Chapter 7.)

The debit and credit entry for each transaction is entered in the journal together with a brief narrative to explain its purpose. Example 6.6 shows some specimen entries.

Solution (to Example 6.5)   **Henry York Cash Book**

Debit side	Discount allowed £	Cash-in-hand £	Cash at bank £	Credit side	Discount received £	Cash-in-hand £	Cash at bank £
March				March			
1 Balance b/d		100	5,672	6 Wages		39	
4 W. Abbot			246	11 Sundry expenses		73	
8 Sales		152		14 Purchases			406
10 G. Smart	29		315	18 J. Sanders	16		185
23 Bank		100		23 Cash			100
26 Sales		94		24 Wages		39	
31 Cash			145	28 Salaries			230
				31 Bank		145	
				31 Balance c/d		150	5,457
	29	446	6,378		16	446	6,378
April							
1 Balance b/d		150	5,441				

Example 6.6   A. Jones, a trader, wishes to record the following in his firm's ledger:

(a) The correction of a wrong posting that entered the purchase of a fixed asset costing £1,000 in the purchase of goods for resale account.
(b) The accrual of rent due for three months of £50.
(c) The introduction by A. Jones of capital in the form of a fixed asset worth £2,500.

Required   Prepare the journal entries to enter the above facts in the firm's ledger accounts.

Solution   The journal entries are as follows:

A. Jones – Journal

	Debit (DR*) £	Credit (CR*) £
(a) Fixed assets	1,000	
Purchases		1,000
Narrative: Transfer to fixed assets of incorrect posting		
(b) Rent	50	
Landlord		50
Narrative: Rent due for three months		
(c) Fixed assets	2,500	
A. Jones – capital		2,500
Narrative: Introduction of capital in the form of a fixed asset		

Note
* 'DR' and 'CR' are usual abbreviations for the words 'debit' and 'credit' respectively.

Although for practical purposes the use of the journal is restricted to those cases where there is no other appropriate book of prime entry, it is theoretically possible to record all entries in journal form, and an exercise on these lines provides a useful way for examiners to test students' understanding of double entry accounting without calling for the preparation of a full set of T accounts. For example, the transactions of Bernard Egin given in Illustration 6.1 can be recorded in journal form:

Illustration 6.1

Bernard Egin – Journal

Transaction Number	Debit £	Credit £
1. Cash	1,000	
Capital		1,000
Receipt of capital in the form of cash		
2. Cash	500	
Loan		500
Loan raised		

3.	Plant	1,000	
	Cash		1,000
	Purchase of plant for cash		
4.	Stock	250	
	Cash		250
	Purchase of stock for cash		
5.	Stock	350	
	Creditor		350
	Purchase of stock on credit		
6(a)	Debtor	550	
&(b)	Sales		550
	Cost of goods sold	350	
	Stock		350
	Sale of goods on credit		
7.	Cash	550	
	Debtors		550
	Collection of cash from debtors		
8.	Creditors	350	
	Cash		350
	Payment of cash to creditors		
9.	General expenses	80	
	Cash		80
	Payment of general expenses in cash		

These entries can be checked to the T accounts in Example 6.1.

CONTROL ACCOUNTS FOR DEBTORS AND CREDITORS

Businesses require two types of information about debtors and creditors:

1. Their total values must be made available both to provide a record of the total amount due to and by the company and to provide the figures for inclusion in the balance sheet.
2. The amount owed to each individual creditor and by each debtor is needed for day-to-day control; the correct amount must be paid or claimed in each case.

The required information is produced by maintaining two records – in the main double entry ledger 'control' or 'total' accounts are kept, which provide the overall values of debtors and creditors, while memorandum debtors and creditors ledgers contain a separate account for each individual debtor and creditor. (The debtors ledger is also referred to as the sales ledger and the creditors ledger is also known as the purchase ledger.) The debtors and creditors ledgers are referred to as 'memorandum' as they are subsidiary to, and do not form part of, the main double entry system.

Records of debtors and creditors

The memorandum accounts for debtors and creditors are written up from the day books and cash book using the entries for each separate transaction. The control accounts in the double entry ledger are compiled using totals from the books of prime entry. Example 6.7 shows the operation of this system for sales; the same method is applicable to purchases.

Example 6.7   Use the following information to prepare (a) a single-column sales day book; (b) the cash book (receipts side only); (c) the debtors control account; and (d) the individual memorandum debtor accounts.

Customer	Balance 1 March	Sales during March	Goods returned	Cash received	Discounts
	£	£	£	£	£
Page	100	150	—	98	2
Book	125	130	10	79	1
Volume	150	160	—	150	—
	375				

(a) Sales Day Book

	£
Page	150
Book	130
Volume	160
	440

The total figure for credit sales is credited to the credit sales account and debited to the sales ledger control account. The individual transactions are debited to the individual memorandum debtor accounts.

(b) Cash Book (debit side)

	Cash £	Discounts £
Page	98	2
Book	79	1
Volume	150	—
	327	3

The total figure for cash received is credited to the sales ledger control account; the individual amounts are credited to the memorandum debtor accounts. The total discount figure is credited to the sales ledger control account; the individual amounts are credited to the individual memorandum debtor accounts.

(c) Sales Ledger (Debtor) Control Account

	£		£
Balance b/d	375	Cash book	327
Sales day book	440	Discounts allowed	3
		Returns inwards	10
		Balance c/d	475
	815		815

(d) Page Account

	£		£
Balance b/d	100	Cash	98
Sales day book	150	Discounts allowed	2
		Balance c/d	150
	250		250

Book Account

	£		£
Balance b/d	125	Cash	79
Sales day book	130	Discounts allowed	1
		Returns inwards	10
		Balance c/d	165
	255		255

Volume Account

	£		£
Balance b/d	150	Cash	150
Sales day book	160	Balance c/d	160
	310		310

Reconciling the control account

The use of control accounts for customers and suppliers reduces the number of entries in the main ledger and enables a cross-check to be performed. The total of the balances on the individual memorandum accounts should agree with the single balance of the control account. Agreement on these lines based on the figures in Example 6.7 is

	£
Balances from individual accounts:	
Page	150
Book	165
Volume	160
Balance as per control account	475

The maintenance of the memorandum debtors and creditors ledgers can be delegated to a responsible person who has no access to the main ledger, which is likely to contain many confidential entries. Where this system is operated, the personnel in charge of the debtors and creditors ledgers should periodically supply a list of balances to the official responsible for the control accounts, who can then check that the totals agree. Any difference must be investigated, but there is the possibility that the totals may agree despite the fact that an error has been made, for example, an invoice may have been posted to the wrong debtor account. However, such an error should be identified when the incorrect amount is demanded from a customer who has been wrongly charged for the goods in question.

Example 6.8

A list of the balances on the memorandum individual personal accounts in a company's sales ledger at 31 December 19X6 had a total of £305,640. This did not agree with the balance on the sales ledger control account at that date of £325,000. The following errors were discovered:

1. A sales invoice of £12,900, included in the sales day book, had not been posted to the personal account in the sales ledger.
2. Discounts allowed to customers of £1,260 had been credited to the individual accounts in the sales ledger, but no other entries had been made in the books.
3. The returns inwards day book had been wrongly totalled; it was overcast by £3,000.
4. A sales invoice of £9,400 had been entirely omitted from the books.
5. A debit balance of £7,400 on the personal account of a customer had been included in the list of balances as £4,700.
6. The balance on a customer's account in the sales ledger of £5,500 had been omitted from the list of balances.

Required

(a) Write up the control account to correct it for those errors by which it is affected.
(b) Revise the total value of the list of balances in respect of those errors by which it is affected.

Solution

(a) **Sales Ledger Control Account**

	£		£
19X6		19X6	
31 Dec. Balance b/d	325,000	31 Dec. Discounts allowed (2)	1,260
Returns inwards (3)	3,000	Balance c/d	336,140
Sales (4)	9,400		
	337,400		337,400

(b)

	£
Value of list of balances	305,640
Invoice not in memorandum account (1)	12,900
Invoice omitted (4)	9,400
Balance wrongly extracted (7,400–4,700) (5)	2,700
Balance omitted (6)	5,500
Correct value of debtors	336,140

Note
The same closing balance now appears in the control account and the list of balances; the results obtained from the two separate sources of information have therefore been reconciled.

The control account is likely to include the following entries in addition to those for sales, cash and discounts:

1. *Credit balances on the debtors ledger and debit balances on the creditors ledger* For example, if a customer overpays, the account in the debtors ledger will be a credit. These balances should be carried down separately in the control account and added to creditors in the balance sheet.
2. *Bad debts* Some debtors are unable to pay, and the amounts they owe are known as bad debts. These balances must be removed from debtors, by a journal entry, as they no longer represent an asset.
3. *Settlement by contra* A firm may both buy from and sell to another company; this gives rise to a debtor account and creditor account in the same name. The balances on the two accounts may be set off, and the net balance settled for cash.
4. *Interest on overdue debts* When a debtor is very slow to pay, a firm may, by agreement, charge interest on the debt; this is added to the amount owed.
5. *Returns* Goods may be returned either to or by the company; the related debt must be cancelled.

Singer Ltd maintains memorandum debtors and creditors ledgers in which the individual accounts of customers and suppliers are kept. The following information relates to 19X1:

Example 6.9

	£
Debit balances on debtors control account 1 January 19X1	66,300
Credit balances on creditors control account 1 January 19X1	50,600
Sundry credit balances on debtors ledger 1 January 19X1	724
Goods purchased on credit	257,919
Goods sold on credit	323,614
Cash received from debtors	299,149
Cash paid to creditors	210,522
Discounts received	2,663
Discounts allowed	2,930
Cash purchases	3,627
Cash sales	5,922
Bad debts written off	3,651

Interest charged on overdue debtor accounts	277
Returns outwards	2,926
Returns inwards	2,805
Accounts settled by contra between debtor and creditor ledgers	1,106
Sundry credit balances on debtors ledger 31 December 19X1	815
Sundry debit balances on creditors ledger 31 December 19X1	698

Required

Prepare the debtors control account and the creditors control account as they would appear in the company's ledger at 31 December 19X1.

Solution

Debtors (Sales Ledger) Control Account

19X1		£	19X1		£
1 Jan.	Balance b/d	66,300	1 Jan.	Balance b/d	724
	Sales	323,614		Cash	299,149
	Interest	277		Discounts allowed	2,930
31 Dec.	Balance c/d	815		Bad debts	3,651
				Returns inwards	2,805
				Contra – creditors	1,106
			31 Dec.	Balance c/d	80,641
		391,006			391,006
19X2			19X2		
1 Jan.	Balance b/d	80,641	1 Jan.	Balance b/d	815

Creditors (Purchase Ledger) Control Account

19X1		£	19X1		£
	Cash	210,522	1 Jan.	Balance b/d	50,600
	Discounts received	2,663		Purchases	257,919
	Returns outwards	2,926	31 Dec.	Balance c/d	698
	Contra – debtors	1,106			
31 Dec.	Balance c/d	92,000			
		309,217			309,217
19X2			19X2		
1 Jan.	Balance b/d	698	1 Jan.	Balance b/d	92,000

Note
The cash sales and cash purchases do not appear in the control accounts. They do not affect the recorded value of debtors or creditors.

Reconciliation with suppliers' statements

Monthly statements should be sent to customers reminding them of the amount due and requesting payment. The customer can then compare this document with the information contained in his or her own ledger. The balances on the statement and in the customers' books are unlikely to be the same, for example, the customer may not have received certain goods appearing on the statement, and so a reconciliation must be prepared. In the same way, the company should receive details of their account from suppliers, and these should be checked with the creditors account in the company's books. This procedure is similar to the preparation of the bank reconciliation (dealt with in Chapter 5) and is illustrated in Example 6.10.

Included in the creditors ledger of J. Cross – a shopkeeper – is the following account, which disclosed that the amount owing to one of his suppliers at 31 May 1984 was £472.13. **Example 6.10**

Creditors Ledger: Nala Merchandising Company

1984		£	1984		£
May 18	Purchases returns	36.67	May 1	Balance b/d	862.07
27	Purchases returns	18.15	16	Purchases	439.85
27	Adjustment		25	Purchases	464.45
	(overcharge)	5.80	25	Adjustment	
31	Discount received	24.94		(undercharge)	13.48
31	Bank	1,222.16			
31	Balance c/d	472.13			
		£1,779.85			£1,779.85
			June 1	Balance b/d	472.13

In the first week of June 1984, J. Cross received a statement (shown below) from the supplier, which showed an amount owing of £2,424.53.

J. Cross in account with Nala Merchandising Company: Statement of Account

1984		Debit £	Credit £	£
May 1	BCE			1,538.70 Dr.
3	DISC		13.40	1,525.30 Dr.
	CHQ		634.11	891.19 Dr.
5	ALLCE		29.12	862.07 Dr.
7	GDS	256.72		1,118.79 Dr.
10	GDS	108.33		1,227.12 Dr.
11	GDS	74.80		1,301.92 Dr.
14	ADJ	13.48		1,315.40 Dr.
18	GDS	162.55		1,477.95 Dr.
23	GDS	301.90		1,779.85 Dr.
25	ALLCE		36.67	1,743.18 Dr.
28	GDS	134.07		1,877.25 Dr.
29	GDS	251.12		2,128.37 Dr.
30	GDS	204.80		2,333.17 Dr.
31	GDS	91.36		2,424.53 Dr.
31	BCE			2,424.53 Dr.

Abbreviations
BCE = Balance; CHQ = Cheque; GDS = Goods; ALLCE = Allowance; DISC = Discount; ADJ = Adjustment.

Prepare a statement reconciling the closing balance on the supplier's account in the creditors ledger with the closing balance shown on the statement of account submitted by the supplier. **Required**

(CACA, Level 1 Accounting, December, 1984)

Solution

	£	£
Balance per creditors ledger		472.13
Add items on statement not in account:		
May 28 Goods	134.07	
May 29 Goods	251.12	
May 30 Goods	204.80	
May 31 Goods	91.36	
		681.35
		1,153.48
Add items in account not on statement:		
May 31 Paid	1,222.16	
May 31 Discount	24.94	
May 27 Goods returned	18.15	
May 27 Overcharge	5.80	
		1,271.05
Balance per statement		2,424.53

Notes
1. The opening balance on the supplier's account in the creditors ledger and the statement balance on 5 May are the same, and so at that point the records are in agreement.
2. Some purchases are combined for entry in the supplier's account: the purchases entered on May 16 of £439.85 consist of the statement entries of May 7 (£256.72), 10 (£108.33) and 11 (£74.80); the purchases entered on May 25 of £464.45 consist of the statement entries of May 18 (£162.55) and 23 (£301.90).

THE TRIAL BALANCE

A set of books maintained in accordance with the double entry method provides a comprehensive and appropriately analysed record of all the transactions undertaken by an entity. This record not only enables the day-to-day control of such items as debtors and creditors but also provides the basis from which the final accounting statements, namely the trading and profit and loss account and balance sheet, are prepared.

The process by which an economic event becomes included in the final accounting statement is as shown in Figure 6.6. It can be seen that the stage prior to the production of the statements from the ledger (covered in Chapter 7) is the preparation of a trial balance. This is a list of all the balances remaining at the end of the accounting period on the many accounts contained in the main ledger; the balances are entered in separate columns according to whether they are debit balances or credit balances. The two columns should possess the same total value since each entry in the books consists of a debit and a credit of equal value and, as described earlier in this chapter, leaves the relationship C + L = A in balance. Although it was not described as such, Example 6.2 part (a) shows the trial balance of Bernard Egin.

Figure 6.6 Process by which an economic event becomes part of final accounting statement

Readers should now work Questions 6.1 to 6.6 at the end of this chapter.

The fact that the trial balance shows equal totals for both debit and credit balances does not necessarily mean that it is correct, since there are some errors that are not revealed by an imbalance. These are as follows:

1. *Error of principle* An entry may be made in the wrong account, for example, wages may be debited to purchases.
2. *Duplication* Both the debits and credits for a transaction could be entered in the accounts twice.
3. *Omissions* A transaction may be omitted altogether.
4. *Compensatory errors* There may be two or more errors, the effects of which cancel each other out.
5. *Error in the original entry* An incorrect figure may be used as the basis for the double entry record.

The suspense account

The trial balance, when it is first extracted, does not always balance, and it is then obvious that some error has been made. The first step to discover the mistake is to review all the balances to ensure that they have been extracted correctly from the books. The next step is to check that subsidiary memorandum ledgers, for such items as debtors and creditors, have been reconciled with their control accounts. Any discrepancy would indicate a likely area in which the error is to be found. Finally, if the difference is material enough to make its discovery essential, a more thorough checking of the records of prime entry to the ledger must be carried out. So as not to delay the preparation of the accounts, a difference on the trial balance may be placed in a suspense account, which is cleared after investigations have been completed. This procedure is shown in Example 6.11.

The trial balance of Wrong at 31 December, as first compiled, contained ***Example 6.11***
total debits of £197,500 and total credits of £210,000. The difference of £12,500 was placed to the debit of a suspense account to balance the trial balance. Subsequent investigation revealed the following errors:

1. The balance from the cash book of £3,750 had not been entered in the trial balance.

2. The debtors balance had been wrongly recorded as £71,560 instead of £75,160.
3. A fixed asset purchased for £10,000 had been credited to the fixed asset account instead of being debited.
4. The previous year's profit of £14,850 had not been added to the profit and loss account balance brought forward.

Required   Prepare the suspense account to record the correction of the errors.

Solution   **Suspense Account**

	£		£
Difference on trial balance	12,500	Cash (1)	3,750
Profit and loss account (4)	14,850	Debtors (2)	3,600
		Fixed assets (3)	20,000
	27,350		27,350

Note
The suspense account now has no value left on it, and the double entry is completed within the trial balance with the following effects:

1. Cash of £3,750 appears as an asset.
2. Debtors are increased by £3,600, to their correct value of £75,160.
3. The incorrect entry in the fixed asset account of £10,000 is cancelled and the correct debit entry of £10,000 is substituted. Note that the total effect of this error was to under-state fixed assets by £20,000.
4. The profit and loss account balance is increased by £14,850, being the previous year's profit omitted.

COMPUTERIZED ACCOUNTING SYSTEMS

A firm's overall accounting system consists of a number of subsystems, for example, a wages system to calculate the amounts due to each employee and allocate them to expense headings, such as production departments, and a purchases system to record creditors and analyse the purchases made between various types of goods and services. Figure 6.7 shows how a firm's accounting system consists of a number of separate, but interlinked, subsystems.

Computer programs are readily available for each subsystem, indicated by an asterisk in Figure 6.7 and, provided they are from an integrated package of programs, the appropriate links will have been established as part of the program. A fact has to be input only once for all the related aspects to be updated, for example, the fact that a sale has been made, when recorded in the sales system, could also update the stock records and form part of the total sales value automatically posted to the nominal ledger. The sales program may also produce the sales invoice and the stock program may check the resulting stock level to see if more of the item needs to be ordered.

The basic requirements of the subsystems are fairly standard, and so little adaptation by the user is needed. For example, the principles of calculating wages and the related tax deductions or running a debtors ledger are generally uniform between businesses. However, before a system is

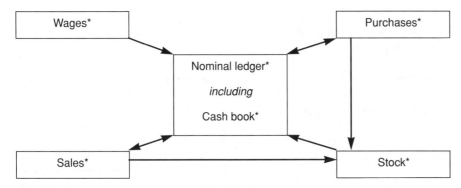

Figure 6.7   Some subsystems in an accounting system

Note
The arrows indicate the direction of information flows.

acquired, the user must determine the basis on which the analysis is to be carried out, and this, in turn, is largely determined by the content of the reports it is desired to produce. Therefore, before a computerized system is put into operation, careful thought must be given to the accounting system as a whole to ensure that the program is capable of performing the necessary analysis and that the first stages of raw data input will eventually lead to the desired output.

Once the desired analysis has been determined, a system of coding must be developed to enable the computer to accumulate data in the appropriate accounts in the nominal ledger. Because each business is likely to have its own organization and analysis requirement, and to give flexibility, accounting programs usually leave the setting of codes to the user. The compilation of a list of codes is a straightforward task, and Figure 6.8 shows the steps used to produce some specimen codes in the context of an organization with a number of branches that are subdivided into departments.

Step 1: Allocate codes to branches, departments and type of transaction. For example:

Code	Meaning
01	Branch 1
02	Branch 2
08	Department 8
09	Department 9
441	Sales
442	Wages

Step 2: Combine the codes from Step 1 to produce detailed codes that can be applied to every transaction the business undertakes:

	Branch	Department	Transaction type
First code	01	08	441
Second code	01	09	441
Third code	02	08	441
Fourth code	01	08	442

Figure 6.8   Specimen transaction codes

Once a code number has been allocated to each branch, department and transaction type in step 1, it is possible, by combining these codes, to develop a code number for each individual transaction as shown in step 2. Thus, as 441 is the code for a sale in Figure 6.8 then the first code number refers to a sale by department 8 of branch 1 and the second code to a sale by department 9 of the same branch; the third code indicates a sale made by department 8 of branch 2. Transaction type 442 relates to wages, and so the fourth code is the payment to an employee in department 8 of branch 1.

As subsequent analysis and reporting of figures is based on the initial coding of each transaction, a system must be established to ensure that the initial coding is carried out correctly. In some cases transactions might be coded automatically, for example, the code for each employee may be held by the computer and wage payments allocated accordingly. If this is done, the employee must be recoded when transferred to another department. In other cases, individual transactions must be examined and coded manually, for example, an invoice for repairs to a branch's premises.

It is possible to add extra codes to give additional analysis, which the computer could carry out on an *ad hoc* basis as required by management – for example, data on sales may be analysed by salesperson, location of customer or value of sale. Such exercises emphasize the need to decide and record in advance the necessary basic data; if this is not done, each analysis would involve the laborious procedure of returning to the prime documents to recode them.

The next stage in computerizing the accounts system is to open a nominal ledger account for each valid code. Such an account would be opened for each code produced under step 2 in Figure 6.8 but, although it could be derived, one would not be needed, for example, for sales by the accounts department that only provides a service for the rest of the organization. The computer can then post every transaction with the appropriate code to an account, and copies of each account can be printed out to show the individual transactions that have been combined to give the closing balance. The usual cross-referencing is done automatically so that each entry can be traced to its source.

The computer is also able to construct and print out the books of prime entry (that is, the day books, cash book and journal) in the form of a list of all the transactions that have been entered in a particular batch. Security is achieved by numbering all such lists consecutively and producing them as an automatic part of the operation; they can then be filed and checked for completeness. Additional security is given if access to parts of the system, such as the cash book and journal, is granted with the use of passwords known only to authorized personnel.

Finally, the trial balance is periodically prepared, usually monthly, and converted into a profit and loss account and balance sheet. This process can be handled by the computer and the reports can be prepared on a number of bases, such as monthly, cumulatively, in comparison with budgets or the same period of the previous year. The production of reports highlights the speed and flexibility of a computerized accounting system as a single set of input data can be manipulated and presented in a number of different ways with great ease.

ADVANTAGES OF DOUBLE ENTRY

The double entry system is very flexible. In this chapter reference has been made to books of account and pages within these books. The records could, in practice, be kept on separate cards or be produced as computer print-outs. Whichever method of operation is employed, however, the benefits derived from the use of double entry are as follows:

1. It enables all types of transactions undertaken by the business, which can be expressed in monetary terms, to be recorded. Provided an economic event has a measurable financial impact, it can be entered into the double entry framework.
2. It enables large numbers of transactions to be recorded in an orderly manner; similar transactions are grouped together.
3. Economic events are recorded both from the personal point of view (that is, their impact on the relationship between the entity and outsiders) and also from their impersonal aspect (that is, their effect on the company itself in terms of assets owned, revenue and expenses).
4. The debits entered to record a particular transaction must be of equal value to the credits. This equality enables a trial balance to be prepared that gives an initial check on the arithmetical accuracy of the records, although there are errors that are not revealed.
5. The trial balance, an end product of the double entry system, is the basis for the preparation of the trading and profit and loss account and balance sheet. The former of these gives an indication of the return made by the entity on the resources invested in it, while the latter presents a picture of the extent to which management has carried out its custodial duties in the form of a statement of the financial position.

Readers should now work Questions 6.7 to 6.14 at the end of this chapter.

Questions

Questions 6.1 to 6.6 trace the transactions of a business from the opening balances of the accounting period through to the closing trial balance. The remaining questions test other aspects covered in this chapter.

6.1 The following are the balances on the accounts of Radio on 1 January:

Credit balances

	£	£
Capital		8,500
Trade creditors:		
Tele	2,300	
Trany	1,000	
Valve	1,300	
	———	
		4,600
		———
		13,100
		———

Debit balances

	£	£
Plant and machinery at written-down value		4,500
Stock		2,700
Debtors:		
Vision	2,500	
Sister	1,500	
Batty	1,200	
	———	
		5,200
Cash		700
		———
		13,100
		———

Required

Prepare the journal entries to record the opening balances in Radio's books on 1 January.

6.2 During January, Radio undertook the following transactions:

Credit transactions with customers during January

Customer	Sales	Returns inwards	Cash received	Prompt payment discount
	£	£	£	£
Vision	7,000	300	6,350	50
Sister	4,000	—	3,500	40
Batty	2,700	200	2,600	25
Flat	200	—	—	—
Broke	300	—	—	—

Credit transactions with suppliers during January

Supplier	Detail	Purchases	Returns outwards	Cash paid	Prompt payment discount
		£	£	£	£
Tele	Goods for resale	3,000	—	2,950	55
Trany	Goods for resale	2,000	100	1,950	35
Valve	Goods for resale	2,400	150	2,200	20
Garage	Motor expenses	100	—	—	—
Paper	Office supplies	50	—	—	—

Other cash transactions during January

Payee	Detail	£
Plantmax	Purchase of plant	1,000
Cash	Wages	1,500
Accom.	Rent for 6 months to 30 June	600
Supplies	Office expenses	250
Garage	Motor expenses	300

£100 was received from Scrap for machinery that was disposed of.

Required

Enter this information in the books of prime entry, i.e. the day books and cash book.

6.3 Use the information in Questions 6.1 and 6.2 to prepare the ledger accounts, other than cash, in Radio's main ledger.

6.4 Use the information in Questions 6.1 and 6.2 to prepare the memorandum debtors and creditors ledger.

6.5 Use the information in Questions 6.3 and 6.4 to prepare reconciliations of the purchases and sales ledger accounts with their memorandum ledgers.

6.6 Prepare Radio's trial balance from the accounts produced in Questions 6.2 and 6.3.

6.7 (a) Define and distinguish, with examples, the following three classifications of ledger accounts:

(i)   Real accounts.
(ii) Personal accounts.
(iii) Nominal accounts.

(b) Give the appropriate classification for each of the following account balances:

(i)   Fixed assets at cost, £10,000.
(ii) Wages paid, £700.
(iii) Discounts received, £1,400.
(iv) Balance due from Double Ltd. £1,500.

6.8 Explain how the accountant makes use of the trial balance.

6.9 The following particulars have been extracted from the books of a trading concern for the year ended 30 September 19X5:

		£
1.	Sales ledger debit balances at 1 October 19X4	102,300
2.	Sales ledger credit balances at 1 October 19X4	340
3.	Credit sales	630,800
4.	Cash sales	140,100
5.	Cash received from debtors	498,660
6.	Returns outwards	8,300
7.	Returns inwards	2,700
8.	Discounts received	15,200
9.	Discounts allowed	11,790
10.	Accounts settled by contra to purchase ledger	5,200

11. Bad debts written off	3,950
12. Sales ledger credit balances 30 September 19X5	510

Required

Prepare the sales ledger control account for the year to 30 September 19X5.

6.10 Ian Error has produced a trial balance for his business for the year to 30 September 19X2 that does not balance, and the error has been placed in a suspense account. An examination of the company's books reveals the following errors:

(a) An invoice from Zed amounting to £1,000, for goods purchased, has been omitted from the purchase day book and posted direct to the purchase account in the nominal ledger and to Zed's account in the memorandum purchase ledger. It has not been included in the creditors control account in the trial balance.
(b) The sales day book has been undercast by £2,400.
(c) Discounts allowed for the month of June amounting to £4,890 have not been debited to the ledger.
(d) Goods received from Wye on 30 June 19X2, which cost £24,100, have been included in the stock but the invoice has not yet been received and entered in the books.
(e) A cheque for £1,920 received from Exe, a debtor, has been debited to cash and credited to the sales account in the nominal ledger.

Required

(i) Prepare the journal entries to correct these errors.
(ii) Prepare a statement that shows the effect of the corrections on the company's profit for the year.
(iii) Calculate the difference between the sides of the trial balance that was placed to suspense account.

6.11 Aries Ltd maintains a creditors ledger control account in its general ledger as part of its double entry system. Individual accounts for suppliers are maintained on a memorandum basis in a separate creditors ledger.

The following totals are available for the financial year ended 30 November 1990:

	£
Discounts received	3,608
Cash and cheques paid to suppliers (per cash book)	231,570
Set-offs to sales ledger control account	818
Credit purchases	249,560
Returns outwards	4,564

The audited total for creditors as at 1 December 1989 was £45,870.

Required

(a) Reconstruct the creditors ledger control account for the year ended 30 November 1990.   *(8 marks)*
(b) The total of the balances on the individual creditors accounts as at 30 November 1990 was £51,120. Following a checking of the records the following errors were discovered:

1. An invoice for £1,125 which was correctly entered into the purchases book has not been posted to the individual supplier's account.
2. Another invoice for £1,850 has been omitted from the purchases book.
3. A credit note from a supplier for £870 has been completely omitted from the records.
4. During the year ended 30 November 1990 petty cash payments to suppliers totalled £625. These have been correctly recorded in the petty cash book and posted to the individual suppliers accounts but no other entry has been made.
5. The total of the individual creditors balances as at 30 November 1990 has been undercast by £2,000.

Required

Prepare a clear calculation of

(i)   the corrected balance on the creditors ledger control account; and
(6 marks)
(ii) the corrected total of the balances on the individual creditors accounts as at 30 November 1990. *(6 marks)*
(Total 20 marks)
(AAT Preliminary, December 1990)

6.12 The following information for the financial year ended 31 May 1991 has been extracted from the accounting system of George Peace Ltd:

	£
Discounts allowed to credit customers	4,170
Cash and cheques received from credit customers	144,700
Discounts received from suppliers	3,910
Cash and cheques paid to suppliers	156,770
Bad debts written off	1,730
Set-offs from customers to suppliers accounts	3,600
Credit sales	167,800
Credit purchases	175,510
Returns in	4,220
Returns out	6,330
Trade debtors as at 1 June 1990	27,490
Trade creditors as at 1 June 1990	21,810

All sales and purchases during the year were made on credit.

Required

(a) Use the above information to prepare a sales ledger control account and a purchases ledger control account for the year ended 31 May 1991.*(14 marks)*
(b) Indicate the source of each of the above totals in the accounting system of George Peace Ltd. *(6 marks)*
(Total 20 marks)
(AAT Preliminary, June 1991)

6.13 The following is a list of typical business transactions:

(a) The purchase of goods on credit.
(b) Allowances to credit customers upon the return of faulty goods.

(c) Refund from petty cash to an employee of an amount spent on entertaining a client.
(d) Credit card sales.
(e) The recovery of a debt previously written off as bad.

Required

For each transaction identify clearly

(i) the original document(s) for the data;
(ii) the book of original entry for the transaction; and
(iii) the way in which the data will be incorporated into the double entry system.

(4 marks each)
(Total 20 marks)
(AAT Preliminary, June 1991)

6.14 After completing a training course at a technical college, Michael Faraday set up in business as a self-employed electrician on 1 January 19X5.

He was very competent at his job but had no idea how to maintain proper accounting records. Sometime during 19X5 one of his friends asked Michael how well his business was doing. He replied, 'All right . . . I think . . . but I'm not quite sure'.

In the ensuing conversation his friend asked whether he had prepared accounts yet, covering his first quarter's trading, to which Michael replied that he had not. His friend then stressed that, for various reasons, it was vital for accounts of businesses to be prepared properly.

Shortly afterwards Michael came to see you to ask for your help in preparing accounts for his first quarter's trading. He brought with him, in a cardboard box, the only records he had, mainly scribbled on scraps of paper.

He explained that he started his business with a car worth £700, and £2,250 in cash of which £250 was his savings and £2,000 had been borrowed from a relative at an interest rate of 10 per cent per annum. It was his practice to pay his suppliers and expenses in cash, to require his customers to settle their accounts in cash and to bank any surplus in a business bank account. He maintained lists of cash receipts and cash payments, of supplies obtained on credit and of work carried out for customers and of appliances sold, on credit.

The list of credit suppliers comprised the following:

Date supplied 19X5	Supplier	Amount owed £	Date paid 19X5	Amount paid £	Remarks
January	Dee & Co.	337.74	March	330.00	Received discount £7.74
	A. B. Supplies	528.20	March	528.20	
February	Simpson	141.34	March	138.00	Received discount £3.34
	Cotton Ltd	427.40	March	130.00	Payment on account
			April	297.40	Remainder
	Dee & Co.	146.82	March	140.00	Received discount £6.82
March	A. B. Supplies	643.43	April	643.43	
	Simpson	95.60			Not yet paid

The purchase in January from Dee & Co. was of tools and equipment to enable him to carry out electrical repair work. All the remaining purchases were of repair materials, except for the purchase in February from Cotton Ltd that consisted entirely of electrical appliances for resale.

In addition to the above credit transactions, he had bought repair materials for cash, as follows:

19X5	£
January	195.29
February	161.03
March	22.06

Other cash payments comprised:

19X5		£
January	Rent of premises for January to June 19X5	400.00
	Rates of premises for January to March 19X5	150.00
	Stationery	32.70
	Car running expenses	92.26
February	Sundries	51.54
	Car running expenses	81.42
March	Sundries	24.61
	Car running expenses	104.52
	Transfer to bank	500.00

He had also withdrawn £160.00 in cash at the end of each month for living expenses.

The list of credit customers comprised:

Date of sale 19X5	Customer	Amount owed £	Date received 19X5	Amount received £	Remarks
January	D. Hopkins	362.80	February	357.00	Allowed discount £5.80
	P. Bolton	417.10	March	417.10	
February	G. Leivers	55.00	March	55.00	
	M. Whitehead	151.72	April	151.72	
	N. John Ltd	49.14	April	49.14	
	A. Linneker	12.53	March	12.53	
March	E. Horton	462.21	April	462.21	
	S. Ward	431.08	March	426.00	Allowed discount £5.08
	W. Scothern & Co.	319.12			Not yet received
	N. Annable	85.41			Not yet received

The above amounts relate to charges for repair work he had carried out, except that the amounts shown in February for G. Leivers, N. John Ltd and A. Linneker are for sales of electrical appliances.

In addition to the above credit transactions, he had cash takings, as follows:

19X5		£
January	Repair work	69.44
February	Repair work	256.86
March	Repair work	182.90
	Appliances	112.81

He estimated that, at the end of March 19X5, his stock of electrical repair materials was £691.02 and of electrical appliances for resale was £320.58, his tools and equipment were worth £300.00 and his car, £600.00.

Apart from loan interest, the only accrual was for heating and lighting, £265.00.

Required

1. Prepare
   (a) purchase day book with analysis columns for type of purchase; and
   (b) sales day book with analysis columns for class of business undertaken.
2. Open, post to 31 March 19X5 only, and balance a columnar cash book suitably analysed to facilitate ledger postings.
3. Open, post to 31 March 19X5 only, and balance a creditors ledger control account and a debtors ledger control account. Use the closing balances in your answer to (7) below. (N.B. Individual accounts for creditors and debtors are *not* required.)
4. Open, post and balance sales and cost of sales accounts, each with separate columns for 'Repairs' and 'Appliances'.
5. Prepare M. Faraday's trading account for the quarter ended 31 March 19X5, distinguishing between gross profit on repairs and on appliance sales.
6. Prepare M. Faraday's general profit and loss account for the quarter ended 31 March 19X5.
7. Prepare M. Faraday's balance sheet as at 31 March 19X5.

(CACA, Preliminary, June)

7

THE DOUBLE ENTRY SYSTEM III: PERIODIC ACCOUNTING REPORTS

The objectives of this chapter are to
- explain how a set of final accounts is prepared from the trial balance;
- show how the value of closing stock is included in a set of accounts;
- demonstrate how depreciation is included in a set of accounts;
- describe how to account for the disposal of fixed assets;
- explain the terms 'prepayments' and 'accruals' and their impact on final accounts;
- show how to account for bad and doubtful debts; and
- illustrate the use of the extended trial balance.

PERIODIC ACCOUNTS

The preparation of accounting statements should be a routine procedure as they are regularly needed by management, ownership and other interested parties, such as debenture holders, to monitor the progress and position of the company. The principal accounting statements used for these purposes are the trading and profit and loss account and the balance sheet. It is normal to prepare these statements at least once a year to comply with legal and taxation requirements, but they can be produced more frequently if required. Their usefulness depends, first, on the ability of the recipients to base decisions on them and, second, on the time lags between the occurrence of events, their financial effects being reported and decisions taken. If decisions are delayed because of a lack of financial information, then opportunities may be missed, possibly with disastrous consequences. For this reason management, and sometimes other interested parties, are provided with statements more frequently than once a year, usually monthly, but possibly even more often. For example, when losses are being made it is important to realize this fact at an early stage; this is helped by the frequent and prompt production of a profit and loss account. The first evidence that losses are being incurred may otherwise be the collapse of the company, an eventuality that might have been avoided if the losses had been identified earlier and remedial action taken.

The procedures described in Chapters 5 and 6 provide the foundations of the accounting process as they are used to record the flows of cash, goods and services and provide a summary of these flows in the form of the trial balance. This chapter deals with the adjustments necessary to the information contained in the trial balance to enable the production of the trading and profit and loss account and balance sheet.

ADJUSTMENTS TO THE TRIAL BALANCE

Adjustments to the trial balance are necessary because the transactions in the ledger accounts do not reflect precisely the economic events that have occurred during the period covered by the accounting statements. Adjustments are therefore needed to take account of the following:

1. *Timing differences* These occur when an item recorded in the books during an accounting period has significance for the business not only in that accounting period but also in previous or subsequent ones. In these circumstances an adjustment must be made to distribute the item accordingly. For example, the purchase of a fixed asset is initially recorded at cost in the year of purchase, but it is necessary to apportion this cost over the years that derive benefit from the expenditure. (For a fuller explanation, see Chapter 8.) Timing differences also operate in the opposite direction. For example, there may be an interval between the receipt of goods and the arrival of the related invoice. (For a fuller explanation, see later in this chapter.)
2. *Incomplete information* The entries in the books may not reflect all the economic changes that must be reported, since some events are not supported by a documented flow of value on which a day book entry is based. For example, a debtor may be unable to pay the sum due to the company, or a machine may be scrapped unsold (see later in this chapter). The routine documentation procedures for a sale or purchase do not apply in these cases, and care must be taken to ensure that allowance has been made for them when the accounts are prepared. The accountant must be satisfied that all the items that relate to the period under review have been included and also that all items that are not relevant have been excluded.

The adjustments made to the trial balance must comply with the rules of double entry – each must comprise a debit and a credit of equal value. The implementation of the adjustments that routinely arise when periodic accounts are prepared are examined in this chapter; the principles of valuation on which the adjustments are based are dealt with in Chapter 8.

STOCKS (INVENTORIES)

Profit is measured by comparing the value of sales for a period of time with their related costs, and so it is necessary to determine the value of goods consumed in the manner described in Chapter 4. Companies may hold many different types of stock, such as raw materials, work-in-progress and finished goods, and the general equation to find the cost of items consumed is

Cost of goods consumed = Opening + Inflow of − Closing
stock   goods   stock

Care must be taken to ensure that all inflows of goods are included. Any items received prior to the accounting date and included in stock, but which have not been entered as purchases as they have not yet been invoiced, must be identified. An adjustment in the form of an accrual is then made, which increases the value of purchases (debit) and is shown as a liability in the balance sheet (credit); for a fuller explanation, see the section on prepayments and accruals in this chapter.

In a system of double entry accounting, unless continuous inventory control as described in Chapter 8 is used, it is usual to enter the opening stock in one account and to accumulate in another account, called purchases, the cost of all acquisitions made during the accounting period. The effect of this procedure is that the trial balance contains separate balances for opening stock and purchases; these provide two of the three elements in the formula given above. The missing element is the figure for closing stock, and this is usually determined by means of a physical stock-take to find the quantities of each type of stock, which are then valued.

To find the cost of goods sold in the trading account the values of opening stock and purchases contained in the trial balance are transferred to the debit of this account. The accounting entry to record closing stock in the final accounts must then be made:

Debit	*Credit*	*With*
Stock account	Trading account	Value of closing stock

The closing balance on the stock account appears as an asset in the balance sheet and is subsequently included as opening stock in the trading account for the following accounting period.

Example 7.1 involves the preparation of final accounts from the trial balance where an adjustment has to be made for closing stock.

The trial balance of Button, a sole trader, at 31 December 19X4 was   ***Example 7.1***

	£	£
Capital		10,000
Drawings	10,000	
Sales		75,500
Purchases	45,250	
Stock 1 January 19X4	6,750	
Debtors	4,300	
Creditors		3,200
Cash	1,125	
Delivery costs	875	
Wages	11,225	
Sundry expenses	3,000	
Freehold premises	6,175	
	88,700	88,700

The stock at 31 December 19X4 was £7,150.

Required   Prepare the trading and profit and loss account of Button for the year to 31 December 19X4 and a balance sheet at that date. The accounts should be presented in vertical format.

Solution   **Trading and Profit and Loss Account year to 31 December 19X4**

	£	£
Sales		75,500
Stock 1 January	6,750	
Purchases	45,250	
Stock 31 December	(7,150)	
Cost of goods sold		44,850
Gross profit		30,650
Wages	11,225	
Delivery costs	875	
Sundry expenses	3,000	
		15,100
Net profit		15,550

Balance Sheet at 31 December 19X4

	£	£
Fixed assets		
Freehold premises		6,175
Current assets		
Stock	7,150	
Debtors	4,300	
Cash	1,125	
	12,575	
Current liabilities		
Creditors	3,200	
		9,375
		15,550
Capital		
At 1 January		10,000
Profit for 19X4		15,550
		25,550
Drawings		10,000
		15,550

Readers should now attempt Question 7.1 at the end of this chapter.

DEPRECIATION

Fixed assets and their related accumulated depreciation are recorded in the double entry ledger by using an account for each type of fixed asset at cost and another for each type of fixed asset's accumulated depreciation. The number of accounts to be opened depends on the nature of the business, but usually separate accounts for land and buildings, plant and machinery, motor vehicles and furniture and fittings suffice. Further accounts can be used if appropriate, for example, computer equipment or assets out on hire may have a value significant enough to warrant separate identification. The totals of these accounts should be backed up by detailed analysis in a fixed asset register so that the individual assets can be identified.

When the trial balance is extracted it contains for each type of fixed asset, as a debit, the cost and, as a credit, the accumulated balance of depreciation brought forward at the start of the accounting period. The value of the depreciation charge for the period for each class of asset has then to be calculated, and the amounts are debited to the profit and loss account and credited to the accounts containing the opening balances of accumulated depreciation. (The calculation of the depreciation charge is dealt with in Chapter 8.) The debit balance on each of the fixed assets (at cost) accounts is entered in the balance sheet, and from it the credit balance on the related accumulated depreciation account is deducted to give the written-down value, that is, the portion of cost not yet written off and therefore carried forward to the next accounting period. It is helpful to the users of the accounts if both the total cost and the total related depreciation are shown in the balance sheet, rather than just the net figure; this procedure indicates how much of the value has been used up and, therefore, how long it is likely to be before replacement becomes necessary. In the case of a limited company, such disclosure is a legal requirement.

The following information relates to the machinery owned by Clip Ltd: **Example 7.2**

	£
At cost, 1 January 19X1	65,000
Accumulated depreciation at 1 January 19X1	25,000
Acquired during 19X1	10,000
Depreciation charge for 19X1	8,000

(a) Prepare the ledger accounts for 19X1 to record the above information. **Required**
(b) Show the balance sheet extract for machinery at 31 December 19X1.

(a) **Machinery at Cost Account** **Solution**

			£			£
1 Jan.	19X1	Balance b/d	65,000	31 Dec. 19X1 Balance c/d	75,000
	19X1	Purchases	10,000		
			75,000		75,000

Accumulated Depreciation Account – Machinery

	£				£
31 Dec. 19X1 Balance b/d	33,000	1 Jan.	19X1	Balance b/d	25,000
		31 Dec.	19X1	Profit and loss account	8,000
	33,000				33,000

(b) **Balance Sheet extract 31 December 19X1**

	£	£
Machinery at cost	75,000	
Less: Depreciation	33,000	
		42,000

Readers should now attempt Questions 7.2 and 7.3 at the end of this chapter. The former question tests the entries for fixed assets and depreciation in the books of account, and the latter puts them in the context of preparing the final accounts from the trial balance.

DISPOSAL OF FIXED ASSETS

When a fixed asset is disposed of, its cost and related depreciation must be eliminated from the books and any profit or loss on disposal calculated. Any proceeds from disposal must not be included in the company's sales figure as they do not relate to routine trading activity. Instead, the proceeds are credited in a disposal of fixed assets account, the balance on which appears as a credit entry in the trial balance. The calculation of the profit or loss arising on disposal may then be made in the disposal of fixed assets account using the following entries:

Account debited	Account credited	With
Disposal of fixed assets	Fixed assets at cost	Historical cost of the asset
Accumulated depreciation	Disposal of fixed assets	Accumulated depreciation on the asset

Example 7.3   In 19X3 Case Ltd sold for £6,500 cash a piece of machinery that had cost the company £25,000. At the time of sale, the accumulated depreciation on the asset was £20,000.

Required   Prepare the disposal of fixed assets account to record the sale of the machinery.

Disposal of Fixed Assets Account			**Solution**

	£		£
Machinery at cost	25,000	Cash	6,500
Profit on sale*	1,500	Accumulated depreciation	20,000
	26,500		26,500

Note
* Balancing figure credited to the profit and loss account.

Sometimes a disposal of fixed assets account is not maintained during the year and instead any proceeds are credited to the fixed assets at cost account. This happens especially where a 'trading-in' allowance is received, for example, when changing motor vehicles, as a reduction in the amount paid for the new asset. In these circumstances, the proceeds or trading-in allowance must be transferred to the disposal account by the following entry:

Account debited	*Account credited*	*With*
Fixed assets at cost	Disposal of fixed assets	Proceeds of disposal or trading-in allowance

Instead of making the appropriate entries in a disposal of fixed assets account, the profit or loss on the disposal of an individual asset may alternatively be calculated by using the following formula:

$$\text{Proceeds on disposal} - \left[\text{Historical cost} - \text{Accumulated depreciation} \right] = \text{Profit/loss on disposal}$$

Questions can be framed so that any one element from this equation is unknown and has to be found as the balancing figure after the others have been determined and entered.

Shed Ltd bought a fixed asset for £10,000 in 19X1, which was sold for £6,250 in 19X5 to give a profit on disposal of £1,250. **Example 7.4**

(a) Calculate the accumulated depreciation that had been charged on the asset up to the time it was sold. **Required**
(b) Explain why, when the amount of profit on disposal is known, it is necessary to calculate the depreciation figure.

(a) **Solution**

£6,250 (Proceeds) – (£10,000 (cost) – Accumulated depreciation
= £1,250 (profit)
∴ £6,250 – £10,000 + Accumulated depreciation
= £1,250
∴ Accumulated depreciation = £10,000 – £6,250 + £1,250
= £5,000

(b) It is necessary to know the value of accumulated depreciation as, when an asset is disposed of, all the related entries in the books must be removed. This is done by using double entry procedures to complete a disposal of fixed assets account:

Disposal of Fixed Assets Account

	£		£
Fixed assets at cost	10,000	Proceeds	6,250
Profit on disposal	1,250	Accumulated depreciation	5,000
	11,250		11,250

When a fully depreciated asset is scrapped, and no proceeds are received, its cost and accumulated depreciation must be eliminated from the books. This is achieved by the entries:

Account debited	*Account credited*	*With*
Accumulated depreciation	Fixed assets at cost	Historical cost of asset scrapped

Readers should now work Question 7.4 at the end of this chapter, which tests all the aspects of asset disposal described in this section.

PREPAYMENTS AND ACCRUALS

A business makes a number of payments that give it a right to enjoy certain benefits over a period of time. Some of these payments, such as rates on the occupation of property, are paid in advance of the receipt of the benefit and give rise to a prepayment, while others, such as for the consumption of gas or electricity, are made in arrears and create accruals. The accruals concept, as explained in Chapter 4, is applied, and so, unless the period of time covered by these payments coincides exactly with the accounting period, an adjustment is needed to take account of the asset created where payments are made in advance, and the liability that arises when benefits are paid for in arrears. The value of accruals and prepayments for items that relate to a period of time is found by apportioning the cost on a time basis.

Prepayments
The entries in the accounts to record a prepayment are:

Account debited	*Account credited*	*With*
Prepayment	Expense	Value of prepayment

The credit of the prepayment in the expense account reduces the expense, and the prepayment is shown in the balance sheet as a current asset. In practice, the prepayment may be carried down in the expense account to which it relates. This is illustrated in Example 7.5.

Gelco Ltd makes up its accounts to 31 December, and made the following cash payments in respect of rates:

Example 7.5

Year	Month	Payment £
19X0	October	900
19X1	April	1,000
19X1	October	1,000

The payments for rates relate to the six-month period starting with the month in which they are paid.

Prepare the rates account for 19X1.

Required

Rates Account

Solution

		£			£
1 Jan. 19X1	Balance b/d	450	31 Dec. 19X1	Balance c/d	500
April	Cash	1,000		Profit and	
October	Cash	1,000		loss account	1,950
		2,450			2,450
1 Jan. 19X2	Balance b/d	500			

The balance brought down at the start of the year is half of the payment of £900 made in October 19X0 and covers January, February and March 19X1. The balance of £500 carried down at the end of 19X1 is an asset since it pays in advance for the first three months of 19X2 and will appear as a current asset in the balance sheet at 31 December 19X1. The transfer to the profit and loss account is found as a balancing figure once all the other entries have been made. The balance brought down on 1 January 19X2 will be charged against profit as an expense in 19X2, even though payment was made in 19X1.

Accruals

The entries in the accounts to record an accrual are:

Account debited	Account credited	With
Expense	Accruals	Value of accrual

The accrual increases the expense figure charged in the profit and loss account (debit) and is included as a current liability in the balance sheet (credit). In practice, the accrual may be carried down in the expense account to which it relates. This is illustrated in Example 7.6.

Example 7.6   Gelco Ltd makes up its accounts to 31 December, and made the following
payments in respect of electricity:

Year	Month	Payment £
19X0	October	400
19X1	January	600
19X1	April	630
19X1	July	400
19X1	October	500
19X2	January	750

The payments are for electricity consumed during the three months immediately prior to the months in which they are made.

Required   Record the above transactions in the company's electricity account for 19X1
and 19X2.

Electricity Account

		£			£
19X1			1 Jan. 19X1	Balance b/d	600
January	Cash	600	31 Dec. 19X1	Profit and loss	
April	Cash	630		account	2,280
July	Cash	400			
October	Cash	500			
31 Dec. 19X1	Balance c/d	750			
		2,880			2,880
19X2			1 Jan. 19X2	Balance b/d	750
January	Cash	750			

The credit balance of £600 brought down would have appeared in the balance sheet at 31 December 19X0 as a liability and relates to the electricity
consumed in the last three months of 19X0. It can be seen that it is cancelled
by the actual cash payment made in January 19X1 since at that point the
balance on the account is zero. The same reasoning relates to the £750 carried down at the end of 19X1.

Readers should now attempt Question 7.5 at the end of this chapter.

BAD DEBTS

When a company makes sales on credit there is a possibility that some of the
customers will not be able to pay their debts, with the result that bad debts
are suffered. Although known bad debts may be written off during the year,
it is usual to review carefully the list of debtors outstanding when the annual
accounts are prepared and write off any additional bad debts. The fact that a
debt is likely to prove bad becomes apparent when a great deal of time has
elapsed since the goods were supplied and no cash has been received despite
repeated efforts to collect the amount outstanding. This emphasizes the im-

portance of monitoring debtors on a routine basis so that, when the terms for payment are exceeded, further supplies can be stopped; such action encourages the customer to pay the amount owed and also minimizes the loss if the debt should prove to be bad. When it becomes apparent that the full amount of the debt will not be received from the debtor, it is necessary to remove the value of the irrecoverable debt from the total debtors account and record the loss. The double entry to achieve this is:

Account debited	*Account credited*	*With*
Bad debts	Debtors control	Value of bad debt

The amount is also credited to the individual personal account of the debtor in the memorandum debtors ledger. The balance on the bad debts account appears as a debit balance in the trial balance, and is written off to the profit and loss account when the annual accounts are prepared since it represents the loss of an asset and, therefore, is an expense.

In addition, a company may know, from experience, that a stable proportion of the debts outstanding at the balance sheet date will prove to be bad, although it is not possible to tell in advance which specific debts will remain unpaid. Prudence suggests that, in these circumstances, an allowance should be made for the likely bad debts contained in the value of debtors outstanding at the year end by the introduction of a provision for doubtful debts. When the amount to be allowed for has been determined, the provision is created by a debit to the doubtful debts account with the corresponding credit to a provision for doubtful debts account; this credit balance is offset against the value of debtors in the balance sheet to show the net amount that is expected to be collected. The fact that this provision is general, or non-specific, means that no consequential adjustments are made in the debtor's individual memorandum personal accounts.

Once a provision has been created, it appears as a credit balance in the trial balance prepared at the end of the subsequent accounting period, and it is necessary only to adjust its value from year to year, rather than charge annually the full required value. This is because the provision created at the end of one year is carried forward to the next, and any debts that in fact prove bad are debited to the bad debts account and then written off to the profit and loss account. The double entry to record adjustments for doubtful debts is:

Account debited	*Account credited*	*With*
Doubtful debts	Doubtful debt provision	Increase in provision
Doubtful debt provision	Profit and loss	Decrease in provision

Example 7.7 The following balances appeared in the books of Fifth Ltd at the end of 19X1:

	Debit £	Credit £
Bad debts written off during 19X1	950	
Provision for doubtful debts brought forward		900
Debtors control account	125,000	

It is decided, after a review of the debtors balances at the end of the year, to write off a further £1,000 of bad debts and create a provision of 1 per cent of the value of the remainder for doubtful debts.

Required Write up the T accounts to deal with these matters and show the appropriate extracts from the profit and loss account and balance sheet.

Solution **Bad Debts Account**

		£			£
19X1	Debtors	950	31 Dec. 19X1	Profit and loss	1,950
31 Dec. 19X1	Debtors	1,000			
		1,950			1,950

Debtors Control Account

		£			£
31 Dec. 19X1	Balance	125,000	31 Dec. 19X1	Bad debts	1,000
			31 Dec. 19X1	Balance c/d	124,000
		125,000			125,000

Provision for Doubtful Debts Account

		£			£
31 Dec. 19X1	Balance c/d	1,240*	31 Dec. 19X1	Balance b/d	900
			31 Dec. 19X1	Doubtful debts	340
		1,240			1,240

Note
* 1% of £124,000 = £1,240.

Doubtful Debts Account

		£			£
31 Dec. 19X1	Provision for doubtful debts	340	31 Dec. 19X1	Profit and loss	340

Profit and Loss Account (extract)

	£		£
Bad debts	1,950		
Doubtful debts	340		
	2,290		

Balance Sheet (extract)

	£	£
Debtors	124,000	
Less: Provision for doubtful debts	1,240	
		122,760

Notes
1. The bad debts of £950 have already been written off the value of debtors and so no further adjustment to the debtors control account is required in respect of this loss.
2. All bad debts arising during 19X1 have been written off against profit. It is therefore necessary only to increase the provision to the revised value, that is, by £340 to £1,240. In some cases the review of debtor balances results in a reduction of the provision and hence a credit to the profit and loss account.

Readers should now work Question 7.6 at the end of the chapter, which tests the book entries related to bad debts, and Question 7.7, which revises the preparation of final accounts from the trial balance with some additional adjustments.

THE ADJUSTED TRIAL BALANCE

The adjustments made to the trial balance when the trading and profit and loss account are prepared must be carried out in a systematic manner that complies with double entry procedures. Examples 7.8 shows how this can be done.

The following trial balance was extracted from the books of T. Jones on 31 December 19X5:   ***Example 7.8***

	£	£
Sales		100,000
Purchases	50,000	
Stock – 1 January	10,000	
Rent	5,000	
Wages	12,000	
Electricity	1,500	
Debtors	9,000	
Trade creditors		8,000
Cash	1,000	
Fixed assets at cost	34,000	
Accumulated depreciation –1 January		13,000
Other expenses	6,000	
Capital – 1 January		17,000
Drawings	9,500	
	138,000	138,000

The following additional information is provided:

1. Goods that cost £1,000 were received during 19X5 and were included in closing stock. No invoice was included in purchases for them in 19X5.
2. Rent of £500 is prepaid.
3. Electricity of £350 is accrued.
4. The depreciation charge for the year is £6,000.
5. Jones took stock for his own use that cost £450. No entry was made in the books in respect of this.
6. The closing stock is £12,000.
7. Bad debts of £150 are to be written off.
8. A provision for doubtful debts of £100 is to be created.

Required

(a) Prepare the adjusted trial balance of T. Jones as at 31 December 19X5.
(b) Prepare the trading and profit and loss account of T. Jones for the year to 31 December 19X5 and the balance sheet as at that date.

Solution (Example 7.8 (a))

Adjusted Trial Balance

	Original trial balance at 31 Dec. 19X5 Dr. £	Cr. £	Adjustments Dr. £	Cr. £	Trading and profit and loss account Dr. £	Cr. £	Balance sheet Dr. £	Cr. £
Sales		100,000				100,000		
Purchases	50,000		1,000 (1)	450 (5)	50,550			
Stock	10,000		12,000 (6)	12,000 (6)	10,000	12,000	12,000	
Rent	5,000			500 (2)	4,500			
Wages	12,000				12,000			
Electricity	1,500		350 (3)		1,850			
Debtors	9,000			150 (7)			8,850	
Creditors		8,000		1,000 (1)				9,000
Cash	1,000						1,000	
Fixed assets at cost	34,000						34,000	
Accumulated depreciation 1 January		13,000		6,000 (4)				19,000
Other expenses	6,000				6,000			
Capital 1 January		17,000						17,000
Drawings	9,500		450 (5)				9,950	
Accruals				350 (3)				350
Prepayments			500 (2)				500	
Depreciation charge			6,000 (4)		6,000			
Bad and doubtful debts			100 (8) } 150 (7)		250			
Provision for doubtful debts				100 (8)				100
	138,000	138,000	20,550	20,550	91,150	112,000	66,300	45,450
					–91,150			20,850
					20,850		66,300	66,300

Notes

1. The adjustment columns show the debit and credit entries needed to give effect to the additional information. The number in brackets by such figures refers to the note in the question on which it is based.

2. The opening balance of each line is taken, adjusted and then entered in the final trial balance.

3. The fact that the two adjustment columns have the same total shows that the double entry rules have been complied with.

4. The final trial balance is separated into the trading and profit and loss account and the balance sheet. This is to aid the preparation of the final accounts. The proof of the trial balance in this format is that each section has an equal, but opposite, difference. This is the profit figure.

5. The accrual of £1,000 for the goods received but not invoiced at the year end represents a trade creditor and so is added to the existing balance of £8,000.

Solution
Example
7.8 (b)

Trading and Profit and Loss Account year to 31 December 19X5

	£	£
Sales		100,000
Opening stock	10,000	
Purchases	50,550	
Closing stock	(12,000)	
Cost of goods sold		48,550
Gross profit		51,450
Rent	4,500	
Wages	12,000	
Electricity	1,850	
Other expenses	6,000	
Depreciation	6,000	
Bad and doubtful debts	250	
		30,600
Net profit		20,850

Balance Sheet at 31 December 19X5

	£	£	£
Fixed assets			
Fixed assets at cost			34,000
Less: Accumulated depreciation			19,000
			15,000
Current Assets			
Stock		12,000	
Debtors	8,850		
Less: Provision for doubtful debts	100		
		8,750	
Prepayment		500	
Cash		1,000	
		22,250	
Current liabilities			
Creditors	9,000		
Accruals	350		
		9,350	
Working capital			12,900
			27,900
Capital			
Balance at 1 January			17,000
Profit for year			20,850
			37,850
Less: Drawings			9,950
			27,900

An adjusted trial balance, as used in Example 7.8, should be completed for inclusion in a set of permanent working papers when final accounts are prepared in practice. In examinations it is often too time consuming to prepare this but, with practice, this process can be avoided. The important requirement is that students should adopt a systematic approach so as to ensure that all necessary adjustments are properly made. One useful technique is to note the double entry effects of all the adjustments to the trial balance on the question paper. The adjusted balances are then used to prepare the final accounts. This approach is now illustrated in Example 7.9, which uses the data given in Example 7.8 for T. Jones. The notes on the trial balance, which would in practice be made by hand, are shown in italics, and the final accounts include notes on how the figures have been calculated.

The following trial balance was extracted from the books of T. Jones on 31 December 19X5 and shows, in italics, the adjustments needed to prepare the final accounts:

Example 7.9

	£			£	
Sales				100,000	
Purchases	50,000	*+1,000*	*–450*		
Stock – 1 January	10,000				
Rent	5,000	*–500*			
Wages	12,000				
Electricity	1,500	*+350*			
Debtors	9,000	*–150*			
Trade creditors				8,000	*+1,000*
Cash	1,000				
Fixed assets at cost	34,000				
Accumulated depreciation – 1 January				13,000	*+6,000*
Other expenses	6,000				
Capital – 1 January				17,000	
Drawings	9,500	*+450*			
	138,000			138,000	
Prepayments	*500*				
Accruals				*350*	
Depreciation	*6,000*				
Bad debts	*150*				
Doubtful debt provision	*100*			*100*	

The additional information on which the adjustments (in italics) are based is given in Example 7.8.

Care must be taken to include workings with the answer submitted to ensure that the examiner understands how the figures were derived. In this example, the workings are given in brackets on the face of the accounts:

Trading and Profit and Loss Account year to 31 December 19X5

	£	£
Sales		100,000
Opening stock	10,000	
Purchases (50,000+1,000−450)	50,550	
Closing stock	(12,000)	
Cost of goods sold		48,550
Gross profit		51,450
Rent (5,000−500)	4,500	
Wages	12,000	
Electricity (1,500+350)	1,850	
Other expenses	6,000	
Depreciation	6,000	
Bad and doubtful debts (100+150)	250	
		30,600
Net profit		20,850

Balance Sheet at 31 December 19X5

	£	£	£
Fixed assets			
Fixed assets at cost			34,000
Less: Accumulated depreciation			
(13,000+6,000)			19,000
			15,000
Current assets			
Stock		12,000	
Debtors (9,000−150)	8,850		
Less: Provision for doubtful debts	100		
		8,750	
Prepayment		500	
Cash		1,000	
		22,250	
Current liabilities			
Creditors (8,000+1,000)	9,000		
Accruals	350		
		9,350	
Working capital			12,900
			27,900
Capital			
Balance at 1 January			17,000
Profit for year			20,850
			37,850
Less: Drawings (9,500+450)			9,950
			27,900

Errors may come to light during the examination of the books that takes place when the periodic accounts are prepared. The correction of these errors must be made in accordance with the double entry techniques described in this chapter. This aspect of preparing final accounts is tested in Question 7.8 at the end of this chapter, which readers should now work.

Questions

7.1 The trial balance of Finis, a sole trader, at 31 December 19X4, was:

	£ Debit	£ Credit
Sales		130,000
Returns inwards	250	
Stock at 1 January 19X4	15,000	
Returns outwards		150
Purchases	80,000	
Capital at 1 January 19X4		27,600
Cash at bank	3,100	
Debtors	15,400	
Creditors		5,000
Premises	8,000	
Wages	17,300	
Discounts received		300
Rents and rates	3,000	
Delivery costs	2,750	
Cash withdrawn by Finis	12,000	
Heat and light	3,500	
Sundry expenses	2,750	
	163,050	163,050

Note
The value of stock at 31 December 19X4 was £17,750.

Required

(a) State the location in the final accounts of each item in the trial balance, i. e . whether it is entered in the trading account, the profit and loss account or the balance sheet.

(b) Prepare the trading and profit and loss account of Finis for the year to 31 December 19X4 and a balance sheet at that date.

7.2 Tip Ltd was established and started trading on 1 January 19X1 and draws up its accounts to 31 December each year. Its purchases and disposals of fixed assets over the subsequent three years were as follows:

Asset	Date of purchase	Cost	Date of disposal	Proceeds on disposal
		£		£
A	1 January 19X1	5,000	—	—
B	1 January 19X1	2,000	1 January 19X3	900
C	1 January 19X3	7,000	—	—

Required

Use this data to

(a) prepare the fixed assets at cost, accumulated depreciation and disposal of fixed assets accounts based on straight-line depreciation of 20 per cent per year for 19X1, 19X2 and 19X3; and

(b) show the fixed asset extracts from the balance sheets at the end of each year.

7.3 The following is the trial balance of Push, a sole trader, at 30 June 19X7:

	£	£
Capital		30,350
Sales		108,920
Purchases	72,190	
Drawings	12,350	
Debtors	7,350	
Creditors		6,220
Cash	1,710	
Stock	9,470	
Plant and machinery at cost	35,000	
Accumulated depreciation at 1 July 19X6		12,500
Rent	1,000	
Wages	14,330	
Other costs	4,590	
	157,990	157,990

Notes
1. The value of stock at 30 June 19X7 was £9,960.
2. The depreciation charge for the year to 30 June 19X7 was £3,000.

Required

Prepare the trading and profit and loss account of Push for the year to 30 June 19X7 and the balance sheet at that date.

7.4 At 31 December 19X3 the trial balance of Damp Ltd contained the following balances in respect of motor vehicles:

	Debit £	Credit £
Motor vehicles at cost	127,000	
Accumulated depreciation at 1 January 19X3		76,000
Disposal of motor vehicles		1,600

You ascertain that during 19X3 the following occurred:

1. A delivery van, which was fully depreciated and had cost £2,000, was scrapped. No proceeds were received.
2. A car that cost £5,000, on which accumulated depreciation was £3,000, had been traded in for a new model with a full cost of £8,000. A trade-in allowance of £1,500 was received, and only the net cost of the new car, £6,500, has been entered in the books.
3. A car that cost £4,000 and had a written-down value of £1,250 was sold for £1,600 (credited to the disposals account).
4. A delivery van was sold for £2,500. This vehicle had cost £10,000 and a loss of £750 was made on its sale. The proceeds have been credited to the fixed asset account.
5. The depreciation charge for the year is £25,000.

Required

(a) Prepare the motor vehicles at cost account, motor vehicles accumulated depreciation account and disposal of motor vehicles account for 19X3 to show the effect of the above information and the transfer to the profit and loss account.

(b) Show the extract for motor vehicles that would appear in the company's balance sheet at 31 December 19X3.

7.5 Prepac Ltd prepared its accounts to 31 December. The following facts relate to 19X8:

	£
Balance on insurance account 1 January	450 (Dr.)
Balance on electricity account 1 January	300 (Cr.)
Balance on rates account 1 January	290 (Dr.)
Balance on gas account 1 January	600 (Cr.)
February – pay for electricity consumed during quarter to 31 January	900
March – pay for gas consumed during quarter to 28 February	850
– pay rates for the half year to 30 September	780
May – pay for electricity consumed during quarter to 30 April	820
June – pay for gas consumed during quarter to 31 May	840
– pay insurance for the year to 30 June 19X9	1,020
August – pay for electricity consumed during quarter to 31 July	690
September – pay for gas consumed during quarter to 31 August	610
– pay rates for 6 months to 31 March 19X9	780
November – pay for electricity consumed during quarter to 31 October	550
December – pay for gas consumed during quarter to 30 November	960
Electricity consumed in November and December 19X8	390
Gas consumed in December 19X8	680

Required

Prepare the insurance account, electricity account, rates account and gas account for 19X8 as they appear in the books of Prepac Ltd and showing clearly in each case the transfer to profit and loss account.

7.6 At 31 December 19X0 the following balances were shown in the books of E. Rider Ltd:

	£
Sales control account	156,937 (Dr.)
Provision for doubtful debts	2,600 (Cr.)
Bad debts	750 (Dr.)

The list of debtors contained balances that were considered to be bad or doubtful as indicated in the 'remarks' column of the schedule below:

Schedule of bad and doubtful debts, 31 December 19X0

Customer	Account number	Account balance	Remarks
B. Clyde	C6	£560	Irrecoverable
S. Wars	W2	£680	In liquidation. At least 50p in the £ is anticipated, but full recovery is a possibility
M. Poppins	P4	£227	Irrecoverable
M. Express	E9	£390	This debt is doubtful to the extent of 20%
M. Ash	A1	£240	A provision of £80 is to be made against this debt

The general provision for doubtful debts in respect of debts other than those dealt with individually above is to be raised to £3,750.

Required

(a) Prepare the sales ledger control account, bad debts account, doubtful debts account and provision for doubtful debts account as they appear after recording the above transactions.

(b) Show the balance sheet extract for debtors at 31 December 19X0.

7.7 The following trial balance was extracted from the books of Dellboy, a retail trader, at 31 December 19X6:

	£	£
Capital account		193,894
Freehold land and buildings at cost	114,000	
Motor vans at cost	37,500	
Provision for depreciation on motor vans at 1 January 19X6		15,450
Purchases	164,770	
Sales		234,481
Rent and rates	3,000	
General expenses	7,263	
Wages	26,649	
Bad debts	693	
Provision for doubtful debts at 1 January 19X6		876
Drawings	18,000	
Debtors and creditors	20,911	13,006
Stock-in-trade at 1 January 19X6	32,193	
Bank balance	32,728	
	457,707	457,707

You are given the following additional information:

1. Wages outstanding at 31 December 19X6 amounted to £271.
2. The provision for doubtful debts is to be increased by £104.
3. Stock-in-trade at 31 December 19X6 was £34,671.
4. Rent and rates amounting to £300 were paid in advance at 31 December 19X6.
5. During 19X6 Dellboy took stock costing £1,250 for his own use. No entry has been made in the books in respect of this.
6. During 19X6 a motor van, which had cost £2,500 and had a written-down

value of £1,000, was sold for £1,500. No entry had been made in the books to record this, other than to credit the cash received to the motor vehicles account.
7. The depreciation charge for the year is £7,000.

Required

A trading and profit and loss account for the year 19X6 and a balance sheet as at 31 December 19X6.

7.8 During the preparation of the accounts from the books of S. Top, a sole trader, for the year to 30 June 19X7, the following items were found:

1. Included in the repairs to machinery account was £2,750, which was paid on 29 June 19X7 and was for the purchase of a new lathe.
2. Manufacturing wages account included £350 paid to an employee for time spent repairing a machine.
3. A debt of £1,290 due from J. Jones was included in debtors, but in fact was irrecoverable.
4. The rates on S. Top's private house of £200 had been paid by the business and charged to the rates account.
5. Goods worth £1,500 had been received into stock on 30 June and included in the value of stock for accounts purposes. No entry had been made in the books to record this purchase.
6. An old machine that had cost £1,000 and was fully depreciated had been scrapped during the year. This fact had not been recorded in the books.
7. S. Top had taken stock to the value of £150 for his own use during the year. No entry appeared in the books in respect of this usage.
8. A payment of £125 for delivery of goods to customers had been entered in the purchases account.

Required

(a) Prepare the journal entries to record the adjustments.
(b) Prepare a statement to show the effect of these adjustments on the profit for the year to 30 June 19X7.

7.9 The following information had been taken from the ledger of Diwan Ltd as at 31 May 1991:

	£
Trade debtors	66,000
Prepaid expenses	1,380
Trade creditors	47,800
Accrued expenses	460
Land	40,000
Buildings	80,000
Fixtures and fittings	88,000
Motor vehicles	45,000
Provision for bad debts	2,570
Provisions for depreciation	
Land and buildings	16,000
Fixtures and fittings	44,000
Motor vehicles	27,000

The above information is before taking the following into account:

(a) Trade debts of £1,340 are to be written off as bad and the provision for bad debts is to be adjusted so that it is 5 per cent of trade debtors.

(b) During the year ended 31 May 1991 motor vehicles which had cost £15,000 and which had a net book value of £3,000 were sold for £4,500.

(c) Depreciation has yet to be provided for as follows:

on buildings	2%	straight-line method
on fixtures and fittings	25%	diminishing balance method
on motor vehicles	20%	straight-line method

No depreciation is charged on land.

Required

Prepare in so far as the above information permits the following ledger accounts for the year ended 31 May 1991:

(i)	Bad debts	*(3 marks)*
(ii)	Provision for bad debts	*(3 marks)*
(iii)	Assets disposals	*(4 marks)*
(iv)	Provision for depreciation – land and buildings	*(3 marks)*
(v)	Provision for depreciation – fixtures and fittings	*(3 marks)*
(vi)	Provision for depreciation – motor vehicles	*(4 marks)*

(Total 20 marks)

(AAT Preliminary, June 1991)

8
ASSET VALUATION, PROFIT MEASUREMENT AND THE UNDERLYING ACCOUNTING CONCEPTS

The purpose of this chapter is to

- explain the effect of different methods of asset valuation on the level of reported profit;
- enable students to distinguish between capital expenditure and revenue expenditure;
- identify and distinguish between different methods of depreciation;
- distinguish between tangible and intangible assets;
- explain the difference between purchased and non-purchased goodwill;
- distinguish between different methods of accounting for purchased goodwill;
- provide an understanding of the methods available for valuing non-purchased goodwill;
- provide an appreciation of the nature of research and development expenditure and its treatment in company accounts;
- explain the effect of the 'lower of cost and net realizable value' rule on the valuation of stock;
- enable students to value stock on the marginal cost basis and total cost basis;
- distinguish between FIFO, LIFO and AVCO as methods of matching purchases with production or sales;
- outline the operation of a system of perpetual inventory; and
- introduce students to the main accounting concepts and indicate the effect of their application on accounting reports.

ASSET VALUATION AND PROFIT MEASUREMENT

The level of profit reported in the accounts depends on the amounts at which assets, listed in the balance sheet, are valued. Any error made when valuing assets has a corresponding effect on the level of reported profit and, therefore, reduces its usefulness as a basis for assessing performance. For example, if closing stock is overvalued by £1,000, the figure for cost of goods sold is understated and reported profit overstated by this amount. Great care should therefore be taken when calculating asset values for inclusion in the accounts. The procedures that are followed, in practice, are examined below.

TANGIBLE FIXED ASSETS

Fixed assets are reported in the balance sheet at cost less accumulated depreciation. The identification of cost and the calculation of the depreciation charge are considered below.

Distinguishing capital expenditure from revenue expenditure

The expenditure incurred by a business must be accounted for as *either* capital expenditure *or* revenue expenditure. The basic test applied to distinguish between the two types of expenditure is the effect that the outlay has on the company's long-run ability to earn profits. If it is enhanced, the expenditure is capital whereas, if the expenditure merely enables the business to continue to operate at its existing level, it is revenue. The distinction is of crucial importance because it affects how the expenditure is reported in the profit and loss account and balance sheet. Capital expenditure on fixed assets is recorded in the balance sheet at cost, and is subsequently charged against revenue over the period of years that benefit from the use of the asset. Revenue expenditure, on the other hand, is normally charged in the profit and loss account against revenue arising during the period when the cost is incurred. A proper classification is important, otherwise the reported balances for profit and net assets will be incorrectly stated and wrong conclusions may be reached regarding the performance and position of the firm. The effects of misallocations are shown in Figure 8.1.

	Effect on	
	Profit	*Net assets*
Capital expenditure wrongly allocated to revenue	Understated	Understated
Revenue expenditure wrongly allocated to capital	Overstated	Overstated

Figure 8.1   Effect of wrongly allocating expenditure to capital or revenue

Most items of expenditure are easily classified as capital or revenue, but there are some 'grey areas' where judgement is needed to help make a proper allocation in the light of all the available facts. The cost of fixed assets acquired or built by the firm itself, to form the basis for business activity, is clearly capital expenditure. Difficulties arise in connection with expenditure incidental to the acquisition of the fixed asset and expenditure on fixed assets currently in use. The following rules should be followed to achieve a proper allocation:

1. Expenditure incurred in getting a new fixed asset ready for business use is a capital expense. This includes, for example, any transport costs, import duties and solicitors' fees. In addition, costs incurred in modifying existing premises to accommodate a new fixed asset should also be capitalized.
2. Expenditure on an existing fixed asset that enhances its value to the business, e.g. by increasing its capacity, effectiveness or useful life, should be capitalized.
3. Expenditure on an existing fixed asset intended to make good wear and

tear and keep it in satisfactory working order is a revenue expense. Where the expenditure contains an element of improvement, as well as repair, an apportionment between capital expenditure and revenue expenditure must be made.

Indicate for each of the following items whether it is capital or revenue expenditure: **Example 8.1**

1. Legal expenses incurred when acquiring a new building.
2. Giving the factory a fresh coat of paint.
3. Replacing 200 tiles on a roof damaged by a gale.
4. Expenditure incurred demolishing part of a wall to make room for a recently purchased machine.
5. Replacing wooden office windows by double-glazed metal windows.
6. Installing a system of ventilation in the factory.

1. *Capital*   This is part of the cost of acquiring the new asset. **Solution**
2. *Revenue*   This makes good wear and tear.
3. *Revenue*   This merely restores the roof to its pre-gale condition.
4. *Capital*   This is part of the cost of bringing the fixed asset into use.
5. *Part capital/part revenue*   The new windows should be more effective in eliminating draughts and making the office soundproof.
6. *Capital*   Working conditions and employee performance should improve.

Readers should now work Questions 8.1. and 8.2 at the end of this chapter.

Depreciation methods
Depreciation is charged in the accounts to reflect the fact that the business has benefited from using fixed assets that, as a result, have declined in value. The pattern of benefit that arises differs from one type of fixed asset to another. For example, some fixed assets produce a greater benefit in the early years of ownership, when the asset is more efficient, whereas others make a fairly steady contribution over their entire useful life. There are a number of different methods of charging depreciation and management should choose the one that most closely reflects the forecast pattern of benefits receivable.

Straight-line (equal instalment) method
Under this method the difference between original cost and ultimate disposal value is spread equally over the asset's estimated useful life. This method is described and illustrated in Chapter 4, and has been used in all previous examples and questions requiring a charge to be calculated. The method assumes that each accounting period benefits to an equal extent from using the fixed asset, and the annual charge is calculated on the basis of the following formula:

$$\frac{\text{Original cost} - \text{Estimated disposal value}}{\text{Estimated useful life}}$$

An attraction of this method is that it is easy to apply once the initial estimates have been made and, for this reason, it is widely used in Great Britain.

Example 8.2   On 1 January 19X1 a manufacturing company acquired a new lathe for
£23,000. It is estimated to have a useful life of four years during which time
it will produce 100,000 units of output: 50,000 units in 19X1; 10,000 units in
19X2; 10,000 units in 19X3; and 30,000 units in 19X4. The lathe is expected
to be sold for £3,000 at the end of four years.

The annual straight-line charge is calculated as follows:

$$\text{Depreciation charge} \quad = \quad \frac{£23,000 - £3,000}{4}$$

$$= \quad £5,000$$

Reducing (declining) balance method

This is the second most popular method. A depreciation rate is decided upon
and then applied to the *net* book value (original cost less accumulated depreciation) of the asset brought forward at the beginning of each accounting
period. The charge is highest in year 1 and then falls, each year, because the
depreciation rate is applied to a declining balance. The rate is usually given
in examinations but, where it is not provided, it may be calculated using the
following formula:

$$\text{Depreciation rate} = \left(1 - n\sqrt{\frac{s}{c}}\right) \times 100$$

where: n is the expected useful life
           s is the expected scrap value
           c the original cost.

Applying this formula to the facts provided in Example 8.2 gives the following results:

$$\text{Depreciation rate} = \left(1 - 4\sqrt{\frac{3,000}{23,000}}\right) \times 100$$

$$= 39.9\%$$

Depreciation charges, 19X1–X4

	£
Original cost	23,000
19X1 depreciation charge, £23,000 × 39.9%	9,177
Net book value at 31 December 19X1	13,823
19X2 depreciation charge, £13,823× 39.9%	5,515
Net book value at 31 December 19X2	8,308
19X3 depreciation charge, £8,308 × 39.9%	3,315
Net book value at 31 December 19X3	4,993
19X4 depreciation charge, £4,993 × 39.9%	1,993
Net book value at 31 December 19X4	3,000

It should be noticed that the charge for 19X1 (£9,177) is over four times higher than the charge for 19X4 (£1,993). Clearly, the method is appropriate only when the bulk of the benefit arises early on. An argument sometimes put forward for this method (and the sum of the digits method, see below) is that repair and maintenance costs normally increase as a fixed asset becomes older and the reducing balance basis therefore helps to ensure that the total annual charge (depreciation + maintenance) remains steady over the asset's useful life.

Sum of the digits method

This method also produces larger charges in the early years, but the differences that occur are less dramatic than with the reducing balance method. Each year of the asset's life is represented by a digit, beginning with 1, and the depreciation charge for each year is calculated by applying the following formula:

$$\frac{\text{Original cost} - \text{Estimated disposal value}}{\text{Sum of the year's digits}} \times \begin{array}{c}\text{Number of years' life remaining}\\ \text{at beginning of year}\end{array}$$

Applying the formula to the facts provided in Example 8.2 gives the following results:

Depreciation charge:

$$19X1 = \frac{£20,000}{(1+2+3+4)} \times 4 = £8,000$$

$$19X2 = \frac{£20,000}{(1+2+3+4)} \times 3 = £6,000$$

$$19X3 = \frac{£20,000}{(1+2+3+4)} \times 2 = £4,000$$

$$19X4 = \frac{£20,000}{(1+2+3+4)} \times 1 = £2,000$$

The units of service method

This method relates the charge to the extent the asset is used during an accounting period. For this purpose usage may be measured on the basis either of the number of units produced or the number of hours in service. The formula used to calculate the annual charge is as follows:

$$\frac{\text{Original cost} - \text{Estimated disposal value}}{\text{Total estimated number of units (hours)}} \times \begin{array}{c}\text{Number of units}\\ \text{(hours) in use}\end{array}$$

Applying the formula to the facts provided in Example 8.2 produces the following results:

Depreciation charge:

$$19X1 = \frac{20,000}{100,000} \times 50,000 = £10,000$$

$$19X2 = \frac{20,000}{100,000} \times 10,000 = £2,000$$

$$19X3 = \frac{20,000}{100,000} \times 10,000 = £2,000$$

$$19X4 = \frac{20,000}{100,000} \times 30,000 = £6,000$$

This depreciation method is considered to be the most rational because it produces a variable charge that depends on the level of activity. The lathe is capable of producing 100,000 units, of which 50,000 are produced in 19X1. Half of the total benefit provided by the asset arises in 19X1 and half of its net cost to the business (£20,000 × ½) should therefore be charged against revenue arising during that year. Only the units of service method produces this result. In the following year, 19X2, when 10,000 units are produced, one-tenth of the asset's net cost, i.e. £2,000, is charged against revenue. The disadvantage of this method is the difficulty of estimating the units of service that a fixed asset will provide, and it is not widely used.

Comparing the methods

The charges made under each of the four methods are as follows:

	19X1 £	19X2 £	19X3 £	19X4 £	Total £
Straight line	5,000	5,000	5,000	5,000	20,000
Reducing balance	9,177	5,515	3,315	1,993	20,000
Sum of the digits	8,000	6,000	4,000	2,000	20,000
Units of service	10,000	2,000	2,000	6,000	20,000

It can be seen that the pattern of charges differs a great deal depending on the method used. For example, the highest charge arises in 19X1 from using the units of service method, in 19X2 from using the sum of the digits method, in 19X3 from using the straight-line method and in 19X4 again from using the units of service method. Within particular years the difference is also marked. For example, in 19X1 the units of service method produces a charge that is twice as high as under the straight-line method. Looked at another way, reported profit for 19X1 is £5,000 more if the straight-line basis is used. This shows that great care should be taken when choosing the depreciation method as this can have a substantial effect on the level of reported profit. The choice is rarely easy, however, as the depreciation policy must be decided upon when the asset is acquired and management does not know, at that stage, the precise benefit that will arise in each future accounting period. The decision is, therefore, to some extent arbitrary and, if an error is made, profit will be either under- or overstated.

Readers should now work Question 8.3 at the end of this chapter.

Estimation errors

In addition to the difficulty of selecting the most appropriate method, there is the problem of making accurate estimates of the useful life of the fixed asset, measured in terms of years or output, and its disposal value at the end of that period. Care should be exercised when making these estimates as errors produce an incorrect charge for depreciation and a consequent understatement or overstatement of profit.

A machine is purchased for £60,000 on 1 January 19X1. It is estimated that *Example 8.3*
the machine will last for five years and then have a zero disposal value.
Management believes that each accounting period will benefit equally
from the use of the machine and the straight-line method of depreciation is
therefore considered appropriate.

(a) Calculate the depreciation charge to be made each year, 19X1–X5.   **Required**
(b) Assuming it turns out that all management's estimates are correct, ex-
     cept that it totally misjudges the second-hand demand for the ma-
     chine, which eventually sells for £20,000, calculate the depreciation
     charge that *would* have been made each year if the disposal value had
     been accurately estimated.

(a) Depreciation charge   = $\dfrac{£60,000}{5}$ =   £12,000   **Solution**

(b) Depreciation charge   = $\dfrac{£60,000 - £20,000}{5}$ =   £8,000

Because the disposal value was wrongly estimated, the annual charge is
overstated and profit is understated by £4,000 during each of the five years
of ownership. This is balanced by crediting £20,000 to the profit and loss account when the fixed asset, by this time completely written off, is sold for
that figure. Where the profit on sale of a fixed asset is abnormally large, as in
this case, the amount should be separately disclosed in the accounts so that
users do not assume that the highly favourable results are derived from normal business operations.

INTANGIBLE FIXED ASSETS

Business assets may be classified as either tangible or intangible. Both categories of asset are valuable because they help the business to earn a profit.
The most common examples of tangible assets are stocks and fixed assets.
The main types of intangible assets are goodwill and research and development expenditure.

Goodwill

Goodwill arises as the result of business connections built up over a period
of time. It was described as follows by Lord MacNaughton in CIR *v.* Muller
(1901), A.C. 217:

> It is the benefit and advantage of the good name, reputation and connection of a business. It
> is the attractive force which brings in custom. It is the one thing which distinguishes an old
> established business from a new business at its first start.

Goodwill may be classified into 'purchased goodwill', which arises on the
acquisition of an existing business, and 'non-purchased goodwill', which has
been created but has no value which has been evidenced by an arm's length
transaction.

Purchased goodwill This is calculated as the difference between the price paid for the business as a whole and the aggregate of the 'fair' (current) values of its various identifiable assets – both tangible and intangible.

Example 8.4

Ted Anthony who had been in business for many years decided to retire and sold his business assets, other than cash and debtors, to William Jones for £30,000. The tangible assets transferred consisted of premises worth £20,000, machinery worth £3,500 and stocks valued at £2,500.

Required

Calculate the value of goodwill arising on the sale of Ted Anthony's business to William Jones.

Note
William Jones took over none of the creditors or other liabilities of Ted Anthony.

Solution

		£	£
Purchase price			30,000
Less:	Tangible assets acquired		
	Premises	20,000	
	Machinery	3,500	
	Stock	2,500	26,000
Goodwill			4,000

The total value of the tangible assets is £26,000, and we can therefore conclude that William Jones was willing to pay an extra £4,000 to cover the goodwill built up by Ted Anthony over the years.

In the above example, goodwill is the 'balancing' figure which results from comparing the agreed purchase price with the total value of the tangible assets acquired. The price paid for goodwill is initially recorded in the books of the acquiring company at cost, but goodwill does not last forever, e.g. the range of customers supplied gradually changes and those 'taken over' with the business eventually leave. Goodwill must therefore be written off either immediately against reserves, or gradually against profits over the estimated useful life of the asset. The latter approach is theoretically more sound as it complies with the accruals concept by attempting to match costs with revenues. Immediate write-off is the option usually selected by companies for two reasons: the difficulty of estimating the asset's useful economic life; and because it enables companies to report a higher profit than would otherwise be the case.

Example 8.5

Shrapnel Ltd purchased the assets including the goodwill of Mr Bullet on 1 January 19X1. The purchased goodwill is shown at cost in the balance sheet prepared for Shrapnel at 31 December 19X1:

Summarized Balance Sheet

	£
Goodwill	50,000
Tangible fixed assets	120,000
Net current assets	26,000
	196,000

Share capital		100,000
Retained profit at 1 January 19X1		72,000
Profit for 19X1		24,000
		196,000

The goodwill is estimated to have a useful economic life of five years.

Required

(a) Revised balance sheets at 31 December 19X1 assuming the decision is made

    (i)   to write off the goodwill immediately against reserves; and
    (ii) to write off goodwill against profit over its estimated useful economic life.

(b) Comment briefly on the results.

(a) **Summarized Balance Sheet**

Solution

	(i)	(ii)
	£000	£000
Goodwill	—	40
Tangible fixed assets	120	120
Net current assets	26	26
	146	186
Share capital	100	100
Retained profit at 1 January 19X1	22	72
Profit for 19X1	24	14
	146	186

(b) The option to write off goodwill over its useful economic life results in a reported profit for 19X1 which is £10,000 or 41. 7 per cent lower than if goodwill is written off immediately against reserves.

In view of the concerns of company directors to report profits which are high rather than low, the attraction of immediate write-off is readily apparent. The widespread use of immediate write-off is a matter of growing concern among those who are responsible for regulating the form and content of company accounts and consideration is being given to the removal of this option.

Non-purchased goodwill Goodwill is built up gradually over the years and, when a business person 'sells up', he or she expects the buyer to pay a price which covers the value of this asset. In these circumstances it is useful to prepare a valuation as a basis for negotiations. The following are two examples of the methods which may be used:

1. *Weighted average profits basis* Goodwill may be valued as a multiple of past profits. For this purpose a number of years' profits may be averaged and 'weights' attached to the profits arising each year.

Example 8.6 The profits of a partnership for the last three years are as follows: 19X1, £20,000; 19X2, £26,000; 19X3, £31,000.

Required Calculate goodwill on the basis of 1.5 times the weighted average profits of the last three years, using weights of 3 for the most recent year, 2 for the previous year and 1 for the earliest year.

Solution Weighted average profits are calculated as follows:

Year	Weight	Profits £	Total £
19X1	1	20,000	20,000
19X2	2	26,000	52,000
19X3	3	31,000	93,000
Total	6		165,000

$$\text{Weighted average} = \frac{£165,000}{6} = £27,500$$

Goodwill = £27,500 × 1.5 = £41,250

2. This method seeks to identify the extra profit, usually called 'super' profit, earned by a firm because of the existence of good connections. It then values goodwill as the capitalized value of this surplus, i.e. at the amount that would have to be invested, assuming a given rate of return, to produce the extra profit for an indefinite time period. The rate of return considered appropriate naturally differs from one type of business to another.

Example 8.7 Leake Ltd has earned profits averaging £20,000 per annum in recent years. It is estimated that £17,000 represents a reasonable return on the existing tangible assets.

Required Calculate goodwill on the 'super' profits basis

Solution

	£
Actual profit	20,000
Normal profit	17,000
Super profit	3,000

The amount a buyer is willing to pay for the 'super profit' depends on what is considered a reasonable rate of return on intangible assets in this line of business. If a return of 20 per cent is considered reasonable, goodwill is worth:

$$\text{Goodwill} = £3,000 \times \frac{100}{20} = £15,000$$

i.e. at a 20 per cent rate of interest, £15,000 must be invested to give an annual return of £3,000.

Both of the above approaches enable goodwill to be valued, but it does not necessarily follow that a buyer will be willing to pay either of these amounts or that the seller will accept them. The price actually paid for goodwill depends on negotiation between these two parties, and the main use of the above calculations is that they produce measures of value which can be referred to during discussions.

SSAP 22 (see Ch. 10 for discussion of SSAPs) categorically states that only purchased goodwill should be recognized in the accounts. The main reason for excluding non-purchased goodwill is that its value is subject to wide fluctuation due to both internal and external circumstances, making any assessment of its worth highly subjective and problematic. It is probably the right conclusion.

Readers should now work Question 8.4 at the end of this chapter.

Research and development expenditure (R & D)

Research is undertaken to discover new products and processes and to improve those products and processes already in existence. The development stage involves the conversion of these ideas into marketable products or services. In large organizations, separate departments are established to undertake these kinds of activities. The record-keeping system normally provides for the accumulation of research and development costs in a separate ledger account. The appropriate accounting treatment of such expenditure, at the end of an accounting period, has been the subject of debate for many years.

Because R & D is undertaken to help a company generate higher revenues in the future, it is reasonable to argue that it represents an asset that should be capitalized and written off against related revenues when they arise. Indeed, the proper application of the accruals concept would seem to require this procedure to be followed. In practice, companies are legally required to write off research expenditure immediately it is incurred, and also development expenditure unless a number of stringent conditions are met. These include requirements that development work should be reasonably well advanced, that the development costs can be accurately identified and that there exists a strong demand for the product.

The reason for the cautious accounting treatment of R & D expenditure is the difficulty of establishing whether a future benefit is likely to occur, and in one particularly well-known case R & D was heavily overvalued and investors and creditors totally misled. The case involved Rolls-Royce, which collapsed in 1971 despite the fact that it had reported satisfactory profits and paid healthy dividends for many years. The company's problems were concealed by the capitalization of large amounts of R & D expenditure that were valueless and should have been written off. A more prudent, and realistic, treatment of this expenditure would have brought the company's difficulties to the attention of the investing public at a much earlier stage.

STOCK VALUATION METHODS

The categories of stock owned by business organizations differ depending on the way in which their affairs are organized. For example:

1. *Trading organizations (i.e. businesses which purchase and sell goods but do not process them)* Stock consists of goods purchased, in their completed state, and remaining unsold at the end of the accounting period.
2. *Manufacturing concerns* Here the term 'stock' covers raw materials, work-in-progress and finished goods awaiting sale.
3. *Service organizations (e.g. accountants and bankers)* These hold very little, if any, stock in the conventional sense of the term, though accountants will have a significant balance of work-in-progress (representing services provided but not yet billed) while banks possess large investments which present their own valuation problems.

For many businesses stock is a large proportion of gross assets. For example, the accounts of Rolls-Royce plc for 1992 included stock amounting to £696,000,000 and this represented 22.8 per cent of its total assets.

The calculation of the figure for stock involves two steps: first, the physical quantities of stocks must be established; and, second, these physical quantities must be valued.

The quantity of stock on hand is usually established by a physical count after close of business at the end of the accounting period. Because of the importance of the 'stock count', stocktaking procedures should be worked out well in advance and the exercise undertaken in a systematic manner by reliable employees who are fully aware of their responsibilities. In these circumstances the likelihood of error, as the result of items being misdescribed, counted twice or completely omitted, is reduced to a minimum. It is also necessary for management to take steps to ensure that all goods sold and invoiced to customers on the last day of the accounting period have been dispatched from the premises by the time the count takes place. Failure to ensure this happens may mean that profit will be substantially overstated as the result of including certain items both in sales for the year and in the year-end stock figure. For similar reasons management operates controls designed to ensure that all goods on the premises, and included in stock, are recorded in the books as purchases made during the year.

We now examine the way in which quantities of stock, once identified, are valued.

The basic rule

The fundamental rule is that stock would be valued at 'the *lower* of cost and net realizable value'. Readers will be broadly familiar with what is meant by cost (examined further in the section on calculating cost in this chapter), but the term 'net realizable value' (NRV) is met here for the first time. Basically,

Example 8.8 The following information is provided relating to a vehicle held in stock by Thornhill Carsales Ltd:

	£
Cost	3,700
Market selling price	5,000

Sales people are paid a commission of 2 per cent on market selling price, and it is the company's policy to allow the customer a full tank of petrol at an estimated cost of £20.

Calculate the net realizable value of the vehicle.

Required

Solution

	£	£
Net realizable value:		
Market selling price		5,000
Less: Further costs – commission	100	
– petrol	20	120
		4,880

NRV is the market selling price of stock less any further costs to be incurred in its sale or disposal by the firm.

NRV normally exceeds cost in a profitable concern, as is the case in the above example – NRV (£4,880) exceeds cost (£3,700) by £1,180. Sometimes NRV is below cost. For example, where an existing model of car is to be replaced, the firm will be anxious to clear its 'old' stock before it becomes unsaleable, and is likely to accept a low price.

The following information is provided for three vehicles held in stock by Reliable Cars Ltd:

Example 8.9

Vehicle	Cost	NRV
	£	£
A	5,400	6,200
B	5,200	8,500
C	7,100	6,200

Calculate the value of Reliable Cars Ltd's stock for the purpose of its accounts.

Required

Vehicle	Cost	NRV	Value for the accounts lower of cost and NRV
	£	£	£
A	5,400	6,200	5,400 (cost)
B	5,200	8,500	5,200 (cost)
C	7,100	6,200	6,200 (NRV)
	17,700	20,900	16,800

Solution

The total cost of the three vehicles is £17,700 compared with a total NRV of £20,900, i.e. total NRV exceeds total cost. It is to ensure that the fall in value of vehicle C is not ignored that the test is applied to each vehicle separately. Where the comparison between the cost and net realizable value of stock on an individual items' basis would be excessively time consuming, for example, because of the large number of items involved, groups of similar items of stock may be compared.

Most of a company's stock is usually valued at cost, with a small number of items reduced to net realizable value either because they are damaged or because they are no longer popular with customers.

Readers should now work Question 8.5 at the end of this chapter.

Calculating cost

The calculation of the cost of stock is a straightforward matter in the case of a trading organization, and normally consists of the price paid to the supplier plus delivery charges (sometimes described as 'carriage inwards') where these are not included in the purchase price. The calculation is more difficult for a manufacturing organization because, in these businesses, cost consists of the price paid for raw materials *plus* the processing costs incurred to convert these materials into finished goods. This raises the question: 'Which processing costs should be included?' Clearly the wages paid to employees working with the materials should be included as part of the cost of the finished item, but what about the wages paid to supervisors and other essential manufacturing costs such as lighting and heating, rent and rates of the factory and depreciation of the machinery? In practice one of the following two procedures is followed:

1. *The marginal cost basis* Only those costs which can be traced directly to the item manufactured are included in the valuation, e.g. materials costs and the wages paid to those employees directly involved in processing the materials.
2. *The total cost basis* All manufacturing costs are included, i.e. the marginal costs plus a fair proportion of incidental manufacturing expenses, called 'manufacturing overheads'.

   The total cost figure for stock therefore exceeds the marginal cost figure by the amount of the fixed manufacturing overhead costs.

Example 8.10   The following data are provided relating to the manufacture of Nexo for the month of January 19X1:

	£
Raw materials used (£5 per unit)	6,000
Wages paid to staff directly involved in manufacture	8,400
Salary paid to supervisor	850
Rent and rates	420
Light and heat	670
Depreciation of machinery	460

During January 1,200 items were manufactured of which 1,000 were sold. There was no opening stock and no work-in-progress at the beginning or end of the month. Closing stock consists of 200 completed items.

Required   (a) Valuations of closing stock on the

   (i) marginal cost basis;
   (ii) total cost basis.

(b) Comment on your results.

Solution   (i) Marginal costs basis:

		£
Direct manufacturing costs:	Raw materials	6,000
	Labour	8,400
		14,400

		£	£
Marginal cost per unit manufactured, £14,400/1,200 =			12
Marginal cost of unsold stock, £12 × 200 =			2,400

(ii) Total cost basis:

		£	£
Direct manufacturing costs			14,400
Manufacturing overheads:	Salary	850	
	Rent and rates	420	
	Light and heat	670	
	Depreciation	460	2,400
			16,800
Total cost per unit manufactured, £16,800/1,200 =			14
Total cost of stock, £14 × 200 =			2,800

(b) The total cost basis produces a cost per unit that is £2 more (£14–£12). This results from the inclusion of a proportion of manufacturing overheads that amount, in total, to £2,400, or £2,400/1,200 = £2 per unit manufactured.

A company must be able to cover all its costs if it is to survive and flourish in the long run and, for this reason, companies are required to use the total cost basis when valuing stock for inclusion in the accounts published for external use. For internal reporting purposes, however, either total costs or marginal costs can be used and management may well regard the latter as the more relevant basis for *short-run* business decisions. For example, a business operating below its full productive capacity may find it worth while to accept orders at prices below total costs, provided marginal costs are covered, since overhead costs will be incurred anyway.

Readers should now work Question 8.6 at the end of this chapter.

First in first out (FIFO) and last in first out (LIFO)
We saw in Chapter 4 that profit is calculated by matching costs with revenues arising during an accounting period. The difficulty, in the case of stocks, is to decide which costs to match with sales revenue in view of the large number of items acquired. It is theoretically possible to identify the actual items sold and, where a firm deals in a relatively small number of high-value items that can be easily identified, for example, cars, this procedure is followed in practice. Where there are a large number of transactions, however, the heavy additional cost involved in keeping such detailed records rules out this option. Instead the matching process is facilitated by making one of a number of arbitrary *assumptions* concerning the flow of goods into and out of the business. Two possibilities are as follows:

1. *First in first out (FIFO)* This assumes that the first items purchased are the first items sold. The items assumed to be in stock are therefore the most recent acquisitions.
2. *Last in first out (LIFO)* This assumes that the last items purchased are the

first sold. The items assumed to be in stock are therefore likely to have been purchased months or even years ago. (It should be noted that the use of LIFO complies with legal requirements but it is not favoured by Standard Accounting Practice – see Chapter 10.)

Example 8.11   The following information is provided for Frame Ltd for 19X2:

	£
Opening stock, 200 units at £5 each	1,000
Purchases during 19X2, 1,000 units at £6 each	6,000
Sales during 19X2, 900 units at £10 each	9,000
Closing stock, 300 units	

Required   Calculate the value of Frame's closing stock using:

(a)   FIFO; and
(b)   LIFO.

	£
Solution (a) FIFO, 300 units at £6	1,800

Note
The 900 items sold are assumed to be made up of the opening stock of 200 units, plus 700 units purchased during the year. Closing stock, therefore, consists of the remaining 300 units purchased during the year and are therefore valued at £6 each.

(b) LIFO:		£
	200 units at £5	1,000
	100 units at £6	600
		1,600

Note
The 900 items sold are assumed to have been made entirely from purchases during the year. Closing stock is, therefore, assumed to consist of the opening stock of 200 units, plus the 100 units purchased during the year that were not sold.

Perpetual inventory

In the previous section the total number of items sold was deducted from the total number of items that came available for sale during the accounting period (i.e. opening stock + purchases), and the balance that remained was valued at latest purchase prices, under FIFO, and earliest purchase prices under LIFO. This is called the 'periodic basis' for matching stocks sold with those available for sale.

Many large companies operate a system of perpetual inventory. In such circumstances the stock records contain details of quantities, and sometimes also values, of the various types of stock on hand throughout the year. This enables the *transaction basis* to be used for matching stocks sold with those available for sale, i.e. each batch of goods dispatched is matched with stock on hand at that point in time, using FIFO or LIFO, as appropriate. Other advantages that result from the maintenance of detailed records are as follows:

1. They provide an element of control by showing the quantity of goods that *should* be in stock at a particular point in time. Any discrepancies compared with *actual* holdings can then be investigated.

2. Steps can be taken, in good time, to replenish stocks when they fall to a predetermined minimum level.
3. Stock values are readily available for the purpose of management accounts, which are perhaps prepared monthly, and the annual accounts published for external use. At least once a year, however, and perhaps more often, it is necessary to have a physical stock-take to check the accuracy of the stock records.

The following purchases and sales are made by Trader Ltd during the first two weeks of January 19X1. There are no opening stocks.   **Example 8.12**

		Purchases		Sales	
		Units	Price per unit £	Units	Price per unit £
January	1	100	7	10	9
	2			20	9
	5			50	9
	7	75	8		
	10			20	9
	12			50	10
		175		150	

The physical stock-take confirmed that there were 25 units in stock at the year end.

Write up the stock records of Trader Ltd using the transaction basis on the following alternative assumptions: **Required**

(a) Issues are made from stock on the FIFO basis.
(b) Issues are made from stock on the LIFO basis.

(a) **FIFO basis: stock card**   **Solution**

Date	Receipts			Issues			Balance		
	Units	Price	£	Units	Price	£	Units	Price	£
Jan. 1	100	7	700	10	7	70	90	7	630
Jan. 2				20	7	140	70	7	490
Jan. 5				50	7	350	20	7	140
Jan. 7	75	8	600				20	7	140
							75	8	600
Jan. 10				20	7	140	75	8	600
Jan. 12				50	8	400	25	8	200
	175		1,300	150		1,100			

(b) **LIFO basis: stock card**

Date	Receipts			Issues			Balance		
	Units	Price	£	Units	Price	£	Units	Price	£
Jan. 1	100	7	700	10	7	70	90	7	630
Jan. 2				20	7	140	70	7	490
Jan. 5				50	7	350	20	7	140
Jan. 7	75	8	600				20	7	140
							75	8	600
Jan. 10				20	8	160	20	7	140
							55	8	440
Jan. 12				50	8	400	20	7	140
							5	8	40
	175		1,300	150		1,120			

Stock valuation methods and changing prices

The adoption of the FIFO and LIFO assumptions have the following different effects on the figure for cost of goods sold and the valuation of stock during a period of *rising* prices:

1. *Cost of goods sold* This is higher under LIFO due to the fact that most recent purchases are matched with sales.
2. *Stock* This is valued at a higher figure under FIFO due to the fact that the most recent purchases are assumed to remain in stock.

The effect on the gross profit of Trader Ltd of using the two different methods (Example 8.12) is shown in the following summarized trading accounts:

Summary Trading Accounts, transaction basis

	FIFO £	LIFO £
Sales (100 × £9) + (50 × £10)	1,400	1,400
Less: Cost of goods sold	1,100	1,120
Gross profit	300	280

The above example shows that, when prices are rising, reported profit is higher using the FIFO cost-flow assumption. The opposite is the case when prices are falling. It is important that readers should recognize that actual events are unaffected by the choice of valuation method, but the selection usually alters the level of reported profit.

Weighted average cost (AVCO)

A further option is for firms to value cost of goods sold and closing stock at its weighted average cost (AVCO). This is fairly popular with companies and produces results that fall between those achieved by using FIFO or LIFO. The procedure is illustrated in Example 8.13.

Example 8.13

Using the information given in Example 8.12:

(a) Calculate the AVCO value of Trader's stock using (i) the periodic basis and (ii) the transaction basis.
(b) Prepare a summary trading account for Trader Ltd using AVCO and the transaction basis.

Solution

(a)(i) Periodic basis:

		Units	Price	£
Purchases:	1 January	100	7.00	700
	7 January	75	8.00	600
		175	7.43*	1,300

Notes
* £1,300/175 = £7.43 per unit.
Stocks are therefore valued at £7.43 × 25 = £186.

(a)(ii) Transaction basis: stock card

Date	Receipts			Issues			Balance		
	Units	Price	£	Units	Price	£	Units	Price	£
Jan. 1	100	7	700	10	7.00	70	90	7.00	630
Jan. 2				20	7.00	140	70	7.00	490
Jan. 5				50	7.00	350	20	7.00	140
Jan. 7	75	8	600				95	7.79*	740
Jan. 10				20	7.79	156	75	7.79	584
Jan. 12				50	7.79	389	25	7.79	195
	175		1,300	150		1,105			

Note
* £740/95 (units).

(b) Summary Trading Account – AVCO (transaction basis)

	£	£
Sales		1,400
Less: Cost of goods sold		1,105
Gross profit		295

Readers should now work Questions 8.7, 8.8, 8.9 and 8.10 at the end of this chapter.

ACCOUNTING CONCEPTS

Accounting records and statements are based on a number of assumptions, called accounting concepts. The ten considered most important are examined below. The treatment is brief in those cases where the concept has already been discussed in an earlier chapter.

Entity concept

This fixes the boundary for the financial affairs contained in an accounting statement and was examined in Chapter 2. The boundary is often the business, but it may be a smaller or even a larger unit. For instance, a business may be split into a number of departments, each of which is treated as a separate entity for the purpose of preparing accounting statements for management (see Chapter 11). At the other extreme, a number of companies may be regarded as a single entity for accounting purposes. This occurs where a company owns the shares of one or more other companies. The connected companies together form a 'group', and their separate accounts are 'consolidated' for the purpose of reporting to shareholders. (See Chapter 10)

Money measurement concept

A business asset is reported in the balance sheet only if its value can be measured in money terms with a reasonable degree of precision. This concept was discussed in Chapter 2. A good example of the application of this concept concerns the accounting treatment of goodwill. We saw earlier in this chapter that goodwill consists of the reputation and business connections built up over a period of time. Most firms enjoy an element of goodwill, but its value continuously fluctuates and is therefore difficult to quantify with any degree of precision. For this reason the existence of goodwill is usually acknowledged by an entry in the accounts *only* when its value is proved by a market transaction involving its purchase and sale.

Matching concept

The accountant measures profit for a period of time, such as a year, by comparing or 'matching' revenue and expenditure identified with that period. The first step is to identify revenues and the second step is to deduct the expenditures incurred in producing the revenues. This concept was examined in Chapter 4. It should be noted that many of the concepts are closely interrelated. For example, the matching concept is put into effect by applying the realization concept and the accruals concept. These are considered next.

Realization concept

Revenue is assumed to be earned when a sale takes place and a legally enforceable claim arises against the customer. The effect of this rule is that stock usually remains in the books at cost until the sale takes place, at which stage a profit arises or a loss is incurred. This concept was discussed in Chapter 4.

The accruals concept

Costs are matched against revenues when the benefit of the expenditure is received rather than when the cash payment is made. Where the benefit is received *before* the payment is made, the amount owed is treated as a *liability* in the balance sheet. Where the benefit is received *after* the payment is made, the amount paid is treated as an *asset* in the balance sheet, and charged against revenues arising during whichever future accounting period benefits from the payments. This concept was examined in Chapter 4.

Readers should now work Question 8.11 at the end of this chapter.

Historical cost concept

Assets are initially recorded at the price paid to the supplier. In certain circumstances further costs may be added. For example in the case of a manufacturing concern, a proportion of the production costs should be added to the cost of raw materials to arrive at the cost of finished goods (see earlier in this chapter). In the case of fixed assets their recorded cost includes not only the price paid to the supplier but also all incidental costs incurred to make the item ready for use (see earlier in this chapter). A major advantage of this concept is that the accounting records are based on objective facts. A disadvantage of using historical cost is that, during a period of rising prices, the reported figures may significantly understate the asset's true value to the business. It is for this reason that some companies periodically revalue their fixed assets and/or publish supplementary accounts designed to take account of the effects of inflation (see further discussion in Chapter 10).

Going concern concept

This assumes that the business is a permanent venture and will not be wound up in the foreseeable future. Many fixed assets, which cost a great deal, have low resale values because they have been specially designed for a particular business. The going concern concept allows accountants to ignore this low resale value and instead spread the cost of an asset over the accounting periods that benefit from its use. The assumption that the business will continue indefinitely as a going concern is, however, in certain circumstances false and must be dropped. For example, if a company is about to be liquidated, forecasts of the amounts likely to be received by various providers of finance should be based on estimates of what the business assets are expected to realize in the market rather than their historical book value.

Consistency concept

The same valuation methods should be used each year when preparing accounting statements. We have seen that there exist a number of methods for valuing fixed assets and stocks. There are arguments in favour and against most of them and, to some extent, an arbitrary choice must be made. The effect on reported profit is unlikely to be significant, however, provided similar procedures are adopted each year. For example, the total cost method of valuing stock produces a higher figure for stock than the marginal cost method, but it does not necessarily produce a higher profit figure. Businesses have both opening and closing stock, and the consistent use of total cost produces a higher figure for stock at both dates.

Example 8.14 The following information is provided for one of the products manufactured by Mill Ltd during 19X8:

Opening stock – 100 units valued as follows:

	£
Marginal cost basis, £5 per unit × 100	500
Total cost basis, £8 per unit × 100	800
Production cost of 500 units:	
Marginal costs, £5 per unit	2,500
Fixed costs	1,500
Sales, 500 units at £12	6,000

Required

(a) Valuations of closing stock using

   (i)   the marginal cost basis; and
   (ii)   the total cost basis.

(b) Profit statements for 19X8 using each of the above bases.

Solution

(a) Opening stock is 100 units and, as the same number of items are produced as are sold, closing stock is also 100 units.

(i)	Marginal cost basis:	£	£
	Marginal costs, £5 × 100		500

(ii)	Total cost basis:	£	£
	Marginal costs	500	
	Fixed costs	300 W1	800

W1 £1,500 (total fixed costs) ÷ 500 (number of items produced) × 100 (number of items in stock at year end)

(b) **Profit Statement, 19X8**

	(i) Marginal cost basis		(ii) Total cost basis	
	£	£	£	£
Sales		6,000		6,000
Less: Opening stock	500		800	
Production costs	4,000		4,000	
Closing stock	(500)		(800)	
Cost of goods sold		4,000		4,000
Gross profit		2,000		2,000

The higher opening and closing valuations, on the total cost basis, cancel out, and gross profit is unaffected by the valuation method adopted. It should be noted, however, that the balance sheet figure for stocks, and therefore gross assets and net assets, are higher if total cost is used. It should also be noted that reported profit does vary when there are changes in the level of stock because, in these circumstances, the opening and closing balances no longer cancel out. However, the difference is unlikely to be large unless the change in the level of stock is substantial, such as occurs when new business operations commence.

The level of reported profit can be significantly inflated or deflated if a company changes from one method to another.

Assume the same facts as for Example 8.14, except that marginal cost is used at the beginning of the year and total cost at the end. **Example 8.15**

The revised profit statement for 19X8. **Required**

Profit Statement, 19X8 **Solution**

	£	£
Sales		6,000
Less: Opening stock (marginal cost)	500	
Production cost	4,000	
Closing stock (total cost)	(800)	
Cost of goods sold		3,700
Gross profit		2,300

Gross profit is £2,300 in Example 8.15 as compared with £2,000 in Example 8.14. Profit is therefore inflated by £300 as the result of switching from one valuation method to another and using the total cost closing stock figure, £800, instead of the marginal cost closing stock figure, £500. As the result of the change, reported profits are greater than actual profits and wrong conclusions may be reached concerning the performance of Mill Ltd. It is therefore important for valuation procedures to be consistently applied so that reported results fairly reflect performance during the year, and valid comparisons can be made with results achieved in a previous accounting period.

While consistency is a fundamental accounting concept (see Chapter 10), it does not mean that methods, once adopted, should never be changed, but sound and convincing arguments must be put forward to justify departures from existing practice. The essential test is whether management can show that the new procedures result in a fairer view of the financial performance and position of the concern. If it is decided that a change should be made to a previously accepted method of valuation, the impact on comparability between two sets of figures must be noted and, wherever possible, also quantified, so that it can be taken into account when measuring performance. For example, when a firm switches from marginal cost to total cost to comply with regulatory requirements, relevant balances for the previous year, which are also reported, must be recomputed, using total cost, so that a proper assessment of comparative performance can be made.

It must be emphasized that inconsistent accounting methods can have a marked effect on the information contained in accounting statements. The changes are not always explained as clearly as they should be, and the user must scrutinize the accounts vigilantly to ensure that distorted financial information does not cause him or her to make a wrong investment decision.

Students should now work Question 8.12 at the end of the chapter.

Prudence concept

The prudence concept (sometimes called the concept of conservatism) requires the accountant to make full provision for all expected losses and not to
anticipate revenues until they are realized. A good example of how this concept affects accounting practice is the basic rule that stock should be valued
at the lower of cost and net realizable value (NRV). Where NRV is above cost,
the profit likely to arise in the near future is ignored and stock remains in the
accounts at the lower figure until the sale occurs, i.e. revenue is not anticipated. On the other hand, where NRV is below cost, stock must be immediately restated at the lower figure so that full provision is made for the
foreseeable future loss.

Approval of a prudent approach to profit measurement is based on the potential dangers of an overoptimistic calculation that may be used as the basis
for an excessive distribution of funds, to ownership, that deprives the concern of much needed resources. Another possible pitfall is that an attractive
presentation of the current position, not justified by the underlying facts,
may cause management to expand the level of operations wrongly and,
when this happens, heavy losses can result. New projects often involve a
substantial commitment of resources, the bulk of which is tied up in fixed assets. The only way the firm is likely to recoup its money is by using the assets
to produce and sell goods at a profit. Caution is, therefore, highly desirable
when management is considering whether to make an investment, and any
accounting statement used to help reach this decision should be prepared on
a prudent basis. This may mean that, occasionally, good opportunities are
missed, but this will not happen often, and the likely loss from an ill con-
ceived investment will be many times greater than the profit possibly for-
gone.

It is important, however, not to take the prudence concept too far. Where
there are a number of likely outcomes it is usually wise to choose the lower
figure, but profit should not be deliberately understated. Accounting statements are used as the basis for decision-making, and they should contain realistic not excessively pessimistic financial information. Understatement can
be just as misleading as overstatement and, although the potential loss from
the misallocation of resources that may result is less, losses can be minimized
by preparers of accounting reports exercising no more than a reasonable
level of caution.

Materiality

Accounting statements should contain only those financial facts that are material, or relevant, to the decision being taken by the recipient of the report. It
is, therefore, important for the accountant to be familiar with the user's requirement so that he or she can decide which information should be included and excluded. For example, if an accounting statement is prepared to
help management assess which departments are most successful, it is clearly
essential for the report to show the profits earned by each of them. This
means identifying the revenues and expenditures that relate to each department, but unnecessary detail is omitted – for example, a manager is interested in knowing the individual amounts expended on materials, wages,
power, depreciation, etc., but not on Christmas gratuities, the ingredients for

morning coffee and paper towels. Trivial items are, therefore, grouped together under the heading 'sundry expenses'. For similar reasons balance sheets contain values for the main categories of assets and liabilities but do not give figures for each item of plant, stock, etc.

Accounting statements prepared for shareholders of limited companies contain even less detail. This is partly because such information is of little interest to them. It is management's job to decide how to allocate resources between various investment opportunities, while the shareholder is primarily interested in assessing whether the overall performance is satisfactory. It is, therefore, considered desirable to keep to a minimum detailed facts that may be difficult to assimilate, and instead concentrate on the broad overall pattern of developments. It must be admitted that the sophisticated institutional investor would welcome far more detail than is sometimes provided in the published accounts, but there is a natural reluctance to publish sensitive material that could be of use to competitors.

There is another aspect of materiality, and this concerns the amount of detail the accountant goes into when measuring profit. A good example is the use of FIFO, AVCO and LIFO instead of attempting to match individual purchases with sales. Another example is the decision not to distinguish between capital and revenue expenditure where the amount spent on a fixed asset is small. For example, minor items of office equipment such as staplers and punches last for a number of years, but it is not usually considered worthwhile to capitalize and depreciate them systematically over their expected useful life. Instead they are written off immediately against revenue. A detailed treatment is justified only if the extra costs involved produce a significant improvement in the quality of the information contained in accounting statements. When applying this test, it must be remembered that, because of the need for estimates to be made and judgement to be exercised, the reported profit figure is at best an approximation and is unlikely to be improved by making precise adjustments for trivial items.

Readers should now work Question 8.13 at the end of this chapter.

Questions

8.1 (a) How would you distinguish between capital and revenue expenditure and why is it important to make a correct allocation?

(b) State, with reasons, in which of the two categories you would place the following items:

(i) Replacement of the blade on a cutting machine damaged as the result of using poor-quality raw material inputs.
(ii) A feeding device costing £1,000 that is fixed to a machine so as to enable a 20 per cent increase in throughput each hour.
(iii) The cost of transporting, to the factory, a new machine supplied by a Japanese company.
(iv) Second-hand plant purchased at a cost of £1,500.
(v) Repairs to the plant mentioned in (iv) above before it is ready for use, £300.

8.2 Simon is a surveyor who purchases old properties in poor condition. He incurs expenditure on improving these properties, which he then resells. His balance sheet at 31 December 19X2 was as follows:

	£		£
Properties on hand (including		Capital	79,000
expenses on purchase)			
1	30,250		
2	29,350		
Bank balance	19,400		
	79,000		79,000

During 19X3 he bought three more properties:

	Cost	Legal expenses borne by Simon	Cost of improvement
	£	£	£
3	36,250	1,000	260
4	24,000	750	1,000
5	25,000	800	520

and sold the following three properties:

	Sale price	Legal expenses borne by Simon
	£	£
1	34,000	400
3	42,500	500
4	31,250	350

General expenses incurred and paid during 19X3 amounted to £2,500.

Required

(a) Simon's bank account for 19X3.
(b) A profit and loss account for the year 19X3 covering Simon's property deals and a balance sheet at 31 December 19X3.

Notes
1. Cash due from the sale of property 4 was not received until 5 January 19X4.
2. There were no other transactions during the year and all receipts and payments were by cheque.

8.3 On 1 January 199X a business purchased a Minilab to process and print films. The Minilab costs £28,000 and has an estimated economic life of 4 years after which it will have no residual value. The financial year of the business ends on 31 December each year. It is estimated that the output from the Minilab will be:

	Films processed
Year 1	40,000
Year 2	50,000
Year 3	55,000
Year 4	55,000
	200,000

Required

(a) Calculate the annual depreciation charges on the Minilab for each of the four years on each of the following bases:

(i) The straight-line basis.
(ii) The diminishing balance method at 55 per cent per annum.
(iii) The units of output method.

Note
Your workings should be to the nearest £. *(10 marks)*

(b) Suppose that the business sold the Minilab half way through the third year for £10,000 and that depreciation had been provided for using the straight-line method applied on a month-for-month basis.
Reconstruct the following accounts *for the third year only*:

(i) The Minilab account.
(ii) The provision for depreciation – Minilab account.
(iii) The assets disposals account. *(10 marks)*
(Total 20 marks)
(AAT, Basic Accounting, December 1990)

8.4 Buy Ltd paid Mr Sale £120,000, cash, to acquire his business, Sale & Co., as a going concern on 1 January 19X1. The assets taken over were considered to be worth the following amounts:

	£
Fixed assets	71,500
Stock	20,000
Debtors	10,000

In addition Buy Ltd assumed responsibility for paying Sale & Co.'s outstanding creditors, which amounted to £5,000. The policy of Buy Ltd is to write off goodwill over a five-year period.

Required

(a) Calculate the goodwill arising on the acquisition of Sale & Co.
(b) Show how goodwill will appear in the balance sheet of Buy Ltd as at 31 December 19X1.

8.5 Give the basic rule for valuing stock. Apply this rule to the facts provided below and calculate the total value of stock to be included in the accounts.

Product	Cost	Net realizable value
	£	£
A	2,400	2,760
B	1,290	740
C	3,680	750
D	2,950	4,760
E	6,280	9,730

8.6 Irwin Brothers manufacture one type of high-quality ornament for the export market. The firm plans its activities three months in advance and its estimates for January, February and March 1994 are as follows:

		Units
Stock of ornaments at 1 January		Nil
Ornaments produced during:	January	450
	February	480
	March	500
Expected sales for:	January	400
	February	450
	March	520
		£
Unit selling price		21
Unit variable manufacturing cost		12
Manufacturing overheads per month		1,800
Fixed administrative expenses per month		600

Required

(a) Prepare profit statements for each of the months January, February and March 1994, adopting

(i) a marginal costing approach; and
(ii) an absorption costing approach.   *(14 marks)*

(b) Using examples from your answer to part (a), explain why the resultant profit figures differ for each approach.   *(4 marks)*
                    (Total: 18 marks)
        (ICSA, Introduction to Accounting, December 1993)

8.7 What do you understand by the terms 'perpetual inventory' and 'periodic stock-take'? In the case of a trader, how is the figure for cost of goods sold obtained under each of these systems?

8.8 D. Hart, a trader dealing in one product only, has the following transactions over a six-month period:

	Date	Quantity (in units)	Unit cost £
Purchases	1 June 1992	1,500	90
	1 August 1992	2,000	92
	1 October 1992	3,000	93
Sales	June 1992	340	140
	July 1992	700	140
	August 1992	800	144
	September 1992	450	144
	October 1992	900	144
	November 1992	630	145

The trader held no stock at 31 May 1992.

Required

(a) Applying the following principles of stock valuation, calculate D. Hart's gross profit or loss for the six months ended 30 November 1992.
(i) First in first out; and
(ii) Last in first out.

(Ignore other expenses which may have been incurred for the period.)

(*14 marks*)

(b) If a trader uses last in first out as the basis of stock valuation, does this mean that he is left with the 'oldest' intake of stock at the end of the period? Briefly explain your answer. (*4 marks*)

(*Total: 18 marks*)

(ICSA, Introduction to Accounting, December 1992)

8.9 Airwaves Ltd are retailers who sell mobile telephones. During January to March 1993 they decided to concentrate their selling activities on the 'Meteor' model, which experienced several cost price fluctuations during the period. The company found that because of this it had to adjust its own selling price.

During the period the following transactions took place:

1. 1 Jan.: an opening stock of 50 telephones was obtained at a total cost of £8,250.
2. 10 Jan.: initial sales were good so extra telephones had to be obtained from abroad; 200 telephones were purchased at a cost of £135 each but in addition there was a freight charge of £3 each, as well as a customs import duty of £5 each.
3. 31 Jan.: during the month 180 telephones were sold at a price of £175 each.
4. 1 Feb.: a new batch of 120 telephones was purchased at a cost of £170 each.
5. 28 Feb.: the sales for February were 120 at a selling price of £215 each.
6. 2 Mar.: a further 220 telephones were purchased at a cost of £240 each and these were subject to a trade discount of 12.5 per cent each.
7. 31 Mar.: 250 telephones were sold during March at a price of £230 each.

All purchases were received on the dates stated.

The accountant of Airwaves Ltd decided he would apply the first in first out (FIFO) and weighted average (AVCO) methods of stock valuation in order that the results could be compared.

Required

(a) Calculate the stock value at 31 March 1993 using each of the methods indicated (if necessary, calculate to one decimal place). (*16 marks*)
(b) Prepare the trading accounts using each of the above methods for the period January–March 1993. (*8 marks*)
(c) What considerations should an accountant bear in mind in deciding on a basis of stock valuation? Reference should be made to relevant accounting concepts. (*20 marks*)

(AEB, Accounting, November 1993)

8.10 Stoval Ltd started to trade on 1 January 19X1. Its purchases of trading stock, at cost, during the first three years of business were

	£
19X1	240,000
19X2	252,000
19X3	324,000

The values of stock at 31 December, under different valuation methods, were

31 December	LIFO cost	FIFO cost	Lower of FIFO cost and net realizable value
19X1	£96,480	£96,000	£88,800
19X2	£87,360	£86,400	£81,600
19X3	£100,320	£105,600	£105,600

Required

(a) Assuming that in any one year prices moved either up or down, but not both in the same year:

   (i) Did prices go up or down in 19X1?
   (ii) Did prices go up or down in 19X3?

(b) Which stock valuation method would show the highest profit for 19X1?
(c) Which stock valuation method applied to opening and closing stock would show the highest profit for 19X3?
(d) Which stock valuation method would show the lowest profit for all three years combined?

8.11 Where accounts are prepared in accordance with the *accruals concept*, cash receipts and payments may precede, coincide with or follow the period in which revenues and expenses are recognized. Give two examples of each of the following:

(a) A cash receipt that precedes the period in which revenue is recognized.
(b) A cash receipt that coincides with the period in which revenue is recognized.
(c) A cash receipt that follows the period in which revenue is recognized.
(d) A cash payment that precedes the period in which expense is recognized.
(e) A cash payment that coincides with the period in which expense is recognized.
(f) A cash payment that follows the period in which expense is recognized.

8.12 The summarized trading account of Change Ltd for 19X1 contained the following information:

Trading Account for 19X1

		£	£
Sales			100,000
Less:	Opening stock	7,000	
	Purchases	80,000	
	Closing stock	(11,000)	
	Cost of goods sold		76,000
Gross profit			24,000

Opening stock is valued at marginal cost, but the directors have now decided that total cost is more suitable, and this basis was used for the purpose of valuing closing stock. The value of opening stock, on the total cost basis, is found to be £10,000.

Required

(a) Prepare a revised trading account for Change Ltd complying with the consistency concept.

(b) Indicate the effect of the revision on the *net* profit figure reported by Change Ltd for 19X1.

8.13
    (i)   Dual aspect;
    (ii) consistency;
    (iii) prudence;
    (iv) matching/accruals; and
    (v)   going concern.

(a) Briefly explain each of the concepts mentioned above.   *(10 marks)*
(b) Explain how each of the concepts will affect the preparation of the final accounts of a company.   *(10 marks)*
                                                          (Total: 20 marks)
(ICSA, Introduction to Accounting, December 1993)

9
PARTNERSHIPS

The objectives of this chapter are to

- explain what a partnership is;
- give an outline of the legal rules governing their operations;
- explain and illustrate how profit is divided;
- describe how the interest of each partner in the firm is recorded;
- show how changes in membership or the profit-sharing ratio are recorded; and
- demonstrate the accounting aspects of dissolving a partnership.

INTRODUCTION

Partnerships use the same basic accounting techniques as those described so far in this book in the context of the sole trader, although some modifications are required in their application to suit the different constitution of the partnership. There is no legal requirement for partnerships to prepare annual accounts, but the need to share profits between the partners and for partners to submit tax returns makes their routine production essential if the conduct of the partnership is to proceed smoothly. As with sole traders, there is no requirement for the contents of partnership accounts to be made public even though they may relate to significant economic entities: this contrasts with the disclosure requirements imposed on limited companies described in Chapter 10.

The legal background is provided by the Partnership Act 1890, which defines a partnership as 'the relation which subsists between persons carrying on a business in common with a view of profit'. There is no formal legal procedure necessary to create a partnership; it can be deemed to exist because people are trading in a way that brings them within the definition. It is very important to determine whether a person is a partner as the liability of each partner for all of the firm's debts is unlimited; if the firm cannot pay, then each partner becomes personally liable to the extent of the entire debt. (The Limited Partnership Act 1907 makes special provision for a partnership to have limited partners whose liability is restricted to the value of their capital investment, provided there is at least one general partner who accepts full liability for all of the firm's debts. This provision is not widely used.)

The most common reasons for forming a partnership are to raise the necessary finance to fund planned operations, and to pool together complementary skills, for example, an engineer who is very capable at developing new products may need the services of a salesman or woman to market them.

The number of partners allowed to combine in a partnership is limited to twenty, although some specific exemptions are granted, for example, firms of chartered accountants can have any number of partners. If a firm limited to twenty partners wishes to seek funds from a larger group, then incorporation as a limited company is first necessary (see Chapter 10).

THE PARTNERSHIP AGREEMENT

The owners of a partnership, the partners, also manage it, and each partner can enter into contracts on behalf of the firm that are binding on the partnership as a whole. In these circumstances, the partners must have a great deal of mutual trust, and it is best for the manner in which the partnership is to be conducted to be set out formally in a legally binding partnership agreement signed by all of the partners. Examples of the matters to be covered by such an agreement are as follows:

1. The purpose for which the partnership is formed.
2. The amount of capital each partner is to contribute.
3. Regulations to be observed when the partnership is created.
4. How profits and losses are to be divided among the partners.
5. Whether separate capital and current accounts are to be maintained.
6. The extent to which partners can make drawings.
7. The frequency with which accounts are to be prepared and whether they are to be subjected to an independent audit.
8. Regulations to be observed when a partner retires or a new partner is admitted, the profit-sharing ratio changes or the partnership is dissolved.

Where no formal agreement exists, the terms of the partnership may be concluded from past behaviour, for example, if profits have always been divided between two partners in the ratio 2:1, without dissent from either partner, then this is presumed to be the agreed ratio. The Partnership Act 1890 provides a 'safety net' of regulations that apply when there is no agreement, either formal or informal, to the contrary. Among the major of these provisions are the following:

1. All profits and losses are to be shared equally among the partners.
2. No interest on capital or remuneration for conducting the partnership business is payable to any partner.
3. A partner is entitled to 5 per cent per annum interest on any loans to the partnership in excess of his or her agreed capital contribution.
4. Every partner is authorized to take part in the firm's management.
5. All existing partners must agree to the admission of a new partner.

THE CREATION OF A PARTNERSHIP

When a partnership is formed, the contribution of each partner is recorded in its books at its current, agreed value. The capital may consist simply of cash or, where the partner already operates as a sole trader, comprise a collection of assets, and possibly liabilities. As was the case with the sole trader, the value of the capital of each partner is equal to, and can be calculated as, the value of the assets contributed less any liabilities. The entries made in the books to record the assets, liabilities (if any) and capital introduced by a partner, on the formation of a partnership, are

Debit	*Credit*	*With*
Various asset accounts		Assets contributed
	Various liability accounts	Liabilities taken over
	Capital account	Value of assets less liabilities

The merging of two sole traders to create a partnership is shown in Example 9.1.

Example 9.1   Beaver and Burroughes are two sole traders who decide to enter into partnership as from 1 March 1986. Their respective balance sheets as at the close of business on 28 February 1986 were as follows:

Beaver

	£		£
Capital account	2,990	Office furniture	500
Creditors	850	Delivery van	660
Bank overdraft	320	Stock	1,440
		Debtors	1,530
		Cash-in-hand	30
	4,160		4,160

Burroughes

	£		£
Capital account	5,200	Office furniture	550
Creditors	920	Delivery van	750
		Stock	1,970
		Debtors	1,730
		Bank	1,120
	6,120		6,120

The partnership acquired *all* the assets and took over *all* the liabilities at the figures shown in the above balance sheets except that:

	Beaver £	Burroughes £
1. Office furniture is to be revalued	400	480
2. Stock is to be revalued	1,300	1,900
3. Goodwill is valued at	—	400
4. Bad debts are to be written off	120	80

5. The bank accounts are to be closed and a new partnership bank account opened.

(i) Calculate the opening capital of each of the two partners. (Calculations *must* be shown.)

(ii) Draw up the *opening* balance sheet of the partnership.

(LCC, Elementary Book-Keeping, winter, 1986)

(i)

	Beaver £	Burroughes £	Total £
Office furniture	400	480	880
Delivery vans	660	750	1,410
Stock	1,300	1,900	3,200
Debtors	1,410	1,650	3,060
Goodwill	—	400	400
Cash	30	—	30
Bank	(320)	1,120	800
Creditors	(850)	(920)	(1,770)
	2,630	5,380	8,010

(ii) **Partnership Balance Sheet, 1 March 1986**

	£	£
Goodwill		400
Office furniture		880
Delivery vans		1,410
		2,690
Stock	3,200	
Debtors	3,060	
Bank	800	
Cash	30	
	7,090	
Creditors	(1,770)	
		5,320
		8,010
Financed by:		
Beaver – capital account		2,630
Burroughes – capital account		5,380
		8,010

THE DIVISION OF PROFIT

The net profit of a partnership is calculated in the usual way, and is then transferred to the appropriation account where it is divided among the partners in the agreed manner. The agreement may provide for a straightforward allocation in accordance with a specific ratio, such as 3:2; alternatively, precise adjustments may be made to take account of the following factors:

1. The partners may provide different amounts of capital; this involves sacrificing different amounts of interest that could have been earned by, for example, putting the money in a bank deposit account. Compensation for this can be achieved by allowing a deduction to be made in the appropriation account for interest on partner's capital. The rate of interest may be fixed in the agreement or, because rates of interest fluctuate, it could be tied to some external indicator, such as the rate paid on long-term deposit accounts by banks. In whichever way the rate is determined, the greater the amount of capital a partner has invested in the firm, the greater is the interest received.
2. By deciding to join a partnership, each partner forgoes potential earnings as an employee of another firm. The sacrifice of alternative income may not be the same for each partner, for example, one may contribute more valuable skills. This can be recognized by giving each partner a salary related to potential 'outside earnings'. Such salaries are also deducted from profit in the appropriation account.
3. Partners make drawings from the firm that reduce the amount of their investment, and it may be decided to recognize this by charging partners interest on their drawings. This interest is then added to the profit to be shared among the partners.
4. After any interest and salaries have been deducted, there must be agreement on how to divide the residual profit or loss. The ratio in which it is shared may be designed to reflect the partner's seniority, or some other basis, such as equality, may be adopted.

The steps necessary to carry out the division of partnership profit are as follows:

1. Determine the manner in which profit is to be divided.
2. Determine the value of profit or loss to be shared. The value found *takes no account* of any payments to the partners, for example, in the form of salaries, and is transferred to the appropriation account.
3. Add to profit any interest charged on drawings made by the partners.
4. Deduct from profit any interest allowed on capital account balances and any salaries payable to partners.
5. Split the residual profit or loss in the agreed ratio.

Steps 3 to 5 are recorded in the firm's books with the following entries:

Debit	Credit	With
Capital account*	Profit and loss appropriation account	Interest charged on drawings
Profit and loss appropriation account	Capital account*	Interest allowed on capital, salaries and share of profit
Capital account*	Profit and loss appropriation account	Share of losses

Note

* These entries are instead made in the current accounts of partners where such accounts are maintained (see the section on capital and current accounts that follows).

The division of profit in the appropriation account is illustrated in Example 9.2.

Example 9.2

Oak and Tree are in partnership and prepare their accounts on a calendar-year basis. They have agreed that profits are to be shared as follows:

1. Oak is to receive an annual salary of £5,000 and Tree one of £10,000.
2. Interest at 10 per cent per annum is to be paid on each partner's capital account balance as on 1 January.
3. Residual profits and losses are to be shared equally.

On 1 January 19X6 the balance on Oak's capital account was £64,000 and on Tree's it was £30,000.

Required

Prepare the partnership's appropriation account on the alternative assumptions that the profit for 19X6 was

(a) £30,000,
(b) £20,000.

Solution

(a) **Appropriation Account**

		£			£
Salary:	Oak	5,000	Profit		30,000
	Tree	10,000			
Interest:	Oak	6,400			
	Tree	3,000			
Residue:	Oak	2,800			
	Tree	2,800			
		30,000			30,000

(b) **Appropriation Account**

		£				£
Salary:	Oak	5,000	Profit			20,000
	Tree	10,000	Share of loss:	Oak		2,200
Interest:	Oak	6,400		Tree		2,200
	Tree	3,000				
		24,400				24,400

> *Note*
> If there is no agreement to the contrary, the profits in the above example would have been divided between the partners in accordance with the terms of the Partnership Act 1890. Each would have received an equal share, namely, £15,000 in (a) and £10,000 in (b).

Readers should now work Question 9.1, which extends the above example to three partners and includes interest charged on drawings, and Question 9.2, both of which are at the end of this chapter.

CAPITAL AND CURRENT ACCOUNTS

The capital each partner invests in the business can be divided into two elements:

1. The part permanently required to finance the ability of the firm to trade. It is invested in fixed assets and working capital and cannot be withdrawn without reducing the capacity of the business.
2. The part that can be withdrawn by the partners as drawings.

The permanent capital of each partner is entered in a 'capital account'. The partnership agreement usually stipulates the amount of permanent capital invested by each partner, and the balances remain constant until the partners agree to a change. Routine transactions among partners and the firm are entered in a 'current account'. The current account balance fluctuates as it is credited with each partner's share of profits, in the form of interest, salary and share of residue, and is debited with drawings and interest on drawings. To prevent partners withdrawing more than their entitlement, the partnership agreement should state that no current account is allowed to have a debit balance without the consent of the other partners.

Example 9.3	Disk and Drive trade in partnership. The following information relates to 19X7:	

	Disk £	Drive £
Current account balance 1 January 19X7	9,130	8,790
Interest allowed on capital	1,000	1,500
Interest charged on drawings	150	390
Salary	5,000	3,000
Share of residual profit	6,250	6,250
Cash drawings	7,160	8,240
Stock drawings	120	80

Required   Prepare the current accounts of Disk and Drive for 19X7. For each entry indicate clearly the location of its corresponding double entry.

Current Accounts

	Disk £	Drive £		Disk £	Drive £
Appropriation Account:			Balance b/d	9,130	8,790
Interest	150	390	Appropriation Account:		
Drawings:			Interest	1,000	1,500
Cash account	7,160	8,240	Salary	5,000	3,000
Purchases a/c	120	80	Residue	6,250	6,250
Balance c/d	13,950	10,830			
	21,380	19,540		21,380	19,540

It is possible for substantial balances to accumulate in the current accounts where partners consistently withdraw less than their share of the profits. The funds represented by these balances may have been invested in trading assets, and so have taken on the aspect of permanent capital, that is, they are not available for quick withdrawal. This position is shown in Figure 9.1.

			£000
Fixed assets			75
Working capital			25
			100

	Paper £000	Clip £000	Total £000
Capital accounts	20	20	40
Current accounts	30	30	60
	50	50	100

Figure 9.1 Summarized balance sheet of Paper and Clip at 31 December 19X9

It is clear that the current account balances could not be withdrawn without reducing the size of the business, since a large proportion of these balances has been invested in fixed assets that would have to be sold to release cash. This is unlikely to happen, and so to bring the balance sheet into line with economic reality, the partners may agree that each of them should transfer, say, £25,000 from current to capital account. The transfer is entered in the books by a debit in each current account and a corresponding credit in each capital account. This increase in capital account balances does not provide the firm with any additional funds, but simply recognizes that the partners have invested funds previously available as drawings in the permanent structure of the undertaking. When *additional* capital funds are required by a partnership, they must be introduced by the partners and credited to their capital accounts.

Readers should now work Question 9.3 at the end of this chapter.

CHANGES IN MEMBERSHIP

The partnership business, unlike a limited company, is not recognized in law as a separate *legal* entity, and so a change in the ownership creates a new business. For accounting purposes, the firm is treated as a continuing entity and the same set of books usually remains in use when a new partner joins or an existing one retires, but entries must be made in the books to give effect to any financial adjustments needed.

Each partner is entitled to their share of the profits, or losses, that have accrued during the period of time for which they have been a partner. Adjustment must be made, when a partner retires or joins, for any increase in value not yet recognized in the accounts, otherwise the retiring partner is not credited with the full amount due and the incoming partner is credited with a share of the assets at below their current value. This is demonstrated in Example 9.4.

Example 9.4   The following is the summarized balance sheet of Lamp and Bulb, who share profits in the ratio 3:2 respectively, at 31 December 19X5:

	£
Net assets	2,000
Financed by:	
Lamp – capital account	1,000
Bulb – capital account	1,000
	2,000

The following is agreed:

1. Bulb is to retire on 1 January 19X6.
2. The net assets have a current value of £3,000.
3. Bulb is to be paid the sum due to him in cash immediately.
4. Socket is to be admitted as a partner on 1 January 19X6.
5. Socket and Lamp agree to share future profits and losses equally.
6. Socket agrees to introduce cash equal to the value of Lamp's capital after the assets have been adjusted to current values.
7. Current accounts shall not be maintained.

Required   (a) Calculate the amount due to Bulb on his retirement.
(b) Calculate the amount of capital to be introduced by Socket.
(c) Prepare the opening balance sheet of the Lamp and Socket partnership.
(d) Comment on the consequences of not adjusting the assets to current values.

Solution   (a)

	£	£
Current value of net assets		3,000
Historical cost of net assets		2,000
Increase in value		1,000

Share of increase:	Lamp	600	
	Bulb	400	
		——	1,000

Amount due to Bulb:		
Capital		1,000
Revaluation surplus		400
		——
Total due		1,400

(b) Lamp and Socket have agreed to share profits equally and the amount Socket should therefore introduce as capital is the same as the balance on Lamp's capital account:

$$1,000 \text{ (balance)} + 600 \text{ (revaluation surplus)} = 1,600$$

(c) **Balance Sheet of Lamp and Socket**

	£
Net assets	3,200*
Financed by:	
Lamp – capital account	1,600
Socket – capital account	1,600
	——
	3,200

Note
* 2,000 (Original value) + 1,000 (Revaluation) – 1,400 (Paid to Bulb) + 1,600 (Cash from Socket) = £3,200.

(d) Without the revaluation, Bulb would withdraw only the balance on his capital account, i.e. £1,000. He therefore leaves £400 in the business that has accrued under his ownership. Socket would introduce only £1,000, the same as the balance on Lamp's capital account, but would be buying a half share in assets with a current value of £3,000.

We will now examine how these matters are recorded in the books of the partnership. To record the revaluation of assets a revaluation account is used in which the following entries are made:

Debit	*Credit*	*With*
Revaluation account	Asset account	Reduction in asset value
Asset account	Revaluation account	Increase in asset value

The revaluation account contains all the increases and decreases in value, and its balance – the net surplus or deficit – is shared among the partners in the agreed ratio. Each partner's share of the net adjustment is entered in his or her capital account as it is permanent in nature. The revaluation account and capital accounts of Lamp, Bulb and Socket, from Example 9.4, would contain the following information:

Revaluation Account

	£		£
Surplus shared:		Increase in value of	
Lamp – capital	600	net assets	1,000
Bulb – capital	400		
	1,000		1,000

Capital Accounts

	Lamp £	Bulb £	Socket £		Lamp £	Bulb £	Socket £
Cash		1,400		Balance b/d	1,000	1,000	
Balance c/d	1,600		1,600	Revaluation	600	400	
				Cash			1,600
	1,600	1,400	1,600		1,600	1,400	1,600

As well as adjusting the values of tangible assets included in the balance sheet, it is also usually necessary to create a balance for goodwill, since the partners are also entitled to share in the value of this intangible asset. The appropriate share of goodwill created during his or her period of ownership is due to a retiring partner, and an incoming partner must expect to pay for a share of existing goodwill.

The partners in the new firm may decide to record the assets taken over at their revalued figures; alternatively they may choose to restate some, or all, of the assets at their pre-revaluation amounts. If the latter course is adopted, the adjustment must be shared among the partners in the new firm in accordance with their agreed profit-sharing ratio. Usually, the revised figures for tangible assets are accepted and goodwill is written off.

Example 9.5   Bill, Ben and Flo are in partnership together and share profits and losses in the ratio of 2:2:1 respectively. The balance sheet of the partnership at 31 December 19X0 was as follows:

	£000	£000
Fixed assets		
Land and buildings		50
Plant and equipment		175
		225
Current assets		
Stock	80	
Debtors	90	
Cash	5	
	175	
Less: Trade creditors	110	

	£000	£000
		65
		290

Financed by:
Capital accounts

	£000	£000
Bill	90	
Ben	80	
Flo	70	
		240

Current accounts

	£000	£000
Bill	10	
Ben	25	
Flo	15	
		50
		290

The following information is relevant:

1. Bill decides to retire on 31 December 19X0, while Ben and Flo intend to continue trading, sharing profits and losses equally.
2. To determine the amount due to Bill, the partners agree that the assets should be revalued as follows:

	£000
Land and buildings	165
Plant and equipment	180
Stock	75
Debtors	85
Goodwill	100

3. After the retirement of Bill, the assets are to be left in the books at their revalued amounts, with the exception of goodwill, which is to be written off. All adjustments are to be made through the partner's capital accounts.
4. All sums due to Bill are to be transferred to a loan account.

Required

Prepare the partnership balance sheet for Ben and Flo after all the above adjustments have been put into effect. Show clearly your calculation of the balances on Ben's and Flo's capital accounts and the amount due to Bill.

Solution

Ben and Flo Balance Sheet

	£000	£000
Fixed assets		
Land and buildings		165
Plant and equipment		180
		345

	£000	£000
Current assets		
Stock	75	
Debtors	85	
Cash	5	
	165	
Less: Trade creditors	110	
		55
		400
Less: Loan from Bill	184	
		216
Financed by:		
Capital accounts		
Ben	114	
Flo	62	
		176
Current accounts		
Ben	25	
Flo	15	
		40
		216

Workings

Revaluation Account

	£000	£000		£000
Stock		5	Goodwill	100
Debtors		5	Land and buildings	115
Surplus			Plant and equipment	5
Bill (loan a/c)	84			
Ben: Capital account	84			
Flo: Capital account	42			
	—	210		
		220		220

Capital Accounts

	Ben	Flo		Ben	Flo
	£000	£000		£000	£000
Goodwill	50	50	Balance b/d	80	70
Balance c/d	114	62	Surplus	84	42
	164	112		164	112

Amount due to Bill

		£000
Balance:	Capital account	90
	Current account	10
	Surplus	84
		184

Note
All sums due to the retired partner are shown as a loan rather than as capital as he is no longer a partner.

Readers should now work Question 9.4 at the end of this chapter.

CHANGE IN PROFIT-SHARING RATIO

It is necessary to revalue the assets when there is an alteration in the ratio in which profits are split, so that changes in value up to that time are shared in the ratio that prevailed while they accrued; subsequent changes are shared in the new ratio. Failure to adopt this approach means that all value changes would be shared in the new ratio, even though this did not apply while some of the changes took place. Some assets may have increased in value while others have lost value, and a value should be assigned to goodwill. The necessary adjustments to values are again made through a revaluation account, the balance on which is shared among the partners in the old profit-sharing ratio. If the original values of any assets are to be reinstated, the adjustments are also made through the revaluation account, the balance on which is transferred to the partners' capital accounts in accordance with the new ratio.

Cut and Hack are in partnership sharing profits and losses equally. The firm's summarized balance sheet at 30 June 19X7 was   **Example 9.6**

	£
Fixed assets	7,000
Working capital	3,000
	10,000

Financed by:
Capital accounts

	£
Cut	5,000
Hack	5,000
	10,000

Hack decides to reduce the amount of time he spends working for the business, and it is agreed that from 1 July 19X7 profits should be shared between Cut and Hack in the ratio 2:1 respectively.

The partners consider that fair current values for the assets on 30 June 19X7 are

	£
Fixed assets	10,000
Working capital	3,500
Goodwill	5,500

The assets are to be recorded in the books at their original values, after the necessary adjustments consequent upon the change in the profit-sharing ratio have been effected.

Required

(a) Prepare the revaluation account of the partnership to record all the adjustments made to asset values.

(b) Prepare the partners' capital accounts showing clearly the balances after all adjustments have been made.

(c) Prepare the revised balance sheet of Cut and Hack.

Solution

(a) **Revaluation Account**

		£		£
Surplus:	Cut	4,500	Fixed assets	3,000
	Hack	4,500	Working capital	500
			Goodwill	5,500
		9,000		9,000
			Written off:	
Fixed assets		3,000	Cut	6,000
Working capital		500	Hack	3,000
Goodwill		5,500		
		9,000		9,000

(b) **Capital Accounts**

	Cut	Hack		Cut	Hack
	£	£		£	£
Revaluation account	6,000	3,000	Opening balance	5,000	5,000
Balance c/d	3,500	6,500	Revaluation account	4,500	4,500
	9,500	9,500		9,500	9,500

(c) **Revised Balance Sheet**

	£
Fixed assets	7,000
Working capital	3,000
	10,000

Financed by:	£
Capital accounts	
Cut	3,500
Hack	6,500
	10,000

DISSOLUTION OF PARTNERSHIPS

When a partnership comes to the end of its life, perhaps because the partners decide to sell up and retire, the firm is dissolved. In these circumstances, the assets are sold, the liabilities settled and the partnership ceases to exist. The Partnership Act 1890 requires that the money raised from the sale of assets must be applied in the following order:

1. To settle all the firm's debts, other than those to the partners.
2. To repay any *loans* owed to partners.
3. To settle amounts due to partners on their capital and current accounts.

A realization account is used to record the dissolution of the partnership. The following entries are made in it:

Debit	*Credit*	*With*
Realization account	Sundry asset accounts	Book values of assets
Cash account	Realization account	Receipts from sale of assets
Realization account	Cash account	Expenses of realization
Capital account	Realization account	Assets taken over by partners at valuation
Capital accounts	Realization account	Share of loss on realization
Realization account	Capital accounts	Share of profit on realization
Creditor accounts	Realization account	Any gains (e.g. discounts) on settlement

Example 9.7 Tape and Ribbon trade in partnership and share profits and losses equally. The firm's summarized balance sheet at 31 December 19X8 is

	£			£
Fixed assets	20,000	Capital:	Tape	15,000
Current assets	12,500		Ribbon	12,500
				27,500
		Overdraft		1,000
		Sundry creditors		4,000
	32,500			32,500

The partners agree to dissolve the firm. Tape is to take over some of the fixed assets at a valuation of £14,000. The remaining fixed assets are sold for £20,000 and the current assets realize £15,000.

The expenses of realization are £1,000 and a prompt payment discount of £200 is received from the creditors.

Required

(a) The firm's realization account.
(b) The partners' capital accounts.
(c) The firm's cash account.

Solution

(a) **Realization Account**

	£		£
Fixed assets	20,000	Tape (fixed assets)	14,000
Current assets	12,500	Cash (fixed assets)	20,000
Cash (expenses)	1,000	Cash (current assets)	15,000
Tape	7,850	Discount received	200
Ribbon	7,850		
	49,200		49,200

(b) **Capital Accounts**

	Tape £	Ribbon £		Tape £	Ribbon £
Realization a/c	14,000	—	Balance b/d	15,000	12,500
Cash	8,850	20,350	Realization a/c	7,850	7,850
	22,850	20,350		22,850	20,350

(c) **Cash Account**

	£		£
Realization account:		Balance b/d	1,000
Fixed assets	20,000	Realization expenses	1,000
Current assets	15,000	Sundry creditors	3,800
		Tape	8,850
		Ribbon	20,350
	35,000		35,000

Readers should now work Question 9.5 at the end of this chapter.

If, after all the assets have been sold, debts settled and loans repaid, any partner has a net debit balance on his or her combined capital and current accounts, he or she must introduce cash to cover the deficiency so that the other partners can receive the amounts due to them. For example, Red, Green and Blue, after trading in partnership for a number of years, decide to dissolve the business. The balance sheet after all of the assets had been sold and the firm's liabilities settled was as shown in Figure 9.2.

	£
Cash	20,000
Capital accounts:	
Red	15,000
Green	10,000
Blue	(5,000)
	20,000

Figure 9.2 Effect of debit balance of one partner at dissolution of a partnership

In these circumstances, Blue must pay £5,000 into the firm's bank account: this raises its balance to £25,000 and eliminates the debit balance on Blue's capital account. Red and Green can then withdraw cash of £15,000 and £10,000 respectively to complete the dissolution.

The rule in Garner v. Murray

If a partner is personally bankrupt and so cannot introduce cash to make good a debit balance on his or her capital account when a partnership is dissolved, then the rule laid down in the case of Garner *v*. Murray must be applied. This requires the deficiency from the realization account to be shared between the remaining partners in the agreed profit-sharing ratio; the irrecoverable debit balance on a partner's capital account is then borne by the solvent partners in the ratio of their capital account balances before the start of the dissolution. The application of this rule is examined in Example 9.8.

The following is the balance sheet of Pink, Blink and Wink, who share trading profits and losses equally, after all the firm's assets have been sold: *Example 9.8*

	£
Cash	20,000
Deficiency from realization account	3,000
	23,000
Capital accounts:	
Pink	15,000
Blink	10,000
Wink	(2,000)
	23,000

Wink is personally bankrupt and cannot contribute anything towards the debit balance on his capital account.

Required

Prepare the capital accounts of the partners showing the distribution of the available cash, and explain the basis on which Wink's deficiency has been shared between Pink and Blink.

Solution

Capital Accounts

	Pink £	Blink £	Wink £		Pink £	Blink £	Wink £
Balance b/d	—	—	2,000	Balance b/d	15,000	10,000	—
Share of loss on realization	1,000	1,000	1,000				
Wink	1,800	1,200		Pink			1,800
Cash	12,200	7,800		Blink			1,200
	15,000	10,000	3,000		15,000	10,000	3,000

The £3,000 debit balance on Wink's account after debiting the loss on realization, is split between Pink and Blink in accordance with the ruling in Garner *v.* Murray, that is, it is shared in the ratio of the capital account balances of the remaining partners prior to the dissolution. Hence, Pink bears 15,000/25,000 × 3,000 = £1,800, and Blink bears 10,000/25,000 × 3,000 = £1,200. The cash balance of £20,000, which remains, is used to pay off the balances on the capital accounts of Pink and Blink.

Questions

Questions 9.1 to 9.5 test individual aspects of partnership accounts specifically dealt with in this chapter; questions 9.6 and 9.7 deal with the preparation of a full set of partnership accounts.

9.1 Jack, Jill and Jane trade together in partnership, and they have agreed to share profits and losses on the following basis:

1. Annual salaries of £10,000, £7,500 and £5,000 are to be paid to Jack, Jill and Jane respectively.
2. Interest of 12 per cent is to be allowed on the average balance of each partner's capital account for the year.
3. Interest of 12 per cent is to be charged on drawings.
4. Residual profits and losses are to be shared: Jack and Jill 40 per cent and Jane 20 per cent.

You are given the following additional information:

1. On 1 January 19X2, the balances on the partners' capital accounts were:

	£
Jack	30,000
Jill	20,000
Jane	40,000

On 30 June 19X2, Jill introduced further capital of £5,000.

2. The charges for interest on drawings for 19X2 are:

	£
Jack	600
Jill	450
Jane	400

3. The firm made a profit of £42,000 in 19X2.

Required

Prepare the partnership appropriation account for 19X2.

9.2

Required

(a) Prepare the partnership appropriation account of the Jack, Jill and Jane partnership using the information given in Question 9.1 above and assuming that no partnership agreement exists.

(b) Explain the basis on which you have divided the profit in part (a).

9.3 Ice and Cube are in partnership, sharing profits and losses equally. The balances on their capital and current accounts at 1 January 19X4 are:

	Capital	Current
	£	£
Ice	50,000	30,000
Cube	60,000	20,000

The trading profit for 19X4 was £45,000, and during the year the cash drawings of Ice were £12,500 and of Cube £14,000. In addition, Ice took over one of the firm's cars at its book value of £1,500 to give to his daughter as an eighteenth-birthday present.

The partners review the accounts for 19X4 and decide that, as some of their current account balances have been invested in the expansion of the firm, Ice should transfer £20,000 and Cube £10,000 from current to capital account.

Required

Prepare the partners' current and capital accounts for 19X4.

9.4 Bush and Shrub are in partnership and share profits and losses in the ratio 1:2 respectively. The firm's balance sheet at 31 December 19X4 was:

	£			£
Fixed assets	15,000	Capital:	Bush	10,000
Working capital	15,000		Shrub	20,000
	30,000			30,000

The following is agreed:

1. Flower is to join the firm as a partner on 1 January 19X5.
2. After 1 January 19X5 the partners are to share profits and losses equally.
3. Flower is to introduce cash of £14,000 as capital.
4. The assets are to be revalued:

	£
Fixed assets	20,000
Working capital	13,000
Goodwill	9,000

5. The original asset values are to be reinstated after the adjustments resulting from Flower's joining have been made, and goodwill is to be written off.

Required

(a) Prepare the revaluation account of the partnership.
(b) Prepare the partners' capital accounts.
(c) Prepare the partnership balance sheet on 1 January 19X5 after Flower has been admitted and all the consequent adjustments made.

9.5 Jupiter, Mars and Saturn are in partnership sharing profits and losses in the ratio 2:1:1. The balance sheet of the partnership as at 30 June 1984 disclosed the following financial position:

	£	£		£	£	£
				Cost	Dep.	Net
Capital accounts			*Fixed assets*			
Jupiter	55,000		Freehold land			
Mars	32,000		and premises	80,000	—	80,000
Saturn	25,000		Equipment	15,000	6,000	9,000
	———	112,000	Motor car	5,000	2,000	3,000
Current liabilities				———	———	———
Creditors	4,100			100,000	8,000	92,000
Bank overdraft	6,400		*Current assets*			
	———	10,500	Stock	24,000		
			Debtors	6,500		
				———		30,500
		———				———
		122,500				122,500

On 30 June 1984 it was agreed that the partnership should be dissolved as from that date. Mars will continue in business on his own account; he agrees to take over the equipment, stock and debtors at valuations of £11,000, £26,000 and £6,100 respectively. He also agrees to purchase the freehold land and premises at an agreed valuation of £120,000, and obtains a bank loan over ten years of £90,000, to help finance the purchase. The proceeds are paid into the partnership. It is agreed that any balance owing by Mars at the finalization of the dissolution transactions will be charged to the capital account of Jupiter as the two parties have agreed that the balance owing by Mars and settled by Jupiter will represent a personal loan to be repaid by Mars, over a four-year period. Saturn agrees to purchase the motor car for £2,900.
Realization expenses amount to £1,500 and, together with amounts owing

to creditors, are paid out of the partnership resources. All transactions were completed on 1 July 1984.

Required

(a) The partnership realization account.   *(6 marks)*
(b) The partnership bank account.   *(4 marks)*
(c) The capital accounts of the partners.   *(7 marks)*
(d) The balance sheet of Mars as at 1 July 1984, indicating what the balance on the capital account of Mars represents.   *(5 marks)*

(Total: 22 marks)
(ICSA, Financial Accounting I, December, 1984)

9.6 Second and Minute started trading as retail grocers in partnership on 1 January 19X4, but did not keep a set of double-entry books. The firm's bank account, for 19X4, prepared from the record of cheques issued and cash paid into the bank, was

	£		£
Capital introduced:		Purchases	160,000
Second	20,000	Wages	17,000
Minute	20,000	Rent and rates	3,500
Sales receipts banked	200,000	Light and heat	1,260
		Delivery van	19,000
		Drawings: Second	18,000
		Minute	16,000
		Balance c/d	5,240
	240,000		240,000

Notes
1. The following payments were made directly from cash sales receipts:

	£
Petrol for van	2,000
Maintenance	1,000
Advertising	900
Purchases	2,500
	6,400

2. The van, purchased on 1 January 19X4, is expected to have a life of five years, at the end of which its scrap value will be £3,000.
3. The partners agree that separate capital and current accounts are to be kept and all profits and losses are to be shared equally.
4. At 31 December 19X4

	£
Debtors	5,460
Trade creditors	3,800
Prepaid rent	100
Light and heat accrued	140
Stock	9,200

5.   During 19X4 both Second and Minute took groceries for personal use at cost price as follows:

	£
Second	1,000
Minute	1,260
	2,260

Required

Prepare the trading and profit and loss account for the year to 31 December 19X4 and the balance sheet at that date.

9.7 The following is the trial balance of Bean and Stalk, who trade in partnership, at 31 March 19X3:

	£	£
Capital account balances at 1 April 19X2:		
Bean		30,000
Stalk		10,000
Current account balances at 1 April 19X2:		
Bean		3,000
Stalk		5,000
Sales		150,000
Stock at 1 April 19X2	30,000	
Wages	14,500	
Rent	5,000	
Expenses	3,000	
Heat and light	1,200	
Debtors/creditors	14,000	11,500
Delivery costs	5,300	
Drawings:		
Bean	7,000	
Stalk	9,000	
Cash	4,500	
Fixed assets	6,000	
Purchases	110,000	
	209,500	209,500

Notes
1.   Stock at 31 March 19X3 was valued at £40,000.
2.   Depreciation of £1,500 is to be written off the fixed assets for the year to 31 March 19X3.
3.   At 31 March 19X3 wages accrued amounted to £500 and rent of £1,000 was prepaid.
4.   On 1 February 19X3 the firm ordered and paid for goods costing £700. These were recorded as purchases but were never received as they were lost by the carrier responsible for their delivery. The carrier accepted liability for the loss during March 19X3 and paid full compensation of £700 in April 19X3. No entries had been made in the books in respect of the loss or claim.
5.   Bean took goods that had cost the firm £340 for his own use during the year. No entry had been made in the books to record this.
6.   The partnership agreement provided that profits and losses should be shared equally between the partners after

(a) allowing annual salaries of £2,000 to Bean and £4,000 to Stalk;

(b) allowing interest of 5 per cent per annum on the balance of each partner's capital account; and

(c) charging Bean £200 and Stalk £300 interest in drawings.

7. The balances on the capital accounts shall remain unchanged, all adjustments being recorded in the current accounts.

Required

Prepare the trading, profit and loss and appropriation accounts for the Bean and Stalk partnership for the year to 31 March 19X3 and the balance sheet at that date.

9.8 Amir and Barry are in partnership with contributed capitals of £70,000 and £50,000 respectively. They have agreed the following appropriation scheme:

(a) Interest is to be allowed on contributed capital at 12 per cent per annum.

(b) Interest is to be charged on drawings.

(c) Amir and Barry are to receive salaries of £10,000 and £13,000 per annum respectively.

(d) Amir and Barry are to share profits and losses in the ratio 3:2 respectively.

During the financial year ended 30 November 1990 Amir and Barry made drawings from the business totalling £37,000 and £40,400 respectively. Amir and Barry are to be charged interest on their drawings amounting to £1,900 and £3,500 respectively.

The balances on the partners' current accounts were Amir £250 and Barry £1,240 as at 1 December 1989. Both were credit balances.

The draft net profit for the partnership for the year ended 30 November 1990 was £95,000 but this is before allowing for the following:

1. It has been discovered that the receipt of a cheque for £3,000 has been correctly recorded in the cash book but has been posted in error to the sales account.

2. The provision for bad debts has still to be adjusted so that it is 2 per cent of trade debtors as at 30 November 1990. The balance on the provision for bad debts account is £3,400 which represents the provision made as at 30 November 1989. Trade debtors totalled £153,000 as at 30 November 1990.

Required

(a) Prepare journal entries to record the correction of the posting error and the adjustment to the provision for bad debts. Dates and narratives are not required. *(4 marks)*

(b) Calculate net profit for the year after taking the above into account. *(2 marks)*

(c) Prepare the partnership appropriation account for the year ended 30 November 1990. *(8 marks)*

(d) Calculate the balances on the partners' current accounts as at 30 November 1990. *(6 marks)*

(Total 20 marks)

(AAT Preliminary Examination, December 1990)

10
COMPANY ACCOUNTS

The objectives of this chapter are to

- explain the procedures followed in the creation of a registered company;
- distinguish between the different types of company;
- distinguish between ownership and control of a company;
- familiarize readers with the main content of the annual report;
- explain the nature and purpose of regulations which set out standard accounting practice;
- indicate the nature of and relationship between 'accounting concepts', 'accounting bases' and 'accounting policies';
- identify sources of information available to external users additional to that contained in the annual accounts;
- distinguish between and show how to account for the issue and forfeiture of shares;
- identify the distinctive features of loan capital and debentures;
- demonstrate how to account for taxation and dividends in the appropriation account;
- introduce readers to the treatment of taxation in company accounts;
- define and distinguish between provisions and reserves;
- explain and identify the impact of fixed asset revaluations on published accounts;
- outline the procedures involved in the redemption of debentures;
- explain the nature of a bonus issue and show how it affects a company's accounts; and
- outline the main limitations of company accounts.

FORMATION OF REGISTERED COMPANIES

A limited company is formed by registering under the Companies Act 1985, hence the term 'registered' company. Registration is a fairly simple process, but certain formalities must be complied with. It is possible for the individuals wishing to form a limited company to do the work themselves; alternatively they may choose to employ a specialist company registration agent who charges a fee in the region of £150. The following information must be filed with the Registrar of Companies at, or soon after, the registration date:

1. The names and addresses of the first directors.
2. A statement showing the amount of the company's authorized share capital.
3. The address of the company's registered office.
4. The company's memorandum of association and articles of association.

A company must have at least two shareholders whose names and addresses appear in the memorandum to demonstrate the fact that this requirement has been fulfilled. The memorandum also gives the company's name and the nature of its proposed operations, which are contained in the 'objects' clause(s).

The articles of association set out the internal rules and regulations of the company, which must be observed by both shareholders and management; they deal with such matters as the voting rights of shareholders, the appointment and powers of directors and the borrowing powers of the company. The Companies Act contains a model set of articles that apply to any limited company not filing articles of its own. The specimen articles also apply to the extent that they are not specifically modified or excluded by any articles the company files. The model articles are rarely entirely suitable and articles 'tailor-made' to the company's individual requirements are usually prepared.

Types of company

There are a number of different types of registered company (see Figure 10.1) and the option chosen will depend on the nature and scale of expected business operations. It is first necessary to decide whether the company is to be registered with limited liability or unlimited liability. Usually the main reason for forming a company is to obtain the protection of limited liability for business activities that, by their very nature, are likely to involve a significant element of risk. For this reason unlimited companies are few and far between, and we do not, therefore, need to consider them further.

There are two basic categories of limited company: the public company and the private company. The public company must include the designatory letters plc after its name, and must have a minimum issued share capital of £50,000, of which at least one-quarter must be collected at the outset. Private companies must use the designatory letters Ltd and are not allowed to make

Figure 10.1   Types of registered company

an issue of shares or debentures (see the section on loan capital and debentures in this chapter) to the general public. For both types of company the minimum number of shareholders is two and there is no maximum. Public companies are able to increase the marketability of their shares and debentures by making arrangements for these securities to be listed on the Stock Exchange, but this is a feasible exercise only for very large concerns.

Ownership and control

The powers delegated to the board of directors, in the articles of association, are considerable but they are nevertheless restricted to those needed to manage a business organization on a day-to-day basis. The shareholder theoretically retains overall control in the following respects:

1. Only shareholders are able to authorize a change in the nature of the company's operations, as set out in the memorandum of association.
2. Shareholders control the extent of the company's operations. The level of share capital and borrowing are both stated in the company's constitution and these levels can be raised only with the approval of the shareholders.
3. Shareholders can remove all or any of the directors by passing an appropriate resolution at a general meeting of the company.

These powers are more apparent than real. In a large company there is likely to be a wide dispersal of shares (for example, the shareholding in Guinness plc set out in Figure 10.2) and most shareholders regard themselves as passive recipients of dividends rather than active participants in policymaking. The directors are usually able to exert effective control through their ownership of a significant block of votes, and the fact that many shareholders absent from the annual general meeting (AGM) empowers the directors to cast their 'proxy' votes in the manner the directors think fit.

Analysis of ordinary shareholders

At 31 December 1992	Holdings Number	Holdings %	Shares Number in millions	Shares %
Category:				
Individuals	84,395	80	261	13
Insurance companies and pension funds	705	1	309	16
Banks	1,703	2	43	2
Bank nominees	1,659	2	203	10
Non-bank nominees	13,884	13	737	37
Other corporate holders	2,027	2	448	22
	104,373	100	**2,001**	100
Size of holdings:				
Up to 1,000 shares	41,385	40	24	1
1,001–10,000 shares	57,644	55	170	8
10,001–50,000 shares	4,024	4	76	4
Over 50,000 shares	1,320	1	1,731	87
	104,373	100	**2,001**	100

Figure 10.2 Analysis of shareholdings in Guinness plc at 31 December 1992

An unusually important issue is required to arouse a sufficient body of shareholders to act, in concert, to outvote the directors. The increased involvement of the institutional investor has made shareholder power a greater reality in recent years. Even then, however, activity is likely to occur behind the scenes resulting in the resignation of a director and the appointment of a capable replacement. In the case of the individual shareholder, dissatisfaction with performance or perhaps policies, for example, lack of attention to environmental issues, simply results in shares being sold.

THE ANNUAL REPORT

The form and content of accounts published, for outsiders is set out in Schedule 4 of the Companies Act 1985 as amended by the First Schedule to the Companies Act 1989. Students are not usually required to prepare accounts in accordance with the detailed legal requirements at an introductory level. However, answers should be presented in a good form and, for this purpose, a specimen layout is given in Figure 10.3, which complies broadly with legal requirements.

Copies of the profit and loss account and balance sheet must be sent to every shareholder and debenture holder at least 21 days before the AGM. A copy of the accounts approved by the AGM must be filed with the Registrar of Companies, at Companies House, where it is available for inspection by any other interested party. In the case of 'small' and 'medium'-sized companies, as defined by the Act, the accounts filed with the registrar maybe abridged versions of the shareholders' accounts. The reason for this concession is to allow what are, in many cases, small, family businesses a measure of confidentiality. A drawback of the information available at Companies House is that accounts need not be filed until seven months (ten months for a private company) after the end of the accounting period to which they relate, and many companies even fail to keep to this generous timetable; hence the material is often hopelessly out of date.

The profit and loss account and balance sheet are normally published in a document called the 'annual report'. For a large company, it is an extensive document; to take an example, the 1992 annual report of Guinness covers 64 pages. A typical annual report, prepared for a large public company, contains the following range of financial and general information in *addition* to the balance sheet and profit and loss account:

1. *The chairperson's review* This is one area of the annual report not subject to any requirements regarding its content. The chairperson is therefore free to say exactly what he or she wishes, but his or her comments will generally cover the following broad areas:

   (a) An assessment of the year's results.
   (b) An examination of factors influencing those results, for example, the economic and political climate or the effect of strikes.
   (c) A reference to major developments, for example, takeovers or new products.

Balance Sheet

Fixed assets		£	£
Intangible asset:	Goodwill		xxx
Tangible assets:	Land and buildings	xxx	
	Plant and machinery	xxx	
	Fixtures and fittings	xxx	xxx
Investments			xxx
			xxx

Current assets	£	£
Stocks	xxx	
Trade debtors	xxx	
Prepayments	xxx	
Temporary investments	xxx	
Cash at bank	xxx	
	xxx	

Less: Current liabilities	£	£
Debenture loans repayable within one year	xxx	
Unsecured loans repayable within one year	xxx	
Bank loans and overdrafts	xxx	
Trade creditors	xxx	
Taxation	xxx	
Dividends payable	xxx	
Accruals	xxx	
Net current assets (working capital)		xxx
Total assets less current liabilities		xxx
Less: Non-current liabilities		
Debentures	xxx	
Unsecured loans	xxx	
	£	£
Taxation	xxx	xxx

Financed by:	£
Share capital: Authorized	xxx
Issued	xxx
Share premium account	xxx
Revaluation reserve	xxx
General reserve	xxx
Retained profit	xxx
	xxx

Trading, Profit and Loss and Appropriation Account

		£	£
Turnover			xxx
Less:	Cost of sales		xxx
Gross profit			xxx
Less:	Distribution costs	xxx	
	Administration expenses	xxx	xxx

Net profit before tax		xxx
Less: Corporation tax		xxx
Net profit after tax		xxx
Less: Dividends	xxx	
Transfer to reserves	xxx	xxx
Retained profit for the year		xxx
Retained profit at beginning of year		xxx
Retained profit at end of year		xxx

In the case of fixed assets, figures for original cost (or revalued amount) and accumulated depreciation should be provided. The above accounting statements broadly comply with the legal requirements concerning the form of company accounts contained in the Companies Act 1985, Schedule 4, format 1.

Figure 10.3 Specimen accounts for a limited company

(d) Capital expenditure plans.

(e) An assessment of future prospects.

The chairperson's message usually conveys a fair amount of optimism even if the financial facts published later in the report make depressing reading. A strong point in favour of the chairperson's review is that it is readable and easily understood by the lay person. A major drawback is that, with regard to future prospects, it must be based on opinion rather than fact, but it is useful background material when attempting to assess progress by an interpretation of the financial information contained in the accounts.

2. *The directors' report* The content of the directors' report is closely regulated by the Companies Act. It must contain a wide range of information, including the following: details of the principal activities and the changes in those activities during the year; recommended dividends and transfers to reserves, if any; significant changes in fixed assets during the year; substantial differences between the book value and market value of land and buildings; details of political and charitable contributions where they exceed specified levels; certain details regarding the company's employment policies; names of the directors and details of their interests in shares and debentures of the company; and details of any acquisitions, by the company, of its own shares.

3. *The auditors' report* We have seen that the directors are legally obliged to prepare accounts that are relied upon by external users to reach a wide range of decisions. The directors usually wish to portray a company's results in the best possible light in order, for example, to persuade the public to buy its shares. It is for this reason that an independent auditor is appointed, by the shareholders, to examine and report on the information contained in the profit and loss account, balance sheet and directors' report. The auditor is not required to report on the chairperson's review, but he or she should not sign an unqualified report if the review contained an erroneous factual statement, for example, where the entire loss for the year was blamed on a strike by the workforce, whereas it was

actually caused by falling demand. The audit report on the accounts of The Boots Company plc for 1993 was as follows:

Auditor's Report

Report of the Auditors to the members of The Boots Company PLC.

We have audited the accounts on pages 38 to 62.

Respective responsibilities of directors and auditors

As described above the company's directors are responsible for the preparation of the accounts. It is our responsibility to form an independent opinion, based on our audit, on those accounts and to report our opinion to you.

Basis of opinion

We conducted our audit in accordance with Auditing Standards issued by the Auditing Practices Board. An audit includes examination, on a test basis, of evidence relevant to the amounts and disclosures in the accounts. It also includes an assessment of the significant estimates and judgements made by the directors in the preparation of the accounts, and of whether the accounting policies are appropriate to the group's circumstances, consistently applied and adequately disclosed.

We planned and performed our audit so as to obtain all the information and explanations which we considered necessary in order to provide us with sufficient evidence to give reasonable assurance that the accounts are free from material misstatement, whether caused by fraud or other irregularity or error. In forming our opinion we also evaluated the overall adequacy of the presentation of information in the accounts.

Opinion

In our opinion the accounts give a true and fair view of the state of affairs of the company and the group as at 31st March 1993 and of the profit of the group for the year then ended and have been properly prepared in accordance with the Companies Act 1985.

KPMG Peat Marwick
Chartered Accountants
Registered Auditors
Birmingham
2nd June 1993

The first section sets out the respective responsibilities of the directors and the auditors while the second section informs shareholders of the scope of the audit, i.e. that work done complies with the instructions issued by the professional accounting bodies for the guidance of auditors. The third section sets out the auditors' findings – their 'opinion'. You will notice that it does not *certify the accuracy* of the accounts, but instead expresses the opinion that the accounts show a *true and fair view*. The auditor of a limited company must be professionally qualified, however, and would be expected to exercise appropriate skill and judgement in reaching his or her conclusions. If the auditors have any reservations regarding the truth and fairness of the accounts, for example, perhaps they believe that the provision for bad debts is inadequate, they must refer to this fact in their report. Details of the qualification, in these circumstances, normally appears at the beginning of the section.

4. *The cash flow statement* The purpose of this statement is to provide a full record of the cash implications of transactions undertaken during an accounting period. It is, therefore, more broadly based than the profit and loss account, which gives details only of revenues and expenditures

during an accounting period. The statement also contains information about capital raised during the year and expenditure on fixed assets. Its function is to provide an insight into the overall financial policy pursued by management and the effect of that policy on the financial structure and stability of the concern. The statement is considered in detail in Chapter 12.

Standard accounting practice

Accounting practices were the subject of a great deal of criticism in the late 1960s. The main reason for this criticism was increased public awareness of the fact that, by adopting alternative valuation procedures, it was possible to report vastly different profit figures. In 1965, Professor Chambers drew attention to the fact that conventionally acceptable procedures provided scope for 'a million sets of mutually exclusive rules' (*Abacus*, September 1965, p. 15) for profit measurement. The event that brought matters to a head, however, was the GEC bid for AEI in October 1967. In an attempt to resist the takeover bid, the directors of AEI issued a profit forecast of £10 million for 1967. The takeover nevertheless went ahead and, when AEI reported in April 1968, the investing public was amazed to discover that its accounts showed a loss of £4.5 million. Subsequent investigations proved that a major cause of the £14.5 million discrepancy between forecast and actual results was simply the adoption of more conservative valuation procedures by the new management.

The result was a public outcry and a great deal of dissatisfaction was expressed with the degree of latitude allowed to those responsible for preparing financial reports. In the endeavour to restore public confidence, the accounting profession established the Accounting Standards Committee (ASC). The job identified for this committee was to prepare SSAPs designed to achieve the following objectives:

1. To encourage the adoption of best accounting practices.
2. To ensure, as far as possible, that companies adopt similar procedures.
3. To disclose the procedures that have actually been adopted.

The ASC did much to raise the standard of financial reporting but it was the subject of increasing criticism during the late 1980s due to its failure to devise a satisfactory system of inflation accounting and because of a growing tendency to issue standards which were sufficiently flexible to gain acceptability by the business community rather than insisting on what it considered to be best practice. For example , we have seen that SSAP 22 permitted companies either to write off purchased goodwill immediately against reserves or to capitalize it and amortize it through the profit and loss account over its estimated useful economic life.

As the result of criticism a review committee was established, in November 1987, under the chairmanship of Sir Ronald Dearing. It reported in 1988 and its recommendations for the revision of the standard-setting process found favour with the government which, on 26 February 1990, announced the establishment of the Financial Reporting Council under Dearing's chairmanship. The Financial Reporting Council has two 'subsidiaries': the Financial Review Panel and the Accounting Standards Board (ASB) (see Figure

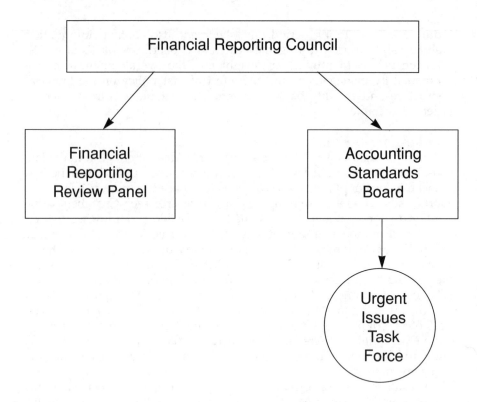

Figure 10.4 The standard-setting regime

10.4). The job of the review panel is to examine published accounts where there is evidence that the requirements of the Companies Act have been breached, particularly where it appears that they failed to show a fair view. The review panel may apply to the Court to issue revised accounts where those previously issued have been shown to be defective. This was done in the case of Trafalgar House which was forced to issue revised accounts for 1991 showing a loss of £38.5 million compared with a profit of £122.4 million in the earlier version.

The function of the ASB is to issue new accounting standards and withdraw any which are considered out of date. It is therefore the successor of the ASC. The ASB is assisted by the Urgent Issues Task Force to deal with conflicts between accounting standards and statutory provisions, which possibly lead to different interpretations.

Although the ASB may be seen as the successor to the ASC, it is different in a number of important respects. The ASB owes its existence to statutory edict and may issue accounting standards in its own name, whereas the ASC merely prepared standards to be issued by the professional accounting bodies. The independence of the ASB is underlined by the fact that it is financed not only by the accounting profession (as was the ASC) but also by the financial community and the government. The fact that there is now a requirement for companies to disclose and explain material departures from accounting standards further increases its authority.

The ASB adopted the 22 SSAPs issued by the ASC and still extant at the date of the latter's demise. The new body issues Financial Reporting Standards of which one, Financial Reporting Standard 1, entitled *Cash Flow Statements*, is considered in Chapter 12 of this book. FRSs will gradually replace SSAPs; for example, FRS 1 replaces SSAP 10 entitled *Source and Application of Funds*.

SSAP 2, entitled *Disclosure of Accounting Policies* (issued November 1971), set out the broad framework for financial reporting by defining and explaining the relationship between accounting concepts, accounting bases and accounting policies. The specific aims of this statement are to ensure that companies

- prepare their accounts in accordance with certain 'fundamental accounting concepts' specified in the statement, with any deviation from those concepts having to be disclosed; and
- report which 'accounting policies' they have chosen from the 'accounting bases' available for the purpose of valuing the assets and liabilities which appear in their accounts. The statement does not establish accounting treatments for individual assets and liabilities; this job is done in other statements, for example, SSAP 12 deals with accounting for depreciation.

The terms 'fundamental accounting concepts', 'accounting bases' and 'accounting policies' are given the following interpretations by SSAP 2.

Accounting concepts

SSAP 2 identifies four 'fundamental' concepts (since incorporated in the Companies Act 1985), which form the basis for financial reporting. These are the going concern concept, the accruals concept, the consistency concept and the concept of prudence. No one would dispute the importance of these concepts, though some would argue that other concepts are of at least equal significance. For example, we believe it is difficult to distinguish, in terms of importance, many of the *ten* accounting concepts discussed in Chapter 8 of this book.

Unless otherwise stated, there is a presumption that the four fundamental concepts have been complied with when preparing the published accounts. In certain circumstances, departure from one or more of the concepts is essential. For example, knowledge that the company is in severe financial difficulties and in imminent danger of liquidation requires the going concern concept to be abandoned. The assets are then restated at their likely realizable values, and the shareholders' attention is drawn to this fact.

Accounting bases

These are the range of options from which valuation procedures may be chosen when preparing the accounts. For a valuation procedure to be acceptable, it must comply with the four fundamental concepts. For example, straight line, reducing balance, sum of the digits and units of service are each acceptable bases for the purpose of valuing fixed assets for inclusion in company accounts, since they all broadly comply with the four fundamental concepts, i.e. they are in accordance with

- the going concept, since they assume that the company will remain in business long enough to allow the original cost to be recovered and do not therefore require assets to be restated at their liquidation values;
- the accruals concept, since the cost less estimated residual value of the fixed asset is written off over the years which the company is expected to benefit from its use, i.e. the cost of a fixed asset does not have to be written off immediately it is acquired;
- the consistency concept. Whichever valuation method is selected must be applied each year and also adopted in the case of similar assets; and
- the concept of prudence. The inclusion of a depreciation charge ensures that provision is made for the loss which will be realized when the asset is scrapped at the end of its useful life.

Accounting policies

These are the accounting bases employed by a particular company – for example, it may be decided to depreciate fixed assets on the straight-line basis. The statement requires companies to set out, in the accounts, the accounting policies used to arrive at 'material' balances reported in the accounts. The accounting policies of the ASDA Group plc are detailed on pages 24–6 of the 1992 annual report. The list includes the following:

> Depreciation, calculated on the basis of estimated useful lives on a straight line basis, is provided on certain elements of the capitalised value of freehold and long leasehold buildings, in particular fixtures, fittings, certain utilities and services.
>
> Other tangible fixed assets are depreciated over their estimated useful lives, on a straight line basis, as follows:

Short leasehold property	over period of lease
Plant and equipment	3–20 years
Motor vehicles	4–10 years

> **Stocks**
> Stocks comprise goods held for resale and development properties and are valued at the lower of cost and net realisable value.

FRSs SSAPs often deal with the valuation and presentation of individual items in the accounts. For example, SSAP 9, entitled *Stocks and Work in Progress*, favours the total cost rather than the marginal cost basis for valuing stocks, and FIFO rather than LIFO. It also requires, where applicable, the classification of stocks into each of its main categories, such as work in progress, raw materials and finished goods. FRS 1, by way of contrast, requires companies to publish an additional accounting statement, i.e. the cash flow statement.

OTHER SOURCES OF INFORMATION

Accounts published by limited companies are an important source, but by no means the only source, of information available for shareholders and other interested parties.

First, there is a whole range of additional information provided by the company itself:

1. A public limited company offering shares to the general public must issue a 'prospectus' containing an accountant's report, which includes the most recent balance sheet and certain specified profit and loss account data for each of the last five years. In addition, the company must provide a forecast of its current year's profits and the planned dividend payment.
2. Companies whose shares are quoted on the London Stock Exchange are required to comply with a range of obligations contained in the *Listing Agreement*. These include the publication, every year, of an interim statement, which is not audited, setting out key profit and loss account and balance sheet data in respect of the first six months of the company's financial year.
3. It is a growing practice for companies to produce house magazines or newsletters for employees. These summarize the company's results in a manner that is easy to assimilate and makes use of pictorial presentations such as bar charts, pie charts and graphs. Although produced principally for employees, it is not unusual for the information to be circulated to shareholders. It is also quite common for such data to be reproduced in the financial press.
4. Shareholders and debenture holders are entitled to attend the AGM where they have the opportunity to ask questions about past performance and the directors' future plans. It is not usual for these meetings to be heavily attended unless the company's affairs are the subject of some controversy, for example, where there is a contested takeover bid. Usually the directors are willing to answer reasonable questions, although they will tend to become evasive if asked for information considered to be particularly sensitive and unsuitable for public disclosure.
5. Shareholders, particularly institutional shareholders, may be able to obtain information about a company's affairs as the result of informal discussions with one or more of a company's directors, perhaps over lunch.

Information about a companys' affairs may also be obtained from *external* sources:

1. A limited company is under a legal obligation to file a copy of its accounts with the Registrar of Companies. This information is available for inspection at Companies House in London and in Cardiff. On payment of £3, an applicant is issued with a microfiche that can be taken away. This contains a copy of the company's accounts, a copy of the company's constitution, details of the company's share capital and debentures, details of each mortgage and charge on the assets of the company, a list of the directors and secretary and the address of the registered office. An extra charge is made for the list of shareholders.
2. Companies such as Extel publish cards setting out key statistics for each of the last ten years and an analysis of published results.

The remainder of this chapter examines a number of important respects in which a limited company's accounts differs from those prepared for sole traders and partnerships.

SHARE CAPITAL

The memorandum of association contains details of the share capital with which the company is to be initially registered and the division of that share capital into shares of a fixed amount. The figure for the company's registered share capital is described as the *authorized* share capital, and the face value of each share is called the 'nominal' or 'par' value. A company may be registered, for example, with an authorized share capital of £500,000 divided into 500,000 shares of £1 each. There is no fixed rule regarding the nominal value of each share, though £1 is often used.

There are a number of different categories of share capital – the two most common are *preference* shares and *ordinary* or *equity* shares. As the name implies, preference shares are given priority over ordinary shares as regards both payment of the annual dividend and repayment of capital on liquidation:

1. *Dividends* The annual dividend payable on preference shares is fixed at, say, 8 per cent per annum, and the dividend is usually paid if profits are sufficient. If profits are insufficient, the dividend is lost, unless cumulative preference shares have been issued, in which case any arrears must be paid, when trading results improve, before any dividend is paid to the ordinary shareholders. The dividend payable on ordinary shares is entirely at the discretion of the directors; if profits are low and/or the directors wish to retain all profits earned within the company, they may decide to pay no dividend whatsoever.
2. *Capital repayment* On liquidation of the company, business assets are applied, first, to settle outstanding liabilities and, second, to repay the preference shareholders the nominal value of their investment. Any balance remaining is paid out to the ordinary shareholders as they possess the equity interest in the concern. If a company is wound up because of financial difficulties, there is often nothing left over, for shareholders, after repaying creditors the amounts due.

The directors do not necessarily issue the company's entire authorized share capital at the outset. The figure initially registered represents the company's estimated financial requirements over, say, the next ten years. To begin with, however, the scale of activity may be relatively modest and the volume of shares issued should be restricted accordingly. The way in which the shares are issued may differ depending on whether the company is private or public. It is likely that the issued share capital of private companies will be acquired entirely by members of the first board of directors, and perhaps also their families and friends. In the case of a public company, an invitation may be made to the general public to acquire some, if not the whole, of the share capital the directors plan to issue. In the latter case the shares are advertised in the prospectus, the content of which is regulated by company law and, in the case of listed companies, also by the Stock Exchange rules.

Shareholders are not necessarily required to pay immediately the full price of the shares. For example, in the case of a £1 share issued at par, 15p may be payable when the shares are applied for, a further 25p when the shares are issued (called the allotment) and two further instalments, designated calls, of 30p each at some future date. Where shares are offered to the general public, it is extremely unusual for applications to match exactly the number of shares available for issue . If the issue is 50 per cent oversubscribed, one way of dealing with the problem is to issue each subscriber with two-thirds of the shares applied for. If the issue is undersubscribed it is likely to fail unless the company has taken the precaution of arranging for the issue to be underwritten. The function of the underwriter, often a finance house or an insurance company, is to guarantee the success of an issue by undertaking to subscribe for a new issue of shares to the extent it is not taken up by the general public. The transaction is in the nature of a speculation: if the issue is popular the underwriter receives a commission and does nothing; if the issue fails to attract the required number of subscriptions the underwriter is obliged to acquire shares for which there is little demand and whose price, initially, is likely to fall.

Griffin Ltd, a newly established private company, is registered with a share capital of £1,000,000 divided into 1,000,000 ordinary shares with a nominal value of £1 each. On 1 January 19X1, 400,000 shares are issued at par to members of the board of directors and paid for immediately in cash. **Example 10.1**

Prepare the capital section of Griffin's balance sheet as at 1 January 19X1. **Required**

Extracts from the Balance Sheet of Griffin Ltd as at 1 January 19X1 **Solution**

	£
Share capital:	
Authorized: 1,000,000 ordinary shares of £1 each	1,000,000
Issued: 400,000 ordinary shares of £1 each fully paid	400,000

The location of these items in a full balance sheet can be seen by referring back to Figure 10.2.

SHARE PREMIUM ACCOUNT

The initial issue of shares is normally made at par value and if, a few days later, one of the shareholders decides to sell his or her investment, he or she is likely to obtain a price not materially different from the issue price. This is because the prospects of the company are unlikely to have altered, materially, during the short space of time since the company was formed. As time goes by the position changes and, assuming the company is successful, the demand for its shares is likely to rise. Where this happens, the original shareholders are able to sell their shares at a profit to new investors. It must be recognized, however, that any rise or fall in the market price of the company's shares has no effect on the finances of the company itself, and the shares continue to be reported in the balance sheet at their issue price, which was £1 in the case of Griffin Ltd.

The directors may decide, at some later stage, to make a further issue of shares to help finance an expansion of the company's scale of operations. This additional issue will be made not at nominal value but at the best price then obtainable. If the market value of the shares has risen to £1.50, the issue price will be fixed at approximately that figure. An accounting problem arises because of a legal requirement that all share issues, not only the first, must be recorded in the share capital account at their nominal value. This problem is solved by recording any excess of the issue price over nominal value in a share premium account.

Example 10.2 Assume the same facts as in Example 10.1. Also, on 31 December 19X5, Griffin Ltd issues, for cash, a further 200,000 ordinary shares at a price of £1.50 each.

Required Prepare the capital section of Griffin's balance sheet as at 31 December 19X5, so far as the information permits.

Solution **Extracts from the Balance Sheet of Griffin Ltd at 31 December 19X5**

	£
Share capital	
Authorized: 1,000,000 ordinary shares of £1 each	1,000,000
Issued: 600,000 ordinary shares of £1 each fully paid	600,000
Share premium account	100,000

SHARE FORFEITURE

A subscriber to a new issue of shares sometimes pays his or her application money but defaults either when required to pay the amount due on allotment or on one of the later calls. This may happen because he or she is short of money or because he or she feels that the shares are no longer a good buy. Since he or she has contracted to acquire the shares, it is possible for the company to sue for the balance due but, even where the defaulting shareholder is perfectly solvent, this course of action is unlikely to be considered worthwhile. The directors are more likely to exercise their right, under the company's articles, to consider the shares forfeited. The directors then endeavour to find an investor who is willing to acquire the shares at a price at least equal to the balance outstanding. Any excess received is credited to share premium account.

Example 10.3 Thatchers Ltd is registered with a share capital of £500,000 divided into 1,000,000 ordinary shares with a nominal value of £0.50 each. On 1 January 19X2, 600,000 shares are issued with the agreement that £0.30 is paid immediately and the balance outstanding on 31 March 19X2. The appropriate amounts are received on the dates due, except that Broke, who acquired 500 shares on 1 January, defaults on the payment of the final call. On 1 June the shares are forfeited and reissued to Wealthy for £0.45 each.

Required Appropriate balance sheet extracts from the capital section of Thatchers Ltd's balance sheet at

(a) 1 January, after the shares have been issued; and
(b) 1 June, after Broke's shares have been forfeited and reissued to Wealthy.

(a) Extracts from the Balance Sheet of Thatchers Ltd at 1 January 19X2

	£
Share capital:	
Authorized: 1,000,000 ordinary shares of £0.50 each	500,000
Issued: 600,000 ordinary shares of £0.50, £0.30 paid	180,000

(b) Extracts from the Balance Sheet of Thatchers Ltd at 1 June 19X2

	£
Share capital:	
Authorized: 1,000,000 ordinary shares of £0.50 each	500,000
Issued: 600,000 ordinary shares of £0.50 each fully paid	300,000
Share premium account	125*

Note
*Collected from:		
	Broke, 500 × £.0.30	150
	Wealthy, 500 × £0.45	225
		375
Total collected		375
Less Nominal value of shares issued, 500 × £0.50		250
Surplus to share premium account		125

THE RIGHTS ISSUE

A rights issue occurs where a company requires additional capital and the shares are offered to existing shareholders on a pro-rata basis according to their existing holdings. If the share issue described in Example 10.2 was a rights issue, it would mean that the existing shareholders of Griffin Ltd were offered one new share at £1.50 each for every two shares presently held. Public companies are legally required to raise additional share capital by way of a rights issue, unless this course of action is impractical, in which case an invitation to subscribe may be made to the general public. A particular attraction to the company of the rights issue is that it is an inexpensive method of raising funds as the formalities associated with the issue are kept to a minimum, for example, a full prospectus need not be issued. From the shareholders' point of view an advantage of this procedure is that control of the company remains in the same hands.

LOAN CAPITAL AND DEBENTURES

A company's memorandum usually authorizes the directors to raise finance by borrowing money as well as by issuing shares. Such loans may be secured or unsecured. A secured loan normally takes the form of a 'debenture', which may be defined as 'the written acknowledgement of a debt usually made under seal'. The security for the loan may take the form of either a fixed charge or a floating charge on the company's assets. A fixed charge exists where the asset on which the loan is secured is specified in the debenture deed. Ideally the asset should be one likely to appreciate rather than depreciate in value over time, such as land and buildings. As a further protection, the company is prevented from selling the charged asset without the debenture holder's express approval. A floating charge exists where the debenture is secured on particular categories of assets, for example, stocks and debtors, or the assets of the company generally. This form of debenture gives the company greater flexibility, since it is allowed to trade in the assets subject to the floating charge, and their composition may well change on a daily basis.

Debentures are usually issued for a specified period of time, after which they are redeemed. The debenture deed will, however, provide for early repayment in certain circumstances. For example, should the company default on an interest payment, a receiver may be appointed by the debenture holders to take control of the secured assets, sell them and repay the amount owed. The main differences between debentures, unsecured loans and share capital are summarized below:

1. Loans carry interest at a fixed rate payable regardless of profit levels. Dividends, even on preference shares, are payable only if profits are sufficient, and the directors decide to make a distribution approved by the shareholders attending the AGM.
2. Loan interest is an allowable expense in calculating taxable profit; dividends are not an allowable expense.
3. Loan interest is debited to the profit and loss account; dividends are debited to the appropriation account (see later in this chapter).
4. Unsecured loans and debentures are reported in the balance sheet as a non-current liability and deducted from the balance of total assets less current liabilities (see Figure 10.3). Each year, of course, loans and debentures come closer to their redemption date, and they must be reclassified as a current liability when repayable during the forthcoming accounting period. Share capital is reported as part of the shareholders' equity.
5. Debentures enjoy priority of repayment on liquidation. Unsecured loans rank alongside other unsecured creditors, such as trade creditors. Share capital is repaid, on liquidation, only if resources remain after all liabilities have been satisfied.
6. Loans are almost always redeemable; share capital is redeemable only if a number of conditions are satisfied. In particular, the redemption must be met either out of a fresh issue of shares or out of profits available for distribution. To the extent the redemption is met out of distributable profits, an equivalent amount must be transferred to a non-distributable 'capital redemption reserve' so as to maintain intact the company's permanent capital.
7. A company may at any time purchase its own debentures in the market; these then remain available for reissue until cancelled. A company may purchase its own shares only if the conditions applicable when there is a redemption of shares are satisfied. Where a company purchases its own shares, they must be cancelled immediately.

THE APPROPRIATION ACCOUNT

Profit is calculated in the trading and profit and loss account; the way in which profit is split between taxation, dividends, transfers to reserves and retention is dealt with in the appropriate account (see Figure 10.3). These allocations are considered, in detail, in the next sections of this chapter.

Corporation tax

Sole traders and partnerships pay income tax on the profits arising from their business activities, whereas the profits of limited companies are subject to corporation tax. The rate of corporation tax differs, depending on the level of profits, and is set out in the budget and, later, incorporated in the annual Finance Act. For example, the Finance Act 1994 fixed the rate of corporation tax for companies whose profits do not exceed £300,000 at 25 per cent and for companies whose taxable profits are above £1.5 million at 33 per cent. Where a company has taxable profits between these two thresholds, corporation tax is paid at the rate of 25 per cent on profits up to £300,000 and 35 per cent on any excess. In the case of a profitable company, corporation tax may well represent the largest single cash outflow during an accounting period, and is therefore of considerable importance.

Corporation tax is levied on taxable profits, and readers must grasp that the figure for taxable profits is rarely the same as the profit figure reported in the company's accounts, which is called accounting profit. The reason for this is that the accountant and the government have different priorities when measuring profit. A good illustration concerns the treatment of capital expenditure. The aim of the accountant is to produce a profit figure that fairly represents the results of the firm for the year. For example, if it is estimated that an item of plant will last ten years, benefit the company equally each year and then be worthless, the accountant would consider it appropriate to make a *straight-line* depreciation charge of 10 per cent for each of those years. A major priority of the government is to ensure equity between taxpayers, and it is for this reason that they replace the depreciation charge, which may vary considerably from one company to another, with fixed rates of capital allowance, which are also laid down in the annual Finance Act. For example, the rate of capital allowance on plant and machinery is presently fixed at 25 per cent per annum on the *reducing balance basis*.

There are many other adjustments that produce less marked differences between accounting profit and taxable profit. For instance, the cost of entertainment, other than for overseas customers, is disallowed for tax purposes but would be treated as a business cost when accounting profit is computed.

Corporation tax is payable nine months after the end of the accounting period to which it relates. The corporation tax charge is disclosed in the profit and loss appropriation account as a deduction from net profit; in the balance sheet the amount payable appears as a current liability.

Example 10.4   Swan Ltd was incorporated on 1 January 19X1, issued 150,000 ordinary shares of £1 each for cash and commenced business on the same day. Plant, purchased at a cost of £130,000, was expected to possess a four-year life and be worth £10,000 at the end of that time. The company reported a profit of £90,000 for 19X1, after charging depreciation of £30,000.

Required   (a) A calculation of corporation tax payable for 19X1, so far as the information permits. For this purpose a writing-down allowance of 25 per cent and a corporation tax rate of 25 per cent are to be used.
(b) Relevant extracts from the appropriation account of Swan Ltd for 19X1.

Solution

	£
(a) Accounting profit	90,000
Add: Depreciation charge disallowed	30,000
	120,000
Less: Capital allowance (£130,000 × 25%)*	32,500
Taxable profit	87,500

Corporation tax payable, £87,500 × 25% = £21,875

Note
* The remaining balance (£130,000 − £32,500 = £97,500) is carried forward and claimed against profits in future years.

(b) **Profit and Loss Appropriation Account for 19X1**

	£
Net profit before tax	90,000
Less: Corporation tax	21,875
Net profit after tax	68,125

Dividends

Investors are willing to finance business activity because they expect that, at some future date, cash returns will exceed their initial investment by an amount sufficient to compensate them for risk and loss of liquidity. The investor in a limited company expects to receive cash returns in two forms, namely, dividends and the proceeds from the eventual sale of the shares. Under British company law it is for management to decide how much the firm can afford to pay as a dividend; the shareholders can only approve the amount proposed or choose to accept a lesser amount. This rule is designed to prevent shareholders from insisting on a level of payout that might undermine the financial position of the concern and prejudice the claims of creditors.

Dividends are expressed in terms of pence per share and appear as a deduction in the appropriation account. Where the directors are fairly confident that results for the year will be satisfactory, it is common practice to pay an interim dividend during the financial year. The final dividend is usually paid some months after the end of the financial year; the amount payable being decided upon when the accounts have been prepared and profit for the year established.

The directors rarely pay out the entire profits in the form of dividends, and shareholders are usually willing to accept a decision to retain resources within the company because, although they forgo immediate income, the expectation is that reinvestment will produce greater future returns. Management usually aims for a reasonable balance between distributions and retentions, although in relatively good years the proportion distributed may be rather lower than in poor years when the bulk of the reported profits may be paid out as dividends to demonstrate management's confidence in the future viability of the concern.

Where the current year's profit is insufficient, dividends can be declared on the basis of undistributed profits brought forward. Where there are accumulated losses brought forward, these must first be made good before a dividend is paid out of the current year's profit.

Example 10.5

Hanbury Ltd has an authorized and issued share capital of £400,000 divided into 800,000 ordinary shares of 50p each. The company made a net profit of £200,000 during 19X1 and, in July of that year, the directors paid an interim dividend of 3p per share. The directors decide to recommend a final dividend of 7p per share, making a total of 10p per share for the year. The retained profit at 1 January 19X1 amounted to £94,000. A provision for corporation tax of £75,000 is to be made on the profits for the year.

Required

The profit and loss appropriation account of Hanbury for 19X1.

Solution

Profit and Loss Appropriation Account of Hanbury Ltd for 19X1

	£	£
Net profit before tax		200,000
Less: Corporation tax		75,000
		────
		125,000
Less: Dividends: Paid	24,000	80,000
Proposed	56,000	────
Retained profit for 19X1	────	45,000
Retained profit at 1 January 19X1		94,000
		────
Retained profit at 31 December 19X1		139,000
		────

Advance and mainstream corporation tax

The payment of a dividend gives rise to an obligation to make an advance payment of corporation tax to the Inland Revenue. The calculation of the amount of the advance payment depends on the basic rate of income tax; for the fiscal year 1994–5, it is calculated by multiplying the dividend by the fraction 20/80. The payment of a dividend of £80,000 therefore gives rise to the need to pay £80,000 × 20/80 = £20,000 to the Inland Revenue.

Advance corporation tax (ACT) is payable on the quarterly date (31 March, 30 June, 30 September, 31 December) following payment of the related dividend. The amount paid over may be offset against the corpora-tion tax charge debited to the profit and loss account in respect of the accounting period during which the ACT payment is made. Assuming a company makes up its accounts on the calendar-year basis, this means that ACT paid *during* 1994 can be offset against corporation tax levied on profits earned during 1994. The balance of corporation tax then remaining out-standing is called mainstream corporation tax (MCT) and is reported in the balance sheet as a current liability. If a final dividend is proposed, for 1994, it is not paid until 1995 and the related ACT is paid some weeks or months afterwards. ACT paid in respect of the final dividend may, therefore, be offset only against tax levied on the profits for 1995. The effect of the ACT regulations is to speed up the payment of corporation tax, but the total amount paid over to the Inland Revenue remains the same.

As far as the shareholders are concerned, they receive dividends net of income tax at the basic rate. For example, the shareholders receiving £80,000, in cash, are deemed to have received a gross dividend of £100,000 from which tax (at the rate of 20 per cent) has been deducted at source. There will be no further liability to income tax unless the shareholder pays higher-rate tax. If, for some reason, a shareholder is not liable to tax at all, for example, because unused personal allowances are available, the tax deducted at source may be reclaimed from the Inland Revenue.

Provisions and reserves

A *provision* is legally defined as any amount written off or retained by way of providing for depreciation, renewals or diminution in the value of assets or retained by way of providing for any known liability of which the amount cannot be determined with substantial accuracy. This definition covers three basic accounting adjustments:

1. The amount written off fixed assets by way of depreciation.
2. The amount written off current assets or investments to reflect the fact that book value exceeds the amount that is ultimately expected to be recoverable. Examples are a provision for bad debts or any provision necessary to reduce stock to net realizable value.
3. The amount set aside to meet a known liability, the amount of which cannot be accurately estimated. This may arise where a company is in breach of contract with an employee, but the amount of damages payable is yet to be decided. A second example is a provision for taxation.

A *reserve* is a transfer made out of profits at the directors' discretion. The reason for retaining profits, as reserves, may be to help finance expansion, to enable dividends to be declared in a future year when profits are low, to ear-mark funds for the redemption of share capital or debentures (see later in this chapter) or to meet unknown contingencies at the date of the accounts.

The distinction between provisions and reserves is very important because it affects the measurement of profit and the way financial informa-tion is presented in the annual accounts. A provision is a cost of carrying on business activity whereas a transfer to reserves is not. Provisions are therefore charged *above the line* (in the profit and loss account) and affect reported profits, whereas transfers to reserves are made *below the line* (in the appropriation account) and leave reported profit unaffected. Clearly it is important for management to identify accurately whether a particular item is in the nature of a provision or a reserve. Equally important, care must be taken when the amount of a provision is estimated, since any under- or over-provision will directly affect the accuracy of the reported profit figure.

For example, let us assume a company is sued by an employee for unfair dismissal and that the company expects the court to allow its former employee damages amounting to £6,000. A provision for this amount is made when computing the reported profit, of £50,000, for 19X1. If the court subsequently awards damages of £15,000, it is clear that the company's liabilities, at 31 December 19X1, have been understated by £9,000 and that profits, for 19X1, have been overstated by a similar figure. If the directors had succeeded in forecasting accurately the damages payable, a profit of £41,000 would have been reported for 19X1.

In the balance sheet provisions are either

1. deducted from the value of the asset to which they relate, e.g. depreciation of fixed assets; or
2. included as a current liability, e.g. provision for taxation.

Reserves, on the other hand, remain part of the shareholders' interest and are listed after issued share capital and any balance on share premium account on the face of the balance sheet (see Figure 10.3).

Most of the matters discussed so far in this chapter are contained in Example 10.6.

Example 10.6

Miskin Ltd commenced business on 1 January 19X2 and the following trial balance was extracted as at 31 December 19X2:

	£	£
Share capital		380,000
8% debentures repayable 19X9		100,000
10% unsecured loan repayable 30 June 19X3		20,000
Tangible fixed assets at cost	480,000	
Gross profit		152,000
Trade debtors	61,500	
Trade creditors		37,870
Bank balance	7,400	
Bad debts written off	320	
Administration and selling expenses	63,200	
Interest paid, 30 June 19X2	5,000	
Interim dividend paid	12,000	
Stock-in-trade at 31 December 19X2	60,450	
	689,870	689,870

The following additional information is provided:

1. The authorized share capital is £500,000 divided into ordinary shares of £1 each. The balance on the share capital account represents the proceeds from issuing 300,000 shares.

2. A provision for doubtful debts is to be made of 2 per cent on outstanding trade debtors.
3. Depreciation is to be charged on fixed assets at the rate of 4 per cent on cost.
4. The directors propose to recommend a final dividend of 5p per share.
5. Corporation tax of £18,000 is to be provided on the profits for 19X2.
6. A transfer of £10,000 is to be made to dividend equalization reserve.

Required

(a) A profit and loss account and an appropriation account for 19X2.
(b) A balance sheet at 31 December 19X2.

Solution

(a) **Profit and Loss Account and Appropriation Account for 19X2**

	£	£
Gross profit		152,000
Less: Administration and selling expenses	63,200	
Bad and doubtful debts, £320 + (2% of £61,500)	1,550	
Interest, £5,000 + £5,000 (1 July–31 Dec. 19X2)	10,000	
Provision for depreciation (4% of £480,000)	19,200	93,950
Net profit before tax		58,050
Less: Corporation tax		18,000
Net profit after tax		40,050
Less: Dividends: Paid	12,000	
Proposed (5p × 300,000)	15,000	
Transfer to dividend equalization reserve	10,000	37,000
Retained profit for 19X2		3,050

(b) **Balance Sheet at 31 December 19X2**

	£	£
Fixed assets		
Tangible assets at cost		480,000
Less: Accumulated depreciation		19,200
		460,800
Current assets		
Stocks	60,450	
Trade debtors (£61,500 – £1,230)	60,270	
Bank	7,400	
	128,120	
Less: Current liabilities		
Unsecured loan repayable 30 June 19X3	20,000	
Trade creditors	37,870	
Taxation due 30 September 19X3	18,000	
Dividend payable	15,000	
Accrual for interest owed	5,000	
	95,870	

	£
Working capital	32,250
Total assets less current liabilities	493,050
Less: Non-current liabilities	
8% debentures repayable 19X9	100,000
	393,050
Financed by:	
Share capital	
Authorized: 500,000 ordinary shares of £1 each	500,000
Issued: 300,000 ordinary shares of £1 each	300,000
Share premium account (£380,000 – £300,000)	80,000
Dividend equalization reserve	10,000
Retained profit	3,050
	393,050

Readers should now work Questions 10.1, 10.2 and 10.3 at the end of this chapter.

REVALUATION RESERVE

Despite determined efforts on the part of successive governments to control inflation, prices have risen almost continuously since 1940. The process has had a significant effect on the usefulness of accounting statements based on the historical cost concept. The major balance sheet items, fixed assets and stocks, are reported at their original cost less, where appropriate, depreciation to comply with this concept. However, fixed assets may have been acquired many years ago when prices were much lower than is the case today; therefore these assets are often reported in the balance sheet at figures far removed from their current value to the concern. This descrepancy has caused many individuals to question the usefulness of the balance sheet as a statement of a company's financial position, and uneasiness increased with the acceleration in the rate of inflation during the 1970s. The revaluation reserve was developed as a means of restoring an acceptable measure of reality to the corporate balance sheet. The adjustment is quite straightforward:

1. The book value of the fixed asset is increased from historical cost less depreciation to the revalued figure.
2. The surplus arising on revaluation is credited to revaluation reserve, which is reported as part of the shareholders' equity in the balance sheet (see Figure 10.3).

The adjustment is entered in the books as follows:

Debit	Credit	With
Revaluation account	Fixed asset at cost account	Historical cost of fixed asset
Provision for depreciation account	Revaluation account	Accumulated depreciation
Fixed asset at revaluation account	Revaluation account	New valuation
Revaluation account	Revaluation reserve	Surplus arising on revaluation

The revaluation reserve is therefore an exception to the general rule that reserves are created as the result of transfers from reported profit.

Example 10.7 The following information is extracted from the balance sheet of Messange plc at 31 December 19X4:

	£000
Freehold land and buildings at cost	2,100
Less: Accumulated depreciation	1,300
	800

The land and buildings were revalued by a firm of chartered surveyors at £5,000,000 on 31 December 19X4. The directors have decided to use the revalued figure for the purpose of the accounts.

Required
(a) The revaluation account of Messange to record the above changes.
(b) Relevant extracts from the balance sheet of Messange plc, at 31 December 19X4.

Solution
(a) **Revaluation Account**

	£000		£000
Fixed asset account	2,100	Accumulated depreciation	1,300
Revaluation reserve	4,200	Fixed asset account	5,000
	6,300		6,300

(b) **Balance Sheet extracts**

	£000
Freehold land and buildings at revalued amount	5,000
Revaluation reserve	4,200

Today some large companies and nationalized industries supplement their historical cost based accounting reports with financial statements fully adjusted to take account of the effect of changing price levels. This important development in corporate financial reporting procedures is the outcome of the inflation accounting debate that raged between 1970 and 1985. Inflation accounting techniques are examined at a more advanced stage of your financial accounting studies.

REDEMPTION OF DEBENTURES

It is essential that the directors plan a company's finances carefully and, in particular, ensure that a proper balance between short-term, medium-term and long-term funds is achieved. Both share capital and loan capital fall into the category of long-term finance, but share capital may be redeemable and loan capital will invariably be redeemable at some future date. It is management's job to ensure that the long-term capital base is not eroded as a result of the redemption. Indeed, in the case of share capital, the directors are under a strict legal obligation to ensure that this does not happen.

Company law imposes no conditions regarding the redemption of debentures. Debenture holders are treated in law as creditors rather than as providers of permanent capital. Consequently, there exists no requirement that the company should take steps to replace the resources paid out when redemption occurs. However, such obligations may either be imposed by the company's articles of association or be assumed voluntarily by the directors. Debentures may be repayable gradually over a period of years or, at the other extreme, the total amount borrowed may be repayable on a single future date. The effect on the company's finances will be less marked in the former situation, and it is often possible to make the necessary repayments out of cash generated from trading operations. In these circumstances the directors may transfer a sum, equal to the value of debentures redeemed, from profits to a debenture redemption reserve in order to acknowledge the fact that resources have been used in this way.

The debentures of Arches Ltd. are repayable by ten equal annual instalments of £10,000 commencing 31 December 19X1. The relevant balance sheet extracts, immediately before the first repayment are as follows: **Example 10.8**

Balance Sheet extracts at 31 December 19X1

	£
Issued ordinary share capital	200,000
Profit and loss account balance	50,000
Shareholders equity	250,000
Debentures redeemable by ten equal instalments, 19X1–19Y0	100,000

The company redeems one-tenth of the debentures on 31 December 19X1, at par, and transfers a similar amount from profit to debenture redemption reserve.

Revised extracts from the balance sheet of Arches after the first repayment   **Required**
of debentures has taken place.

Solution

Balance Sheet extracts as at 31 December 19X1

	£
Issued ordinary share capital	200,000
Debenture redemption reserve	10,000
Profit and loss account balance (£50,000 − £10,000)	40,000
Shareholders equity	250,000
Debentures redeemable by nine equal instalments, 19X2–19Y0	90,000

Note
The company's cash balance will also be reduced by £10,000.

Where the debentures are to be repaid on a single date, transfers to the debenture redemption reserve may be made over a number of years in anticipation of this event. Additional action must be taken, of course, to ensure that the necessary amount of cash is available to finance repayment when it falls due. One approach is to invest separately, each year, an amount of cash equal to the figure transferred to the debenture redemption reserve. These investments may be described, in the balance sheet, as 'debenture redemption investment fund', and the balance on this account appears as a separate item among the current assets of the company. The investments are sold, when the redemption date approaches, and the debentures redeemed out of the proceeds. The debenture redemption investment fund is seldom employed today.

The balance to the credit of the debenture redemption reserve remains legally available for distribution but, in reality, it forms part of the company's permanent capital. To acknowledge this fact, a further transfer may be made from debenture redemption reserve to a non-distributable capital redemption reserve after the redemption has taken place; a second alternative is to capitalize the credit balance on debenture redemption reserve by making a bonus issue (see the next section).

BONUS (CAPITALIZATION, SCRIP) ISSUE OF SHARES

Figure 10.5 shows a typical balance sheet of a manufacturing company that has traded successfully for a number of years and financed a great deal of its expansion out of retained profits. Over the years Star has generated and retained profits amounting to £575,000 and the whole of this amount is legally available for distribution to the shareholders of the company. An examination of the information contained in the balance sheet in Figure 10.5 clearly shows that, in practice, the company would find it difficult to pay any dividend whatsoever. The company has a cash balance of just £2,000 to meet day-to-day cash outgoings and there is a bank overdraft of £136,000. Clearly the profits retained in the company, although initially in the form of cash, have since been reinvested in business assets. Consequently, although £575,000 remains legally available for distribution, in practice the company is unable to adopt this course of action. It is therefore argued that the equity section of the balance sheet does not fairly represent the financial position of Star.

	£	£
Fixed assets		
Plant and machinery at cost		850,000
Less: Accumulated depreciation		360,000
		490,000
Current assets		
Stock and work in progress	426,000	
Trade debtors and prepayments	250,000	
Cash-in-hand	2,000	
	678,000	
Less: Current liabilities		
Trade creditors and accruals	207,000	
Bank overdraft	136,000	
	343,000	
Net current assets		335,000
		825,000
Financed by		
Share capital (£1 ordinary shares)		250,000
Reserves (all distributable)		575,000
		825,000

Figure 10.5   Balance Sheet of Star plc as at 31 December 19X1

The directors are able to rectify the position by converting reserves into share capital. The procedure followed is to issue shareholders with additional shares in proportion to their existing holdings, and to make necessary adjustments to the relevant ledger accounts. The process is described as a capitalization of profits and the share issue to existing investors is called a bonus issue or a scrip issue. The adjustment is entered in the books as follows:

Debit	Credit	With
Retained profit (or reserves)	Share capital	The amount of the bonus issue

Assuming the directors of Star make a bonus issue of two shares for every one share presently held, the capital section of the balance sheet is revised as follows:

Balance Sheet extract, Star plc as at 31 December 19X1

Financed by:	£
Share capital (£1 shares)	750,000
Reserves	75,000
	825,000

The term 'bonus issue' is misleading. The implication is that the shareholder has received some additional financial benefit he or she did not previously enjoy. This is not the case. It is true that after the issue has taken place each shareholder holds three times as many shares, but the company receives nothing extra and its profit earning potential remains unchanged. This can be demonstrated by examining the net asset value per share both before and after the bonus issue:

Net asset value per share

$$\text{Before} \qquad \frac{£825,000}{£250,000} \quad = \quad £3.30$$

$$\text{After} \qquad \frac{£825,000}{£750,000} \quad = \quad £1.10$$

A person who initially owned 100 shares had a total interest in the book value of the company's net assets of $100 \times £3.30 = £330$. After the bonus issue he or she owns 300 shares, but their underlying asset value has fallen to £1.10 each and the total book value of his or her interest remains unchanged at £330 ($300 \times £1.10$). The market price of the share falls by a similar proportion to reflect the larger number of shares in circulation.

It has been noted earlier that the source of a bonus issue of shares is not limited to distributable profits; in particular, balances on the share premium account, revaluation reserve, debenture redemption reserve and capital redemption reserve may be applied in this way.

Readers should now attempt Questions 10.4, 10.5 and 10.6 at the end of this chapter.

GROUPS OF COMPANIES

There has been a substantial increase in the average size of the business unit during the present century which started with many industries still characterized by the 'one man business'. Today the sole trader remains an important feature of business life but, in many industries, large-scale limited liability is dominant. This development has occurred as the result of both internal and external growth.

Internal expansion is brought about by the reinvestment of profits, whereas external growth involves combining together the activities of two or more separate entities in either of two ways: by purchasing either the assets of another business or its shares in order to obtain effective control of its operations. There are many reasons for business combinations, which include the desire to safeguard essential sources of raw material or to guarantee wholesale and retail outlets for the products the company manufactures. The economic term used to describe the process whereby companies expand backwards or forwards along the chain of production and distribution is vertical integration. In contrast, horizontal integration occurs when companies at the same stage in the chain join together; this strategy may be adopted in order to reduce competition and perhaps also to reap some of the benefits commonly associated with large-scale production. Diversification occurs when companies expand into unrelated fields for such reasons as risk spreading or to utilize available funds when there is no room for further expansion in their present line of business.

The accounting problems associated with either of these types of business combination are not the subject for an introductory textbook. However, students should have an appreciation of the nature and impact of business combination and so a few further comments are in order.

A combination based on the purchase of assets is dealt with in a straightforward manner. The assets acquired are revalued and incorporated into the purchasing company's books; any excess of price paid over the value attached to the assets purchased is attributed to goodwill. Once this has been done, the assets are subsequently accounted for in the normal way.

A combination based on the purchase of shares arises where one company acquires sufficient shares in another to achieve effective control of its operations. For example, company A may acquire the entire share capital of company B. In these circumstances the arrangement is made between company A and the *shareholders* of company B; a transaction does not affect company B directly and it remains in existence as a separate legal entity. The reason for basing a combination on the acquisition of shares rather than assets are as follows:

- *Economy*   It is not necessary to purchase all the target company's shares, merely enough to ensure effective control of its operations.
- *Continuity*   Where the acquired company maintains a separate identity, its goodwill is more likely to survive unimpaired.
- *Decentralization*   Decentralization of both managerial and decision-making processes is facilitated where companies retain their own identity.

Combinations based on shares give rise to a group of companies within which the company that purchases the shares is called the 'holding company' and the company whose shares are acquired is called the 'subsidiary'. The relationship between these is demonstrated in Figure 10.6. HC plc purchases the entire share capital of SC Ltd. The arrow in Figure 10.6 indicates that HC is the holding company and SC is the subsidiary, while the percentage superimposed on the arrow indicates the extent of the shareholding. Together HC and SC comprise a group of companies.

Figure 10.6   Relationship between holding company and subsidiary company

The shares in the subsidiary may be purchased for cash or in exchange for shares in the holding company, and the impact on the balance sheet of the holding company is indicated in Example 10.9.

Example 10.9

A Limited purchases 50,000 shares with a par value of £1 each in B Limited. The agreed price is £70,000.

Required

State the effect of this transaction on the balance sheet of A Limited assuming

(a) the transaction is paid for in cash; and
(b) the purchase consideration is satisfied by the issue of 40,000 shares in A Limited each with a par value of £1.

Solution

(a) The balance of cash in the balance sheet of A Limited is reduced by £70,000 and there appears instead an asset described as 'Investment in subsidiary £70,000'.
(b) The investment in the subsidiary is again shown at £70,000. The corresponding credit entries are to increase the issue share capital of A Limited by £40,000 with the excess of £30,000 to share premium account.

One company does not need to purchase the entire share capital of another for the latter to become its subsidiary – merely sufficient shares to obtain effective control of its operations. Acquisition of over 50 per cent of the voting share capital will normally be sufficient to achieve that objective.

The Companies Acts impose additional reporting requirements on holding companies. They must prepare both a profit and loss account and a balance sheet that cover the entire affairs of the group they control. In other words, the profit and loss account reports the combined turnover, costs and profits (or the share attributable to the holding company) of the holding company and its subsidiaries, while the group balance sheet combines together the assets and liabilities of the constituent companies. Where only a proportion of the shares are acquired, the amount of profit attributable to 'minority interests' must be shown in the profit and loss account and the proportion of assets attributable to them must be shown in the balance sheet (see Figure 1.2 which contains the relevant figures in relation to The Boots Company plc for 1993).

Almost all companies of significant size in the UK are holding companies. The largest have many subsidiaries. For example, the most recently published accounts for The Boots Company plc list 38 subsidiaries and those of Guinness plc 57.

Readers should now attempt Question 10.7 at the end of this chapter.

LIMITATIONS OF COMPANY ACCOUNTS

There is general agreement that shareholders and other external users find company accounts a useful basis for performance assessment and decision-making. At the same time it is accepted that they suffer from a number of important deficiencies. Some criticisms are as follows:

1. The accounts are usually well out of date. If they are prepared on a calendar-year basis, they are unlikely to be available until March or April of the following year. These will be of limited use to, say, a potential creditor as the financial position of a company may have changed dramatically since the accounts were prepared.

2. The information contained in the accounts is based on original cost rather than current value. For example, a freehold property purchased in 1950, for £100,000, might still be reported at this figure despite the fact that it is today worth £5 million. Most people would agree that this is absurd, but the use of £100,000 is fully in accordance with accepted accounting procedures.

3. The balance sheet reports some, but by no means all, the assets belonging to an organization. In broad terms, an asset must possess a fairly readily identifiable cash value for it to be reported in the accounts. Certain assets, although extremely valuable, do not possess this characteristic and are not reported. For example, the favourable trading connections or 'goodwill' of a company, built up over the years, is omitted from the accounts.

4. Annual accounts are past history, whereas the user wants to know what is likely to happen to a company in the future. Last year's accounts may show a good profit and a stable financial position , but trading conditions are subject to constant change, and a series of setbacks may result in heavy losses and a rapid deterioration in the company's financial structure.

Demands for the publication of information about future financial developments, such as cash forecasts and profit forecasts, have been resisted by management and accountants for a number of reasons that include the problem of accurately forecasting future results, the scope which forecasts provide for management to take an overoptimistic view of likely future outcomes and the difficulties that would arise for the auditor if he or she was required to report on the reliability of forecast data. It is interesting to note, however, that management overcomes its opposition to the publication of forecasts when its company is under threat. For example, the directors often publish profit forecasts as a defensive measure to counter an unwelcome takeover bid. In general, however, information about future developments is restricted to the broad comments made by the chairperson in his or her report.

It must therefore be admitted that, although the improvement of financial reporting procedures continues to be the aim of most businessmen and women and accountants, much work remains to be done. The above limitations must therefore be borne in mind in assessing the usefulness of information reported in company accounts.

Questions

10.1 The following information is provided in respect of the affairs of Newton Ltd, a trading company, for 19X0 and 19X1:

Draft Profit and Loss Account, year to 31 December

	19X0	19X1
	£000	£000
Administration expenses	1,620	1,809
Selling costs	520	572
Distribution costs	140	164
Transfer to general reserve	—	500
Depreciation charge	250	300
Proposed dividend	100	200
Balance of profit	300	60
	2,930	3,605

Draft Balance Sheet, 31 December

	£000	£000
Debit balances:		
Stock	724	771
Debtors	570	524
Plant and machinery at cost	1,840	2,650
Cash at bank	92	305
	3,226	4,250
Credit balances:		
Trade creditors	416	480
Provision for depreciation	520	820
General reserve	—	500
Dividend	100	200
Share capital (£1 shares)	1,600	1,600
Profit and loss account	590	650
	3,226	4,250

Required

(a) Redraft the above accounts in order to make them more informative. The profit and loss account should show figures for gross profit, net profit and retained profit; the balance sheet should include an appropriate classification of assets and liabilities.

(b) Comment on the view expressed by one of Newton Ltd's directors that the company should not pay the proposed increased dividend because profits have declined.

10.2 The following trial balance was extracted from the accounts of Minto plc at 31 October 1986:

	£	£
Called-up share capital		200,000
Share premium		100,000
12% debentures		225,000
Fixed assets at cost:		
Freehold premises at cost	435,000	

Machinery and equipment	60,000	
Motor lorries	225,000	
Provisions for depreciation to 1 November 1985:		
Freehold premises		30,000
Machinery and equipment		24,000
Motor lorries		62,000
Sales		791,600
Discounts allowed	14,200	
Discounts received		9,800
Purchases	458,200	
Debtors and creditors	54,100	31,400
Provision for doubtful debts at 1 November 1985		3,700
Bad debts	2,900	
Wages and salaries	68,400	
Administrative expenses	32,800	
Research and development expenditure	9,600	
Debenture interest paid	13,500	
Directors' remuneration	40,000	
Retained profits at 1 November 1985		115,200
Stock at 1 November 1985	113,400	
Goodwill at cost	30,000	
Bank balance	35,600	
	1,592,700	1,592,700

Additional information relevant to the year ended 31 October 1986 is as follows:

(i) Share capital is divided into 200,000 ordinary shares of £1 each and is all issued and fully paid.

(ii) Stock held at 31 October 1986 is detailed as follows:

	Cost	Net realizable value
Category – small	£36,200	£26,700
Category – large	£47,800	£58,600
Category – magnum	£56,300	£46,800

(iii) The provision for doubtful debts is to be increased to £4,500.

(iv) Provision is to be made for depreciation as to

machinery and equipment at 10 per cent per annum of cost;
motor lorries at 20 per cent per annum of cost; and
freehold premises – £6,000.

(v) Corporation tax on the profits of the year is to be provided for at £33,000.

(vi) Goodwill is to be amortized at 20 per cent of cost.

(vii) A machinery replacement reserve is to be created of £15,000.

(viii) An ordinary share dividend is proposed at the rate of 10p per share.

(ix) Wages and motor expenses accruals amount to £1,500 and £900 respectively.

Required

(a) Trading and profit and loss account for the year ended 31 October 1986.

(15 marks)

(b) The balance sheet as on the above date in vertical format, and with appropriate subtotals.   *(10 marks)*

(Total: 25 marks)

(ICSA, Introduction to Accounting, December, 1986)

10.3 (a) Within the field of periodic financial reporting, comment on and distinguish between 'accounting bases' and 'accounting polices' and relate them to the following fundamental accounting concepts:

(i)   The 'going concern' concept.
(ii) The 'accruals' concept.
(iii) The 'consistency' concept.
(iv) The 'prudence' concept.

(13 marks)

(b) Explain how the directors of a company attempt to ensure that the annual published financial statements portray a 'true and fair view'.

(12 marks)

(Total: 25 marks)

(ICSA, Financial Accounting l, December, 1984)

10.4 The following trial balance was extracted from the books of Porchester Ltd on 31 March 19X6:

	£	£
Ordinary share capital (£1 shares)		500,000
Retained profit to 1 April 19X5		1,039,000
10% debentures repayable 19X9		300,000
Freehold land and buildings at cost	400,000	
Plant and machinery at cost	1,300,000	
Provision for depreciation on plant and machinery at 1 April 19X5		512,000
Debtors and prepayments (including trade debtors, £360,000)	370,080	
Stock and work-in-progress at 31 March 19X6	984,020	
Bank balance	268,000	
Provision for doubtful debts at 31 March 19X6		15,000
Creditors and accrued expenses		351,500
Gross profit for the year		1,020,800
Administration expenses	216,900	
Selling expenses	150,400	
Bad debts written off	8,700	
General repairs and maintenance	25,200	
Debenture interest to 30 September 19X5	15,000	
	3,738,300	3,738,300

Additional information is provided as follows:

1. The company's freehold property was revalued at £900,000 on 1 October 19X5. The directors have decided to use this figure for the purpose of the accounts.
2. The company made a bonus issue of two ordinary shares, fully paid, for each share held on 1 October 19X5. No entry has been made in the books in respect of the issue.
3. The directors propose to pay a dividend of 5 pence per share of the ordinary share capital at 31 March 19X6.
4. The company purchased additional plant costing £120,000 on 31 March 19X6. The plant was delivered to the company's premises on that date together with the purchase invoice to be paid within seven days, but no entry has been made in the books in respect of the transaction.
5. Depreciation is to be provided at 25 per cent, reducing balance, on all plant and machinery owned by the company at the year end, except the plant referred to under 4 above. Ignore depreciation of freehold property.
6. Corporation tax of £150,000, due for payment on 1 January 19X7, is to be provided out of the trading profit for the year.
7. The company's authorized share capital is £2,000,000 divided into ordinary shares of £1 each.

Required

The profit and loss account and profit and loss appropriation account of Porchester Ltd for the year ended 31 March 19X6, together with the balance sheet at that date. Particular attention should be given to layout, although the accounts need not necessarily be in a form appropriate for publication.

10.5 What is the purpose of a bonus issue of shares? Using the information prepared in your answer to Question 10.4, consider whether the issue was reasonable in amount.

10.6 The trial balance of Southgate plc at 31 December 19X9 was as follows:

	£	£
Ordinary share capital (shares £1 each)		500,000
Freehold property at cost	500,000	
Furniture and equipment at cost	375,000	
Provision for depreciation of furniture and equipment, 1 January 19X9		59,500
Debtors and prepayments	105,000	
Stock and work-in-progress at 31 December 19X9	104,200	
Creditors and accruals		85,300
Balance at bank	72,000	
Gross profit on trading		416,500
Rent and rates	30,000	
Office salaries	142,600	
Advertising costs	21,000	
Transport costs	23,600	
Profit and loss account balance, 1 January 19X9		278,500
Taxation due but unpaid on 19X8 profits		103,600
Deposit on new equipment	10,000	
Temporary investment	60,000	
	1,443,400	1,443,400

You are given the following additional information:

1. The company has contracted to purchase new equipment at a cost of £50,000. A deposit of £10,000 was paid during December 19X9 and the remainder will be paid during January when delivery is expected.
2. Depreciation is to be provided on furniture and equipment, other than the new equipment referred to under 1, at the rate of 10 per cent on cost.
3. The figure for rent and rates in the above trial balance covers the 15 months to 31 March 19Y0.
4. During December 19X9 the company used part of the profit and loss account balance at 1 January 19X9 to make a bonus issue of one new share for every five shares already held. The issue was made at par but has not yet been written into the books.
5. During November 19X9 the company's freehold premises were valued at £650,000 by a firm of professional valuers. The company's directors have decided to write the revaluation into the 19X9 accounts and credit the surplus arising to revaluation reserve.
6. Taxation is to be provided at 50 per cent on the company's net profit from trading operations.

Required

(a) The profit and loss account of Southgate for 19X9 and balance sheet at 31 December 19X9. Each accounting statement should be presented in vertical format.
(b) Your comments on the suggestion, from one director, that the company should pay a dividend of 10p per share on the issued share capital in view of the large bank balance and the fact that no dividend was paid for 19X8.

Note
Ignore depreciation of freehold property.

10.7 The following information is available for three companies, Lander plc, Yelstet plc and Oviedo plc, as at 31 December 1992, and after the preparation of the annual accounts:

	Lander plc £000	Yelstet plc £000	Oviedo plc £000
Issued share capital:			
£1 ordinary shares, fully paid	1,500	700	—
25p ordinary shares, fully paid	—	—	100
£1 11% preference shares, fully paid	400	—	200
Share premium	1,100	450	500
General reserve	600	200	150
Retained earnings	750	280	110
9% debentures 2,005	—	400	—
Current liabilities	550	350	400
Fixed assets	2,300	1,510	960
Current assets	1,900	870	500
Investment in Yelstet plc			
350,000 £1 ordinary shares at cost	700	—	—

Additional information:

1. Lander plc had paid the preference share dividend for the year and had also declared a final ordinary dividend for the year of 5p a share.

2. For the year ended 31 December 1992, the net trading profits for each of the companies were:

	£000
Lander plc	350
Yelstet plc	110
Oviedo plc	90

3. The directors of Lander plc had made a transfer of £200,000 to general reserve on 31 December 1992.
4. After the completion of the annual accounts Oviedo plc made a bonus issue of one ordinary share for every two shares held. The issue was funded from the share premium account.
5. Lander plc wanted to strengthen its market position within the European Community. Thus it decided to acquire the following shares; the terms of issue were agreed by the companies involved:

    (i) 50,000 ordinary £1 shares in Yelstet plc at £2.50 per share. The transaction was settled in cash.
    (ii) 320,000 ordinary 25p shares in Oviedo plc. It was agreed that the shares in Oviedo plc were to be valued at £1 a share. Lander plc issued £250,000 new £1 convertible stock at par with the balance in cash to the ordinary shareholders in Oviedo plc who had accepted the offer.

    This share purchase occurred after Oviedo plc had made the bonus issue.

Required

(a) A profit and loss appropriation account for Lander plc for the year ended 31 December 1992.   *(10 marks)*
(b) A balance sheet for Lander plc after the acquisition and issue of shares as identified in item (5) above.   *(16 marks)*
(c) Explain what is meant by a subsidiary company. By making appropriate calculations determine whether Yelstet plc and Oviedo plc are subsidiaries of Lander plc.

    Your calculations should be made after taking into account items (4) and (5) above.   *(14 marks)*
(d) Explain why Lander plc believes that after acquiring further shares in Yelstet plc and Oviedo plc it will be able to strengthen its market position. Identify any further advantages that may accrue to Lander plc.   *(10 marks)*

11
SOME SPECIALIZED ACCOUNTING TECHNIQUES

The objectives of this chapter are to

- demonstrate how to prepare a manufacturing account;
- show how to analyse and report information on a departmental basis;
- explain how to use the double entry system to prepare the accounts of an organization with branches;
- outline the use of instalment credit arrangements and how they are recorded in the books of the seller and buyer;
- demonstrate the accounting entries to record the transfer of a business;
- outline the operation of value added tax and show how it is recorded; and
- show how accounting techniques can be used to identify losses of stock and cash.

INTRODUCTION

The techniques of information collection and analysis described so far have related mainly to trading concerns that operate in a single location and buy and sell goods without further processing; transactions where the amount due is settled in one payment, either immediately or in the near future; and the 'going' concern. There are many occasions when the activities of a business or the information requirements of ownership, management or other interested parties, such as the firm's bankers, do not fit into this framework. This chapter covers the specialized accounting techniques to be used in the following instances:

1. Businesses concerned with manufacturing which buy raw materials and other supplies and spend further sums to process them into finished goods.
2. Businesses that operate a number of distinct departments, require reports on the results achieved by each of them to be provided to management so that their contribution to the overall results is identified and action can be taken to maximize each department's effectiveness, and hence the performance of the entity as a whole.
3. A business that conducts its activities through a number of branches spread over a wide geographical area.

4. Where transactions are entered into on terms that involve the receipt of the total sum due in a number of instalments spread over a fairly long period of time; this occurs especially in the retail trade. Similar terms may be used by companies to purchase their fixed assets.
5. Businesses are themselves sometimes the subjects of purchase and sale or are dissolved.
6. A business has to account for Value-Added Tax.

The system of double entry book-keeping is extremely flexible and can be extended to meet not only the circumstances described above but also many others that may arise. However, extensions of the system often introduce complications of data accumulation, recording and interpretation, and the cost of these additional impositions should be weighed against the benefits derived from the possession of additional information to decide whether the extra effort is justified. In some instances these extra costs have to be met to comply with legal requirements, such as the collection of value added tax on behalf of the government; the manner in which this may be achieved as part of the routine accounting system is described later in this chapter. Finally, consideration is given to the steps that must be taken to identify losses of stock and cash when the basic records are lost or are considered unreliable.

THE MANUFACTURING ACCOUNT

Where a company manufactures the product in which it trades, it is useful for management to identify separately the cost of production. This is done by preparing a manufacturing account in which all the costs related to production are combined. The total cost of completed items, established in the manufacturing account, is then transferred to the trading account, where it takes the place of purchases and is adjusted for the opening and closing stocks of finished goods, in the usual way, to calculate the cost of goods sold.

The manufacturing account shows how much it has cost to produce the goods sold during a period and so enables management to compare individual elements of cost with either the results of previous periods or predetermined standards. Also, the total cost of production can be compared with the cost of purchasing similar completed products from an outside supplier to give an indication of the efficiency of the manufacturing section. If it is discovered, for example, that finished goods can be purchased elsewhere at a total cost lower than that of internal manufacture, then the cessation of manufacturing should be investigated and the possibility of simply buying the completed product for resale examined.

Management may decide to use the accounting system to identify the manufacturing profit or loss by making the transfer from the manufacturing account to the trading account at the market value for which similar finished goods could be purchased. The manufacturing profit or loss is transferred to the profit and loss account where it is combined with the gross profit on trading.

The technique of making transfers at other than historical cost can be extended. For example, a company may make subassemblies for incorporation into a finished product; these may be charged to production at 'outside' prices to allow the performance of the various departments to be assessed. This process may be illustrated by reference to a car manufacturer that produces its own gear boxes – the market price can be used for transfers from the gear-box department to the main car-assembly section to show the profit or loss on internal production. The greater the number of separate departments it is desired to monitor, then the more detailed the analysis of costs has to be.

The preparation of the manufacturing account

When preparing the final accounts of a manufacturing organization, the first step is to examine the data contained in the trial balance to determine which entries relate to manufacturing; these are transferred to the manufacturing account. Typical manufacturing costs are raw materials and depreciation of plant, and these can be identified solely with the production process. However, in some cases it is not possible to relate a cost entirely to one function, for example, a single rent payment may be made for premises that contain a factory, warehouse, transport depot and offices. When this occurs, the total cost recorded in the trial balance must be apportioned, that is, the proportion that relates to the factory is shown in the manufacturing account and the remainder in the profit and loss account. Such apportionments should be made on a rational basis, for example, rent can be divided on the basis of the area occupied by each section. (The usefulness and limitations of apportionments are discussed in the section on departmental accounts later in this chapter.)

The costs entered in the manufacturing account should be classified, for presentation purposes, between prime costs and production overhead costs. Prime costs are the materials and labour used directly in the production process; they vary with the level of production and would not be incurred at all if output fell to zero. Overhead costs are those that do not usually vary with the rate of production, for example, the rent must be paid whether the factory is producing very little or operating at full capacity. (The importance of the behaviour of costs in response to changes in output is discussed in Chapter 14.) The sum of the prime costs and overhead costs is the total factory cost of production.

To determine the cost of raw materials consumed, the value of purchases during a period must be adjusted by the opening and closing stocks by applying the formula:

$$\frac{\text{Opening stock of}}{\text{raw materials}} + \text{Purchases} - \frac{\text{Closing stock of}}{\text{raw materials}} = \frac{\text{Cost of materials}}{\text{consumed}}$$

There may also be stocks of 'work-in-progress', that is, units of output that are partly completed at the accounting date; closing work-in-progress is valued and deducted from total factory cost of production to give the cost of completed production. The cost of work-in-progress is carried forward to the next period, when further costs are incurred to complete the items involved and to make them ready for sale; work-in-progress appears in the balance sheet as part of the stock included in current assets. The adjustment is made by applying the formula:

$$\begin{array}{ccccc}
\text{Opening work-} & + & \text{Total factory} & - & \text{Closing work-} & = & \text{Cost of completed} \\
\text{in-progress} & & \text{cost} & & \text{in-progress} & & \text{items}
\end{array}$$

The following balances were among those extracted from the books of **Example 11.1**
Worker, a manufacturing business, on 31 December 19X4:

	Debit £	Credit £
Sales		270,000
Production wages	50,000	
Purchase of raw materials	100,000	
Depreciation of manufacturing equipment in 19X4	10,000	
Production overhead expenses	7,500	
Rent	9,000	
Depreciation of office equipment in 19X4	2,000	
Salaries of sales personnel	16,000	
Delivery costs	12,000	
Advertising costs	6,000	
General administration expenses	22,000	
Stocks at 1 January: Raw materials	15,000	
Work-in-progress	1,500	
Finished goods	20,000	

Notes
1. Stocks at 31 December were

	£
Raw materials	12,500
Work-in-progress	2,500
Finished goods	27,000

2. Two-thirds of the rent charge relates to the factory.

Prepare the manufacturing, trading and profit and loss accounts of Worker **Required**
for 19X4.

Manufacturing, Trading and Profit and Loss Account of   **Solution**
Worker for the year to 31 December 19X4

	£	£
Stock of raw materials at 1 January	15,000	
Purchases of raw materials	100,000	
Less: Stock of raw materials at 31 December	(12,500)	
Raw materials consumed	102,500	
Production wages	50,000	
Prime cost	152,500	
Production overhead costs		
Depreciation	10,000	
Expenses	7,500	
Rent	6,000	
Total factory cost	176,000	

	£	£
Total factory cost (brought forward)	176,000	
Work-in-progress at 1 January	1,500	
Less: Work-in-progress at 31 December	(2,500)	
Cost of completed items transferred to trading account	175,000	
Sales		270,000
Stock of finished goods at 1 January	20,000	
Transferred from production	175,000	
	195,000	
Less: Stock of finished goods at 31 December	(27,000)	
Cost of goods sold		168,000
Gross profit		102,000
Rent	3,000	
Depreciation of office equipment	2,000	
Sales personnels' salaries	16,000	
Delivery costs	12,000	
Advertising	6,000	
General administration	22,000	
		61,000
Net profit		41,000

The identification and elimination of profit on manufacture

The identification of profit on manufacture enables management to judge the efficiency of manufacturing operations, but a problem arises when preparing final accounts for external use. For this purpose, the realization concept (see Chapter 4) allows profit to be recognized *only* when a sale takes place, and this means that unsold stock must be valued at cost. Where transfers of stock have been made within the firm at a value in excess of cost, an adjustment must be made to remove any unrealized profit at the year end. This is done by creating a provision for unrealized profit that is set off against the stock value reported in the balance sheet. As was demonstrated with the provision for doubtful debts (see Chapter 7), once a provision has been created it is only necessary to adjust its value each year with one of the following entries:

	Debit	*Credit*	*With*
either	Profit and loss account	Provision for unrealized profit	An increase in the provision
or	Provision for unrealized profit	Profit and loss account	A decrease in the provision

Doer Ltd was established on 1 January 19X8. The summarized trading and *Example 11.2* profit and loss accounts at historical cost for the first year of operations to 31 December 19X8 are:

	£	£
Cost of manufacture: Prime		150,000
Overheads		75,000
Factory cost of completed items		225,000
Sales		375,000
Transfer from manufacturing account	225,000	
Less: Closing stock of finished goods at cost	(50,000)	
Cost of goods sold		175,000
Gross profit		200,000
All other costs		150,000
Net profit		50,000

The company's management wishes to know the profit on manufacturing. It discovers that it could have purchased a similar product at a price 10 per cent greater than its own cost of manufacture. Prices were stable throughout the period, and there was no work-in-progress at the accounting date.

(a) Prepare the manufacturing, trading and profit and loss accounts of **Required** Doer Ltd for the year to 31 December 19X8, making the transfer from the manufacturing account at cost plus 10 per cent.
(b) Show the entry in the balance sheet at 31 December 19X8 for the stock of finished goods.

Note
A provision should be made, in the profit and loss account, for the unrealized profit on unsold stock.

(a)   **Solution**

	£	£
Costs of manufacture: Prime		150,000
Overhead		75,000
Factory cost of completed items		225,000
Profit on manufacturing		22,500
Transfer to trading account		247,500
Sales		375,000
Transfer from manufacturing account	247,500	
Less: Stock at 31 December at		
transfer price (cost + 10%)	(55,000)	
		192,500

Gross profit on trading		182,500
Profit on manufacturing		22,500
		———
		205,000
Less: All other costs	150,000	
Provision for unrealized profit	5,000	
	———	
		155,000
		———
Net profit		50 000
		———

(b) Balance Sheet extract

	£
Stock of finished goods	55 ,000
Less: Provision for unrealized profit	5,000
	———
	50,000

Notes
1. The identification of the manufacturing profit results in the following double entry: a debit to the manufacturing account and a credit to the profit and loss account.
2. The revised accounts show that the company makes £22,500 profit by manufacturing its own product, and £182,500 profit from trading.
3. The value of net profit, after providing for an unrealized profit in manufacture, remains unchanged.

Readers should now attempt Question 11.1 at the end of this chapter, which combines the various aspects of the manufacturing account dealt with in this section. Note that the presentation of the profit and loss account is improved if similar items are grouped together under such headings as 'finance costs' and 'selling costs' and their subtotals calculated.

DEPARTMENTAL ACCOUNTS

Where a business has a number of separate departments, management needs to know which of these are performing well and which poorly so that areas of weakness can be strengthened and successful activities built upon. To achieve this, the costs and revenues of each department must be identified in a way that makes them controllable.

The production of departmental accounting statements relies on the careful analysis of the flows of expense and revenue at the time of their initial recording in the day books. Where possible, costs should be *allocated*, that is, recorded as belonging directly to a particular department. For example, the wages of an employee who works in a particular department can be allocated directly to that department. However, there are some costs that cannot be allocated, and these have to be *apportioned*. Costs that are apportioned can alternatively be described as 'joint costs' as they give benefit to more than one department, and the benefit itself is not divisible. For example, the cost of overall administration has to be met, but relates to all of the departments of the firm; each department, therefore, has to contribute towards this cost, but does not make its own direct payment in respect of the charge.

It is usual to present departmental accounts in columnar format as this makes comprehension easier and facilitates easy comparison between the separate areas to which the report relates. In columnar presentation, the results of each separate department are entered in a column alongside the results of the others. This technique is illustrated in Example 11.3.

The following list of balances was extracted from the books of Bucket Ltd in respect of the year to 31 March 19X9:

Example 11.3

	£	£
Sales: Department X	68,000	
Y	54,000	
Z	41,000	163,000
Purchases: Department X	44,880	
Y	37,060	
Z	29,060	111,000
Lighting and heating		3,570
Delivery expenses		1,956
Commission paid		3,260
Printing and stationery		750
Salaries and wages		27,000
General expenses		6,900
Opening stock: Department X		12,410
Y		9,550
Z		7,750
Closing stock: Department X		10,540
Y		7,350
Z		8,280

Expenses are to be apportioned between the departments as follows:

1. Delivery expenses in proportion to sales.
2. Commission at 2 per cent of sales.
3. Printing and stationery and wages and salaries in the proportion 6:4:5.
4. Other expenses equally.

A columnar trading and profit and loss account for the year ended 31 March 19X9.

Required

Solution

Departmental Trading and Profit and Loss Account for the year to 31 March 19X9

	X £	Y £	Z £	Total £
Sales	68,000	54,000	41,000	163,000
Less:				
Opening stock	12,410	9,550	7,750	29,710
Purchases	44,880	37,060	29,060	111,000
Closing stock	(10,540)	(7,350)	(8,280)	(26,170)
Cost of goods sold	46,750	39,260	28,530	114,540
Gross profit	21,250	14,740	12,470	48,460
Less:				
Delivery expenses	816	648	492	1,956
Commission	1,360	1,080	820	3,260
Printing and stationery	300	200	250	750
Salaries and wages	10,800	7,200	9,000	27,000
Lighting and heating	1,190	1,190	1,190	3,570
General expenses	2,300	2,300	2,300	6,900
Total expenses	16,766	12,618	14,052	43,436
Net profit (loss)	4,484	2,122	(1,582)	5,024

Readers should now work Question 11.2 at the end of this chapter.

BRANCH ACCOUNTS

A company that operates branches has to organize its accounting function so that proper control can be exercised over each branch's activities. The alternative approaches that may be adopted are to keep all of the records at the head office and maintain a single set of books for the whole business, or to allow branches to keep their own separate sets of double entry records. The system adopted in a particular instance is likely to depend, in part, on the degree of autonomy with which branches are allowed to operate; the former approach is more applicable where strict central control is exercised, while the latter suits circumstances where branches are, within limits, allowed to function as autonomous units. This chapter now examines how these alternative accounting methods are operated in practice.

Integrated records at head office
When the branch records are fully integrated with those of the head office, a single set of double entry accounting records is maintained, at head office, which covers the whole organization and so, at the end of each accounting

period, a single trial balance is produced. To enable the results of individual branches to be identified, each entry must clearly indicate the branch to which it relates. This method is the same as that used for departmental accounts, described earlier in this chapter, and effectively treats each branch as a department, despite the fact that they are located in different places. To see how this system operates, readers may refer back to Example 11.2 and substitute 'branch' for each occurrence of the word 'department'.

In some instances, goods purchased by head office are entered in its purchases account and then transferred to branches for sale. The transfer to the branch is recorded in the books by the following entry:

Account debited	Account credited	With
Goods to branch	Head office purchases	Costs of goods sent to branch

The balance on the goods sent to branch account is transferred to the branch's trading account at the end of the accounting period and is added to any purchases recorded as specifically relating to the branch.

If the head office provides a wholesale facility for the branches by buying in bulk, it may be desired to identify the profit head office generates from this function. To achieve this, the goods are charged to the branch at a price in excess of cost and the profit element in the transaction is recorded in a 'mark-up' or 'branch stock adjustment' account as follows:

Account debited	Account credited	With
Goods sent to branch		Transfer price of goods (cost plus profit)
	Head office purchases	Cost of goods transferred
	Mark-up	Profit element of transfer price

For *internal* reporting purposes the branch's opening and closing stocks are valued at transfer price, and the profit on the wholesale aspect of the head office operation is given by the balance on the mark-up account. For *external* reporting purposes the stock held by branches must be restated at the cost to the business, and so a 'provision for unrealized profit' must be made in the same way as that described earlier in this chapter.

Organizer operates a head office and two branches, A and B. All purchases of goods for resale are made by the head office and then transferred to the branches at cost plus 25 per cent. The firm's books of account are kept by the head office, and the trial balance at 31 December 19X4 was: ***Example 11.4***

	£000	£000
Goods sent to branches		
Branch A	250	
Branch B	375	
Mark-up account		125
Sales		
Branch A		350
Branch B		450

	£000	£000
Capital at 1 January		345
Stock at 1 January at transfer price		
Branch A	50	
Branch B	75	
Provision for unrealized profit at 1 January		
Branch A		10
Branch B		15
Fixed assets	350	
Debtors	60	
Cash	35	
Drawings	45	
General expenses		
Branch A	40	
Branch B	65	
Head office	25	
Creditors		75
	1,370	1,370

The following information is relevant:

1. No stocks were held at the head office at either the beginning or end of the year.
2. At 31 December 19X4 the stocks held at the branches at transfer price were:

Branch A	£55,000
Branch B	£100,000

Required

Prepare, in columnar format, the trading and profit and loss accounts of the branches, and the whole organization, for the year to 31 December 19X4 and the balance sheet as at that date.

Solution (£000)

Trading and Profit and Loss Account for the year to 31 December 19X4

	Branch A	Branch B	Total
Sales	350	450	800
Less:			
Opening stock	50	75	125
Plus: Goods at transfer prices	250	375	625
Less: Closing stock	(55)	(100)	(155)
Goods sold at transfer price	245	350	595
Gross profit on branch trading	105	100	205
General expenses	40	65	105
Branch profit	65	35	100

Mark-up	125	
Less: Increase in provision for unrealized profit	6 (W1)	
		119
		219
Head office general expenses		25
Net profit		194

Balance Sheet at 31 December 19X4

	£000	£000
Fixed assets		350
Stock	124 (W2)	
Debtors	60	
Cash	35	
	219	
Creditors	(75)	
		144
		494
Financed by:		
Capital 1 January		345
Profit for 19X4		194
Less: Drawings		(45)
		494

Workings

Stock is transferred at cost plus 25 per cent and so cost is 80 per cent and profit 20 per cent of the transfer price.

	Closing stock at transfer price	W1 Profit = 20%	W2 Cost = 80%
Branch A	55	11	44
Branch B	100	20	80
		31	
Less: Opening provision (10 + 15)		25	
Increase in provision		6	
Closing stock at cost			124

If any transfers of goods take place between branches, an adjustment to reflect this must be made in the accounting records kept at head office:

Account debited	Account credited	With
Goods sent to receiving branch	Goods sent to sending branch	Value of goods transferred

It is possible for the head office to transfer stock to branches at the retail selling price, i.e. the value at which the branch is to sell the goods to its customers. The records relating to the branch are all maintained at selling price, and its profit is identified in the mark-up account after adjusting for unrealized profit. This approach enables the head office to maintain a tight control over branches, as it sets the prices at which sales are to be made, and therefore determines margins, and is able to calculate the theoretical value of closing stock, at selling prices, by using the formula:

$$\frac{\text{Opening stock}}{\text{at selling prices}} + \frac{\text{Goods from head office}}{\text{at selling prices}} - \text{Sales} = \frac{\text{Closing stock}}{\text{at selling prices}}$$

The theoretical closing stock value can then be compared with the results of a physical stock check, valued at selling prices, and any discrepancies investigated.

Separate branch records

The maintenance by a branch of its own complete set of double entry books requires that 'current accounts' are used to enable transactions between the head office and the branch to be recorded. In the head office books there is a 'branch current account' and in the branch's books there is a 'head office current account'. The head office current account in the branch's books can be regarded in the same light as the sole trader's capital account as it represents the amount due to ownership, in this case the head office; conversely, the branch current account in the head office books represents the net investment that has been made in the branch. Example 11.5 shows some specimen entries in current accounts.

Example 11.5   Highlight has a branch that maintains its own set of double entry books. At 1 January 19X5 the balances on the current accounts were

In the head office books: Branch current account – £50,125 (debit).
In the branch books: Head office current account – £50,125 (credit).

The following transactions took place in January 19X6:

1. The branch sent cash of £2,500 to the head office.
2. The head office sent goods to the branch at cost £7,250.
3. The head office bought for cash a delivery van for the branch at a cost of £10,750.
4. The branch returned to the head office damaged goods that had been transferred to it at a cost of £550.
5. The branch paid wages of £1,000 to its staff in cash.

Required   Show the entry of the above information in the branch current account in the head office books and the head office current account in the branch books and show the closing balances.

Head office books
Branch Current Account

	£		£
Balance b/d	50,125	1. Cash	2,500
2. Goods to branch	7,250	4. Goods returned	
3. Cash – van	10,750	from branch	550
		Balance c/d	65,075
	_____		_____
	68,125		68,125

Branch books
Head Office Current Account

	£		£
1. Cash	2,500	Balance b/d	50,125
4. Goods returned		2. Goods from	
to head office	550	head office	7,250
Balance c/d	65,075	3. Van	10,750
	_____		_____
	68,125		68,125

Note
Transaction 5 does not appear in the current accounts as it does not involve a transaction between the head office and the branch. It appears only in the books of the branch: debit wages £1,000 and credit cash £1,000.

The current accounts record all transfers between the head office and the branch and so the balances should be equal, but of opposite value, once all the relevant transactions have been entered in each of them. It is possible for the balances to differ at the accounting date, however, and when this occurs a reconciliation must be carried out to identify the causes of the difference. It may be found, for example, that goods or cash were sent on the final day of the accounting year but were not received until the following day so that at the accounting date they were entered in the sender's book but not the receiver's. After all such items have been identified and adjusted, the balances will agree; trial balances can then be extracted from both sets of books and used as the basis for preparing the final accounts.

Example 11.6

Sundowner has a head office in London and branches in Cardiff and Bristol. Each branch maintains its own set of full double entry books, from which the following trial balances were extracted on 31 December 19X6:

	London		Cardiff		Bristol	
	Dr.	Cr.	Dr.	Cr.	Dr.	Cr.
	£000	£000	£000	£000	£000	£000
Capital		350				
Sales		200		100		150
Purchases	125		30		70	

Goods sent to branches		25				
Goods from head office			20		5	
Fixed assets at book value	130		70		100	
Stock at 1 January	10		18		22	
Debtors	30		21		28	
Cash at bank	15		3		5	
Creditors		24		26		17
Advertising	52		9		19	
Selling expenses	33		13		23	
Head office administration	17					
Drawings	20					
Head office current account				52		105
Cardiff branch current account	52					
Bristol branch current account	115					
	599	599	181	181	272	272

Notes

1. The Bristol branch sent £10,000 to the head office on 31 December 19X6; it was not entered in the head office books until 2 January 19X7.
2. Depreciation of 10 per cent of the book value is to be written off fixed assets.
3. Stocks at 31 December were:

	£000
London	15
Cardiff	23
Bristol	30

4. All transfers of goods were made at cost.

Required

Prepare, for the head office, the individual branches and the firm as a whole, the trading and profit and loss accounts for the year to 31 December 19X6 and the balance sheets as at that date.

Solution

Trading and Profit and Loss Accounts for the year to 31 December 19X6

	London £000	Cardiff £000	Bristol £000	Total £000
Sales	200	100	150	450
Opening stock	10	18	22	50
Purchases	125	30	70	225
Goods sent to branches	(25)	20	5	
Closing stock	(15)	(23)	(30)	(68)
Cost of goods sold	95	45	67	207
Gross profit	105	55	83	243
Advertising	52	9	19	80
Selling expenses	33	13	23	69
Depreciation	13	7	10	30
Total costs	98	29	52	179

Branch profit	7	26	31	64
Head office administration				17
Net profit				47

Balance Sheets at 31 December 19X6

	London £000	Cardiff £000	Bristol £000	Total £000
Fixed assets at book value	117	63	90	270
Current assets:				
Stock	15	23	30	68
Debtors	30	21	28	79
Cash	25(W1)	—	5	30
	70	44	63	177
Less: Current liabilities				
Creditors	24	26	17	67
Overdraft	—	3	—	3
	24	29	17	70
Working capital	46	15	46	107
Cardiff branch current account	78 (W2)			
Bristol branch current account	136 (W3)			
	377	78	136	377
Financed by:				
Capital at 1 January	350			350
Plus: Profit	47	26	31	47
Less: Drawings	(20)			(20)
Head office current account		52	105	
	377	78	136	377

Workings (£000)
W1: 15 (balance) + 10 (cash in transit)
W2: 52 (balance) + 26 (profit)
W3: 115 (balance) – 10 (cash in transit) + 31 (profit)

Note
The (intracompany) transfers of goods in the trading accounts cancel out to prevent the overstatement of purchases and sales. Similarly, the current account balances shown in the separate balance sheets cancel to avoid overstatement of assets and liabilities.

It is possible to make transfers of goods at above cost when branches keep their own sets of books in the same way as when all the records are at the head office. The head office identifies and records the profit element in a mark-up account and charges the full transfer price in the branch's current account while the branch enters the full transfer price in its books as the cost of acquiring goods for resale. Any unrealized profit in the stock valuation at the balance sheet date must be eliminated in the usual way when external accounting reports are prepared.

INSTALMENT CREDIT

It is possible for businesses to make both sales and purchases on the basis of instalment credit. This involves the settlement of the total amount due by a number of instalments spread over an agreed period of time. To compensate for the delay in settling the amount outstanding, it is usual to add to the cash price an amount of interest. This chapter now deals with how such transactions can be accounted for in the books of the seller and the buyer.

The seller's books

The application of the realization concept (explained in Chapter 4) means that profit is recognized at the point of sale, and this rule applies whether the sale is on cash or credit terms. There are some circumstances where the strict application of this rule is not, however, believed to portray fairly the underlying economic facts, such as when a sale is made under a hire-purchase or instalment credit agreement whereby the debt is settled by a number of payments spread over a fairly long period of time. It is possible to determine the point of sale for such transactions in strictly legal terms: in the case of hire purchase it is at the time of the last instalment; in the case of instalment credit, the sale is deemed to take place at the outset when the entire debt is created. However, to recognize the whole profit at either the beginning or the end of the entire transaction is generally thought to be misleading. The economic fact is that completion of the sale takes place over a period of time, and this should be recognized when profit is measured.

A rational basis of apportionment is required to spread the expected profit, and a good measure of the degree of completeness is the proportion of the total sales price received during the period for which profit is to be calculated. The application of this approach is shown in Example 11.7.

Example 11.7 A company's accounting date is 31 December. On 1 June 19X1 it made a sale under an instalment credit agreement. The total value of the sale is £480 to be settled by a deposit of £96 and 24 monthly instalments of £16, the first to be made on 30 June 19X1. The cost of the goods sold is £360.

Required Calculate the profit to be recognized on the sale in 19X1, 19X2 and 19X3 assuming that profit is recognized as cash is received.

The total gross profit on the sale is £480 – £360 = £120.   **Solution**

				Cash received	Proportion of total cash received	Profit taken	
				£			£
19X1	96 +	(6 × £16)	=	192	40%	40% × 120 =	48
19X2		12 × £16	=	192	40%	40% × 120 =	48
19X3		6 × £16	=	96	20%	20% × 120 =	24
				480			120

The phased recognition of profit on instalment credit transactions can be entered in the books of account in a number of ways. Two of the most common are:

1. to credit the total value of the sale to the trading account in the accounting period during which the sale takes place and create a provision for unrealized profit; or
2. to credit each period's trading account with the cash received during the period and to assign a value to stock on the basis of cash not yet collected.

In both cases it is best to operate a separate trading account in which to enter all instalment credit sales so that their results can be separately monitored.

The provision for unrealized profit on instalment credit sales method

With this method, the full value of the sale is entered in the trading account and recorded as a debtor. At the accounting date the value of unrealized profit is calculated and debited to the profit and loss account. The credit balance on the provision account is deducted from the value of instalment sales debtors, which should be disclosed separately in the balance sheet.

Prepare the trading and profit and loss account for 19X1 based on the information given in Example 11.7, using a provision for unrealized profit, and show the relevant extract from the balance sheet.   ***Example 11.8***
Required

	£	**Solution**
Sales	480	
Cost of goods sold	360	
Gross profit	120	
Provision for unrealized profit (£48 + £24)	72	
Profit	48	

Balance Sheet extract

	£
Instalment sales debtors	288 (W1)
Provision for unrealized profit	72
	216

W1

£480 (Total selling price) – £96 (Deposit) – (£16 × 6) (19X1 instalments).

Notes

1. In 19X2, £48, and in 19X3 the remaining £24, of the provision are credited to the profit and loss account.
2. There will usually be a number of transactions each year and the provision is adjusted at the year end in the same way as the provision for doubtful debts (see Chapter 7).

The cash receipts method

The cash received as a deposit and the instalments receivable during the accounting period are entered in the trading account, and 'stock out on instalment sales' is carried down as an asset in the balance sheet; no entry for debtors appears in the balance sheet other than for any instalments due but unpaid at the accounting date.

The value of the stock out on instalment sales is found by applying the proportion of sales price still outstanding to the cost of stock sold. The following formula may be used:

$$V = \frac{I}{S} \times C$$

where
    V = Value of stock out on instalment sales.
    I = Instalments due in future accounting periods.
    S = Total selling price.
    C = Cost of stock sold.

Example 11.9
Required

Prepare the trading and profit and loss accounts for 19X1, 19X2 and 19X3 based on the information given in Example 11.7, using the stock out on instalment sales method.

Solution

To value stock at 31 December:

			19X1	19X2
I	(Instalments due in future accounting periods)	=	288	96
S	(Total selling price)	=	480	480
C	(Cost of goods sold)	=	360	360
$V = \dfrac{I}{S} \times C$		=	216	72

Instalment Sales Trading Accounts

	19X1		19X2		19X3	
	£	£	£	£	£	£
Deposit and instalments receivable		192		192		96
Stock out on instalment credit b/f	—		216		72	
Goods sold	360		—		—	
Stock out on instalment credit c/f	(216)		(72)		—	
		144		144		72
Profit		48		48		24

The examples in this section have dealt with only a single sale. Readers should now work Question 11.3, which extends the principle to multiple sales.

The buyer's books

The total amount payable when a company buys a fixed asset on instalment credit terms consists of the cash price of the asset plus interest. To comply with the historical cost concept, the cash price of the asset is recorded in the fixed asset account. The matching concept requires that the interest charge is apportioned between the accounting periods over which the instalments are paid; this concept also requires the cost of the asset to be depreciated in the usual way over its useful life. For a hire-purchase transaction, the following entries are made to record the initial purchase of the fixed asset:

Account debited	Account credited	With
Fixed asset at cost		Cash price of asset
Interest suspense		Total interest payable over the life of the agreement
	Hire-purchase creditor	Total amount payable under the agreement

The deposit paid or trade-in allowance is debited to the hire-purchase creditor account as are the individual instalments as they fall due. At the end of each accounting period the portion of interest that relates to the period is transferred to the profit and loss account, and the balance remaining on the interest suspense account is set against that on the hire-purchase creditor account and the net sum entered in the balance sheet.

Jacobin Ltd purchased a new delivery van under a hire-purchase agreement on 1 July 19X5. The cash price of the van was £10,000 and Jacobin paid a deposit of £4,000. Hire-purchase interest charges of £1,272 were added to the outstanding balance, the total of which was to be paid off by 24 equal monthly instalments starting on 31 July 19X5.

Jacobin makes up its accounts to the 31 December. It is calculated that the hire-purchase interest charges should be apportioned 19X5 – £424, 19X6 – £652, 19X7 – the remaining balance.

Example 11.10

(a) Prepare the hire-purchase creditor and interest suspense accounts as they would appear in the books of Jacobin for the years 19X5, 19X6 and 19X7.

(b) Show the balance sheet extract for the hire-purchase creditor at 31 December 19X5 and 19X6.

Required

Solution

(a) **Hire-Purchase Creditor Account**

	£		£
19X5		19X5	
Cash deposit	4,000	Delivery van	10,000
Cash 6 instalments	1,818	Interest suspense	1,272
Balance c/d	5,454		
	11,272		11,272
19X6		19X6	
Cash 12 instalments	3,636	Balance b/d	5,454
Balance c/d	1,818		
	5,454		5,454
19X7		19X7	
Cash 6 instalments	1,818	Balance b/d	1,818

Hire-Purchase Interest Suspense Account

	£		£
19X5		19X5	
Hire-purchase creditor	1,272	Profit and loss	424
		Balance c/d	848
	1,272		1,272
19X6		19X6	
Balance b/d	848	Profit and loss	652
		Balance c/d	196
	848		848
19X7		19X7	
Balance b/d	196	Profit and loss	196

Working

Amount of each instalment:

11,272 (HP price of asset) − 4,000 (deposit) =
7,272/24 (instalments) = £303.

(b) **Balance Sheet extracts 31 December**

	19X5	19X6
Hire-purchase creditor	5,454	1,818
Less: Interest not yet due	848	196
	4,606*	1,622

Note
* For the purpose of the published accounts this sum must be split between that part that is a current liability, i.e. due for payment on or before 31 December 19X6, and that payable in more than a year's time.

The method shown above is equally applicable where, instead of hire purchase, an instalment credit agreement is used. In these circumstances, an account titled 'instalment creditor' is used in place of the 'hire-purchase creditor' account.

TRANSFER OF BUSINESS

It is possible for a business to grow by acquiring an existing undertaking. This is known as 'external' expansion and contrasts with 'internal' expansion, which involves the purchase of new trading assets and the creation of additional activity to utilize them. The advantage of external expansion is that management does not have to develop new products or outlets. For example, the owner of a shop may wish to open a branch in another town: internal expansion involves acquiring premises and stock, training staff and attracting customers; external expansion involves the purchase of an existing shop together with its stock, as a going concern, and possibly the retention of the bulk of its staff and customers.

The accounting entries that result from the transfer of a business can be divided into three areas:

1. The record of the assets and liabilities taken over in the books of the purchaser.
2. The record of any transactions carried out by the purchaser on behalf of the vendor of the business.
3. The record of the sale of the business in the vendor's books.

The initial record

The agreement under which an existing business is acquired must contain a clear statement of which assets and liabilities are to be transferred under the deal. This is to avoid any future disputes about, for example, where the responsibility lies for such liabilities as an overdraft or trade creditors created before the takeover, or whether a specific piece of property is included in the price.

The transferred assets should be recorded in the purchaser's books at the agreed price, which is unlikely to be the same as the historical cost at which they are recorded in the vendor's books as they are acquired at current values. A difficulty may arise because a global figure is paid for the acquired business that is not allocated between specific assets taken over. In these circumstances, the price paid must be apportioned between the tangible assets and liabilities acquired, on the basis of their current values, with any excess recorded as goodwill. (See Chapter 8 for a full discussion of goodwill.)

Example 11.11   The balance sheet of Firefly at 31 December 19X4 was

	£	£		£
Premises		14,000	Capital	20,000
Stock	12,000		Creditors	15,000
Debtors	7,000			
Cash	2,000			
		21,000		
		35,000		35,000

Required

Gloworm agreed to buy the business on 1 January 19X5 for £30,000 cash. The cash balance was not part of the deal and was to be retained by Firefly. The current value of the premises was £20,000; the other assets and liabilities are fairly stated at their balance sheet values.

(a) Calculate the value of goodwill purchased from Gloworm.
(b) Show the journal entry made in Gloworm's books to record the acquisition.

Solution

(a) **Calculation of goodwill**

		£	£
Price paid			30,000
Acquired:	Premises	20,000	
	Stock	12,000	
	Debtors	7,000	
		39,000	
Less: Liabilities assumed		15,000	
Net assets acquired at current value			24,000
Goodwill			6,000

(b) **Journal**

	Debit £	Credit £
Premises	20,000	
Stock	12,000	
Debtors	7,000	
Creditors		15,000
Goodwill	6,000	
Cash		30,000
	45,000	45,000

Readers should now work Question 11.4 at the end of this chapter.

Transactions on behalf of the vendor

The purchasing company may carry out some transactions on behalf of the vendor, such as collecting debtors or paying creditors that are not taken over. This is a useful way of maintaining continuity with customers and suppliers. All such transactions are entered in a separate account, in the name of the vendor, and a net settlement made as agreed. Care must be exercised not to confuse these transactions with the trading activity that takes place after the acquisition.

Hotter purchased the business of Colder on 31 December 19X5. It was agreed that the following items should not be included in the acquisition: **Example 11.12**

	£
Debtors	15,000
Creditors	6,000
Overdraft	1,700

Hotter agreed to collect the sums due from debtors, use this cash to settle the creditors and overdraft, and pay the remaining balance to Colder. By 31 January 19X6, £14,500 had been collected from debtors, the rest being considered bad debts, and Hotter had settled the agreed debts of Colder.

Prepare the account of Colder in the books of Hotter and show the balance due to Colder on 31 January 1986. **Required**

Colder's Account **Solution**

	£		£
Cash paid to creditors	6,000	Cash collected from debtors	14,500
Cash paid – overdraft	1,700		
Balance due to Colder	6,800		
	14,500		14,500

Readers should now work Question 11.5 at the end of this chapter.

The vendor's books

When the business of a sole trader is sold, entries must be made in the firm's books to calculate the resulting profit or loss and to record the dissolution of the undertaking. A 'realization account' is opened and the same basic procedure followed as was described for partnerships in Chapter 9. When a limited company is wound up, any surplus or deficit in the realization account is transferred to the profit and loss account. Each ordinary shareholder then receives a share of the cash, which remains after all other liabilities have been paid, on the basis of the proportion of shares owned.

Some modifications to the method of recording dissolution are required when, instead of ceasing to trade, a firm is converted into a limited company. The following discussion and example relate to a partnership, but the same method is used for a sole trader.

The conversion of a partnership into a limited company brings the partnership to an end, and so a realization account is opened that is credited with the value of the shares, debentures, cash and any other form of consideration the limited company has agreed to give in exchange for the net assets it is to acquire. The realization account is then closed by transferring the profit or loss to the partners' capital accounts. The assets of the partnership now consist of the securities and/or any cash, received from the limited company. The securities are shared between the partners on the agreed basis, and any balances remaining on the capital accounts are cleared by the introduction or withdrawal of cash. The process is dealt with in Example 11.13.

Example 11.13 Wing, Beat and Flap trade in partnership and share all profits equally. The firm's balance sheet was as follows:

	£	£		£
Fixed assets		25,000	Capital accounts:	
Current assets	16,000		Wing	9,000
Current liabilities	8,000		Beat	9,000
			Flap	15,000
		8,000		
		33,000		33,000

The partners decide to transfer the business to a limited company and, at the same time, adjust the balance of investment between the partners. To achieve this the partners set up Flyer Ltd and arrange to transfer to it all the assets and liabilities of the partnership in exchange for 27,000 ordinary shares of £1, and debentures worth £15,000. Wing is to receive 50 per cent of the shares and Beat and Flap 25 per cent each; the debentures are to be divided equally between the partners.

Required Prepare the realization account, the shares in Flyer account, the debentures in Flyer account and the partners' capital accounts to record the transfer of the business to Flyer Ltd and the dissolution of the partnership.

Solution **Realization Account**

	£		£
Fixed assets	25,000	Current liabilities	8,000
Current assets	16,000	Shares in Flyer	27,000
Profit on realization:		Debentures in Flyer	15,000
Wing	3,000		
Beat	3,000		
Flap	3,000		
	50,000		50,000

Shares in Flyer Account

	£		£
Realization account	27,000	Capital account:	
		Wing	13,500
		Beat	6,750
		Flap	6,750
	27,000		27,000

Debentures in Flyer Account

	£			£
Realization account	15,000	Capital account:		
		Wing		5,000
		Beat		5,000
		Flap		5,000
	15,000			15,000

Capital Accounts

	Wing £	Beat £	Flap £		Wing £	Beat £	Flap £
Shares in Flyer	13,500	6,750	6,750	Balance b/d	9,000	9,000	15,000
Debentures in				Profit on			
Flyer	5,000	5,000	5,000	realization	3,000	3,000	3,000
Cash				Cash			
withdrawn		250	6,250	introduced	6,500		
	18,500	12,000	18,000		18,500	12,000	18,000

Readers should now work Question 11.6 at the end of this chapter.

VALUE ADDED TAX (VAT)

Every business that trades in taxable items and has an annual turnover, including VAT, in excess of £46,000 (from 1 December 1999) must register for VAT purposes. The consequence of registration is that VAT at the appropriate rate (at the time of writing the rate is 17.5 per cent) must be added to the selling price of goods and services and charged to the customer. Every three months the VAT collected, known as the output tax, is paid to the government after deducting any VAT the firm has itself paid on its purchases (the input tax). It is usually possible for a trader to reclaim VAT if the amount of input tax paid in any three-month period exceeds the amount of output tax collected. This may arise if, for example, a particularly expensive fixed asset is purchased as VAT is charged by the supplier of such items and is immediately recoverable in full.

The accounting records of a registered trader have to be kept in such a way that all input tax and output tax is routinely identified so that the correct settlement can be made. This objective is achieved by identifying and recording separately the VAT element of transactions in a separate column in the books of prime entry. The total from the VAT analysis column of the sales day book is credited to a VAT account in the main ledger: the total from the VAT analysis column of the purchases day book is debited to the VAT account. Similar action must be taken in other books of prime entry, such as the cash book, goods returned day book or petty cash book, where transactions involving VAT are recorded. The VAT account is balanced every three months to find the amount due to HM Customs and Excise. The trading results of the enterprise are therefore reported net of VAT, and any balance on the VAT account at the balance sheet date is shown as a current asset or current liability. For example, if a company sells on credit an item for £235, of which £35 is VAT, the following entries are made in the books:

1. Debit the customer's account with £235. This is the full amount that has to be collected in respect of the sale.
2. Credit sales account £200. The company retains this amount after paying over the tax.
3. Credit VAT account with £35. This is the sum owed to the tax authorities as a result of the transaction and is a current liability until it is paid.

Note that the amount due from the customer is 117.5 per cent of the sales revenue which accrues to the company. Therefore, to find the VAT element of the gross price, it is multiplied by 17.5/117.5, and to find the sales value it is multiplied by 100/117.5. In the above example:

$$£235 \times 17.5/117.5 \ = \ £35$$
$$£235 \times 100/117.5 \ = \ £200$$

It is clear from the above that VAT is accounted for on the accruals basis at the time of purchase or sale, and not when the related cash is payable. A possible result is that, if a customer takes a long period of credit, VAT has to be paid before the cash for the sale has been received. This is partially offset if a correspondingly long period of credit is taken from suppliers. However, although in general accounting for VAT takes place every three months on an invoice basis, a number of 'special schemes' are operated, for example:

- Retailers who sell directly to the general public base their output tax on cash receipts.
- Businesses with an annual turnover of less than £300,000, excluding VAT, may be authorized to account for VAT on an annual basis; nine interim payments, based on the previous year's figures, are made during the year followed by a final balancing payment within two months of the end of the VAT year.

Example 11.14 The following are summaries of the totals on the sales and purchases day books of Collector at the end of its three-monthly VAT accounting period:

Sales Day Book

Total	VAT	Sales
£	£	£
111,625	16,625	95,000

Purchases Day Book

Total	VAT	Materials	Cleaning	Advertising
£	£	£	£	£
66,975	9,975	37,500	5,000	14,500

Petty Cash Book

Total	VAT	Stationery	Sundries	Motor expenses	Subscriptions
£	£	£	£	£	£
470	70	150	100	90	60

Prepare the VAT account to record the above items, showing the balance due. **Required**

VAT Account **Solution**

	£		£
Purchases day book	9,975	Sales day book	16,625
Petty cash book	70		
Balance due	6,580		
	16,625		16,625

Some items, such as food, are not subject to VAT and carry a *zero rate*. A business that sells zero-rated items still has to maintain a VAT account so that input tax can be entered and reclaimed. Other items, such as the provision of health care, are *exempt* from VAT, which means that no tax is charged on their sale, but none of the related tax paid on inputs can be reclaimed; firms that trade only in exempt items do not need to register for VAT or keep a VAT account.

LOSSES OF STOCK AND CASH

The accounts of businesses only reflect those economic events the initial data collecting process has been designed to record. Some activity remains unrecorded, such as losses of stock or cash. Stock may be lost through theft or accident, such as fire, and cash may be lost if, for example, the employee responsible for handling it steals some before recording the amount received. It is possible, where such losses are known or suspected, to calculate their value by using the techniques of incomplete records described in Chapter 4. This ability relies on the fact that the accounting process uses known relationships between the elements it reports, and if all the elements are known, except one, then the unknown value can be determined. For example, if all of the balances in a balance sheet are known with the exception of capital, the missing figure can be found as the amount needed to balance the balance sheet (see Chapter 3 where this technique is used).

Stock losses
The value of stock lost is calculated by constructing the trading account from the date at which reliable data was last available to the time of the suspected loss. A theoretical value for closing stock is estimated as the balancing figure in the account and is compared with the actual value found by a physical stock check; the difference between these two figures is the amount of the loss. The figures in the trading account are determined as follows:

1. *Sales* Sales are known where a business maintains a system of double entry ledger accounts; alternatively, it may be necessary to convert cash received into the value of sales by adjusting for such matters as opening and closing debtors and discounts given to customers.
2. *Purchases* The value of purchases is known where a business maintains a system of double entry ledger accounts; alternatively, it may be necessary to convert cash paid into purchases by adjusting it for opening and closing creditors and discounts received.
3. *Opening stock* This is taken from the closing balance sheet of the previous period, the date of which must be the starting point from which sales and purchases are measured.
4. *Gross profit* The difference between the selling price and the cost of goods sold is the 'gross profit' or 'margin' and can be assumed with some accuracy for a particular trade. The appropriate margin, expressed as a percentage, for the trade concerned is assumed to apply to the business under consideration. Care must be taken to ascertain whether the percentage relates to the value of sales or to the cost of goods sold. For example, if sales are £100 and the cost of goods sold £80, then the margin is £20; this is 20 per cent of the value of sales, or 25 per cent of the cost of goods sold.

The value of stock lost may now be calculated as follows:

1. Calculate the expected gross profit by applying the assumed mark-up to the value of sales.
2. Calculate the cost of goods sold by deducting the expected gross profit (found in 1) from sales.
3. Calculate the theoretical closing stock by using the formula:

    Closing stock = Opening stock + Purchases – Cost of goods sold
    (found in 2)

4. Calculate the value of stock lost by deducting the value of any stock that remains from the theoretical value of stock (found in 3).

Example 11.15   During the night of 14 March 19X2 a fire occurred in the premises of Smoke and Company, which destroyed a large quantity of stock and all the stock records. The following information was found from the accounting records:

	£
Stock at 31 December 19X1 as shown in the balance sheet	15,865
Sales 1 January to 14 March 19X2	78,640
Purchases 1 January to 14 March 19X2	57,103
Value of stock not destroyed as counted on the morning of 15 March 19X2	2,856

The company makes a gross profit of 25 per cent calculated on selling prices.

Required   Calculate the value of stock lost in the fire.

Step   **Solution**
1. Expected profit = 25% × 78,640 = 19,660.
2. Cost of goods sold = 78,640 – 19,660 = 58,980.
3. Theoretical closing stock = 15,865 + 57,103 – 58,980 = 13,988.
4. Stock lost = 13,988 – 2,856 = £11,132.

Note
It is possible to reconstruct directly the theoretical closing stock from the trading account:

	£	£
Sales		78,640
Opening stock	15,865	
Purchases	57,103	
Closing stock	(13,988)‡	
Cost of goods sold		58,980 †
Gross profit		19,660 *

Notes
*   Calculated as 25 per cent of sales.
†   Found as first balancing figure.
†† Found as second balancing figure.

Readers should now work Question 11.7 at the end of this chapter, which tests the calculation of the value of lost stock with adjustments for debtors and creditors.

Cash losses

Businesses must establish adequate control over their cash as it is a mobile asset that is difficult to trace and easily exchanged. Receipts from cash sales are potentially vulnerable because control is only established once the sale has been recorded; prior to that point theft would not be highlighted by, for example, the failure of the amount of money taken from the till to agree with the till roll recording receipts. The value of suspected losses can be calculated as follows:

1. Calculate the cost of goods sold applying the formula:

    Opening stock + Purchases – Closing stock = Cost of goods sold

2. Calculate the theoretical value of sales by applying the expected mark-up to the cost of goods sold (found in 1).
3. Deduct recorded sales from theoretical sales (found in 2) to calculate the shortfall in recorded sales, and hence cash.

Example 11.16   The manager of a shop suspects that takings are being stolen. He ascertains the following for the month of July 19X9:

	£
Stock at 1 July	15,762
Purchases during July	68,570
Stock at 31 July	17,056
Recorded sales	80,840

All goods are sold at a price to yield a gross profit of 20 per cent on selling price.

Required   Calculate the value of any cash discrepancy.

Solution   *Step*
1. The cost of goods sold is £15,762 + £68,570 − £17,056 = £67,276.
2. Of the selling price, 20 per cent is gross profit, and so the cost of goods sold is 80 per cent of the selling price. The theoretical value of sales is therefore:

$$£67,276 \times 100/80 = £84,095$$
(i.e. goods are sold at cost plus 25%).

3. The value of takings stolen is: £84,095 − £80,840 = £3,255.

Note
The usefulness of this technique is reliant on the accuracy of the assumed gross margin.

Questions

11.1 Note: This question tests the principles dealt with at pp. 239–44 of this chapter. The following is the trial balance of Midwich, a manufacturer, at 31 March 19X6:

	£	£
Capital		50,000
Sales		208,000
Loan		30,000
Raw materials: Purchases	40,000	
Stock at 1 April 19X5	12,000	
Production wages	30,000	
Production equipment: At cost	70,000	
Provision for depreciation at 1 April 19X5		14,000
Rent	6,400	
Light, heat and power	12,000	
Production overhead expenses	17,500	
Administration expenses	7,500	
Administration salaries	15,000	
Work-in-progress at 1 April 19X5	2,000	
Finished goods stock at 1 April 19X5	11,500	
Provision for unrealized profit at 1 April 19X5		1,500
Hire of office equipment	7,000	

Postage and telephone	5,350	
Loan interest	3,000	
Bank charges	1,250	
Overdraft		10,000
Hire of delivery vans	2,000	
Van driver's wages	7,000	
Petrol and other van expenses	1,000	
Debtors	20,000	
Creditors		5,000
Drawings	48,000	
	318,500	318,500

Notes

1. The production equipment has a life of 10 years and a zero scrap value.
2. Stocks at 31 March 19X6 were:

	£	
Raw materials	14,000	(at cost)
Work-in-progress	7,000	(at cost)
Finished goods	13,800	(at transfer price)

3. Of the rent and light, and heat and power, 75 per cent relates to the factory.
4. Transfers are made from the manufacturing account at cost plus 15 per cent.

Required

The manufacturing, trading and profit and loss account of Midwich for the year to 31 March 19X6 and the balance sheet at that date.

11.2 Calc Ltd has a head office and three branches. The company's results for 19X6 were:

		£000	*£000*
Sales:	Branch 1	250	
	Branch 2	300	
	Branch 3	175	
			725
Cost of goods sold:	Branch 1	125	
	Branch 2	160	
	Branch 3	67	
			352
Gross profit			373
Running costs:	Branch 1	60	
	Branch 2	85	
	Branch 3	47	
			192
			181
Head office costs			90
Profit			91

Required

Redraft the accounts to show the results achieved by each branch.

11.3 Lingwood commenced business as a hire-purchase trader on 1 January 19X5, with a cash capital of £10,000. He decided to sell vacuum cleaners (VC) and electric polishers (EP) and his terms were that payment should be made in eight equal instalments, the first payable on the date of sale, and the remainder at quarterly intervals thereafter.

The following information is extracted from Lingwood's books at the end of 19X5:

	Numbers purchased	Numbers sold	Cost per unit £	Cash selling price per unit £	Total selling price per unit £
VCs	300	250	96	144	168
EPs	250	200	144	216	252

Bank Account for 19X5

	£		£
Opening balance	10,000	Purchases	
Receipts in respect of sales:		Vcs – 250 at £96	24,000
VCs – 250 at £84	21,000	EPs – 250 at £144	36,000
EPs – 200 at £63	12,600	Expenses	1,980
	———	Drawings	3,500
	43,600	Bank interest	1,086
Overdraft at 31 Dec. X5	22,966		
	66,566		66,566

All instalments due from customers were received on due date. On 31 December 19X5, Lingwood still owed his suppliers for 50 VCs; creditors for expenses were £460.

Note

Credit for profit on sales is only to be taken in respect of instalments received.

Required

The hire-purchase trading and profit and loss account of Lingwood for 19X5 and his balance sheet at 31 December.

11.4 The following are the balance sheets of Sharpner and Pencil at 31 December 19X7:

	Sharpner £	Sharpner £	Pencil £	Pencil £
Fixed assets				
Land and buildings		32,100		10,000
Motor vans		20,000		3,000
		52,100		13,000
Current assets				
Stock	10,700		6,000	
Debtors	7,600		3,000	
Cash	5,200		700	
	23,500		9,700	

Current liabilities				
Trade creditors	7,000		3,200	
Working capital		16,500		6,500
		68,600		19,500
Financed by:				
Capital		68,600		19,500

On 1 January 19X8 Sharpner purchased all of the assets, except cash, and liabilities of Pencil for £29,000 cash. The current values of Pencil's assets were:

	£
Land and buildings	15,000
Motor van	2,700
Stock	5,800

To finance the acquisition, Sharpner took out a loan of £25,000 repayable in ten years' time.

Required

Prepare the balance sheet of Sharpner on 1 January 19X8 after the acquisition of Pencil's business has been completed.

11.5 The balance sheet of the business owned by I. Sellup at 31 December 19X2 was as follows:

	£			£
Fixed assets				
Freehold land and			Capital	28,694
buildings	22,100		Trade creditors	7,462
Motor vans	1,975		Bank overdraft	1,893
	24,075			
Current assets	£			
Stock	8,992			
Debtors	4,982			
	13,974			
	38,049			38,049

Mr Buyit agrees to purchase Sellup's business on 1 January 19X3 for £40,000 cash. He sells some investments and opens a business bank account with a deposit of £50,000 and immediately pays from it the sum due to Sellup. Buyit did not take over the debtors or liabilities, and accepted no responsibility for Sellup's bank overdraft. He did agree to collect the debts and to account to Sellup for the amount collected. Land and buildings, the van and stocks were taken over and were recorded in the books of Buyit at the values reported above.

The following balances were extracted from Buyit's books, maintained strictly in accordance with double entry principles, as at 31 December 19X3:

	£
Sales revenue	92,968
Cost of sales	71,034
Expenses	13,168
Collected from Sellup's debtors	2,740
Paid to Sellup	2,610
Debtors	6,949
Creditors for supplies	4,972
Stock-in-trade	15,594
Creditors for expenses	192

Depreciation on the van is to be charged at 20 per cent per annum on the takeover price.

Required

(a) A summary of Buyit's bank account for 19X3.
(b) The trading and profit and loss account of Buyit's business for 19X3 and a balance sheet at 31 December 19X3.

11.6 The following is the balance sheet of Purlin at 30 June 19X5:

	£		£	£
Fixed assets		Capital		50,000
Premises	27,000	Trade creditors	10,000	
Equipment	5,000	Overdraft	3,000	
Motor car	2,000		———	13,000
	———			
	34,000			
Stock and debtors	29,000			
	———			———
	63,000			63,000

Lintel Ltd acquired the business of Purlin on 1 July 19X5 for £50,000, with the exceptions of the equipment, motor car and overdraft. Purlin sold the equipment separately for £4,000 cash and took the car over at book value for his own use.

Required

Prepare the realization account, equipment account, cash account and capital account to record the dissolution of the firm as they appear in the books of Purlin.

11.7 The premises of Advance & Co. suffered a fire during the night of 18 February 19X4, which destroyed a quantity of stock together with the stock records. The stock was insured against fire and the company wishes to submit a claim. The following information is available:

(a) The company's accounting date is 31 December, and the balance sheet at that date in 19X3 showed stock-in-trade of £66,000, debtors of £54,000 and creditors for purchases of £42,000.
(b) During the period 1 January to 18 February 19X4, the following transactions took place:

	£
Cash collected from debtors	97,000
Discounts allowed	1,000
Cash paid to creditors	68,000
Discounts received	400
Cash sales	36,000
Stock drawings by owner at cost	600

(c) The company's ledger shows that on 18 February 19X4 debtors owed £57,000 and creditors were owed £39,000.

(d) A stock-take, carried out immediately after the fire, showed the value of undamaged stock to be £18,000.

(e) The company makes a gross profit of 25 per cent on the selling price of its goods.

Required

A calculation of the cost of stock lost in the fire.

11.8 Sensible Software Ltd issued the following invoices to customers during the week commencing Monday 19 November 1990. All sales are subject to VAT at 15 per cent and the following list gives the *gross* value of each invoice issued:

Date issued 1990	Invoice number	Customer	Gross amount
23 November	CS 1233/90	B. Pain	£460.00
22 November	CS 1232/90	Milne Consultancies Ltd	£1,380.00
21 November	CS 1231/90	Moussin & Sons Ltd	£402.50
20 November	CS 1230/90	Cherebin plc	£262.20
19 November	CS 1229/90	B. Pain	£179.40

On 23 November Cherebin plc returned the goods invoiced on 20 November to Sensible Software Ltd (invoice number CS 1230/90) along with their debit note (number DN 90/125) dated 22 November. Sensible Software Ltd confirmed receipt of the goods on 23 November by issuing a credit note (number SR 770/90) for £262.20 gross.

On 24 November Sensible Software received back some of the goods shipped to B. Pain on 19 November. On the telephone Sensible Software Ltd agreed an allowance of £89.70 gross with B. Pain and on the same day sent out a credit note (number SR 771/90) for this amount.

Required

(a) Write up Sensible Software Ltd's sales book and sales returns book for the week commencing 19 November 1990 totalling the columns off as at the close of business on 24 November 1990 *(9 marks)*

(b) Describe how the information in the sales book and the sales returns book would be incorporated into Sensible Software Ltd's ledger. *(7 marks)*

(c) The balance brought forward on B. Pain's account as at 1 November 1990 was £440.00. Sensible Software Ltd received a cheque on 7 November 1990 for this amount less 5 per cent cash discount which B. Pain was entitled to deduct. There were no other transactions with B. Pain during the month of November other than those detailed above.

Reconstruct B. Pain's personal account as it would appear for the month of November 1990 in Sensible Software Ltd's ledger. Balance off the account as at 30 November 1990. *(4 marks)*

(Total 20 marks)

(AAT Preliminary Examination, December, 1990)

11.9 Ian Crowther, a sole trader, has decided to draw up a cash book to start recording his cash and bank transactions as from the week commencing 25 November 1991.

His cash and bank transactions during the week were as follows:

Nov. 25   Mr Crowther counted £117 cash in the business till at the start of business and confirmed a favourable balance in the business bank account of £391 with his bankers.

Nov. 25   Mr Crowther paid £222 rent for the business premises by cheque.

Nov. 25   Cash sales for the day totalled £235 including VAT at 17.5 per cent.

Nov. 26   Mr Crowther incurred business travelling expenses totalling £71 which he paid in cash.

Nov. 26   An invoice from A. Young, one of Mr Crowther's suppliers, was paid in full by a cheque for £60. Mr Crowther was able to deduct 10 per cent discount because he paid the invoice promptly.

Nov. 26   Mr Crowther received a cheque from A. Berry, one of his credit customers, in full settlement of an invoice for £450. Mr Berry has taken advantage of 10 per cent discount for settling within the discount period. Mr Crowther pays all cheques received into the business bank account the day they are received.

Nov. 27   Cash sales for the day amounted to £470 inclusive of VAT.

Nov. 28   Paid employees their wages for the week – partly by cheque for £350 and partly in cash £120.

Nov. 28   Mr Crowther withdrew £75 from the business till for private expenditure.

Nov. 29   Mr Crowther paid a telephone bill by cheque for £102. The invoice from the telephone company included VAT of £16.

Nov. 29   Mr Crowther received cheques from the following credit customers:

| C. Dundas | £144 |
| E. Ferguson | £171 |

Nov. 29   Mr Crowther was informed by his bankers that bank charges of £45 had been debited to his account.

Nov. 29   Mr Crowther transferred £450 from the business till into the business bank account.

The following is a summary of the cash book as maintained by Mr Crowther for the week:

I. Crowther – Cash Book

Date	Narration	Folio	VAT disc. received		Bank	Cash	Date	Narration	Folio	VAT disc. allowed		Bank	Cash
			£	£	£	£				£	£	£	£
Nov. 25	Balance	b/f			391	117	Nov. 25	Rent	NL 27			222	
Nov. 25	Sales	NL 44	41.13			235	Nov. 26	Trvl. exps.	NL 50				71
Nov. 26	A. Berry	SL 02		45	450		Nov. 26	A. Young	SL 30		6	60	
Nov. 27	Sales	NL 44	82.25			470	Nov. 28	Wages	NL 67			350	120
Nov. 29	C. Dundas	SL 10			144		Nov. 26	Drawings	NL 13				75
Nov. 29	E. Ferguson	SL 21			117		Nov. 29	Telephone	NL 48	16.00		102	
Nov. 29	Bank chrgs.	NL 04			45		Nov. 29	Cash	C				450
Nov. 29	Bank	C			450		Nov. 30	Balance	c/f	107.38	39	863	106
			123.38	45	1,597	822				123.38	45	1,597	822

Required

Check Mr Crowther's transactions off against the entries he has made in his cash book and draw up a list of any errors you think may have been made in the cash book by Mr Crowther.

(Total 20 marks)
(AAT Preliminary Examinations, December 1991)

12
INTERPRETATION OF ACCOUNTS: THE CASH FLOW STATEMENT

> The objectives of this chapter are to
>
> - explain the uses of the cash flow statement as part of the annual accounts package;
> - outline the required format of a cash flow statement so that it complies with FRS 1;
> - show how the individual figures contained in a cash flow statement are derived;
> - illustrate the construction of a complete cash flow statement; and
> - demonstrate the interpretation of the information contained in cash flow statement.

INTRODUCTION

For many years limited companies have been legally obliged to publish each year a balance sheet and profit and loss account. During the 1960s, a number of companies voluntarily added to these two reports a third financial statement called 'the statement of source and application of funds', which was often abbreviated to 'statement of funds'. The production of the statement of funds was regulated in 1975 with the issue of SSAP 10, which required virtually all companies to include one as part of their annual accounts. SSAP 10 was replaced in 1993 by FRS 1, *Cash Flow Statements*, which changes the focus of the published statement from funds, generally defined as working capital, to cash. These developments reflect the recognition of an important gap in the information provided to external users of accounting reports.

The balance sheet sets out the financial state of a business at a particular point in time, whereas the profit and loss account reports some, but not all, transactions undertaken during an accounting period; it includes only those transactions that directly give rise to revenues and expenditures. Other transactions, such as issues of shares and debentures and the purchase or disposal of fixed assets, are not reported in the profit and loss account since they are *capital* as opposed to *revenue* transactions. The inclusion of a cash flow statement as part of the annual accounts brings the following benefits:

- The concept of a cash flow is one which lay people can be expected to understand and so it helps to remove some of the misunderstanding which may arise when users of accounts do not understand the concepts and conventions that underlie such features as the depreciation charge.
- The survival of a company depends on its ability to meet its liabilities when they fall due, and this requires cash. The cash flow statement allows the user to judge an enterprise's ability to generate positive future cash flows and meet its financial obligations, such as the payment of dividends or repayment of loans.
- It enables the effect of investments undertaken during the financial period on the organization's financial position to be *assessed*.
- It explains the reasons for differences between profits and cash flows arising from trading activity.
- The value of a business reflects the amount of cash it is expected to generate in the future, and so the cash flow statement, although reporting historical events, provides a useful input to business valuation models based on estimates of likely future cash flows.

The next part of this chapter shows how the cash flow statement is presented, explains the calculation of the various figures it contains and describes the way in which it can aid interpretation.

FORMAT

A cash flow statement can be defined as follows: *The cash flow statement sets out, in an orderly manner, the cash which has been raised and generated by a business during the year and the ways in which this cash has been spent.* For publication purposes, FRS 1 requires that the cash flows are classified under the following standard headings:

- *Net cash flow from operating activities* These are the cash flows which result from trading activities. Therefore this section contains the cash flows resulting from operations that are reported in the profit and loss account. All of the cash flows are to be reported net of value added tax, and the net amount, payable or recoverable in respect of VAT, is to be included as an item within this section.
- *Returns on investments and servicing of finance* These are the receipts, such as interest received, resulting from the ownership of investments and payments, for example, dividends, made to providers of finance.
- *Taxation* This covers cash flows resulting from the taxation of revenue and capital profits that, for most companies, means corporation tax.
- *Investing activities* These cash flows arise from the purchase or sale of fixed assets, including long-term investments made in the shares or debentures of other companies and their eventual sale or repayment.
- *Financing* These are cash flows that take place between the company and its suppliers of long-term finance. Cash receipts come from issuing shares, loans or debentures, and cash payments from their redemption.

The overall effect of the cash transactions is a net increase or decrease in the cash balance. In outline, the cash flow statement appears as shown in Figure 12.1.

	£000
Net cash flow from operating activities	X
Returns on investment and servicing of finance	X
Taxation	X
Investing activities	X
Financing	X
Increase (decrease) in cash	X

Figure 12.1   Outline cash flow statement

The preparation of the cash flow statement for a company usually starts with the profit and loss account for a year together with its opening and closing balance sheet. It is then necessary to convert the flows of resources, such as sales or dividends, into cash flows, using the techniques given in Chapter 4 where the reverse operation was carried out, namely converting cash flows into resource flows. The next section shows the practical application of these methods.

STATEMENT CONSTRUCTION

The profit and loss account and balance sheet from which a cash flow statement is to be prepared are given in Figure 12.2.

Final Accounts of Tide Ltd

		£000	£000
Sales			3,620
Less:	Opening stock	224	
	Purchases	1,760	
	Closing stock	(293)	
Cost of goods sold			1,691
Gross profit			1,929
Less:	Depreciation	104	
	Loss on sale of fixed assets	25	
	Administration expenses	1,136	
	Distribution costs	275	
			1,540
Operating profit			389
Interest received		26	
Interest paid		(10)	
			16
Profit on ordinary activities before tax			405
Corporation tax			90
			315
Dividends:	Paid	45	
	Proposed	180	
			225
Retained profit for the year			90
Profit brought forward			178
Profit carried forward			268

Balance Sheets at 31 December 19X4 and 19X3

	19X4 £000	19X3 £000
Fixed assets		
Plant at book value, 1 January	945	1,000
Additions	530	20
Disposals at book value (Note 1)	(40)	—
Depreciation charge	(104)	(75)
	1,331	945
Current assets		
Stock	293	224
Debtors	586	549
Cash at bank	—	53
	879	826
Current liabilities		
Bank overdraft	171	—
Trade creditors	181	156
Proposed dividend	180	120
Corporation tax due	90	117
	622	393
Working capital	257	433
Total assets less current liabilities	1,588	1,378
Debentures	—	(200)
	1,588	1,178
Financed by:		
Ordinary shares of £1 each	1,200	1,000
Share premium	120	—
Profit and loss account	268	178
	1,588	1,178

Figure 12.2 The following information is provided for Tide Ltd in respect of the year to 31 December 19X4

The information contained in Figure 12.2 is now used to calculate the values to be included in a cash flow statement. Each of the elements identified in Figure 12.1 is dealt with separately and is then included in the complete statement. After the complete statement has been compiled, a number of related complications are considered.

Net cash flow from operating activities

There are two alternative ways in which this may be calculated: the direct method and the indirect method.

The direct method calculates the cash flow by comparing the cash received from customers with the outflows for goods and services paid to suppliers and employees. The calculation of the cash flow from operating activities for

Tide Ltd calculated in this way is given in Figure 12.3.

	£000
Cash from sales (W1)	3,583
Cash paid for:	
Purchases (W2)	(1,735)
Administrative expenses	(1,136)
Distribution costs	(275)
Net cash flow from operating activities	437

Workings

	W1 Sales £000	W2 Purchases £000
From profit and loss account	3,620	1,760
Add: Opening debtors/creditors	549	156
Less: Closing debtors/creditors	(586)	(181)
Cash flow	3,583	1,735

Figure 12.3   Cash flow from operating activities: direct method

The opening debtors and creditors are added to the figures from the profit and loss account as they represent revenues and expenditures which took place in the previous year but are not converted to cash until the current year. The closing debtors and creditors are deducted because the sale or purchase took place in 19X4, but the related cash flow will occur next year.

The indirect method produces exactly the same net cash flow as the direct method, but starts with the operating profit and makes adjustments for items in the profit and loss account which do not match their corresponding cash flow. The calculation for Tide Ltd is shown in Figure 12.4.

Adjustments are made for changes in the value of stocks, debtors and trade creditors because values recognized in the profit and loss account are not represented by a corresponding cash flow. For example, a credit sale is included in the profit and loss account even though the cash has not yet been received; when accounts are drawn up before the debt is settled, the sales for the period differ from the cash received by the value of the debt. However, the cash from debts due at the start of the year are received during the current year and add to cash inflows. Therefore the difference between

	£000
Operating profit	389
Depreciation charge	104
Loss on sale of fixed assets	25
Increase in stocks	(69)
Increase in debtors	(37)
Increase in trade creditors	25
Net cash flow from operating activities	437

Figure 12.4   Cash flow from operating activities: indirect method

the cash received from sales and the entry in the profit and loss account is measured by the change in the value of debtors between the start and end of the year.

FRS 1 requires companies to publish

- a single figure for net cash flow from operating activities on the face of the cash flow statement; and
- a note which shows the reconciliation of the cash flow from operating activities with the profit from operating activities.

In addition, companies are free to publish additional information showing the results calculated on the direct method if they so wish.

The direct method of calculation has the advantage of being a clear statement of cash inflows and outflows and so is easily comprehended, while the indirect method highlights the reasons for differences between operating profit and operating cash flow.

Returns on investment and servicing of finance

This section contains the cash receipts and payments of interest and dividends. The calculation for Tide Ltd is shown in Figure 12.5.

	£000
Interest received	26
Interest paid	(10)
Dividends paid (W1)	(165)
Net cash flow	(149)
Working (W1)	
Interim dividend for 19X4 from profit and loss account	45
Final dividend for 19X3 from opening balance sheet	120
	165

Figure 12.5   Returns on investment and servicing of finance

Taxation

The tax paid in 19X4 is the amount included in the opening balance sheet as a current liability, in this case £117,000. The charge for 19X4 is a liability in that year's closing balance sheet and will cause a cash outflow in 19X5.

Investing activities

This covers the cost of acquiring fixed assets and investments and the cash inflow from the disposal of any of these items. The flows for Tide Ltd are given in Figure 12.6.

	£000
Payments to buy fixed assets	(530)
Receipts from sale of fixed assets	15
	(515)

Figure 12.6   Investing activities

Financing

The issue of shares or debentures and their repayment are recorded under this heading, and so the figures are calculated by comparing the opening and closing balance sheets for these items to see whether there has been any increases.or decreases. The results for Tide Ltd are given in Figure 12.7.

	£000
Issue of shares (W1)	320
Repayment of debentures	(200)
	120
Working (W1)	
Increase in share capital	200
Increase in share premium	120
	320

Figure 12.7   Financing

It is now possible to combine all of the calculations made so far to produce a full cash flow statement for Tide Ltd, and this is shown in Figure 12.8.

SOME COMPLEXITIES OF THE CASH FLOW STATEMENT

This section examines some of the complexities associated with the cash flow statement:

- The depreciation charge as a source of cash.
- Reconstructing the profit and loss account.
- Movements in fixed assets.

Depreciation and cash flow

The fact that the year's depreciation charge is added to operating profit as a source of cash requires further consideration. During the course of trading activity, a company generates revenue, principally in the form of sales receipts, and incurs expenditure comprising a wide range of different outlays, some of which result in an outflow of cash in the current accounting period and others which do not. Most outlays fall into the first category, for example, expenditure on purchases of materials, wages, salaries and rent. There are, however, a small number of items, the most important of which is depreciation, that are charged against profit but do not result in a current outflow of cash.

The purpose of the depreciation charge is to reflect the fact that sales revenue has benefited, during the period under review, from the use of fixed assets acquired in a previous accounting period. The effect of making the charge is to earmark an equivalent amount of cash for retention within

	£000	£000
Net cash flow from operating activities (Note 1)		437
Returns on investment and servicing of finance:		
Interest received	26	
Interest paid	(10)	
Dividends paid (W1)	(165)	
Net cash flow	——	(149)
Taxation		(117)
Investing activities:		
Payments to buy fixed assets	(530)	
Receipts from sale of fixed assets	15	
	——	(515)
Net cash outflow before financing		(344)
Financing:		
Issue of shares (W1)	320	
Repayment of debentures	(200)	
	——	120
Decrease in cash (Note 2)		(244)

Note 1 Reconciliation of operating profit to net cash inflow from operating activities:

	£000
Operating profit	389
Depreciation charge	104
Loss on sale of fixed assets	25
Increase in stocks	(69)
Increase in debtors	(37)
Increase in trade creditors	25
	437

Note 2 Change in cash balance during the year:

	£000
Opening balance in hand	53
Closing overdraft	171
Decrease in cash	224

Figure 12.8   Tide Ltd, Cash Flow Statement for the year to 31 December 19X4

the business, which may be used, in due course, to help finance replacement of the asset when it is worn out.

Because depreciation is charged in the profit and loss account, but does not result in a current outflow of funds, it must be added back to reported profit in order to identify cash generated from operations, i.e.:

Cash generated from operations = Profit + Depreciation

Students often find it difficult to grasp the fact that the depreciation charge is *represented* by an equivalent *inflow* of cash. The link is demonstrated in Example 12.1.

Example 12.1   The balance sheet of Pencil Ltd, which purchases and sells goods for cash, is as follows at 31 December 19X1:

Balance Sheet at 31 December 19X1

	£	£
Fixed assets at cost		1,800
Less: Depreciation		540
		1,260
Current assets		
Stock	400	
Cash	200	600
		1,860
10% Loan repayable 19X7		500
		1,360
Financed by:		
Share capital		1,000
Retained profit		360
		1,360

During 19X2 cash sales and cash purchases amounted respectively to £4,000 and £2,500. The stock level remained unchanged during the year and £600 was *paid out* for wages and other operating expenses. In addition, loan interest was paid on 31 December 19X2, and depreciation of £240 was charged on fixed assets.

Required

(a) The cash account for 19X2.
(b) The trading and profit and loss account for 19X2.
(c) The balance sheet at 31 December 19X2.
(d) A calculation of cash generated from operations during 19X2, i.e. profit + depreciation.

Solution

(a) **Cash Account for 19X2**

	£		£
Opening balance	200	Purchases	2,500
Sales	4,000	Wages, etc.	600
		Interest	50
		Closing balance	1,050
	4,200		4,200

(b) Trading and Profit and Loss Account for 19X2

	£		£
Opening stock	400	Sales	4,000
Purchases	2,500		
Less: Closing stock	(400)		
Cost of goods sold	2,500		
Gross profit	1,500		
	4,000		4,000
Wages, etc.	600	Gross profit	1,500
Interest	50		
Depreciation	240		
	890		
Net profit	610		
	1,500		1,500

(c) Balance Sheet at 31 December 19X2

	£	£
Fixed assets at cost		1,800
Less: Depreciation		780
		1,020
Current assets		
Stock	400	
Cash	1,050	1,450
		2,470
10% Loan repayable 19X7		500
		1,970
Financed by:		
Share capital		1,000
Retained profit (360 + 610)		970
		1,970

(d) Cash generated from operations:

	£
Profit	610
Add: Depreciation	240
Cash from operations	850

The cash balance has increased from £200 to £1,050 and the cash account shows, in detail, how this increase of £850 has been brought about. The profit and loss account shows a profit figure of £610, and this is less than the increase in the cash balance because a 'non-cash' item of expenditure, i.e. depreciation, £240, has been debited to the profit and loss account. It is, therefore, necessary to add back depreciation to reported profit in order to reconcile the opening cash balance with the closing cash balance:

	£	£
Opening cash balance		200
Add: Profit	610	
Depreciation	240	
Cash generated from operations		850
Closing cash balance		1,050

In practice, it is rare for the change in the cash balance to be entirely due to cash generated from operations. There are numerous other transactions that cause it to change, for example, new plant is purchased or additional shares issued.

A note of warning

A common misconception is that the depreciation charge *produces* an inflow of cash, and that the amount of cash available can be increased by raising the charge. This is wrong. Cash is generated from trading transactions, and the depreciation charge is simply a 'book entry' that earmarks a proportion of funds generated from operations for retention within the business. If the depreciation charge, in Example 12.1, is increased from £240 to £400, profit falls from £610 to £450 and cash generated from operations remain unchanged at £850 (depreciation £400 + profit £450). An effect of raising the charge is, however, to earmark a *larger* amount of cash for retention within the business in the current year; later in the asset's life, charges and retentions will be correspondingly lower because the balance that remains to be written off at 31 December 19X2 is reduced by £240.

Example 12.2   Assume the same facts as appear in the solution to Example 12.1.

Required   Calculate the closing cash balance of Pencil, on 1 January 19X3, in each of the following circumstances:

(a) The entire profit of £610 is paid out as dividends on 1 January 19X3.
(b) The depreciation charge is amended to £400 and the entire profit of £450 is paid out as dividends on 1 January 19X3.

Note
No other transactions occur on 1 January 19X3.

	(a)	(b)	**Solution**
	£	£	
Cash balance at 31 December 19X2	1,050	1,050	
Less: Dividends	610	450	
Cash balance at 1 January 19X3	440	600	

Note
The increase in the depreciation charge, under (b), reduces the maximum dividend payable by £160 and, as a result, the remaining cash balance is £160 higher at £600.

Reconstructing the profit and loss account

In some cases a profit and loss account may not be provided, and so the operating profit for the year has to be reconstructed from examining the changes between the opening and closing balance sheets. This technique is illustrated in Example 12.3.

The following are the summarized balance sheets of Ebbs Ltd at 31 December 19X2 and 19X1:   *Example 12.3*

	19X2	19X1
	£000	£000
Fixed assets at book value	1,300	1,200
Current assets		
Stock	220	200
Debtors	300	250
Cash	15	10
	535	460
Current liabilities		
Trade creditors	160	140
Corporation tax	50	45
Dividend	55	35
	265	220
Working capital	270	240
	1,570	1,440
Financed by:		
Ordinary shares of £1 each	1,000	1,000
Profit and loss account	570	440
	1,570	1,440

The company paid an interim dividend of £15,000 during 19X2.

Required Calculate the profit from trading activities of Ebbs Ltd for 19X2.

Solution

	£000
Retained profit 31 December	570
Retained profit 1 January	440
Increase	130
Tax charge	50
Interim dividend	15
Final dividend	55
Profit for the year	250

Movements in fixed assets

Quite often a company purchases *and* sells fixed assets during the year. The balance sheet may only show the 'net' change and it is necessary to prepare a fixed asset schedule that shows gross changes during the year. The preparation of the schedule is based on the following known relationships:

Cost of fixed assets Opening balance + Additions – Cost of assets sold
= Closing balance

Accumulated depreciation Opening balance + Charge for the year –
Accumulated depreciation on asset sold = Closing balance

Example 12.4 The following information is extracted from the balance sheet of Staple Ltd at 31 December:

Fixed assets	*19X0*	*19X1*
Motor vehicles at cost	£40,000	£57,500
Less: Accumulated depreciation	22,700	31,600
	17,300	25,900

On 1 July 19X1, Staple sold a motor vehicle for £750. The machine had cost £6,000 some years ago, and accumulated depreciation at 31 December 19X0 was £4,900. The company's policy is to charge a full year's depreciation in the year of purchase and none in the year a vehicle is sold.

Required
(a) Calculations of additions during the year and depreciation charged.
(b) Calculate the profit or loss on disposal of vehicles.
(c) Show the information to be included in the cash flow statement relating to motor vehicles, and indicate in which section of the statement each item would appear.

(a)

	Cost £	*Dep.* £
Opening balance	40,000	22,700
Add: Purchases/depreciation charge for year	23,500*	13,800*
Less: Sales	(6,000)	(4,900)
Closing balance	57,500	31,600

Note
* These are the balancing figures.

(b)

	£
Book value (cost £6,000 – depreciation £4,900)	1,100
Less: Sales proceeds	750
Loss on sale	350

(c)

	£	*Location*
Depreciation charged	13,800	Reconciliation of profit and cash
Loss on sale of vehicle	350 *	flow from operating activities
Sale proceeds	750	Investing activities
Purchase of motor vehicles	23,500	

Note
* The loss on disposal, of £350, is debited to the profit and loss account to make up for the fact that insufficient depreciation has been charged. Like depreciation, the loss on sale is a non-cash expense and must be added back to the profit to produce the figure for cash generated from operations. Any profit on sale, credited to the profit and loss account, must likewise be deducted from profit, as the entire sale proceeds appear in the statement in the 'investing activities' section.

INTERPRETATION USING THE CASH FLOW STATEMENT

The preparation of a cash flow statement is not an end in itself, and its purpose is to provide some insights into the financial policy pursued by management during the year and to show the effects of that policy on the changes in the financial position of the company which have taken place. The interpretation of the information contained in the statement is now discussed.

Overcapitalization
A company sometimes finds itself with cash in excess of operating requirements. This may occur because initial financial requirements were over-estimated and too much capital was raised at the outset. A second possible reason is a sharp contraction in the level of business operations, for example, the closure of a segment of a business or the sale of a valuable freehold property. It is essential that excess funds should not be allowed to lie idle, and the usual solution is for management to make plans for the investment of these resources. Where this is not possible, cash should be returned to the shareholders in the form of a reduction of capital. Stringent legal formalities must be complied with, when undertaking such a scheme, to ensure that the position of the creditors is not jeopardized.

Financing long-term investment

It is management's job to ensure that inflows and outflows of cash are properly matched, i.e. cash available for only a short period of time should only be used for a short-term application while long-term investment must be paid for out of long-term finance. For example, the purchase of a fixed asset should be paid for by raising a long-term loan, or by issuing shares, or by retaining profits permanently within the business. The reason for this is that a company is likely to suffer acute financial embarrassment if it attempts to finance the purchase of factory premises, for example, using a short-term source of finance such as a bank overdraft. The new acquisition is expected to generate sufficient revenue to cover its cost and produce an adequate balance of profit, but this process will probably take a number of years and short-term finance will have to be repaid long before it is complete.

Overtrading

Overtrading is a condition that arises when a company attempts to do too much too quickly and, as a result, fails to maintain a satisfactory balance between profit maximization and financial stability. Overtrading usually occurs when a company rapidly expands its scale of business activities but fails, first, to make available sufficient long-term finance for this purpose. Where a company has overtraded some, or all, of the following features will be apparent from an examination of consecutive balance sheets:

- A sharp increase in expenditure on fixed assets.
- A decrease in the balance of cash, and perhaps the emergence of a bank overdraft.
- The structure of the current assets becomes less liquid, probably because the proportion of current assets 'tied up' in stock increases dramatically.
- A sharp increase in creditors caused by the company's inability to pay debts as they fall due.

The actual *causes* of overtrading are clearly demonstrated in the cash flow statement, which shows how much long-term finance has been made available during the year and how it has been used.

Example 12.5 Madoc is confused and worried and has come to you for advice. He tells you that, although he made a bigger profit in 19X7 than in 19X6, and has also made fewer drawings, he does not seem to be any better off and is finding it difficult to pay his creditors.

The balance sheets of Madoc's business at the end of 19X6 and 19X7 are shown below:

Balance Sheets at 31 December

	19X6 £	19X7 £
Machines as cost	10,000	20,500
Less: Depreciation	3,000	5,500
	7,000	15,000

Stock	1,700	4,900
Debtors	1,800	3,700
Bank	3,500	400
	7,000	9,000
Creditors	3,000	10,000
Working capital	4,000	(1,000)
Net assets	11,000	14,000
Financed by:		
Opening capital	12,000	11,000
Add: Net Profit	5,000	7,000
Less: Drawings	(6,000)	(4,000)
Closing capital	11,000	14,000

Required

Explain to Madoc what has happened, and support your explanation with an appropriate numerical statement. Briefly advise Madoc on future policy.

Solution

The causes of Madoc's problems can be identified from a cash flow statement:

	£
Cash flow from operating activities:	
Profit	7,000
Depreciation	2,500
Increase in stock	(3,200)
Increase in debtors	(1,900)
Increase in creditors	7,000
	11,400
Investing activities	
Purchase of fixed assets	(10,500)
Financing:	
Drawings	(4,000)
Decline in cash balance	(3,100)

The cause of Madoc's confusion is that he mistakenly believes that profit produces an equivalent increase in the bank balance. This may happen in certain circumstances, but only if no additional investment takes place. The above cash flow statement shows that Madoc has invested heavily in additional fixed assets, and there have also been substantial increases in stocks and debtors. In total, these outlays significantly exceed cash generated from operations; the result is that the bank balance has fallen dramatically and the amount owed to creditors has more than trebled.

Madoc is in a very difficult financial position, as a result of *overtrading*, and it is important that he undertakes no further investment at this stage. He should also keep drawings to a minimum and use future profits to reduce his firm's reliance on short-term credit.

Readers should now work Question 12.4 at the end of the chapter.

The situation shown in Example 12.5 is a relatively simple one. The principles of interpretation are now applied to the cash flow statement of Tide Ltd, as shown in Figure 12.8, to see what messages it contains:

- The company has a substantial net cash flow from operations, and Note 1 explains the extent to which this differs from operating profit. Funds from operations (represented by operating profit, depreciation charge and loss on sale of fixed assets) are mainly responsible for cash generation, some of which has been used to finance the increase in stock and debtors, to the extent that this has not been covered by the increase in trade creditors.
- The 'Returns on investment and servicing of finance' shows that the main outflow is dividends paid, which absorbs about one-half of net cash flow from operating activities.
- 'Taxation' discloses that paying corporation tax during the year has absorbed about 40 per cent of the net cash flow.
- 'Investing activities' reveals that a substantial outlay has been made during the year. This is the largest single item in the cash flow statement and is mainly responsible for a net outflow of cash before financing of £344,000.
- The company has made a significant issue of shares, most of the cash from which has been used to repay the debentures. A net balance of £120,000 is shown in the 'Financing' section to help defray the net investment made during the accounting period.
- The overall outcome is a substantial decrease in cash of £224,000, with a cash balance of £53,000 at the start of the year turning into an overdraft of £171,000 at the end as a result of these developments.
- The concluding impression is of a company which has undertaken a significant expansion with the result that its liquidity position has been put under strain.

Retrieving financial stability

The management of a company that has overtraded must take prompt steps to correct the financial imbalance, otherwise it is quite possible that the company will fail. There are a number of possible courses of action open to management. These include the following:

1. *Reduce the level of business investment*   Money is tied up in both fixed assets and current assets, and management should look carefully at the feasibility of releasing cash resources by reducing the amount invested in each of these areas. It is also possible that there is a building or a piece of land that can be sold without any unfavourable repercussions for the company's operating capability. Ratio analysis may be used to examine stock levels and debtor levels to discover whether these are unduly inflated. The company's stock ordering, processing and distribution policies will come under scrutiny as will the effectiveness of the company's system of credit control. The possibility of reducing the investment in debtors, by offering discounts for prompt payment, may also be examined. It must, of course, be borne in mind that discounts, although helpful in improving cash flow, reduce sales proceeds and therefore profit. The employment of the

services of a debt factor and the sale and lease back of freehold property are other options that need to be investigated if there is a substantial liquidity problem that cannot be solved by more conventional means.

2. *Raise additional finance* The total finance to be raised depends on the period over which the cash shortage is expected to persist. Temporary cash difficulties may be overcome by arranging a bank overdraft facility or a short-term loan. Severe overtrading is likely to be corrected, however, only by raising long-term finance in the form of share capital or debentures. Access to either of these sources of long-term finance depends on the particular circumstances of the company under review. If loan finance is presently at a low level and the company has adequate security in the form of tangible assets, the issue of a debenture may well be appropriate. A share issue is, however, more likely to be the answer to the company's financial problems.

   The fact that the company is in financial difficulties obviously places a question mark against the competence of the management team. They have not been successful in anticipating the present cash flow problems, and a potential lender might be doubtful whether management is able to do better in the future. It is the shareholders who will be at greatest financial risk if the company goes into liquidation. They are the last source of finance to be repaid and, in a forced sale, assets are likely to realize significantly less than their book values, often leaving little or nothing over for the providers of equity finance. On the other hand, if the company recovers, the shareholders have most to gain in the form of profits distributed to them in dividends or reinvested on their behalf. At a time of financial difficulty, it will therefore be necessary for the shareholders to confirm their confidence in the future of the company and subscribe to a rights issue.

3. *Cash generated from operations* The third possibility is for the company to recover on the basis of internally generated funds. The component elements of internal funds flow are usually net profit before tax plus depreciation. Tax must, of course, be paid out of this balance, but management is able to exercise a fair amount of discretion concerning the disposition of what remains. Usually, of course, a dividend is paid and investments are made in fixed assets, stocks and debtors. At a time of severe cash shortage, it is important that such outlays are kept to a minimum so that funds generated from operations may instead be used to improve the financial stability of the concern. Indeed, it may be necessary to abandon the payment of a dividend and, if possible, delay the replacement of old plant until the financial position improves. In the case of a profitable company, funds generated from operations and retained within the business can quickly restore an element of financial stability.

4. *A combination of remedies* A number of possible schemes have been considered to help the recovery of a company that has overtraded. It is unlikely that any individual course of action will be the complete solution to the problem. Steps may be taken to economize on working capital and raise, say, a two-year loan to 'tide the company over' until sufficient finance has been generated internally to complete the recovery. Quite

obviously, the appropriate remedy will depend entirely on the particular circumstances of the company in difficulty.

Readers should now work Question 12.5 at the end of this chapter.

The kind of problems discussed in this section are often avoidable. Financial imbalance is usually the result of management's failure to plan future financial developments. Forward planning and the use of forecast accounts to help management decide how to allocate resources are discussed in Chapter 14.

Questions

12.1 The balance sheets of Southall Ltd at 31 December 19X1 and 31 December 19X2 are as follows:

	19X1		19X2	
	£	£	£	£
Fixed assets				
Plant at cost	52,000		70,000	
Less: Depreciation	16,500	35,500	22,700	47,300
Transport at cost	10,000		10,000	
Less: Depreciation	3,600	6,400	4,800	5,200
		41,900		52,500
Current assets				
Stock	10,200		12,600	
Debtors	8,300		13,700	
Bank	4,900		—	
	23,400		26,300	
Less: Current liabilities:				
Trade creditors	5,100		5,800	
Bank overdraft	—		1,300	
	5,100		7,100	
Working capital		18,300		19,200
		60,200		71,700
Financed by:				
Share capital		50,000		54,000
Profit and loss account		10,200		17,700
		60,200		71,700

Required

A cash flow statement for 19X2.

12.2 The following summarized balance sheets of Sticker Ltd for the two years to 31 August 1984 and 31 August 19X5 are made available for your further analysis:

Balance Sheets at 31 August

	19X4	19X5		19X4	19X5
	£	£		£	£
Called-up share			Fixed assets		
capital	60,000	75,000	(tangible) at cost	116,100	153,000
General reserve	16,500	21,000	Less: Depreciation	41,100	50,250
Retained profits	6,750	11,700			
Debentures	10,500	7,500		75,000	102,750
Current liabilities			*Current assets*		
Taxation	8,550	9,750	Stock	28,500	31,500
Creditors	9,450	10,800	Debtors	12,000	9,450
Proposed dividends	6,750	9,000	Bank	3,000	1,050
	118,500	144,750		118,500	144,750

Note

No fixed assets were sold in the year ending 31 August 19X5.

Required

A cash flow statement for the year ended 31 August 19X5.

(15 marks)

(Adapted from ICSA, Financial Accounting I, December, 1985)

12.3 The following balances relate to the affairs of Tufton Ltd as at 31 March 19X0 and 31 March 19X1:

	19X0	19X1
	£	£
Share capital	500,000	600,000
Retained profit	395,800	427,100
10% debentures	200,000	300,000
Creditors	179,800	207,500
Proposed dividend	50,000	60,000
Bank overdraft	—	36,900
	1,325,600	1,631,500
Plant at cost	658,300	796,900
Less: Depreciation	263,500	371,600
	394,800	425,300
Freehold property at cost	300,000	350,000
Stock	327,100	608,300
Debtors	265,700	247,900
Cash at bank	38,000	—
	1,325,600	1,631,500

You are given the following information:

(i) During the year to March 19X1, plant with a written-down value of £202,500 was sold for £169,500. This plant had originally cost £390,000.

(ii) A bonus issue of one ordinary share for every five held was made out of retained profit on 1 June 19X0.

Required

A cash flow statement for the year to 31 March 19X1.

12.4 The following information is provided for Sharpener Ltd:

Balance Sheets 31 December

	19X4		19X5	
	£	£	£	£
Fixed assets				
Cost		650,000		680,000
Less: Accumulated depreciation		176,500		203,700
		473,500		476,300
Current assets				
Stock	126,400		127,500	
Trade debtors	97,700		95,000	
Bank balance	23,600		—	
	247,700		222,500	
Less: Current liabilities				
Trade creditors	72,900		87,100	
Proposed dividend	44,000		44,000	
Bank overdraft	—		37,900	
	116,900		169,000	
Working capital		130,800		53,500
		604,300		529,800
Share capital		400,000		400,000
Retained profit		104,300		109,800
		504,300		509,800
6% debentures repayable 19X9		100,000		20,000
		604,300		529,800

During 19X5 the directors offered to repay the debentures, and this invitation was accepted by the majority of the debenture holders.

Required

(a) A cash flow statement for 19X5.

(b) A brief explanation for the decline in the bank balance based on the information contained in the statement.

12.5 The following information is provided in respect of a small public company:

Profit and Loss Account for the year ended 30 September

	1993 £000	1992 £000
Turnover	6,206	5,621
Net operating costs:		
Raw materials and consumables	2,932	2,747
Staff costs	609	616
Depreciation	152	150
Other operating charges (including goodwill written off)	1,150	982
	4,843	4,495
Operating profit	1,363	1,126
Interest charges	180	162
Profit on ordinary activities before taxation	1,183	964
Tax on profit on ordinary activities	285	255
Profit after taxation	898	709
Proposed final dividend	270	220
Retained profit for the year	628	489
Retained profit brought forward	647	158
Retained profit carried forward	1,275	647

Balance Sheet at 30 September

	1993 £000	1992 £000
Fixed assets:		
Tangible assets		
Acquired brands at cost	2,800	2,500
Land and buildings at valuation (1992 cost)	2,500	1,765
Plant and machinery at book value	2,160	1,100
Intangible assets		
Goodwill	216	250
	7,676	5,615
Current assets		
Stocks	2,833	2,261
Debtors and prepayments	1,690	1,348
Cash and deposits	450	306
	4,973	3,915

Creditors: Amounts falling due within one year		
Trade creditors	351	307
Mainstream corporation tax	285	255
Proposed dividend	270	219
	906	781
Net current assets	4,067	3,134
Total assets less current liabilities	11,743	8,749
Creditors: Amounts falling due after more than one year		
Debentures and other loans	1,500	1,602
	10,243	7,147
Share capital and reserves		
Called-up share capital	7,400	6,500
Share premium account	833	—
Profit and loss account	2,010	647
	10,243	7,147

During the financial year 1992–3 the company purchased new plant at a cost of £1,314,000 and sold items with a book value of £102,000 for £131,000.

Required

(a) A reconciliation of the operating profit with the cash inflow from operating activities.
(b) A cash flow statement for the year to 30 September 1993 so far as the information permits.
(c) A calculation of the net cash flow from operating activities using the direct method of calculation.
(d) An analysis of the information prepared under (a) and (b).

Note
Ignore advance corporation tax and deferred taxation.

(ICSA, Financial Accounting, December 1993, modified)

13
Interpretation of Accounts: Ratio Analysis

The objectives of this chapter are to

- explain the need for profitability and financial stability in both the short and long term;
- introduce ratios as a tool to investigate corporate performance together with their strengths and weaknesses;
- illustrate the calculation of significant accounting ratios and discuss the interpretation of the results;
- classify ratios and examine the relationships between them; and
- show how the cash flow statement and ratios can be used together to investigate the financial performance and position of a company.

THE NEED FOR PROFIT AND CASH

It is widely accepted that the maximization of profit is a major business objective, and it is part of management's job to devise an effective means of achieving this aim. Management must, however, recognize that there exists an effective constraint on the rate of expansion, and this limitation is the quantity of cash available at any point in time. If management pursues a policy of expansion without first taking steps to ensure that sufficient cash is available for this purpose, the consequence will be, at the very least, financial embarrassment and, at worst, bankruptcy or liquidation.

It is, therefore, important for management to plan carefully future business developments, and this planning process should concentrate attention on two separate, but related, areas:

- profitability; and
- financial stability.

Each area is of equal importance, and any tendency to emphasize one aspect to the exclusion of the other is likely to produce unfavourable repercussions. For instance, preoccupation with financial stability is likely to discourage innovation. Constant changes in consumer demand are facts of business life, and the failure of management to anticipate, or at least respond to, these changes will result in a decline in the demand for the company's products to a level where the business is no longer viable. On the other hand, investment in a project that promises high profits in the near future, without first attempting to assess whether the company can afford the project, is equally ill-advised. Recognition of the importance of financial stability should not cause management to ignore the need for profit, but it will cause management to follow a policy of *long-run* rather than *short-run* profit maximization.

A proper assessment of business performance must therefore focus attention on the adequacy of both profit and cash. The way in which ratio analysis is used to achieve such an assessment is examined in this chapter.

PRINCIPLES OF RATIO ANALYSIS

Accounting ratios are calculated by expressing one figure as a ratio or percentage of another with the objective of disclosing significant relationships and trends that are not immediately evident from the examination of individual balances appearing in the accounts. The ratio that results from a comparison of two figures only possesses real significance, however, if an identifiable economic relationship exists between the numerator and the denominator. For example, one would expect there to be a positive relationship between net profit and the level of sales. Assuming that each item sold produces a profit, one would expect a higher sales figure to produce more profit. So the knowledge that profit is £5 million is not particularly illuminating. What is of greater interest is net profit expressed as a percentage of sales (see later in this chapter).

The significance of an accounting ratio is enhanced by comparison with some yardstick of corporate performance. There are three options available, namely comparison with

1. results achieved during a previous accounting period by the same company (trend analysis);
2. results achieved by other companies (interfirm comparisons); and
3. predetermined standards or budgets.

The advantage of making comparisons is that it enables users to classify a company's performance as good, average or poor in certain key areas. However, the user must realize that there are certain attractions and limitations attached to each of the three bases for comparison listed above.

1. Last year's results are readily available, in the case of limited companies, because there is a legal requirement for them to publish accounts giving corresponding figures for the previous accounting period. In the case of sole traders and partnerships, the ability to obtain access to the relevant data will depend on the particular circumstances of each case. For example, a banker can insist on the provision of relevant accounting information as a precondition for granting a loan. A limitation of trend analysis is that it provides little useful guidance about whether a business is doing as well as it should. For example, a comparison may show that there is an improvement in the net profit percentage, but last year's results may have been disastrous.

2. Problems with interfirm comparisons include the difficulty of finding a company engaged in a similar range of business activities, while differences in accounting policies might detract from the significance of any findings. It is, however, important to discover how a company is performing in relation to its competitors since this throws a great deal of light on the efficiency of management and the long-term prospects of the concern.
3. A comparison of actual results with predetermined budgets or standards should, in theory, be the best test of whether the workforce has achieved a reasonable level of efficiency. There is, however, the difficulty and cost of establishing realistic standards. Also, it is of little consolation to discover that work is being carried out efficiently if, due to the existence of a declining market, profits are falling. In practice, management rarely publishes budgeted future results, or standards, and so external users of accounting reports usually have to confine their attention to trend analysis and interfirm comparisons.

CLASSIFICATION OF ACCOUNTING RATIOS

A meaningful accounting ratio is calculated by comparing two financial balances between which there exists some identifiable economic relationship, such as profit and sales. The most important accounting ratio is the return on capital employed examined next in this chapter, while ratios designed to analyse profit margins, solvency, asset utilization and gearing are dealt with later. Finally, the relationship between the various financial ratios is examined.

Accounting ratios are used to build up a corporate profile of the company under investigation. The ratios rarely point unanimously in the same direction; profits, for example, may have declined during the same accounting period that solvency has improved. This emphasizes the importance of not attaching too much attention to individual accounting ratios, and a balanced assessment of the company's progress requires a careful examination to be made of the relative significance of the ratios that are calculated.

RETURN ON CAPITAL EMPLOYED (ROCE)

The amount of profit earned by a business is important but, to assess the relative performance of a number of businesses, or even the performance of the same business over a number of years, it is necessary to examine the figure for profit in relation to the amount of money invested (capital employed) in the business. The return on capital employed is calculated as follows:

$$\text{Return on capital employed} = \frac{\text{Net profit}^*}{\text{Capital employed}} \times 100$$

Note
* It is generally acceptable to use either net profit *before* or net profit *after* tax for the purpose of this calculation. Whichever approach is adopted it should be consistently applied. When tax complications are introduced later in this chapter, the pretax version is used.

Example 13.1   The following information is provided for 19X1:

	Company A £	Company B £
Net profit	100,000	150,000
Capital employed	500,000	1,500,000

Required   Calculate the return on capital employed for each company.

Solution   Company A $= \dfrac{£100,000}{£500,000} \times 100 = 20\%$

Company B $= \dfrac{£1,50,000}{£1,500,000} \times 100 = 10\%$

Company A has reported a net profit of £100,000 whereas company B has reported a net profit of £150,000, i.e. company B has generated 50 per cent more profit than company A but, to achieve this, three times as much has been invested. When profit is related to the amount invested we find that company A has earned a return of 20 per cent compared with 10 per cent by company B, i.e. on every £1 invested in company A, a return of 20p is earned whereas, on every £1 invested in company B, a return of 10p is earned. It is therefore clear that, contrary to the initial impression conveyed by the figures provided in the question, company A is by far the better business proposition for, say, the prospective investor.

Calculation of capital employed

Capital employed is the amount of money invested in the business. The two most common methods of calculating capital employed are as follows:

1. *Owners' (proprietors') capital employed* This is the amount invested by the owner or owners. It is the balance on the sole trader's capital account; the aggregate of the balances on the partners' capital and current accounts or, in the case of a limited company, the ordinary shareholders' capital plus share premium account, retained profits and any balances on reserve accounts. Using the asset-based approach, owners' capital employed is calculated by taking total assets and deducting non-ownership liabilities.
2. *Total capital employed* This is found by adding together all sources of finance, i.e. capital, non-current liabilities and current liabilities. Using the asset-based approach, total capital employed is calculated by combining the balances for each category of asset belonging to the business.

Example 13.2   The following balances were extracted from the books of Compass Ltd at 31 December 19X2:

	£
Fixed assets	130,000
Ordinary share capital	100,000
Share premium account	20,000
10% loan repayable 19X8	50,000

Trade creditors	25,000
Current assets	105,000
Revaluation reserve	12,000
Proposed dividend	10,000
Retained profit	18,000

Required

(a) The balance sheet of Compass Ltd at 31 December 19X2, presented in horizontal format.

(b) The figures for

(i) owners' capital employed; and
(ii) total capital employed.

Solution

(a) **Balance Sheet of Compass Ltd at 31 December 19X2**

	£	£
Fixed assets		130,000
Current assets	105,000	
Current liabilities		
Trade creditors	25,000	
Proposed dividend	10,000	
	35,000	
Working capital		70,000
		200,000
10% loan repayable 19X8		50,000
		150,000
Financed by:		
Ordinary share capital		100,000
Share premium account		20,000
Revaluation reserve		12,000
Retained profit		18,000
		150,000

(b) (i) Owners' capital employed, £150,000.
  (ii) Total capital employed, £235,000 (£130,000 fixed assets + £105,000 current assets).

Matching profit with capital employed

The profit figure used for the purpose of calculating ROCE will differ depending on the version of capital employed under consideration:

- *Owners' capital employed* Use net profit before tax reported in the accounts.
- *Total capital employed* Use net profit before tax and before deducting interest charges, including interest on any bank overdraft.

The different purposes of these calculations are as follows: the former measures the return earned for ordinary shareholders; the latter directs attention to the efficiency with which management utilizes the total resources at its disposal.

Example 13.3   Assume the same facts as for Example 13.2. In addition, the summarized profit and loss account of Compass Ltd for 19X2 is as follows:

Profit and Loss Account of Compass Ltd for 19X2

	£	£
Gross profit		100,000
Less: Administrative costs	54,000	
Selling and distribution costs	17,000	
Interest on long-term loan	5,000	76,000
Net profit before tax		24,000
Less: Taxation		8,000
		16,000
Less: Dividends		10,000
Retained profit for 19X2		6,000
Retained profit at 1 January 19X2		12,000
Retained profit at 31 December 19X2		18,000

Required

Calculations of the return on

(a) owners' capital employed; and
(b) total capital employed.

Solution

(a) Owners' capital employed:

$$\text{Return} = \frac{24,000}{150,000} \times 100 = 16\%$$

(b) Total capital employed:

$$\text{Return} = \frac{29,000*}{235,000} \times 100 = 12\ 3\%$$

Note
* £24,000 (net profit) + £5,000 (all interest charges).

The directors of Compass have managed to achieve a return of 12.3 per cent on the total resources at their disposal. The return earned on the owners' capital employed is significantly higher, at 16 per cent. There are two reasons for this:

1. Compass benefits from 'free' finance amounting to £35,000, consisting of the dividend not yet due (£10,000) and trade credit (£25,000). It is for this reason that businessmen or women usually take the maximum amount of finance offered in the form of credit by suppliers.

2. The directors have raised a long-term loan at a favourable rate of interest, i.e. the £50,000 loan repayable in 19X8 attracts interest at the rate of 10 per cent per annum and, because the return earned on total capital employed is higher (12.3 per cent), the surplus accrues to the ordinary shareholders who are, as a result, better off. The division of total capital between shares and loans – technically referred to as gearing – is discussed further later in this chapter.

The rates of return, calculated in this section, are based on capital employed at the *year end*. Profit arises throughout the twelve-month period, however, and a more precise calculation is made by using *average* capital employed during the year. Because the information needed to calculate average capital employed is rarely provided, and because absolute accuracy is not a priority, it is perfectly acceptable to use the year-end figure, which usually produces a close approximation.

PROFIT RATIOS

The purposes of profit ratios are to help assess the adequacy of profits earned, to discover whether margins are increasing or declining and to help choose between alternative courses of action. A proper appreciation of the significance of the gross profit margin and the net profit percentage is dependent upon a thorough understanding of the different ways in which business costs, both fixed and variable, respond to changes in the levels of production and sales (see Chapter 14).

Gross profit margin (ratio)
The gross profit margin is calculated, as a percentage, using the formula:

$$\text{Gross profit margin} = \frac{\text{Gross profit}}{\text{Sales}} \times 100$$

In the case of a trader, where cost of goods sold is a variable cost, the ratio is expected to remain *constant* when the level of sales rises or falls.

The sales, cost of goods sold and gross profit of Printer Ltd for 19X4 and 19X5 were: **Example 13.4**

	19X4 £	19X5 £
Sales	162,000	196,000
Cost of goods sold	121,500	147,000
Gross profit	40,500	49,000

Calculate the gross profit margin for each year. **Required**

Solution Gross profit margin:

$$19X4: \quad \frac{40,500}{162,000} \times 100 = 25\%$$

$$19X5: \quad \frac{49,000}{196,000} \times 100 = 25\%$$

The constant gross profit margin results from the fact that for each additional unit sold, an extra unit is purchased, and prices, both for buying and selling, are unchanged. In practice, the margin does not always remain stable for reasons that include the following:

1. *A reduction in the unit cost of goods sold* Increased purchases, for example, may enable bulk purchase discounts to be obtained.
2. *Under or overvaluation of stocks* If stocks are undervalued, for example, cost of goods sold is inflated and profit understated. An incorrect valuation may be the result of an error during stock-take or it may be due to fraud, for example, a businessman or woman might intentionally undervalue his or her stocks so as to reduce the amount of tax payable. The closing stock of one period is the opening stock of the next, of course, and so the effect of errors cancels out unless repeated.
3. *Price variations* The directors may decide to cut the selling price in an attempt to increase sales. This reduces the gross profit margin but, provided sufficient extra units are sold, gross profit may still increase.

The gross profit margin of manufacturing businesses varies with changes in the level of activity even where prices are stable and stocks correctly valued. This is because manufacturing expenses include some *fixed* costs and, as production increases, the fixed costs are spread over a greater number of units with the result that the total cost per unit falls.

Example 13.5 Yale Ltd incurs annual fixed manufacturing costs of £75,000 and a variable manufacturing cost per unit of £5. Each unit sells for £10. In 19X1, 20,000 units were produced and sold and 25,000 in 19X2. There were no opening or closing stocks in either year.

Required (a) Calculate the average fixed manufacturing cost per unit.
(b) Calculate the company's total gross profit and gross profit margin for each year.
(c) Comment briefly on the results prepared in answer to parts (a) and (b).

Solution (a)

	19X1		19X2	
Average fixed manufacturing cost per unit	$\dfrac{£75,000}{£20,000}$	= £3.75	$\dfrac{£75,000}{£25,000}$	= £3

(b)

	19X1 £	19X1 £	19X2: £	19X2: £
Sales		200,000		250,000
Less: Variable costs	100,000		125,000	
Fixed costs	75,000		75,000	
		175,000		200,000
Gross profit		25,000		50,000

Gross profit margin:

19X1: $\dfrac{£25,000}{£200,000} \times 100 = 12.5\%$

19X2: $\dfrac{£50,000}{£250,000} \times 100 = 20\%$

(c) An increase in sales of 25 per cent has resulted in an increase in gross profit of 100 per cent and in the gross profit margin of 60 per cent. This is because the average fixed cost per unit has fallen from £3.75 to £3.00.

Net profit percentage (ratio)
The net profit percentage expresses net profit as a percentage of sales. It is calculated as follows:

$$\text{Net profit percentage} = \frac{\text{Net profit}}{\text{Sales}} \times 100$$

The expenses debited to the profit and loss account are both fixed and variable with respect to sales. For example, interest paid on debentures is a fixed expense, provided that no further loans are taken out, while delivery costs are likely to respond to changes in the level of sales. The net profit percentage of traders *and* manufacturers can be expected to increase or decrease in line with the level of sales.

Crackle is a trader who buys and sells goods. His trading results for 19X6 and 19X7 were **Example 13.6**

Summarized trading results

	19X6 £	19X7 £
Sales	80,000	100,000
Cost of goods sold	60,000	75,000
Gross profit	20,000	25,000
Expenses	10,000	12,000
Net profit	10,000	13,000

There were no opening or closing stocks in either year. The cost of goods Crackle sells rose by 10 per cent on 1 January 19X7.

Required

(a) Calculate Crackle's gross profit margin and net profit percentage for 19X6 and 19X7.

(b) Comment on the changes in the percentages calculated in part (a).

Solution

(a)

19X6 19X7

Gross profit margin $\quad \dfrac{20,000}{80,000} \times 100 = 25\% \qquad \dfrac{25,000}{100,000} \times 100 = 25\%$

Net profit percentage $\quad \dfrac{10,000}{80,000} \times 100 = 12.5\% \qquad \dfrac{13,000}{100,000} \times 100 = 13\%$

(b) The gross profit margin has remained constant at 25 per cent, and so we can conclude that Crackle has been able to pass on the 10 per cent increase in costs to his customers. The growth in the value of sales is due not only to the price rise but also to an increase in the volume of sales. If sales had simply risen in line with the price rise, they would have amounted to only £80,000 + (80,000 × 10 %) = £88,000.

The value of sales has increased by 25 per cent, while expenses have increased by only 20 per cent (some of them must be fixed costs). As a result, the net profit percentage has increased from 12.5 to 13 per cent.

To examine the relative impact of changes in level of activity on the cost structure, it is useful to express all costs as a percentage of sales. This is demonstrated in Example 13.7, which also shows that changes in the gross profit margin have a 'knock-on' effect on the net profit percentage.

Example 13.7   Stamp Ltd, a trading company, did not increase its selling prices between 19X6 and 19X7, but the cost of the goods it sells rose 1.25 per cent on 1 January 19X7. Its trading and profit and loss accounts for 19X6 and 19X7 were:

Summarized Trading and Profit and Loss Accounts

	19X6 £	19X7 £
Sales	50,000	60,000
Cost of goods sold	40,000	48,600
Gross profit	10,000	11,400
Rent	1,200	1,200
Other expenses	2,000	2,400
	3,200	3,600
Net profit	6,800	7,800

(a) Prepare statements for 19X6 and 19X7 in which each of the cost cate-
    gories, the net profit and the gross profit are expressed as percentages
    of sales.

Required

(b) Comment on the results shown in the statement prepared in part (a).

(a)

Solution

	19X6	19X7
	%	%
Sales	100.0	100.0
Cost of goods sold	80.0	81.0
Gross profit	20.0	19.0
Rent	2.4	2.0
Other expenses	4.0	4.0
	6.4	6.0
Net profit	13.6	13.0

(b) The gross profit has risen, but the gross profit margin has fallen by 1 per
    cent as a result of the rise in the cost of the goods it sells (1.25 per cent
    of cost is equivalent to 1 per cent of sales price where the gross margin
    is 20 per cent).

    Turning to the profit and loss account, rent is a fixed cost, and its
    impact has fallen from 2.4 to 2 per cent. Other expenses continue to
    account for 4 per cent of sales. The net result is a fall in total profit and
    loss account costs from 6.4 to 6 per cent.

    The overall impact is a fall in the net profit percentage by 0.6 per cent,
    although the amount of net profit has risen. If the gross profit margin
    could have been maintained by passing on the price rise to customers,
    the net profit percentage would also have risen.

Readers should now work Question 13.1 at the end of this chapter.

Earnings per share and the price/earnings ratio

SSAP 3 requires quoted companies to state their earnings per share (EPS) in
the accounts, and shareholders use this figure as one basis for assessing the
performance of their investment. The EPS is calculated as follows:

$$EPS = \frac{\text{Earnings}}{\text{Equity shares}}$$

where

1. earnings is defined as profit, in pence, after deducting taxation and any
   preference dividends (this is the amount available for the equity shareholders); and
2. equity shares are the number of ordinary shares in issue and a ranking for
   dividend.

Example 13.8   Walnut has an issued share capital of £1 million, divided into ordinary shares of 25p each, and 500,000 £1 preference shares carrying a dividend of 7 per cent. The following information is provided in respect of 19X0 and 19X1:

Profit and Loss Account extracts

	19X0 £	19X1 £
Profit before taxation	700,000	900,000
Less: Taxation	165,000	200,000
Profit after taxation	535,000	700,000
Dividends: Ordinary shares	(100,000)	(150,000)
Preference shares	(35,000)	(35,000)
Retained profit	400,000	515,000

Required   A calculation of the earnings per share for 19X0 and 19X1.

Solution

$$\text{EPS} = 19\text{X0} \quad \frac{50000000\text{p}}{4000000} = 12.5\text{p}$$

$$\text{EPS} = 19\text{X1} \quad \frac{66500000\text{p}}{4000000} = 16.6\text{p}$$

The earnings per share is also used as the basis for calculating the price/earnings ratio, which is widely used by financial analysts as a means of assessing the performance of an individual company and comparing it with the performance and prospects of other companies in the same industry. The price/earnings ratio is calculated as follows:

$$\text{P/E ratio} = \frac{\text{Market price of share}}{\text{Most recent EPS}}$$

We can, therefore, see that the ratio is calculated by expressing the current market price of the share as a multiple of *past* earnings per share. The figure for market price is taken from the daily list issued by the London Stock Exchange and the earnings per share can be obtained from the company's most recent accounts. A number of daily newspapers give an up-to-date calculation of the P/E ratio of quoted companies. A high P/E ratio indicates that the market believes the company has good prospects whereas a low P/E ratio suggests that the experts think that the next results published for the company are likely to show a deterioration. It follows from this that companies favoured by the stock market will have higher P/E ratios.

SOLVENCY RATIOS

Working capital ratio
A business must be able to meet its debts as they fall due if it is to maintain its credit worthiness and continue as a going concern. For this desirable state

of affairs to exist, a business must have an adequate balance of working capital (i.e. current assets – current liabilities). A secure financial position is illustrated in Example 13.9.

Example 13.9

The following balances were extracted from the books of Campion Ltd as at 31 December 19X1:

	£
Share capital	100,000
Reserves	75,000
Taxation due at 30 September 19X2	10,000
Trade creditors	15,000
Balance of cash at bank	5,000
Fixed assets at cost less depreciation	150,000
Stock	22,000
Trade debtors	23,000

Required

A calculation of Campion's working capital balance at 31 December 19X1.

Solution

Calculation of working capital:

		£	£
Current assets:	Stock		22,000
	Trade debtors		23,000
	Bank balance		5,000
			50,000
Less: Current liabilities:	Trade creditors	15,000	
	Taxation payable	10,000	25,000
Working capital			25,000

The above calculation shows that Campion is able to pay its current liabilities out of resources made available by the conversion of current assets into cash and, in addition, it shows that £25,000 will remain after the necessary payments have been made. The fact that business activity is continuous means that additional purchases will be made during January 19X2 and more sales will also occur. Consequently, the £25,000 surplus will never actually arise in a single lump sum. Nevertheless, the working capital calculation provides a useful indication of the company's ability to meet its short-term debts as they fall due for payment, i.e. it focuses attention on the solvency position of the firm.

The significance that can be attached to the balance for working capital, taken in isolation, is limited. A figure of £25,000 suggests financial stability in the case of a small business, such as Campion, but probably not in a much larger enterprise. In another company, the deduction of current liabilities amounting to, say, £975,000 from current assets of £1,000,000 would also show a working capital balance of £25,000 but, in view of the much larger scale of short-term commitments, it would probably be regarded as a totally inadequate financial 'cushion'. It is for this reason that users of accounting statements pay more attention to the working capital (or current) *ratio*, which examines the proportional relationship between current assets and current liabilities. It is calculated as follows:

$$\text{Working capital ratio} = \frac{\text{Current assets}}{\text{Current liabilities}} : 1$$

The working capital ratio of Campion is:

$$\text{Working capital ratio} = \frac{£50,000}{£25,000} : 1$$
$$= 2:1$$

The purpose of the working capital ratio is to help assess the solvency position of a business, and a question naturally asked by students and businessmen and women is, 'What is an acceptable ratio?' Unfortunately it is not possible to give a definite answer because much depends on the nature of the trade in which the company is engaged. It may be assumed, for the purpose of illustration, that Campion is a trading company that purchases and sells goods on credit, and also that the company receives from suppliers the same period of credit it allows to customers. Thirty days is the normal credit period, although the exact duration is unimportant because, provided a company allows customers, on average, the same period of credit as is granted by its suppliers, the amount of money due from customers will be received in time for the creditors to be paid as their debts fall due. Because Campion sells goods on credit none of the money presently tied up in stock will be converted into cash in time to pay the existing current liabilities as they mature. It is true that some stock will be sold in the next few days, but it will be a further thirty days, at least, before the cash is collected from the customer. It will be even longer before the remaining stock is converted into cash. The conclusion that arises from this analysis is that the working capital ratio must be sufficiently high to accommodate the inclusion of stock among the current assets. If stock comprises no more than 50 per cent of total current assets, as is the case at Campion, an adequate ratio of current assets to current liabilities is in the region of 2:1.

In practice a ratio of 2:1 is conventionally regarded as the acceptable 'norm'. It cannot be emphasized too strongly, however, that this is a broad generalization that should be treated with great caution. For example, companies in certain sectors of the economy turn stock into cash very quickly and, for them, a ratio of well below 2:1 is quite acceptable (the Boots Company plc's working capital ratio at 31 March 1993 was 1:42:1). This state of affairs usually exists in the retail trade where sales are made mainly for cash. In circumstances where resources are tied up in stock for a much longer time period, as happens in the construction industry, a working capital ratio of perhaps 4:1 may be regarded as essential.

Readers should now work Question 13.2 at the end of the chapter.

Liquidity ratio
The purpose of the liquidity ratio is similar to the working capital ratio, in that it is designed to assess the ability of a business to meet its debts as they fall due. The calculation is as follows:

$$\text{Liquidity ratio} = \frac{\text{Liquid assets}}{\text{Current liabilities}} :1$$

It is a more rigorous test of solvency than the working capital ratio because it omits current assets that are unlikely to be converted into cash in time to meet liabilities falling due in the near future. The ratio is for this reason sometimes described as the 'acid test' of solvency. Non-liquid current assets that must be left out of the calculation include stock (unless sales are made on the cash basis, as in the case of a food supermarket, in which case stock is a liquid asset) and any trade debts not receivable in the near future because customers have been allowed an extended period of credit.

The liquidity ratio of Campion (Example 13.9) is as follows:

$$\text{Liquidity ratio} = \frac{£23,000+£5,000}{£25,000} :1$$

$$= 1.1:1$$

This calculation shows that Campion Ltd has sufficient liquid assets to cover its current liabilities. A ratio of 1:1 is generally considered desirable in practice and, on the whole, this is a fair test. However, readers should be aware of the fact that the conventional method of calculation can understate the short-term financial position of the firm because, although current assets are carefully examined and less liquid items excluded, the same distinction is not made in the case of current liabilities. Normally all current liabilities are included despite the fact that some of the amounts outstanding, particularly taxation, may not be payable for a number of months. In Campion's case, for example, current liabilities include taxation that is not due for payment until 30 September 19X2, nine months after the balance sheet date. Readers should therefore be aware of the fact that the conventional method of calculating the liquidity ratio, which includes all current liabilities, is consistent with the accounting concept of 'prudence' but may, in certain circumstances, be a little overcautious.

Readers should now work Question 13.3 at the end of the chapter.

ASSET TURNOVER RATIOS

The ratios calculated in this section are designed to answer the following question: 'Is management making full enough use of the resources placed at its disposal by shareholders and creditors?'

Rate of stock turnover
This ratio measures the speed with which a company turns over its stock. The calculation is made as follows:

$$\text{Rate of stock turnover} = \frac{\text{Cost of goods sold}}{\text{Average stock level}}$$

Example 13.10   The accounts of Treadmill Ltd show figures for cost of goods sold and average stock levels of £150,000 and £25,000 respectively.

Required   Calculate the rate of stock turnover of Treadmill.

Solution $$\text{Rate of stock turnover} = \frac{150,000}{25,000} = 6 \text{ times a year}$$

Two queries often raised by students concerning the calculation of the above formula are as follows: 'Why use cost of sales rather than sales?' 'Why use average stock levels rather than closing stock?' The reason, in both cases, is to ensure that both the numerator and denominator are computed on a comparable basis.

Stocks, which make up the denominator, are valued at cost for accounting purposes, and the numerator must be computed on a similar basis. The sales figure can be used to produce a ratio that enables users to make helpful inter-period comparisons, when cost of sales figures are not available, but there is a risk that wrong conclusions will be drawn when there are changes in the gross profit margin from one accounting period to another.

Turning to the reason for using *average* stock levels, the numerator measures the cost of goods dispatched to customers *during* an accounting period, and the denominator should therefore represent the average investment in stocks during the same period. The average is usually based on opening and closing stock figures but, because stock levels fluctuate a great deal, a more precise calculation would make use of stock levels at various dates during the year, perhaps at the end of each month.

The term 'ratio' is used loosely, in accountancy, to cover all the calculations that measure the relationship between two financial totals. We have already seen, for example, that net profit is conventionally expressed as a percentage of sales rather than as an actual ratio. In the case of the stock turnover ratio, many analysts prefer to present it in terms of the number of days (weeks or months) that elapse between the date that goods are delivered by suppliers and dispatched to customers, i.e. the stockholding period. This can be done by dividing the result of the calculation presented in Example 13.10 into 365 (52 or 12), or by modifying the formula so as to achieve the desired result in a single step.

Rate of stock turnover, in days:

$$= \frac{\text{Average stock}}{\text{Cost of goods sold}} \times 365$$

$$= \frac{25,000}{150,000} \times 365 = 61 \text{ days}$$

Companies strive to keep the stockholding period as low as possible in order to minimize associated business costs. If Treadmill held its stock for an average of four months, rather than 61 days, its investment in stocks would double to approximately £50,000. Extra finance would then have to be raised, handling costs would increase and the potential loss from stock damage and obsolescence would be much greater. Although management's aim is to keep stocks to a minimum, it must nevertheless ensure that there are sufficient raw materials available to meet production requirement (in the case of a manufacturer) and enough finished goods available to meet consumer demand. It is, therefore, management's job to maintain a balance between these conflicting priorities.

Example 13.11

The following information is provided in respect of the affairs of Hutchinson, which makes up its accounts on the calendar-year basis:

	19X5 £	19X6 £
Sales	500,000	600,000
Purchases	350,000	400,000
Cost of goods sold	330,000	360,000
Stock at 31 December	60,000	100,000
Debtors at 31 December	102,000	98,000
Creditors at 31 December	25,000	40,000
Total assets at 31 December	185,000	300,000

Stock and debtors at 1 January 19X5 amounted to £70,000 and £98,000 respectively.

Required

(a) Calculations of the rate of stock turnover expressed (i) as a ratio and (ii) in days, for each of the years 19X5 and 19X6.
(b) Comment briefly on your results.

Solution

(a) (i) *Ratio*

$$19X5: \quad \frac{330,000}{\frac{1}{2}\,(70,000 + 60,000)} \quad :1 \quad = 5:1$$

$$19X6: \quad \frac{360,000}{\frac{1}{2}(60,000 + 100,000)} \quad :1 \quad = 4.5:1$$

(ii) *Days*

$$19X5: \quad \frac{\frac{1}{2}\,(70,000 + 60,000)}{330,000} \quad \times 365 \quad = 72 \text{ days}$$

$$19X6: \quad \frac{\frac{1}{2}\,(60,000 + 100,000)}{360,000} \quad \times 365 \quad = 81 \text{ days}$$

(b) In 19X6 Hutchinson achieved a 20 per cent increase in sales from £500,000 to £600,000. In these circumstances, a proportionate increase in the volume of stock held might be expected. However, a disproportionate increase in stock levels, from £60,000 to £100,000, has occurred. This has been caused by a growth in the average stockholding period from 72 days to 81 days, i.e. it has taken the company, on average, 9 days longer to turn over stock in 19X6 compared with the previous year.

Rate of collection of debtors

The period of credit allowed to customers is an important business decision. Too little credit makes it difficult to achieve a satisfactory level of sales, whereas too much credit deprives a company of essential liquid resources. The 'normal' credit period varies between industries but, in practice, it is quite usual for customers to take from six to eight weeks to pay their bills. The rate of collection of debtors is calculated, in days, as follows:

$$\text{Rate of collection of debtors} = \frac{\text{Average trade debtors}}{\text{Credit sales}} \times 365$$

Note that the denominator is confined to credit sales, since only these give rise to debts outstanding. Where the split between cash and credit sales is not given, the total sales figure may be used to calculate a ratio that gives useful comparative information provided there is no significant change in the proportion of total sales made for cash.

The debt collection ratio measures the effectiveness of a company's system of credit control. When an order is received, the credit controller (usually the owner in the case of a small business but a specialist function in the case of a large corporation) must assess the credit worthiness of the potential customer. This may involve taking up references, from say a bank, speaking to colleagues in the trade and perhaps examining a recent copy of the company's accounts. If it is decided to supply the goods requested, it is important that they should be invoiced immediately following dispatch. Any time lag inevitably increases the credit period and the volume of resources tied up in debts outstanding.

At the end of the credit period, often 30 days, a check should be made to ensure that cash has been received. Indeed, a list of debtor balances, classified by the length of time outstanding, should be prepared as a matter of systematic routine. If the credit period is exceeded, the customer's attention should be drawn to this fact by sending either a statement or a letter requesting immediate payment. The debt should subsequently be kept under continuous scrutiny and no further goods supplied until payment is made. Failure to respond to the second request for payment should result in determined attempts to recover the balance outstanding by such devices as persistent telephone calls or a solicitor's letter threatening legal action. Whether legal action will in fact be taken depends on the amount outstanding, the likelihood of recovery (has the customer the money?) and the costs involved.

Example 13.12   Using the information given in Example 13.11, calculate the rate of collection of debtors, in days, for each of the years 19X5 and 19X6 and comment briefly on your results.

Solution   Rate of collection of debtors:

$$19X5: \quad \frac{\frac{1}{2}(98,000+102,000)}{500,000} \times 365 = 73 \text{ days}$$

$$19X6: \quad \frac{\frac{1}{2}(102,000+98,000)}{600,000} \times 365 = 61 \text{ days}$$

The company has reduced the average period taken to collect debts from 73 days to 61 days. As a result, the average debtor balance outstanding has remained at £100,000, despite a significant increase in sales. Possible explanations are a strong demand for the company's product, enabling credit periods to be cut or improved efficiency in the credit control department.

Rate of payment of creditors

This ratio measures the average period of time taken by companies to pay their bills. As a general rule, companies extract the maximum credit period from suppliers since, in the absence of discounts for prompt payment, it represents a free source of finance. At the same time, undue delays should be avoided as these will have a harmful long-run effect on the company's credit standing. The result of the calculation must be interpreted with particular care since not all suppliers grant similar credit terms but, provided there are no significant changes in the 'mix' of trade creditors, the average payments period should remain stable. The rate of payment of creditors is calculated, in days, as follows:

$$\text{Rate of payment of suppliers} = \frac{\text{Average trade creditors}}{\text{Credit purchases}} \times 365$$

A change in the rate of payment of suppliers' invoices may well reflect an improvement or decline in a company's liquidity. For instance, if a company is short of cash it is likely that creditors will be made to wait longer for the payment of amounts due to them. This may be an acceptable short-term strategy, particularly where suppliers are familiarized with their customer's 'temporary' predicament and are willing to accept an extension of credit terms. Management should, however, take prompt steps to arrange for additional finance; otherwise supplies of goods will eventually be curtailed.

Using the information given in Example 13.11, calculate the rate of payment of creditors, in days, for each of the years 19X5 and 19X6 and comment briefly on your results.   **Example 13.13**

Hutchinson's figure for trade creditors at 1 January 19X5 is not provided. It is, therefore, impossible to calculate the ratio by using the *average* creditors figure for that year. We could make the calculation, based on averages, for 19X6 but, without a comparative figure for 19X5, this would be of little interpretive value. The best course is to make calculations, for each year, using the closing figures, instead of average figures, for trade creditors. This measures the approximate number of days' purchases represented by the closing balances of trade creditors. The result of the calculation is open to criticism since purchases are unlikely to have occurred at a uniform rate throughout the year. It must be remembered, however, that too much weight ought not to be attached to an individual ratio that should be used only to help build up an overall business profile.   **Solution**

Rate of payment of creditors:

$$19X5: \quad \frac{25,000}{350,000} \times 365 = 26 \text{ days}$$

$$19X6: \quad \frac{40,000}{400,000} \times 365 = 36.5 \text{ days}$$

Trade creditors have increased disproportionately between the end of 19X5 and 19X6; at the latter date the volume of creditors outstanding represents 10½ days additional purchases. One possible explanation is that the company is now making full use of credit periods allowed by suppliers. Alternatively, the company may simply be short of cash. As usual, ratios merely measure change and investigation is needed to discover what actions have caused these changes to occur.

The cash operating cycle

The period of time that elapses between the payment for goods supplied and the receipt of cash from customers in respect of their sale is called 'the cash operating cycle'. During this time period the goods acquired must be financed by the company. The shorter the length of time between the initial outlay and the ultimate collection of cash, the smaller the value of working capital to be financed. The length of the cycle is calculated as follows:

Stockholding period + Debt collection period – Credit from suppliers

Using the figures calculated above, the cash operating cycle of Hutchinson is as follows:

	19X5 Days	19X6 Days
Stockholding period	72.0	81.0
Debt collection period	73.0	61.0
	145.0	142.0
Credit from suppliers	(26.0)	(36.5)
Cash operating cycle	119.0	105.5

Total asset turnover

It is management's job to make the fullest use of available resources; only if this objective is achieved are profits likely to be maximized. The stock turnover and debt collection ratios are designed to measure management's ability to control the level of investment in certain selected areas, whereas 'total asset turnover' has the broader aim of assessing the extent to which management utilizes all available resources. It is computed as follows:

$$\text{Total asset turnover} = \frac{\text{Sales}}{\text{Average total assets}} :1$$

A high ratio indicates that management is using the assets effectively to generate sales; most probably the company is working at, or near, full capacity. Possible reasons for a decline in the ratio include the following:

1. A fall in either the stock turnover or debt collection ratios which have a 'knock-on' effect on the total asset turnover ratio.

2. Temporary inconveniences such as a strike or a fire, which destroys essential equipment.
3. The collapse in demand for a product line, unless steps are promptly taken to dispose of the equipment or transfer it to an alternative use.
4. The acquisition of fixed assets. A new company needs to make arrangements for accommodation and for the installation of any necessary plant and equipment. These facilities are unlikely to be used to their full capacity immediately but, as business builds up, the level of utilization increases. The point is eventually reached where existing fixed assets are used to their full capacity, and further expansion of business activity involves the acquisition of additional plant. It normally takes some time before demand increases sufficiently to absorb the extra capacity and, meanwhile, fixed asset turnover declines.

Example 13.14

Using the information given in Example 13.11, calculate the total asset turnover for each of the years 19X5 and 19X6 and comment briefly on your results.

Solution

Total asset turnover:

$$19X5: \quad \frac{500,000}{185,000} \quad :1 = 2.7:1$$

$$19X6: \quad \frac{600,000}{300,000} \quad :1 = 2:1$$

The ratio may be expressed either in the above form or as an amount of sales per £1 invested in assets, i.e. sales were £2.70 per £1 invested in 19X5 and £2 per £1 invested in 19X6. It is therefore apparent that a significant reduction in asset utilization has occurred.

A limitation of the asset turnover ratio is that it gives a high result for companies using older assets. This is partly the effect of inflation, but also because company accounts show fixed assets at net book value, which declines each year.

RELATIONSHIP BETWEEN ACCOUNTING RATIOS

Analyses of corporate performance made by students, and even by trained accountants, are often unsatisfactory; a common weakness is the failure to explore the *relationship* between the various ratios that have been calculated. The essence of the relationship is contained in the following formula:

Primary ratio	**Secondary ratios**	
	Margin	× *Utilization*
Return on total capital employed	= Net profit percentage	× Total asset turnover

A principal managerial objective is to maximize the return on total capital employed, sometimes referred to as the 'primary ratio'. It can accomplish this objective in the following ways: it can increase the net profit percentage and/or it can achieve a higher rate of asset utilization. It may well happen that greater asset utilization, for instance more sales, can only be achieved by lowering prices, and management has to judge whether the larger volume of activity will be sufficient to justify the lower gross and net margins that result from implementing a policy of price reductions.

Example 13.15   Double and Quick are suppliers of computer software. Double rents premises and advertises his products in popular magazines. He supplies goods by mail order and insists on the receipt of cash before the software is dispatched. Quick owns a shop in the centre of town and advertises heavily on local radio and television, as well as in trade journals. Goods are supplied over the counter for cash or on a credit basis. The following information is provided in respect of 19X9 for each of these businesses:

	Double £	Quick £
Net profit	120,000	200,000
Sales	600,000	800,000
Average total capital employed	400,000	1,000,000

Required   Calculate the primary and secondary ratios for Double and Quick and comment on the results.

Solution   Applying the formula:

Return on capital employed = Net profit percentage × Total asset turnover

$$\text{Double:} \left(\frac{120,000 \times 100}{400,000}\right) = \left(\frac{120,000 \times 100}{600,000}\right) \times \left(\frac{600,000}{400,000}\right)$$

$$30\% \qquad = \quad 20\% \qquad \times \quad 1.5$$

$$\text{Quick:} \left(\frac{200,000}{1,000,000} \times 100\right) = \left(\frac{200,000 \times 100}{800,000}\right) \times \left(\frac{800,000}{1,000,000}\right)$$

$$20\% \qquad = \quad 25\% \qquad \times \quad 0.8$$

The above calculations show that Double achieves the greater asset utilization (£1.50 of sales per £1 invested as compared with the £0.80 achieved by Quick) but his net profit percentage is lower (20 per cent compared with Quick's 25 per cent). Overall, Double's policy of maintaining a retail outlet in the centre of town seems to be more successful, i.e. the greater asset utilization more than compensates for the lower margins, and he achieves a rate of return on gross assets of 30 per cent.

The above analysis may be extended by producing a 'pyramid' of accounting ratios in the form demonstrated in Figure 13.1. The pyramid can be used to tackle questions in a structured manner. It is not, of course, necessary to reproduce the ratios in pyramid format, though readers may decide that such a presentation is helpful. The first step is to calculate the primary ratio, i.e. the return on gross assets. Ideally, it will be possible to calculate comparative figures for a previous accounting period or another company in the same industry. The secondary ratios can then be calculated to discover profit

Figure 13.1 Pyramid of accounting ratios

margins and the extent of asset utilization. The discovery that the net profit percentage is stable would suggest that further investigation of profit margins is probably unnecessary. A significant variation in asset utilization, however, points to the need to calculate ratios further down the pyramid to discover the reasons for observed changes.

Readers should now attempt Questions 13.4 and 13.5 at the end of this chapter.

GEARING (OR LEVERAGE)

The return earned for shareholders is dependent on management's achievements in three key areas:

1. Profit margins.
2. Utilization of assets.
3. Gearing.

The previous section demonstrates the fact that the rate of return on gross assets is a function of profit margins and asset utilization, but it takes no account of the company's capital structure. The effect of gearing on the return earned for the equity shareholders is now examined.

Capital is derived from two sources: shares and loans. Quite often only shares are issued when a company is formed, but loans are usually raised at some later date. There are numerous reasons for issuing loan capital. For instance, the owners might want to increase their investment but minimize the risk involved, and this can be done by making a secured loan. Alternatively, management might require additional finance that the shareholders are unwilling to supply, and so a loan is raised instead. In either case, the effect is to introduce an element of gearing or leverage into the capital structure of the company. There are numerous ways of measuring gearing, but the debt/equity ratio is perhaps most commonly used. It is calculated as follows:

$$\text{Debt/equity ratio} = \frac{\text{Total financial debt*}}{\text{Shareholders' equity}} \times 100$$

Note
* Includes preference shares, loans from directors and bank overdrafts.

The use of debt capital is likely to affect the amount of profit accruing to the ordinary shareholders, and expansion is often financed in this manner with the objective of increasing, or 'gearing up', the rate of return on shareholders' capital employed. This objective can be achieved, however, only if the rate of return earned on the additional funds raised exceeds that payable to the providers of the loan.

Example 13.16   The directors of Beulah Ltd are planning to undertake a new project that involves an investment of £10 million in fixed assets and working capital. The directors plan to finance the whole investment with a long-term loan bearing interest at 15 per cent per annum. The company's accountant forecasts an annual profit, before finance charges, of £2 million from the new project (taxation ignored).

Required   Calculate the financial benefit accruing to the equity shareholders from undertaking the project. Comment on the implications of your calculation.

Solution

	£m
Additional profit contributed by new project	2.0
Less: Interest charge, 15% of £10 million	1.5
Surplus	0.5

The existing shareholders are expected to be better off to the tune of £0.5 million, each year, as the result of undertaking the new project. This is because the new venture yields a return of 20 per cent whereas the loan creditors have contracted for interest at the lower rate of 15 per cent. Profit may, of course, not come up to expectations, and if it is less than £1.5 million the introduction of gearing will be detrimental to the ordinary shareholders. For example, if the new project generates profits before interest charges of £0.8 million, interest of £1.5 million must still be paid and the shortfall of £0.7 million (£1.5 million–£0.8 million) must be borne by the ordinary shareholders.

The shareholders of a highly geared company reap enormous benefits when there are increases in earnings before interest and tax. The interest payable on loan finance remains unchanged and a growing surplus accrues to a relatively small group of equity shareholders. The converse is also true, and a highly geared company is likely to find itself in severe financial difficulties if it suffers a succession of trading losses. It is not possible to specify an optimal level of gearing for companies but, as a general rule, gearing should be low in those industries where demand is volatile and profits are subject to fluctuation.

Readers should now attempt Question 13.6 at the end of this chapter.

CASH FLOW STATEMENT RATIOS

The cash flow statement, the preparation of which was explained in Chapter 12, shows the sources from which the company has derived cash during the year, how it has spent the cash and the resulting net impact on its cash position. Percentages can be used to show the relative balance between the inflows and outflows of cash, with the choice of which figure to use as a base (i.e. which one equals 100 per cent) depending on the purpose of the analysis. This is shown in Example 13.17.

The cash flow statement of Tide Ltd, as given previously in Figure 12.8, for the year to 31 December 19X4 is as follows: **Example 13.17**

	£000	£000
Net cash flow from operating activities		437
Returns on investment and servicing of finance:		
Interest received	26	
Interest paid	(10)	
Dividends paid	(165)	
Net cash flow	—	(149)
Taxation		(117)
Investing activities:		
Payments to buy fixed assets	(530)	
Receipts from sale of fixed assets	15	
	—	(515)
Net cash outflow before financing		(344)
Financing:		
Issue of shares	320	
Repayment of debentures	(200)	
	—	120
Decrease in cash		(224)

(a) Explain how the cash flow generated from operations has been used.   **Required**
(b) Discuss the manner in which the new fixed assets have been financed.

(a) Of the cash flow from operations, 34 per cent has been used to finance returns on investments, and 27 per cent was absorbed in paying taxation. The remaining 39 per cent contributed to the acquisition of fixed assets.   **Solution**
(b) The acquisition of fixed assets caused a cash outflow of £530,000. This was financed as follows:

- 3 per cent by selling other fixed assets.
- 32 per cent by cash generated from operations after taxation and servicing of finance.
- 23 per cent from issuing shares after repaying debentures.
- The balance of 42 per cent by running down the cash balance.

LIMITATIONS OF ACCOUNTING RATIOS

The various calculations illustrated in this chapter suffer from a number of limitations that should be borne in mind by anyone attempting to interpret their significance. The main limitations are as follows:

1. Accounting ratios can be used to assess whether performance is satisfactory, by means of interfirm comparison, and also whether results have improved, worsened or remained stable, by comparing this year's results with those achieved last year. The ratios do not, however, provide explanations for observed changes, and further inquiry is needed for this purpose. The external users' ability to obtain further information is usually extremely limited, for example, the shareholder may ask questions at the annual general meeting. It is only management that has direct access to the information needed to provide the right answer.
2. A deterioration in an accounting ratio cannot necessarily be interpreted as poor management. For example, a decline in the rate of stock turnover might appear undesirable, but further investigation might reveal the accumulation of scarce raw materials that enable the plant to continue working when competitors are forced to suspend production.
3. Too much significance should not be attached to individual ratios, for example, a rate of return on total capital employed of 30 per cent might indicate that all is well, but this conclusion would be unjustified if further analysis revealed a liquidity ratio of 0.4:1.
4. Company financial statements are usually based on historical cost and, therefore, accounting ratios based on these figures would be expected to improve, irrespective of efficiency, during a period of rising prices, for example, total asset turnover of £3 per £1 invested might be computed from historical cost accounts, whereas a figure of £1.80 per £1 invested might be obtained if assets were restated at their current worth.
5. Differences in accounting policies may detract from the value of interfirm comparisons, for example, the valuation of stock on the AVCO basis rather than the FIFO basis would probably produce a much lower working capital ratio.
6. Financial statements and accounting ratios can be distorted as the result of 'one-off' large transactions such as cash raised from issuing a debenture and awaiting investment, or a profit on the sale of a fixed asset. Analysts should similarly be on their guard for evidence of 'window-dressing', perhaps designed to conceal a deteriorating financial position.
7. Particular care must be taken when interpreting accounting ratios calculated for seasonal businesses. Where sales are high at a particular time during the year, for example, at Christmas, stock might be expected to increase and cash to decline in the months leading up to the busy period. In these circumstances deteriorations in both the liquidity ratio and the rate of stock turnover are not necessarily causes for concern.
8. Consideration must be given to variations in commercial trading patterns when assessing the significance of accounting ratios computed for particular companies. For example, a retail chain of supermarkets would be expected to have a much lower liquidity ratio and a much higher rate of

stock turnover than a constructional engineering firm. In this context, accepted 'norms' such as a working capital ratio of 2:1 must be used with care.

LINKING TOGETHER CASH FLOW ANALYSIS AND RATIO ANALYSIS

Accounting ratios can be used to assess the performance of a company during an accounting period. Comparisons with earlier years and the performance of other businesses provide useful yardsticks for assessing whether or not an improvement has occurred and for gauging whether or not results are as good as they could be. The cash flow statement complements these calculations by helping to explain how improvements in a company's financial position have been brought about or why a deterioration has occurred. Example 13.18 illustrates how the two forms of financial analysis may be employed, alongside one another, to gain an understanding of the financial performance and position of a business enterprise. In addition, it shows how the annual accounts, although relating to a *past* time period, may be used as a basis for estimating likely future prospects.

Expansion Ltd is a private company that has carried on copper-mining activities for a number of years. At the beginning of 19X2 the company purchased a small established tin mine at a cost of £350,000; production commenced at once. Tin extracted from the new mine in 19X2 amounted to 600 tonnes. This is expected to increase to 900 tonnes by 19X8 and then decline gradually. Finance for the new mine was partly provided by an overdraft to be repaid by the end of 19X3.

Example 13.18

The summarized balance sheets for 31 December 19X1 and 19X2 are as follows:

	19X1 £	£	19X2 £	£
Fixed assets				
Mines as cost	465,000		815,000	
Less: Depreciation	150,000	315,000	190,000	625,000
Plant and equipment at cost	213,250		263,250	
Less: Depreciation	56,200	157,050	75,200	188,050
		472,050		813,050
Current Assets				
Stocks of tin and copper	143,100		169,000	
Debtors	86,250		118,250	
Cash at bank	44,100		—	
	273,450		287,250	

Current liabilities
Trade creditors and accrued

expenses	63,000		138,100	
Overdraft	—		148,200	
	63,000		286,300	
Working capital		210,450		950
		682,500		814,000

Financed by:

Share capital	500,000	500,000
Profit and loss account	182,500	314,000
	682,500	814,000

The net profit earned during 19X2 was £181,500 (19X1 £103,000) of which £50,000 (19X1 £25,000) was paid out in dividends. Turnover increased from £1,060,000 in 19X1 to £1,500,000 in 19X2.

Required

Examine the financial policies pursued by the directors of Expansion Ltd during 19X2 and comment on proposals to develop further by acquiring an additional site in the early months of 19X3. You should use a cash flow statement and relevant accounting ratios to support your analysis.

Solution: examination of solvency

Cash Flow Statement for 19X2

	£
Cash flow operations (Note 1)	257,700
Dividends paid	(50,000)
Purchase of fixed assets	(400,000)
Decrease in cash	(192,300)

Note 1: Cash flow from operations

Profit	181,500
Depreciation	59,000
Increase in stock	(25,900)
Increase in debtors	(32,000)
Increase in creditors	75,100
	257,700

Ratios	19X1	19X2
Working capital ratio	4.3:1	1:1
Liquidity ratio	2.1:1	0.4:1

The company had surplus funds at the end of 19X1 and so decided to expand. It financed the remainder of the expansion with a two-year loan to be repaid out of funds generated from operations. The financial position at the end of 19X2 is weak due to the failure to raise sufficient long-term finance to meet the cost of the investment programme.

Examination of profitability

Ratios

	19X1 %	19X2 %
Net profit percentage	9.7	12.1
Return on total capital employed	13.8	16.5
Return on owners' equity	15.1	22.3

A significant improvement in profitability has occurred, which might be expected to continue with further increases in output from the new mine. The company has paid a good dividend.

Expansion has been funded out of short-term finance and the financial position at the end of 19X2 is weak. This is risky and an element of over-trading has undoubtedly occurred. The project is profitable, however, and it seems that the company will recover on the basis of funds generated from operations that, in 19X2, amounted to £240,500. Further expansion appears undesirable at present; there should be a delay of a year to 18 months. If this is not possible, the company should raise medium- or long-term finance to cover the cost of the additional site.

Conclusions and prospects

Readers should now work Question 13.7 at the end of this chapter.

Questions

13.1 The summarized trading and profit and loss account of Rubber Ltd for 19X1 and its summarized balance sheet at 31 December 19X1 are as follows:

Trading and Profit and Loss Account for 19X1

	£		£
Cost of sales (variable)	126,000	Sales	180,000
Gross profit	54,000		
	180,000		180,000
Expenses (fixed)	39,000	Gross profit	54,000
Net profit	15,000		
	54,000		54,000

Note
A dividend of £10,000 is proposed for 19X1.

Balance Sheet as at 31 December 19X1

	£	£
Fixed assets		113,000
Current assets	70,000	

Current liabilities
General	23,000	
Dividend	10,000	
	33,000	
Working capital		37,000
		150,000
Financed by:		
Share capital		100,000
Retained profit		50,000
		150,000

The company could expand production to a sales level of £255,000 with no increase in fixed expenses and the cost of sales would remain the same percentage of sales as for 19X1.

Required

(a) Calculate the gross profit percentage, net profit as a percentage of sales and the return on capital employed for 19X1.
(b) A calculation of the level of sales that would have been necessary to increase the return on capital employed by 2 per cent.

Note
For the purpose of the answer, capital employed is to be interpreted as issued capital plus retained profit on 31 December.

13.2 The balance sheets of Galston Ltd as at 31 December 19X5 and 19X6 are as follows:

	19X5		19X6	
	£	£	£	£
Fixed assets at cost		303,000		367,500
Less: Accumulated depreciation		124,500		157,500
		178,500		210,000
Current assets				
Stock	37,500		75,000	
Debtors	34,500		43,500	
Bank	18,000		1,500	
	90,000		120,000	
Current liabilities	45,000		55,500	
Working capital		45,000		64,500
		223,500		274,500

Financed by:		
Share capital	150,000	150,000
Retained profit at 31 Dec. 19X5	73,500	73,500
Profit for 19X6	—	51,000
	223,500	274,500

The figure of current liabilities as at 31 December 19X5 includes a proposed dividend of £7,500 for the year to that date. No decision has been taken yet about the dividend to be paid for 19X6, and nothing is included in the 19X6 balance sheet for such a dividend.

The directors are considering the dividend that should be paid for 19X6 in the light of the excellent results for that year.

Required

(a) Calculations of Galston's working capital and working capital ratio as at 31 December 19X5 and 31 December 19X6.
(b) A calculation of the maximum dividend that should be declared for 19X6 if the working capital ratio at 31 December 19X6 is to be the same as at 31 December 19X5.
(c) A brief discussion of the financial policy pursued by the directors of Galston Ltd in 19X6.

13.3 The following information has been extracted from the accounts of Lock Ltd, a wholesale trading company:

Balances at 31 December

	19X1	19X2
	£000	£000
Fixed assets	500	550
Trade debtors	125	150
Cash at bank	25	—
Proposed dividend	20	60
Overdraft	—	20
Trade creditors	80	100
Stocks	150	200

Results for the year to 31 December

	19X1	19X2
	£000	£000
Sales	2,000	3,000
Cost of sales	1,000	1,450
Overhead costs	800	1,300

Required

(a) A statement showing the return on capital employed, the working capital ratio and the liquidity ratio. Your answer should be presented in the following form:

	19X1	19X2
Return on capital employed	——	——
Working capital	——	——
Working capital ratio	——	——
Liquidity ratio	——	——

(b) A brief discussion of the implications of the information calculated above.

Note

For the purpose of your calculations, capital employed is defined as shareholders' equity.

13.4 The summarized accounts of Brunel, a trader, for the years 1983 and 1984 are as follows:

Trading and Profit and Loss Account

		1983			1984
	£	£		£	£
Sales		240,000			300,000
Less: Opening stock	24,000			25,000	
Purchases	191,000			265,000	
Closing stock	(25,000)			(60,000)	
Cost of sales		190,000			230,000
Gross profit		50,000			70,000
Less: Running expenses		28,000			30,000
Net Profit		22,000			40,000

Balance Sheet at 31 December

	1983	1984
	£	£
Fixed assets at cost less depreciation	75,000	73,500
Current assets		
Stock	25,000	60,000
Trade debtors	21,000	29,000
Bank balance	5,000	—
	51,000	89,000
Current liabilities		
Trade creditors	25,500	37,000
Bank overdraft	—	11,000
	25,500	48,000
Working capital	25,500	41,000
	100,500	114,500
Financed by:		
Capital	99,500	100,500
Net profit	22,000	40,000
Drawings	(21,000)	(26,000)
	100,500	114,500

At 31 December 1982, trade debtors and trade creditors amounted to £19,000 and £23,500 respectively. All sales and purchases are on credit.

Required

(a) Calculate the following ratios for 1983 and 1984:

    (i)   The rate of stock turnover.
    (ii) The rate of debtors turnover.
    (iii) The rate of creditors turnover.
    (iv) The working capital ratio.
    (v) The percentage return on capital employed.

(20 marks)

(b) Examine the progress and position of Brunel's business based on your calculations under (a). You should indicate whether each ratio has improved or declined over the two years.

(10 marks)

Note
Calculations to *one* decimal place.

(Amended, RSA, Accounting, Stage II, May, 1985)

13.5 The following information is obtained in connection with the affairs of two companies, manufacturing specialized metal products, in respect of the year ended 31 December 19X5:

	Metalmax Ltd £000	Precision Products Ltd £000
Sales	800	950
Administration expenses	30	30
Selling expenses (including promotional costs)	45	60
Plant and machinery at cost	360	360
Depreciation to 31 December 19X4	110	110
Current assets	240	400
Trade creditors	120	320
Share capital (£1 ordinary shares)	200	200

It is also established that both companies incur variable costs of sales, excluding depreciation, of 80 per cent on sales. Depreciation should be charged at 15 per cent on the cost of machinery. Reserves may be treated as the balancing figure in the balance sheets.

Required

(a) Summary trading and profit and loss accounts for the year ended 31 December 19X5 and balance sheets at that date for each company in vertical format to facilitate comparison.

(b) A comparison of the profitability of the two companies during 19X5 and of their respective financial positions at the end of the year. Relevant accounting ratios should be used to support the discussion.

Notes
1. Within the current asset totals are included balances in respect of stocks and work-in-progress as follows:

    Metalmax Ltd   £120,000
    Precision Products Ltd   £200,000

2. Ignore taxation.

13.6 The following information is provided relating to the affairs of two companies engaged in similar trading activities:

	Hot Ltd	Cold Ltd
	£	£
Ordinary share capital	800,000	500,000
15% debentures	200,000	500,000

Each company earned a trading profit before finance charges of £110,000 in year 1 and £190,000 in year 2. Corporation tax is charged at 50 per cent on the trading profits after finance charges have been deducted. The company pays out as dividends its entire post-tax profits, i.e. there are no reserves.

Required

(a) Summary profit and loss accounts, dealing with the results of each of the two companies' activities during years 1 and 2, so far as the information given above permits.
(b) Calculations of profits before tax expressed as percentages of ordinary share capital for each company in respect of both years 1 and 2.
(c) A discussion of the returns earned for shareholders over the two-year period.

13.7 The following information relates to the affairs of General Engineering plc:

Balance Sheets at 31 December

	19X7		19X8	
	£000	£000	£000	£000
Plant at cost less depreciation		2,600		2,760
Property at cost less depreciation		800		700
Investments at cost		300		250
		3,700		3,710
Current assets				
Stock and work-in-progress	900		2,120	
Debtors	660		700	
Deposits at bank	290		620	
	1,850		3,440	
Current liabilities				
Creditors	520		720	
Proposed final dividend	400		400	
	920		1,120	
Working capital		930		2,320
		4,630		6,030
Long-term loan (12%)		—		300
		4,630		5,730

Financed by:

Issued share capital	2,000	2,500
Share premium account	—	200
Retained profit	2,630	3,030
	4,630	5,730

Extracts from the Profit and Loss Account for 19X8

	£000
Trading profit for the year after charging all costs, including depreciation of plant, £250,000, and depreciation of property, £100,000	700
Interest and dividends received, less interest paid	20
Net profit from ordinary activities	720
Add: Profit from the sale of an investment	80
	800
Less: Proposed dividend	400
Retained profit for the year	400
Retained profit at 1 January 19X8	2,630
Retained profit at 31 December 19X8	3,030

During 19X8 investments that had cost £50,000 some years earlier were sold for £130,000.

Required

(a) A cash flow statement for the year to 31 December 19X8.
(b) A discussion of the change in the financial position of General Engineering between the end of 19X7 and the end of 19X8. You are not required to examine the profitability of the firm, but should use the working capital and liquidity ratios to help assess financial developments.

Note
Ignore taxation.

13.8 The following financial information is available for Span Ltd:

Profit and Loss Appropriation Account for the year ended 30 June 1992

	£000	£000
Net Profit		290
Less: Transfer to general reserve	80	
Dividends:		
Interim ordinary (paid)	20	
Final ordinary (proposed)	50	150
To retained earnings		140

Balance Sheets as at 30 June

1991 Cost £000	Aggregate depreciation £000	Net £000	Fixed assets	1992 Cost £000	Aggregate depreciation £000	Net £000
650	—	650	Freehold premises	900	—	900
340	90	250	Plant and machinery	450	130	320
60	20	40	Motor vehicles	90	31	59
1,050	110	940		1,440	161	1,279
			Current assets			
221			Stocks at cost	400		
85			Trade debtors	120		
78			Balance at bank	2		
45	429		Cash-in-hand	27	549	
			Less: Current liabilities			
71			Trade creditors	84		
—			Bank overdraft	58		
32	103	326	Proposed dividend	50	192	357
		1,266				1,636
			Called-up capital £1 ordinary shares			
		600	fully paid			750
		300	Share premium			150
		—	General reserve			80
		366	Retained earnings			506
		1,266				1,486
			Long-term liabilities			
		—	11% debentures 1998–2000			150
		1,266				1,636

Additional information for the year to 30 June 1992:

1. During the financial year additional premises had been acquired at a cost of £250,000.
2. On 30 June 1992 it was decided to revalue all freehold premises held at 30 June 1991. The valuation was increased by £950,000. No adjustment had been made for this in the above figures.
3. During the financial year a bonus issue was made to ordinary shareholders on a one for four basis.
4. New plant and machinery had been purchased during the year for £160,000. Old plant which cost £50,000 was sold in December 1991 for £10,000. The aggregate depreciation on this plant at 1 July 1991 was £20,000. There were no other sales or purchases of plant and machinery.
5. No motor vehicles were disposed of during the year.

6. In the latter part of the financial year the company negotiated a bank over-draft with a limit of £180,000.
7. No disposals or purchases of land occurred during the year.

Required

(a) A cash flow statement for Span Ltd for the year ended 30 June 1992. Show the movement in working capital over the year. *(13 marks)*
(b) Comment on the change in the cash balance. *(5 marks)*
(c) Explain how the following items affect the liquidity of Span Ltd:

    (i)   The bonus issue of shares.
    (ii) The issue of debentures.
    (iii) The acquisition of a bank overdraft.
    (iv) The revaluation of the freehold premises. *(7 marks)*
                    (Adapted from AEB, A-level, November 1992)

13.9 The last two years final accounts of Emmerson plc are outlined below:

Profit and Loss Accounts for the years ended 30 November

	1991 £m	1992 £m
Sales	100	110
Cost of goods sold	(60)	(67)
Gross profit	40	43
Distribution costs	(10)	(10)
Administration expenses	(15)	(16)
Operating profit	15	17
Interest payable	(5)	(9)
Net profit	10	8
Corporation tax	(3)	(2)
Dividends	(6)	(6)
Retained profits for the year	1	—
Retained profits brought forward	47	48
Retained profits carried forward	48	48

Balance Sheets as at 30 November

	1991 £m	1992 £m
Fixed assets	146	244
Stock-in-trade	9	12
Debtors	24	18
Trade creditors	(12)	(12)
Bank overdraft	(5)	(6)
Dividends	(6)	(6)
Corporation tax	(3)	(2)
Debenture	(45)	(90)
	108	158

Ordinary 50 pence shares	60	90
Share premium	—	20
Retained profits	48	48
	108	158

Note
(If required) Stock-in-trade at 30 November 1990 was valued at £11 million.

Required

(a) Clearly showing your workings, calculate, for each of the two years, the following ratios:

Creditor days
Debt/equity ratio
Debtor days
Earnings per share (use number of shares in issue at the financial year end)
Interest cover
Liquid ratio
Operating profit % sales
Return on equity
Sales % capital employed
Stock-turnover

(10 marks)

(b) Giving reasons for your choice, select two different ratios from the above list which would be of particular interest to each of the following user groups:

(i)   shareholders;
(ii)   senior management;
(iii) suppliers of stock; and
(iv) debenture holders.

(You may quote a total of eight ratios, that is two different ratios for each user group.)

(10 marks)
(Total: 20 marks)
(ICSA, Introduction to Accounting, December 1992)

13.10 The following trial balance has been extracted from the ledgers of JK Ltd at 31 March 1993:

	£	£
Sales (all on credit)		647,400
Stock (1 April 1992)	15,400	
Trade debtors and creditors	82,851	41,936
Purchases (all on credit)	321,874	
Carriage in	13,256	
Carriage out	32,460	
Electricity	6,994	
Business rates	8,940	
Wages and salaries	138,292	

Postage and stationery	6,984	
Rent	14,600	
VAT control		16,382
PAYE control		4,736
Motor vehicles: At cost	49,400	
Depreciation		21,240
Bank deposit account	90,000	
Bank current account	77,240	
Ordinary shares of £1 each		50,000
Profit and loss – unappropriated profit		76,597
	858,291	858,291

The following notes are also relevant:

(i)   Stock at 31 March 1993, valued at cost, was £19,473.
(ii) Prepaid rent amounted to £2,800.
(iii) Accruals are estimated as follows:

	£
Electricity	946
Wages and salaries	2,464

(iv) Depreciation on motor vehicles is to be provided at 25 per cent per annum using the reducing balance method.
(v)   Accrued interest on the bank deposit account amounts to £7,200.
(vi) A provision for corporation tax of £30,000 is to be made on the profits of the year.
(vii) No interim dividend was paid but the directors propose a final dividend of £0.05 per share.

You are required

(a) to prepare JK Ltd's trading, profit and loss and appropriation account for the year ended 31 March 1993, in vertical format;   *(10 marks)*
(b) to prepare JK Ltd's balance sheet at 31 March 1993, in vertical format; and *(7 marks)*
(c) to calculate and comment briefly on the debtors' and creditors' payment periods and the stockholding period of JK Ltd.   *(10 marks)*

(Total: 27 marks)
(CIMA, Accounting, May 1993)

14
DECISION-MAKING

The objectives of this chapter are to

- introduce the use of accounting information as part of the decision-making process;
- show how costs behave in response to changes in the level of activity;
- define and distinguish between fixed costs and variable costs and direct costs and indirect costs;
- define and distinguish between cost centres and cost units;
- differentiate between production cost centres and service cost centres;
- show how to trace direct costs (materials and labour) to cost centres and cost units;
- demonstrate how to apportion overhead costs to cost centres;
- explain the calculation of overhead recovery rates;
- assess the relative merits of different methods of overhead recovery and introduce students to activity-based costing;
- explain and illustrate the use of break-even analysis;
- show how to carry out investment appraisal using payback, return on capital employed and net present value techniques;
- compare and contrast the different methods of investment appraisal; and
- show how to prepare forecasts of cash flows, the profit and loss account, the balance sheet and the cash flow statement.

INTRODUCTION

The accounting process has many aspects and, so far, this book's emphasis has been on recording, reporting and analysing the financial consequences of past economic activity. The essence of this approach is that it is a post-fact exercise and concentrates on events that have already taken place. An important application of accounting techniques is to provide a basis on which management decisions of the following type can be taken:

1. Whether existing activity should be expanded or reduced.
2. Whether a new product should be introduced.
3. How existing production techniques could be improved.

4. Whether new products should be manufactured or purchased ready-made.

5. The manufacturing techniques to be used for new products.

All possible business decisions must be examined in the light of their expected impact on profit, and management must be satisfied, before resources are committed, that any proposed activity, or change in existing activity, will add to overall profit. Financial forecasts are therefore needed so that the likely outcomes of alternative courses of action can be analysed and the most profitable ones adopted.

This chapter introduces the study and interpretation of cost behaviour that must be understood as the basis for preparing forecasts; it reviews some of the analytical techniques available to assist management when it makes investment decisions; and it examines the impact of anticipated activity on cash flow, and funds flow, profit and the balance sheet.

COST BEHAVIOUR

The manner in which production or trading activity is organized sets the capacity of the undertaking and influences its costs. For example, the acquisition of a particular machine sets the maximum output that can be achieved before an additional machine must be bought; similarly, the size of premises used by a shop determines their cost and the maximum number of product lines that can be displayed and stored; above a certain level, further space is needed. The capacity of the business sets the upper level of activity and the output of a firm is the extent to which the available capacity is utilized – the lowest level is zero, and the greatest is the largest amount permitted by available capacity. Management must decide what the likely output will be and arrange capacity accordingly, bearing in mind the costs of servicing the capacity and that growth may take place. In the long run it may prove cheaper to acquire at the start of a project the additional capacity likely to be needed so as to take advantage of the economies of scale that can result from the use of capital intensive techniques.

It is necessary for management to understand how costs behave, or are likely to behave, so that they can be controlled, and the most appropriate mix of inputs, with their related costs, selected. This section examines a number of ways in which costs can be analysed to enable management to gain this understanding.

FIXED AND VARIABLE COSTS

Business costs may be classified according to how they behave in response to changes in output:

Fixed costs These remain constant over a range of output and include such items as rent and depreciation. For example, the rent for premises or a straight-line depreciation charge related to a machine are constant irrespective of whether these assets are being used at full capacity or well below. However, if an output in excess of the existing full capacity is contemplated, then an additional set of fixed costs must be incurred to provide additional capacity.

Variable costs These vary in direct proportion to output, and include the costs of raw material and manufacturing wages. For example, if no production takes place, then no raw materials have to be purchased while, at full capacity, the total cost of materials is the number of units produced times the material cost per unit.

Forecast output is unlikely to be achieved exactly in practice, and calculations of the profit expected at different levels of output are helpful in making a decision about whether a new project should be undertaken. This is shown in Example 14.1.

Example 14.1 The management of Glass Ltd is considering the possibility of manufacturing a new product that will sell at £15 per unit. Existing capacity is fully utilized, and so a new factory would have to be rented and plant, with a life of ten years, purchased. The expected costs are

	£
Annual factory rent	10,000.00
Purchase price of plant	75,000.00
Raw material cost per unit	2.10
Labour cost per unit	1.50
Other variable costs	1.00
Fixed costs (excluding rent and depreciation)	6,500.00

Note

The company depreciates plant on the straight-line basis assuming a zero residual value.

Required Forecast the profit that will be made from sales of the new product at the alternative annual rates of

(a) 2,500 units,
(b) 5,000 units.

Solution **Profit forecasts at different sales levels**

	£	(a) £	£	£	(b) £	£
Sales			37,500			75,000
Fixed costs						
Rent	10,000			10,000		
Depreciation	7,500			7,500		
Other	6,500			6,500		
			24,000			24,000

Variable costs					
Raw materials	5,250			10,500	
Labour	3,750			7,500	
Other	2,500			5,000	
		11,500			23,000
			35,500		47,000
Profit			2,000		28,000

Output has doubled, but profit has increased fourteen times. This result is examined later in the chapter.

Another use of forecasts, of the type prepared in Example 14.1, is to help decide the method of production; the choice often lies between 'capital intensive' and 'labour intensive' techniques. Capital intensive production uses automatic machines, such as the 'robots' seen on car production-lines, and requires a large investment in plant with a consequent high level of fixed costs. Variable costs are lower as each additional unit produced requires only a small labour input. Additional potential benefits from capital intensive methods are that raw materials are used more efficiently, and therefore cost less per unit, and there is a lower rejection rate at the stage of inspecting the finished product. Labour intensive methods use relatively little plant and have low fixed costs, but high variable costs per unit as each additional item produced requires a large input of labour.

Example 14.2

The directors of Hasard Ltd are sure that 10,000 units a year of a newly developed product can be sold at £90 each. They are undecided about how to produce it. The alternatives are

	Method 1 £	Method 2 £
Investment in plant with a ten-year life	125,000	750,000
Fixed costs (excluding depreciation)	185,000	200,000
Variable cost per unit		
Raw materials	35	30
Labour	20	5
Other	6	2

Note
The company calculates depreciation on the straight-line basis assuming a zero scrap value.

Prepare financial statements to show the likely profit from each of the two methods at the expected level of sales.

Required

Solution   **Forecast trading results**

	Method 1			Method 2		
	£	£	£	£	£	£
Sales			900,000			900,000
Fixed costs						
Depreciation	12,500			75,000		
Other	185,000			200,000		
		197,500			275,000	
Variable costs						
Raw materials	350,000			300,000		
Labour	200,000			50,000		
Other	60,000			20,000		
		610,000			370,000	
			807,500			645,000
Profit			92,500			255,000

Readers should now work Question 14.1 at the end of this chapter.

Some costs are neither completely fixed nor fully variable – they are termed 'semi-variable'. Although semi-variable costs respond to volume changes, they do not change in direct proportion to them. It is possible for semi-variable costs to remain constant over a relatively small range of activity, and each successive set of costs may differ in price from its predecessor. For example, an increase in manufacturing output creates additional work in the accounts department. The initial load may be carried by an accountant who alone performs all the necessary activities. When his or her capacity is exceeded, a book-keeper may be added to the staff, and then a clerk. Each additional employee, hired to increase the capacity of the accounts department in response to an increase in manufacturing output, adds relatively less to costs as an accountant is paid more than a book-keeper, who in turn earns more than a clerk. This type of response to changes in output occurs in the case of general expenses in Question 14.2 at the end of this chapter, which should now be worked.

Direct and indirect costs

Direct costs are those that can be traced in full to an individual costing unit. Indirect costs are those that relate only partially to a particular costing unit and must be apportioned to it. Care has to be taken when interpreting results based on apportioned (joint) costs as they have to be met in full irrespective of whether activity in a particular department continues or is discontinued. An initial examination of results may produce the conclusion that a department or branch is making a loss and so should be closed, but it must be remembered that its share of apportioned costs will then have to be met by the remaining cost centres.

The business of Bits & Co. is divided into three departments of equal size: **Example 14.3**
A, B and C. The departmental results for 19X7 were (£000):

Departmental trading results

	Department			Total
	A	*B*	*C*	
Sales	50	120	180	350
Cost of goods sold	25	60	90	175
Gross profit	25	60	90	175
Departmental wages	10	20	30	60
	15	40	60	115
Rent (shared equally)	20	20	20	60
Profit (loss)	(5)	20	40	55

Mr Bits is considering closing department A because it is making a loss. He
says it is better to leave the floor space empty than to use it to lose money.

Prepare a statement to show Mr Bits the effect on total profit if department   **Required**
A is closed.

Revised departmental trading results   **Solution**
                                                                                  (£000)

	Department		Total
	B	*C*	
Sales	120	180	300
Cost of goods sold	60	90	150
Gross profit	60	90	150
Departmental wages	20	30	50
	40	60	100
Share of rent*	30	30	60
Profit (loss)	10	30	40

Note
* Rent shared equally between the remaining departments.

Department A should be kept open as it meets 75 per cent of its share of
apportioned costs. Total profit is reduced by £15,000 if it is closed. The
revised departmental trading results show that the plan of Mr Bits to close
department A is based on his failure to appreciate the difference between
direct and indirect costs.

It is sometimes argued that, because the accounting information that results
can lead to wrong decisions, the apportionment of indirect costs should not
be made. If indirect costs are not apportioned, the departmental trading
results of Bits & Co. would be presented as follows (£000):

	Department			Total
	A	B	C	
Sales	50	120	180	350
Cost of goods sold	25	60	90	175
Gross profit	25	60	90	175
Departmental wages	10	20	30	60
Departmental surplus	15	40	60	115
Rent	—	—	—	60
Profit				55

The above presentation highlights the fact that all departments are making a positive *contribution* to general overhead costs that are not controllable at the departmental level. In the short run, therefore, the question is whether the continued operation of a particular department or the acceptance of a sales order will make a *contribution* towards fixed costs (which are broadly equivalent to overheads or indirect costs). We will also see that the theory of contribution costing underpins break-even analysis as a means of planning business activity and making investment decisions.

The nature of a cost, that is whether it is direct or indirect, has to be decided in accordance with the costing unit under examination. For example, if the costing unit is a manufacturing department, then the depreciation of machines located in it and the salary of the departmental supervisor are direct costs. However, if the costing unit is a single item of output, then the depreciation and supervisor's salary are indirect costs as they also relate to the rest of the output. Raw materials and manufacturing wages are examples of direct costs where the costing unit is a single item of output.

TOTAL COSTING AND OVERHEAD RECOVERY RATES

Earlier in this chapter we have seen that direct costs (usually these are the variable costs) are of most relevance for the purpose of decision-making. For example, a company will keep a department open provided revenues cover variable costs that, in the short run, may well consist mainly of direct materials and direct labour costs. In the longer run, more costs become avoidable – the next annual rental becomes payable and fixed assets must be replaced – with the result that at this stage avoidable costs (which now include fixed as well as variable costs) may not be covered and the department closed.

For a company to survive and prosper in the long run, therefore, it must cover not only its direct costs but also its indirect costs. A company therefore needs to be aware of the total costs involved in supplying a particular product despite the fact that, in certain circumstances, it may be willing to accept a price below that figure. It is therefore normal practice for companies to operate a system of total or absorption costing, despite some doubts concerning its validity as the basis for many business decisions.

The operation of a system of total costing requires the collection of costs at cost centres which may be defined as: *A department or section of a department or any other convenient basis on which it is helpful to collect costs for decision-making purposes.* The first problem is to devise a satisfactory system for allocating and apportioning costs to cost centres. This is examined in the next section.

The following stage is to recharge the costs collected at the cost centres to the cost units, which are usually the products manufactured. This is examined in the section below entitled 'Total unit cost'.

Accounting for materials, labour and overheads

Materials

The usual approach is to raise a materials requisition note to authorize the issue of goods from the stores to production. The requisition note identifies the cost centre to which the materials have been allocated and is used as the originating document for the purpose of recharging material issued from the stores to the cost centre. The method of pricing the issue may be FIFO, LIFO, AVCO or some other acceptable basis.

Labour

Job cards are kept for each employee to show where each individual is spending his or her time. The weekly or monthly pay-roll is then analysed in conjunction with the job cards to determine the charge to various cost centres. Not all labour costs can be charged directly to cost centres and the remainder are treated as part of the indirect costs or overheads.

We can therefore see that, provided a suitable system of record-keeping is developed, it is a fairly straightforward matter to trace direct material costs and direct labour costs to cost centres. The costs are incurred at the cost centre and it is merely necessary to ensure that the records are capable of identifying that fact.

Overheads

In this case it is not possible to identify the cost directly with a cost centre and so the approach adopted is to apportion overheads between cost centres on some logical basis. Some examples are as follows:

Expense	Basis of apportionment
Rent and rates	Square metre of floor space occupied
Wages of timekeeper	Number of employees in department
Canteen costs	Number of employees in department
Insurance costs	The insurable value of items in the department
Lighting	The number of power points
Heating	The number of radiators

We can see that the aim is to establish a logical relationship between the cost incurred and the method of apportionment. For example, the rent and rates payable in respect of a building are related to the size of the building, and it would therefore seem sensible to apportion the total cost between departments located within the building based on their relative size.

There is one further problem. Cost centres are made up of two types: production cost centres where goods are manufactured; and service cost centres which assist the production cost centres but do not themselves produce goods. The costs of the service cost centres, once established, must therefore be recharged to the production cost centres on a logical basis.

Example 14.4 Jones Ltd has two production departments and a service department. Each department produces a single product. The budgeted costs for 19X0 are as follows:

Direct costs	£
Materials:	
Production department A	100,000
Production department B	250,000
Service department	150,000
Labour:	
Production department A	55,000
Production department B	250,000
Service department	100,000
Indirect costs	
Depreciation	100,000
Stores	20,000
Rent	36,000
Power	120,000

The following further information is provided:

Department	Value of plant	Stores requisitions	Floor space m^2	Machine horse power	Labour hours	Machine hours
A	200,000	300	10,000	200	70,000	20,000
B	160,000	600	8,000	120	30,000	80,000
Service	140,000	100	2,000	80	—	—

It is agreed that the service department serves the two production departments equally.

Required

A statement (overhead analysis sheet) showing the apportionment of the overhead (indirect) costs to the three departments and the overhead costs of the service department recharged to the operating departments.

Solution

Overhead Analysis Sheet

Type of expense	Basis of apportionment	Total £	Production department A £	Production department B £	Service department £
Depreciation	Book value of plant	100,000	40,000	32,000	28,000
Stores	Material requisitions	20,000	6,000	12,000	2,000
Rent	Floor space	36,000	18,000	14,400	3,600
Power	Machine horse power	120,000	60,000	36,000	24,000
		276,000	124,000	94,400	57,600

Materials and labour	250,000			250,000
Recharged equally		153,800	153,800	(307,600)
Total cost	526,000	277,800	248,200	

Based on the information provided, the most appropriate basis for allocating the total depreciation charge of £100,000 would seem to be the book value of plant. For similar reasons, stores costs are allocated on the basis of material requisitions, rent on the basis of floor space and power on the basis of machine horse power. The result of this process is to apportion £57,600 to the service department. These costs, together with the material and labour costs of the services department, amounting to £250,000, are then reallocated to the two production departments on equal basis.

Total unit cost

It may be helpful to summarize, at this stage, the process involved in the recovery of total manufacturing costs. The three steps are as follows:

1. Apportion overhead costs to *cost centres* (usually departments) in the manner described above.
2. Recharge the costs of service cost centres to production cost centres on some logical basis as demonstrated above.
3. Recharge the total overheads apportioned to a cost centre to *cost units* (usually products) based on the selected overhead recovery rate (see below).

The process may be shown diagrammatically as in Figure 14.1. The elements of cost are direct materials, direct labour and overheads. The continuous arrow shows that the material and labour costs can be traced directly to each of the two production departments and the service department and, in due course, to the products produced (where there are a large number of homogeneous products – for example, car tyres – an *average* cost is used for this purpose). The broken arrow represents the apportionment of overheads to each of the three departments and the second broken arrow rising upwards from the service department indicates its total costs are recharged to production departments. The final stage (arrows with dots and dashes) is the use of overhead recovery rates to recharge overheads to products. In the case of production department A, it can be seen that its overhead costs are split between two products (X and Y) whereas production department B's overheads must be recovered as part of the cost of the product Z.

The calculations involved in the final stage are now considered.

Overhead recovery rates

The overheads allocated to each production centre must now be recharged to the cost units – products X, Y and Z. The method of recovering these overheads is to attach them to a variable with which there can be established some kind of causal relationship. Traditionally, five methods have been employed in British industry:

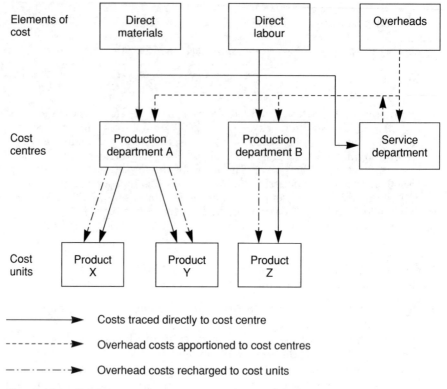

Costs traced directly to cost centre

Overhead costs apportioned to cost centres

Overhead costs recharged to cost units

Figure 14.1   Tracing costs to cost centres and cost units

- Percentage on direct materials.
- Percentage on direct labour.
- Percentage on total direct (prime) costs.
- Machine hour rate.
- Direct labour hour rate.

The justification for adding a 'percentage' based on direct material, or direct labour, or total direct cost is that the level of overheads attaching to a particular product is a consequence of one or other of these variables. It is unlikely that the causal relationship would be strong but, where direct materials or direct labour are the dominant element of total cost and the level of overheads fairly modest, any distortion of the total cost figure resulting from its adoption is unlikely to be great.

Because overheads are usually a function of time, an hourly rate is therefore more appropriate. In circumstances where production is labour intensive, a labour hour rate might be seen as most appropriate; where production is capital intensive a machine hour rate should be preferred. It is a criticism of British industry that the percentage on direct labour method remains in widespread use; it has the merit of simplicity but, in circumstances where the ratio of overhead costs to direct labour is substantial, its adoption may well mean the provision of highly misleading figures for total cost and wrong decisions being reached.

The calculation of overhead recovery rates will be illustrated using the information contained in Example 14.4 (percentage on total direct cost is not calculated):

Percentage on direct materials

$$\frac{\text{Allocated overheads}}{\text{Budgeted direct material costs}} \times 100$$

Department A = $\dfrac{277,800}{100,000}$ $\times 100 = 277.8\%$

Department B = $\dfrac{248,200}{250,000}$ $\times 100 = 99.3\%$

Percentage on direct labour

$$\frac{\text{Allocated overheads}}{\text{Budgeted direct labour costs}} \times 100$$

Department A = $\dfrac{277,800}{55,000}$ $\times 100 = 505.1\%$

Department B = $\dfrac{248,200}{250,000}$ $\times 100 = 99.3\%$

Direct labour hour rate

$$\frac{\text{Allocated overheads}}{\text{Budgeted labour hours}}$$

Department A = $\dfrac{277,800}{70,000}$ = £3.97 per hour

Department B = $\dfrac{248,200}{30,000}$ = £8.27 per hour

Machine hour rate

$$\frac{\text{Allocated overheads}}{\text{Budgeted machine hours}}$$

Department A = $\dfrac{277,800}{20,000}$ = £13.90 per hour

Department B = $\dfrac{248,200}{80,000}$ = £3.10 per hour

Example 14.5 The following information is provided in respect of a single unit manufactured of each of the three products, X, Y and Z, manufactured in departments A and B (see Example 14.4 and Figure 14.1):

	X	Y	Z
	£	£	£
Direct materials cost	500	1,200	1,000
Direct labour costs	450	850	800
Labour hours	360	850	120
Machine hours	100	245	360

Required Calculate for each product its total cost using

(a) percentage on direct labour method; and
(b) Machine hour rate method.

Note
Calculations to the nearest £.

Solution

	X		Y		Z	
	(a)	(b)	(a)	(b)	(a)	(b)
	£	£	£	£	£	£
Direct materials cost	500	500	1,200	1,200	1,000	1,000
Direct labour cost	450	450	850	850	800	800
% on direct labour						
505.1%	2,273		4,293			
99.3%						794
Machine hour rate						
£13.90 per hour		1,390		3,405		
£3.10 per hour						1,116
	3,223	2,340	6,343	5,455	2,594	2,916

We can therefore see significant differences in total costings depending upon the method used to recover overheads. For example, product X is costed at £3,223 using the percentage on direct labour and £2,340 using the machine hour rate. Clearly both figures for total cost cannot be correct (of course they may both be incorrect), and the use of an inappropriate method leads to misguided pricing decisions and assessments of profitability.

We do not know which method is correct without further investigation of the circumstances prevailing within the factory. However, it does seem that production of products X and Y is relatively labour intensive (note the larger number of labour hours worked compared with machine hours and the high level of direct labour cost) suggesting that the labour hour method may be most appropriate. Product Z, on the other hand, is relatively capital intensive (note the large number of machine hours and low labour costs) and the machine hour rate may be more appropriate in this case.

Activity-based costing
The traditional models for recovering overheads have come under increasing criticism in recent years. The main objection is that a single (global)

method is used to recover the entire overheads allocated to a cost centre. It is argued that this is misguided on the grounds that there is likely to be a range of different factors which affect individual types of overhead cost, and this fact is ignored by the traditional methods. Different factors are of course recognized for the purpose of allocating overheads to cost centres but this procedure is not carried through in the identification of overhead costs with cost units.

Advocates of activity-based costing (ABC) argue that, as the result of improvements in information technology, links between individual overheads and cost units, which may have been impossible in earlier times when the traditional methods were developed, can now be forged. ABC involves the following:

- The identification of 'cost drivers', i.e. the activity which causes the overhead to be incurred. For example, the cost of running the buying department may be a function of the number of orders placed and so the cost of the buying department should be allocated to individual product lines based on the number of orders placed during the accounting period.
- The accumulation of overhead costs, by cost unit (product), in accordance with the cost drivers.
- The apportionment of batches of overheads to product lines in accordance with the extent to which they utilize the cost driver.

The outcome is that the product bears a fairer share of overheads and more relevant data is generated for the purposes of pricing and monitoring business performance.

Readers should now work Question 14.3 at the end of this chapter.

Contribution costing

A useful technique to apply when examining the way in which fixed and variable costs respond to changes in the level of activity is to calculate the 'contribution' each unit sold makes towards fixed costs. Analysis based on this approach assumes that the revenue from each unit is applied first to meet its related variable costs, and any surplus, the contribution, is then set against total fixed costs. Once the fixed costs have been completely recovered, the contribution of each additional unit sold adds to profit. The contribution of each unit is calculated by the formula

Contribution = Selling price per unit – Variable cost per unit

Product Z incurs the following variable costs per unit:

Example 14.6

	£
Materials	5.00
Wages	4.50
Expenses	1.25

Required

Calculate the contribution of product Z if its selling price per unit is:

(a) £12,
(b) £15.

Solution   The total variable cost is

	£
Materials	5.00
Wages	4.50
Expenses	1.25
Total	10.75

(a) Contribution = £12 − £10.75 = £1.25.
(b) Contribution = £15 − £10.75 = £4.25

The technique of contribution costing is used in break-even analysis and margin of safety and target profit calculations, which are dealt with later in this chapter.

Break-even analysis

A forecast of sales should be prepared as part of the appraisal of whether a particular project should be undertaken. The volume of anticipated sales sets the capacity that has to be provided and also determines the total value of variable costs. Forecasts cannot be wholly accurate, and so it is usual to examine results based on a number of alternative outcomes. A particularly useful piece of information to know is the volume of sales needed to achieve break even, which occurs where total costs equal total revenues and neither a profit nor loss is made. Looked at another way, a company breaks even when the contribution from sales is exactly equal to fixed costs. The break-even point is calculated with the formula:

$$\text{Break-even point, measured in units sold} = \frac{\text{Fixed costs}}{\text{Contribution}}$$

The break-even point in terms of the value of sales can be calculated by multiplying the number of units by the selling price per unit.

The importance of the break-even point is that below it a loss is suffered, and above it a profit is earned. It is, therefore, very important that management selects projects that are likely to achieve at least enough sales to break even.

Example 14.7   The directors of Cumberland Ltd are considering an investment project that has a maximum output of 50,000 units and is expected to involve the following costs and revenues:

	£
Annual fixed costs	100,000
Selling price per unit	10
Variable cost per unit	6

Required   (a) Calculate the sales in terms of both units and value that have to be made for the project to break even.
(b) Calculate the profit or loss that would occur if sales are

(i) 1,000 units less than those needed to break even; and
(ii) 1,000 greater than those needed to break even.

(a) Contribution $= £10 - £6 = £4$ **Solution**

Break-even point
(in units) $= \dfrac{£100,000}{£4} = 25,000$ units

or Break-even point
(in value) $= 25,000$ (units) $\times £10$ (selling price per unit)
$= £250,000$

(b)

	(i) 1,000 less	*(ii) 1,000 more*
Sales in units	24,000	26,000
	£	£
Contribution (unit sales $\times$ 4)	96,000	104,000
Fixed costs	100,000	100,000
Profit (loss)	(4,000)	4,000

Note
An alternative way to calculate the effect of changes in the level of sales on profit is to calculate the increase, or decrease, in the contribution. In this case, the starting profit is zero, and the contribution from sales of 1,000 units = 1,000 $\times$ £4 = £4,000. Therefore, an increase in sales of 1,000 units gives a profit of £4,000, and a decrease of 1,000 units gives a loss of £4,000.

The certainty with which sales can be forecast may influence the choice of production method and also affect decisions about which products to trade in. Where there is great uncertainty, production methods and products with low break-even points may be chosen to minimize the risk of losses. However, the choice of a method or product with a low break-even point may restrict the total profits that can be earned if high sales are achieved.

The directors of Trestle Ltd are considering the following alternative meth-   **Example 14.8**
ods of manufacturing a new product:

	Method 1	Method 2
	£	£
Plant with a life of ten years	50,000	150,000.00
Other annual fixed costs	3,000	3,000.00
Variable cost per unit	7	6.50
Selling price per unit	8	8.00

The plant is expected to have a zero scrap value at the end of its life, and the company uses the straight-line method of depreciation.

Method 2 has a lower variable cost because it uses less labour and has lower wastage rates for raw materials.

(a) Calculate the break-even point for each method of production.   **Required**
(b) Calculate the profit or loss for each method that results from sales levels of 10,000 units, 20,000 units and 30,000 units.
(c) What is the greatest loss that might be suffered under each method?
(d) Advise management on which method should be adopted.

Solution

		Method 1 £		Method 2 £	
(a)					
	Fixed costs				
	Depreciation	5,000		15,000	
	Other	3,000		3,000	
		8,000		18,000	
	Contribution	£8 – £7	= £1	£8 – £6.50	= £1.50
	Break-even point	8,000		18,000	
		——	= 8,000	——	= 12,000
		1	units	1.50	units
(b)					
	10,000 units				
	Contribution	10,000		15,000	
	Fixed costs	8,000		18,000	
	Profit (loss)	2,000		(3,000)	
	20,000 units				
	Contribution	20,000		30,000	
	Fixed costs	8,000		18,000	
	Profit	12,000		12,000	
	30,000 units				
	Contribution	30,000		45,000	
	Fixed costs	8,000		18,000	
	Profit	22,000		27,000	

(c) The greatest loss occurs when there is no contribution (i.e. zero output), and is equal to the fixed costs. Therefore, the maximum loss of method 1 is £8,000 and of method 2 is £18,000.

(d) Once method 2 breaks even, £1.50 is added to profit by every additional unit sold, while method 1 adds only £1. However, method 1 breaks even at a lower level of sales. Both methods make the same profit at sales of 20,000 units.

The decision about which method to select therefore rests on expected sales. If 20,000 is the maximum level of expected sales, then method 1 is better; if sales are expected easily to exceed that level, then method 2 is better.

Readers should now work Question 14.4 at the end of this chapter.

It is sometimes useful, for example, when preparing a report for consideration at a meeting, to present the results of break-even analysis in the form of a graph. Figure 14.2 shows how this is done using the information given in

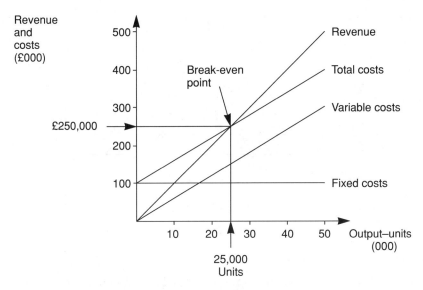

Figure 14.2 A break-even graph

Example 14.7. All of the relationships expressed in the graph are represented by straight lines, and so each of them can be plotted by calculating two points. This is done by considering the costs and revenues that arise at levels of output of zero and full capacity which, in Example 14.7, was 50,000 units:

	Zero output	*Full capacity*
Revenue	$0 \times £10 = £0$	$50,000 \times £10 = £500,000$
Fixed cost	£100,000	£100,000
Variable cost*	$0 \times £6 = £0$	$50,000 \times £6 = £300,000$
Total cost	£0 + £100,000	£300,000 + £100,000
(Variable plus fixed costs)	= £100,000	= £400,000

Note
* It is possible to omit this line without reducing the usefulness of the chart, especially to save excessive contents when the results of two alternatives are being plotted on the same graph.

The break-even point can be found in terms of either units or value and is where the total cost line crosses the revenue line. At levels of sales below this point a loss is made, and above it a profit. The extent of the divergence between the revenue and total cost lines above the break-even point indicates the rate of growth in profit as sales increase.

The graph should not be extended beyond the stated full capacity as, after this point, an additional set of fixed costs has to be incurred, and no information is given on the resulting cost structure, or how demand in this region would be met.

Question 14.5 at the end of this chapter should now be worked.

Profit-volume graph
The relationship between the volume of activity and profit can also be expressed in a profit-volume graph which shows the profit (or loss) arising at

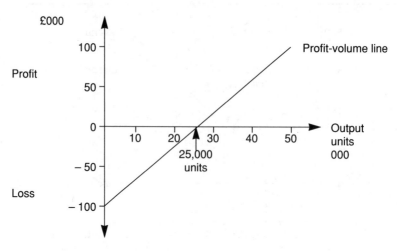

Figure 14.3 A profit-volume graph

various levels of output. When output is zero, a loss equal to the fixed costs is suffered; each additional unit sold reduces the loss by an amount equal to its contribution until the break-even point is reached. Thereafter, each extra unit's contribution adds to profit until maximum output is achieved. Figure 14.3 shows the profit-volume graph using the information given in Example 14.7. The relationship between profit and volume is a straight line, and so can be plotted using figures for profit or loss at zero and maximum levels of activity. In the case of Figure 14.3 these two figures are:

1. at zero output a loss of £100,000, the fixed costs, results; and
2. at full capacity the profit is

(50,000(output) × £4 (contribution per unit)) – £100,000 (fixed costs) = £100,000

The break-even point is found where the profit-volume line crosses zero, indicating that neither a profit nor loss is made at that point.

The margin of safety
The margin of safety gives an indication of how vulnerable a company is to changes in the volume of sales. It shows, as a percentage, how far sales can fall from their expected level before the break-even point is reached – a fall to below this point results in a loss. The margin of safety is calculated, using data on either value or units, by the formula:

$$\frac{\text{Expected sales} - \text{Sales at break-even point}}{\text{Expected sales}}$$

Example 14.9 Using the information in Example 14.7, calculate, using both values and quantities, the margin of safety of the project under consideration by Cumberland if the expected annual sales are 40,000 units.

Quantity:

$$\frac{40{,}000 \ (\text{Expected sales}) - 25{,}000 \ (\text{Break-even point})}{40{,}000 \ (\text{Expected sales})} = 37.5\%$$

Value:

$$\frac{400{,}000 \ (\text{Expected sales}) - 250{,}000 \ (\text{break-even point})}{400{,}000 \ (\text{Expected sales})} = 37.5\%$$

Note
The same result is obtained using either values or quantities.

The margin of safety can also be calculated using actual results, in which case the formula is

$$\frac{\text{Actual sales} - \text{Actual break-even point}}{\text{Actual sales}}$$

Target profit calculation

Once the contribution is known, it is also possible to calculate the level of sales needed, in terms of either value or quantity, to earn a given amount of profit. First, sales have to be sufficient to earn a total contribution equal to fixed costs, and then sufficient additional sales must be made to give the required profit. The formula to calculate the sales, in units, for a particular profit is

$$\text{Sales in units} = \frac{\text{Fixed costs} + \text{Required profit}}{\text{Contribution}}$$

The value of sales can then be calculated by multiplying the number of units by the selling price per unit.

Example 14.10

The directors of Carp Ltd are considering the manufacture of a new product that sells at £16 per unit. Its manufacture would involve annual fixed costs of £147,500 and a variable cost per unit of £9.50. The directors are only willing to undertake the project if a profit of £80,000 can be made.

Required

Calculate the sales required, in terms of both quantity and value, to produce the desired profit.

Solution

	£
Selling price per unit	16.00
Variable cost per unit	9.50
Contribution per unit	6.50

$$\text{Required sales} = \frac{£147{,}500 + £80{,}000}{£6.50}$$

$$= 35{,}000 \text{ units}$$
$$or \ 35{,}000 \times £16 = £560{,}000$$

Readers should now work Question 14.6 at the end of this chapter.

INVESTMENT APPRAISAL

Management must decide how to invest the resources at its disposal, and usually the funds available are not sufficient to carry out all the possible projects that have been put forward, even if they all appear profitable. Some decisions still remain even after an initial decision of which projects to pursue has been taken, for example, once it has been decided to acquire a piece of machinery the options remain of whether to buy it or lease it. Therefore, a selection process has to be carried out to choose those projects to be undertaken, and to decide how the plans are to be put into operation. A number of techniques have been developed to help management make such decisions, and some of the more common ones are described in the following sections.

Payback

The payback method of investment appraisal is based on the time taken by a project to generate the amount of cash that has been invested in it. The decision of which projects to undertake depends on the speed with which the available projects recover their initial investment:

1. If there is no limit on the funds available, all projects that recover their investment within a set period of time are chosen.
2. If funds are limited, those projects that recover their investment the quickest are selected.

Example 14.11 The management of Applause Ltd is considering the following proposed investment projects. All of the fixed assets are expected to have a life of five years at the end of which their value will be zero:

	Project A £	Project B £	Project C £
Initial investment in fixed assets	25,000	50,000	60,000
Inwards cash flow:			
Year 1	10 000	30,000	10,000
Year 2	10,000	20,000	20,000
Year 3	10,000	15,000	20,000
Year 4	10,000	5,000	40,000
Year 5	10,000	5,000	60,000

Assume that the cash flows arise evenly throughout the year.

Required
(a) Calculate the payback period of each project.
(b) State which projects would be chosen if all projects that pay back in three or less years are selected.
(c) State which projects would be chosen if only £70,000 is available for investment, i.e. only one of the projects can be undertaken.

Solution
(a) Project A pays back the initial investment of £25,000 in 2.5 years, i.e. £10,000 + £10,000 + (£10,000 × 0.5). Project B pays back £50,000 in 2 years, i.e. £30,000 + £20,000. Project C pays back £60,000 in 3.25 years, i.e. £10,000 + £20,000 + £20,000 + (£40,000 × 0.25).

(b) Projects A and B would be chosen as they both pay back in three or less years. Project C is rejected as it takes more than three years to earn a sum equal to its initial investment.

(c) Only one of the projects can be chosen as the combination of any two of them involves an outlay in excess of the £70,000 available. Project B recovers the sum invested most quickly, and so it would be selected.

The selection of investment projects on the basis of their payback periods has been criticized because it ignores cash received after the payback period and so it may exclude a very profitable project if the bulk of its returns are not expected until near the end of its life, for example, project C in Example 14.11. A counter to this argument is that companies do not like to take risks and are exposed to less risk if projects are chosen that recover their cash outlay most quickly. A further advantage of payback is that it focuses on earlier rather than later forecasts, which become less reliable the further they are projected into the future.

Return on capital employed (ROCE)

The calculation of the ROCE was explained in Chapter 13 and can be used to choose between alternative investment projects:

1. If there is no limit on the funds available, all projects that have a ROCE in excess of a stated minimum are chosen.
2. If funds are limited, those projects that have the higher ROCE are selected.

It is usual to base the calculation of the forecast ROCE on the average investment as, over the life of the project, the value of the fixed assets decreases from their cost price at the start of the project to their scrap value at the end. The average investment is found by the formula

$$(\text{Cost of fixed assets} - \text{scrap value}) \div 2$$

The management of the Applause Ltd in Example 14.11 decide to use the expected ROCE of the projects under consideration as the basis on which to make their investment decision. **Example 14.12**

(a) Calculate the ROCE of each project. **Required**
(b) State which projects would be selected if all those with a ROCE of 25 per cent or more are to be undertaken.
(c) State which project would be carried out if only one can be selected.

(a) **Solution**

	Project A £	B £	C £
Annual Profit (loss)*			
Year 1	5,000	20,000	(2,000)
Year 2	5,000	10,000	8,000

Year 3	5,000	5,000	8,000
Year 4	5,000	(5,000)	28,000
Year 5	5,000	(5,000)	48,000
	25,000	25,000	90,000
Average annual profit	5,000	5,000	18,000
Average capital invested	12,500	25,000	30,000
Expected ROCE	5,000/12,500	5,000/25,000	18,000/30,000
	= 40%	= 20%	= 60%

Note
* Calculated by deducting a straight-line depreciation charge from the forecast cash flows of each project. The depreciation charges are: project A £5,000 (£25,000/5); project B £10,000 (£50,000/5); and project C £12,000 (£60,000/5).

(b) Projects A and C are selected as they give a return on capital employed of 25 per cent or more.
(c) Project C is chosen as it has the highest ROCE.

Example 14.12 produces a different selection of projects compared with pay-back. Because all the returns over the life of the project are included, project C becomes the most desirable whereas project B is excluded. However, it can be argued that the returns in the more distant future should not be given the same weight as the more imminent ones, as they carry greater uncertainty and, even if they transpire as predicted, they are less valuable as it has been necessary to wait longer for them.

Net present value (NPV)

The NPV method of investment appraisal brings into consideration all the cash flows over the life of a project, but gives decreasing weight to them the further into the future they are expected to arise. The weights applied are based on the *time value of money*, a concept that holds that sums of money received in the future are worth less than the same sum received today. The link between the present and future values is determined by the rate of interest, also known as the discount rate, faced by the entity making the calculation. For example, if a firm's discount rate is 10 per cent per annum, then £100 receivable in two year's time is worth only £82.65 today as £82.65 invested at a compound annual interest rate of 10 per cent will accumulate as follows:

	£
Invested today	82.65
Year 1 interest	8.26
Value at the end of year 1	90.91
Year 2 interest	9.09
Value at the end of year 2	100.00

Based on this calculation, it can be stated that the present value of £100 in two year's time at a 10 per cent discount rate is £82.65. Note the operation of compound interest whereby the interest earned is added to the sum invested at the end of each year, and so itself earns interest from then on.

To avoid the need to make complicated calculations, tables of discount factors are available that show, for different discount rates, the present value of £1 received at various times in the future. Such a table of discount factors is shown in Table 14.1. This table is used to find the present value of future sums of money by multiplying the sums by the appropriate discount factor. For example,

1. the present value of £10,000 receivable in 4 years' time by a firm with a cost of capital of 15 per cent is £10,000 × 0.572 = £5,720; and
2. the present value of £15,000 receivable in 3 years' time by a firm with a cost of capital of 10 per cent is £15,000 × 0.751 = £11,265.

The steps to carry out an investment appraisal using NPV are as follows:

1. Calculate the cash flows of the project. The cash outflow of the initial investment takes place immediately and is given a weight of 1. The other cash flows are assumed to take place at the end of the year in which they occur.
2. Determine the discount rate. This is the rate of interest paid to borrow funds to carry out the project – it is also known as the firm's cost of capital.
3. Use a discount factor table to find the factors appropriate to the timing of the cash flows (from step 1) and the discount rate (from step 2).
4. Calculate the present values of the cash flows from step 1 by applying the factors found in step 3.
5. The present values, positive and negative, from step 4 are summed to find the NPV.
6. If there is no limit on the funds available, all projects with a positive NPV are chosen. If funds are limited and the initial investments are the same, the project with highest positive NPV is selected. Where the initial investments are not equal, the project with the highest profitability index in excess of 1 is selected. The profitability index is calculated by the formula:

$$\text{Profitability index} = \frac{\text{Present value of cash inflows}}{\text{Initial investment}}$$

Table 14.1 A discount table showing the present value of £1

| Discount rate | Discount factor | | |
	10%	15%	20%
Year			
0	1.000	1.000	1.000
1	0.909	0.870	0.833
2	0.826	0.756	0.694
3	0.751	0.658	0.579
4	0.683	0.572	0.482
5	0.621	0.497	0.402

Example 14.13 The directors of Applause Ltd determine that the company's cost of capital is 15 per cent.

Required Using the information on cash flows in Example 14.11, but assuming that the annual cash inflow from project A is £5,000

(a) calculate the NPV of each project;
(b) calculate the profitability index of each project;
(c) state which projects would be accepted if unlimited funds are available; and
(d) state which project would be accepted if limited funds are available and only one can be undertaken.

Solution (a)

	Discount factor	Project A Cash flow £	Present value £	Project B Cash flow £	Present value £	Project C Cash flow £	Present value £
Investment	1.000	−25,000	−25,000	−50,000	−50,000	−60,000	−60,000
Year 1	0.870	5,000	4,350	30,000	26,100	10,000	8,700
2	0.756	5,000	3,780	20,000	15,120	20,000	15,120
3	0.658	5,000	3,290	15,000	9,870	20,000	13,160
4	0.572	5,000	2,860	5,000	2,860	40,000	22,880
5	0.497	5,000	2,485	5,000	2,485	60,000	29,820
NPV			(8,235)		6,435		29,680

(b) **Profitability index**

Project A	Project B	Project C
16,765/25,000	56,435/50,000	89,680/60,000
= .67	= 1.13	= 1.49

(c) If funds are unlimited, projects B and C are chosen as they both have positive NPVs.
(d) If only one project can be undertaken, project C is chosen as it has the highest profitability index, i.e. it gives the greatest NPV per £ invested.

As is the case with all techniques of investment appraisal, it must be remembered that NPV analysis is only a guide for management and relies on forecasts of the future that must be subject to uncertainty. Management also has to contend with the fact that different techniques can give different advice, and so judgement must be exercised when making a final selection.

Readers should now work Question 14.7 at the end of this chapter.

FORECAST RESULTS

Management is often faced with a number of alternative courses of action, especially when it is considering the long-term development of the company.

It is of great assistance to management to prepare forecasts that predict the likely outcome of alternatives so that choices are based on the best possible information available.

Forecasts cannot be completely accurate, as many of the factors that influence actual results, such as the cost of raw materials and the actual demand for the product, are outside the control of management. However, this does not invalidate the exercise of preparing forecasts since the alternative is to make decisions without evaluating the outcome of management's expectations. To prepare forecasts, management must answer such vital questions as, 'How many units do you expect to sell?' 'What will be the selling price per unit?' 'How much labour, at what cost, will it take to produce each unit?' Forecasts bring together the answers to all these questions in accounting statements, and show the expected impact of alternatives on key financial magnitudes such as cash, profit and working capital. Cash forecasts are considered in the next section of this chapter, the forecast trading and profit and loss account and balance sheet are then dealt with, and finally how to prepare a forecast cash flow statement of funds.

The availability of spreadsheets for use on computers has greatly assisted the preparation of forecasts. Any reader familiar with these programs will see clearly how they could be used and appreciate their benefits when studying the following sections. However, the fact that a forecast has been prepared on a computer does not mean that the underlying techniques are correct, and so it is important that the correct approaches, as described in this section, are understood and used. One of the main benefits of using a spreadsheet to prepare a forecast is the ability, with careful design, to compute revised solutions in response to changes in key variables; this facility is so useful that readers are advised to acquire the ability to use spreadsheets if they have to prepare forecasts on a routine basis.

Cash forecasts

Management must ensure that the company can afford any new project that is under consideration, that is, the company will not run out of cash if a particular plan is followed. Additional external finance, such as a bank overdraft, can be sought if the company's own cash resources are insufficient, but lenders will only be willing to provide funds that are likely to be repaid. The impact of plans on the cash resources of a company can be predicted using a cash forecast, and this is also of great interest to any person or organization, such as a bank, which is approached for funds. If cash forecasts are not prepared, a company may suddenly find itself short of cash or holding unproductive surplus funds in its bank account. A cash forecast enables a company to foresee a deficit, for which appropriate funding can be sought, or a surplus for which uses can be prepared in advance.

The preparation of a monthly cash forecast involves the identification of the cash flows expected to take place in each month and the calculation of the forecast cash position at the end of each month. The following techniques are used to predict cash transactions:

1. *Sales* Cash sales are entered in the forecast as receipts for the month in which they take place. The time lag has to be taken into account for credit

sales, for example, cash from March sales may be received in April.
2. *Purchases* Cash purchases are entered in the month in which they take place. The time lag has to be taken into account for credit purchases, for example, cash for October purchases may be paid in November.
3. *Regular items* Regular payments are entered in the appropriate month, possibly with adjustment for a lag between the date when the expense is incurred and when it is paid.
4. *Irregular items* Irregular items, such as the purchase of fixed assets or the payment of tax, are also entered according to their incidence.

Example 14.14

Hamel runs a shop that makes all of its sales for cash. Forecasts for the first half of 19X6 are

Sales	January to March – £25,000 per month. April to June – £30,000 per month.
Purchases	A gross margin of 20 per cent on selling prices is made. Every item sold is immediately replaced. Suppliers are paid in the month following delivery.
Payments	Wages and other expenses, £4,000 per month. Drawings, £1,000 per month. Delivery van cost £7,000; received on 1 January and paid for in February.
Opening balances	Owed to suppliers £16,000. Cash £1,000.

Ignore interest on any overdraft that may arise.

Required

(a) Calculate the value of monthly purchases.
(b) Prepare a cash forecast for Hamel for the first six months of 19X6 that shows the cash balance at the end of each month.
(c) Comment on the position shown by the forecast.

Solution

(a)

	Sales	*Purchases* *(Sales – 20%)*
	£000	*£000*
January	25	20
February	25	20
March	25	20
April	30	24
May	30	24
June	30	24

(b)

	Jan. £	*Feb.* £	*March* £	*April* £	*May* £	*June* £	*Total* £
Cash in							
Sales	25,000	25,000	25,000	30,000	30,000	30,000	165,000

Cash out							
Purchases	16,000	20,000	20,000	20,000	24,000	24,000	124,000
Wages and							
other							
expenses	4,000	4,000	4,000	4,000	4,000	4,000	24,000
Drawings	1,000	1,000	1,000	1,000	1,000	1,000	6,000
Delivery van		7,000					7,000
	21,000	32,000	25,000	25,000	29,000	29,000	161,000
Opening							
balance	1,000	5,000	(2,000)	(2,000)	3,000	4,000	1,000
+Cash in	25,000	25,000	25,000	30,000	30,000	30,000	165,000
–Cash out	21,000	32,000	25,000	25,000	29,000	29,000	161,000
Closing							
balance	5,000	(2,000)	(2,000)	3,000	4,000	5,000	5,000

(c) The purchase of the van creates a cash deficit in February and March, but this is made good from trading cash inflows by April. The bank should be approached for a temporary loan – an overdraft would be best. By the end of June the business is accumulating a cash surplus that will continue to increase if trade stays at the same level. Thought should be given to how any permanently spare cash is to be used.

Note the columnar layout of the solution to part (b) of the example. The use of this presentation is recommended because:

1. it saves time as the descriptions of cash flows do not have to be repeated for each month;
2. errors are less likely to occur as any inconsistent entries are more easily identified; and
3. it aids comparison throughout the period covered by the forecast of the individual elements of cash flow.

Readers should now work Question 14.8 at the end of this chapter.

Forecast trading and profit and loss account and balance sheet

The preparation of a trading and profit and loss account and balance sheet from the cash account, and opening and closing values for assets and liabilities, was explained in Chapter 4 in the context of past results. Once the cash forecast has been prepared, the same techniques may be applied to prepare a forecast trading and profit and loss account and balance sheet.

Example 14.15 The balance sheet of Hamel at 31 December 19X5 was:

	£	£
Fixed assets		
Premises		10,000
Current assets		
Stock	18,500	
Cash	1,000	
	19,500	
Current liabilities		
Trade creditors	16,000	
		3,500
		13,500
Capital		13,500

Hamel expects to undertake the transactions given in Example 14.14 during the first six months of 19X6. You may assume that the monthly cash forecast has been prepared, which gives a summary of cash transactions in the 'total' column.

The van is expected to have a life of five years and a zero scrap value at the end of that time. Hamel uses the straight-line method to calculate depreciation.

Required Prepare Hamel's forecast trading and profit and loss account for the six months to 30 June 19X6 and a balance sheet at that date.

Solution **Forecast Trading and Profit and Loss Account**

	£	£
Sales		165,000
Less: Cost of goods sold (W1)		132,000
Gross profit		33,000
Wages	24,000	
Depreciation $(0.5 \times 7,000/5)$	700	
		24,700
Net profit		8,300

Balance Sheet

	£	£
Fixed assets		
Premises		10,000
Van	7,000	
Less: Depreciation	700	
		6,300
		16,300

Current assets		
Stock	18,500	
Cash	5,000	
	23,500	
Current liabilities		
Trade creditors (June purchases)	24,000	
		(500)
		15,800
Capital		
Opening balance		13,500
Plus: Profit		8,300
		21,800
Less: Drawings		(6,000)
		15,800

Working 1

Purchases = Payments – Opening creditors + Closing creditors.
Purchases = 124,000 – 16,000 + 24,000 (June purchases) = 132,000.

The level of stock has remained unchanged, and so purchases and cost of goods sold have the same value.

Readers should now work Question 14.9 at the end of this chapter.

Forecast cash flow statement

The preparation of the cash flow statement from historical data was dealt with in Chapter 12. The same principles can be applied to prepare a cash flow statement from forecast data such as that in Example 14.15 (question and solution).

Prepare the forecast cash flow statement of Hamel for the six months to 30 June 19X6 using the information given in Example 14.15 (question and solution).

Example 14.16
Required

Cash Flow Statement for the six months to 30 June 19X6

Solution

	£
Net cash flow from operating activities (Note 1)	17,000
Returns on investment and servicing of finance	
Drawings	(6,000)

Investing activities	
Payments to buy fixed assets	(7,000)
Increase in cash	4,000

Note 1: Net cash flow from operating activities	
Profit	8,300
Depreciation	700
Increase in creditors	8,000
	17,000

Students should now work Questions 14.10–14.12.

Questions

14.1 Rock Ltd manufactures a single product that passes through two separate processes, designated X and Y, in two separate factories; all products must pass through both processes before they are ready for sale.

Rock's summary revenue account for 19X5 is as follows:

	£
Process X	
Raw materials	20,000
Wages	30,000
Depreciation	12,000
Rent	8,000
Transfer to process Y	70,000
Process Y	
Raw materials	10,000
Wages	40,000
Depreciation	12,000
Rent	8,000
Cost of production	140,000
General expenses	36,000
Net profit	24,000
Sales (100,000 units)	200,000

There are no stocks of any type at the beginning or at the end of the year.

There is a heavy demand for the product. Production costs and selling price are to be maintained at the same level as in 19X5.

Consideration is being given to three proposals for increasing production as follows:

(i) The expansion of manufacturing capacity at both factories. The cost of rent and the depreciation charge will in both cases be double that for 19X5. Materials consumed and wage rates would continue for both factories at the same unit cost as for 19X5.

(ii) The purchase of the additional process X components from an outside source at a price of 80p per unit. Expansion of manufacturing capacity at factory Y on the same terms and the same cost as for proposal (i).

(iii) The purchase of the additional finished goods from an outside source at 180p per unit and their sale at 200p per unit. No additional capacity would be required.

General expenses will increase in all cases at the rate of £2,000 per additional 25,000 units sold.

Required

Prepare a financial statement for management that shows the forecast *additional* profit under each of the three proposals if outputs and sales increase by (a) 25,000 units and (b) 50,000 units.

14.2 Glen Eagles is the proprietor of a small but long-established manufacturing business that has consistently made an annual profit of £20,000. The financial results of the business have shown little change in recent years, and the financial position has been very stable, supported by the fact that annual drawings have generally been lower than the profit. The expectation is that there will be little change over the next few years and that the level of profit will be maintained.

Eagles has recently been invited by Troon Ltd to increase his production to meet an export demand in a market where the prospects of development and increased sales are very substantial. Additional plant with a life of ten years, and a zero residual value at the end of that period, will be needed for such an expansion. Machines that will produce 46,000 items per annum are available at a cost of £36,000 each.

The selling price per item is £1, and the variable costs of manufacture for the export market will be 55p per item. Additional general expenses will amount to £10,000 for the first £46,000 increase in sales, but will fall to £4,000 for each £46,000 block of additional sales above the first £46,000.

Eagles has no private resources. The existing liquid resources of the business would cover any additional working capital required, and also provide £10,000 towards the capital cost of the new project. A bank is willing to lend up to £100,000 to Eagles at an interest rate of 15 per cent per annum.

An alternative proposal is made to Eagles. Troon Ltd offers him £120,000 in cash for his entire business and is prepared to retain his services as a manager on a ten-year contract at a salary of £14,000 per annum plus an additional £3,000 per annum for each £46,000 increase in turnover.

Eagles can expect to invest the proceeds of the sale of his business to earn interest of 10 per cent per annum.

Required

(a) Statements reporting on the profit likely to be received from overseas sales at the rate of £46,000, £92,000 and £138,000 per annum respectively.

(b) Prepare a report to Eagles that shows the results of the alternative course of action open to him.

14.3 Tassell Ltd is a manufacturing company specializing in the production of two machines, XX and YY. The manufacturing process for the two machines is different and this necessitates a separate production department for each.

The managing director of the company is considering a revised selling price for each machine.

The estimated costs for the next twelve months are as follows:

	Admin. & Support Services £	Dept. of Manufacturing XX £	YY £	Stores Dept. £
Direct wages	—	891,880	144,900	—
Direct materials	—	2,043,216	5,924,800	—
Rent and rates	81,000			
Power	23,200			
Heat and light	11,740			
Salaries and indirect wages	196,300	128,640	64,185	144,415
Insurance of:				
Buildings	8,910			
Machinery	5,750			
Office equipment	1,000			
Depreciation of:				
Buildings	5,940			
Machinery	23,000			
Office equipment	4,000			
Miscellaneous expenses	2,190	12,210	6,875	5,775

Other than salaries and indirect wages and miscellaneous expenses, the overheads have not yet been spread on to individual cost centres.

Additional information for the forthcoming year is as follows:

	Admin. & Support Services	Dept. of Manufacturing XX	YY	Stores Dept.
No. of employees	14	71	17	12
Stores requisitions	20	600	840	—
Value of:				
Buildings (whole site)	£540,000	—	—	—
Machinery	—	£110,000	£420,000	£45,000
Office equipment	£60,000	—	—	—
Floor area (square metres)	220	800	600	1,080
Cubic capacity (metres)	—	3,200	2,300	5,540
Direct labour hours	—	121,620	22,560	—
Machine operating hours	—	12,000	46,000	—
Units produced	—	162,160	322,000	—

Required

(a) Prepare an overhead analysis sheet for Tassell Ltd in respect of the year. Clearly show the basis for apportionment where appropriate.

(15 marks)

(b) Calculate an appropriate overhead recovery rate for each productive cost centre.   *(2 marks)*

(c) The managing director of Tassell Ltd has decided to add £1.80 to each unit of XX and YY to cover other costs and profit element. Establish a selling price for each product which covers the company's

direct costs;
overheads;
other costs; and
profit element. *(5 marks)*
(Total: 22 marks)
(ICSA, Introduction to Accounting)

14.4 During 19X4 Feather Ltd, which has a maximum possible output of 100,000 units, sold 60,000 units of a product and made a net profit of £20,000. The contribution per unit was £2, and the selling price was £5 per unit.

A competitor entered the market in November 19X4, and is selling a very similar product to Feather's at £4.60 per unit. The management of Feather decides that it must introduce automation to meet this challenge and decides upon the following plan for 19X5:

(a) Reduce the selling price per unit to £4.50. This should increase sales to 90,000
(b) Introduce new machinery with the result that annual fixed costs increase by £80,000.
(c) The new machinery will decrease variable costs by £1 per unit.

Required

(a) Prepare the summary profit and loss account for 19X4, showing sales, variable costs, fixed costs and profit.
(b) Calculate the break-even level of sales for 19X4 in terms of units and £s.
(c) Prepare the forecast profit and loss account for 19X5, showing sales, variable costs, fixed costs and profit.
(d) Calculate the break-even level of sales for 19X5 in terms of both units and £s.

14.5 Use the information in Question 14.4 to prepare a break-even chart that shows the results of both 19X4 and 19X5.

14.6 The summarized profit and loss account of Latchmere Ltd for 19X6 is as follows:

	£		£
Raw materials	50,000	Sales (100,000	
Wages	100,000	units at £2 each)	200,000
Depreciation	10,000		
Gross profit	40,000		
	200,000		200,000
General expenses	20,000	Gross profit	40,000
Net profit	20,000		
	40,000		40,000

The company's plant has now reached its maximum level of production and the directors are considering proposals for expansion.

Two plans have been suggested:

1. The purchase of additional plant of the same type and capacity as that in use at present, and which will operate at exactly the same raw materials and wages costs per unit as the existing plant, in the expectation of

doubling the level of sales. It is thought that a market exists at the current selling price of £2 per unit. The plant will cost £100,000.

2. The purchase of additional plant, at a cost of £200,000, capable of manufacturing a similar product with the same raw material content as the current product, but for which the wages cost will be reduced to 15 per cent of the expected selling price of £2 per unit.

Under both plans, *additional* general expenses amounting to £5,000 will be incurred for any increase in turnover up to £100,000 (total sales £300,000) and a further £10,000 will be incurred for any increase in turnover above £100,000 and up to £200,000 (total sales £400,000). The cost of production and the selling price per unit of the first £200,000 of sales will be the same as for 19X6, and the profit on those sales will be unchanged.

For both plans, the life of the new plant will be ten years at the end of which it will have a zero scrap value. The purchase will be financed by a fixed-term ten-year loan at 10 per cent per annum.

Required

(a) Prepare a trading and profit and loss account of Latchmere Ltd for 19X7 assuming that plan 1 is implemented and that the expected sales increase of £200,000 is achieved.

(b) Calculate the minimum increase in sales needed under plan 2 to ensure that the net profit after charging interest is equal to the profit it is calculated will be produced under plan 1.

(c) Calculate the sales necessary in 19X7 under plan 2 that give the company as a whole the same net profit, after interest, as was earned in 19X6, that is, £20,000.

14.7 The directors of Axmede Ltd have decided that it has £100,000 available for investment in fixed assets and is considering the following two alternative projects, both of which are expected to have a life of four years at the end of which the plant will have a zero scrap value:

	Project Zero £000	Project Nemo £000
Initial investment in fixed assets	80	90
Cash inflows		
Year 1	50	30
2	40	30
3	30	40
4	20	60
	140	160

The company's cost of capital is 20 per cent.

Required

(a) Calculate the payback period of each project.
(b) Calculate the return on capital employed of each project.
(c) Calculate the net present value of each project.
(d) Calculate the profitability index of each project.
(e) Advise management as to which project it should undertake.

14.8 Grant commences business on 1 January 19X6 and introduces £20,000 cash as capital. He also borrows £8,000 from his brother at 10 per cent per annum interest, payable half yearly in June and December. He makes the following estimates about the first six months of 19X6:

Fixed assets	£20,000 purchased for cash in January.
Sales	£12,000 per month. Two months' credit to be given to customers.
Purchases	£16,000 in January and £8,000 per month thereafter. Suppliers will allow one month's credit.
Expenses	£800 per month average, excluding interest, payable in the month in which they are incurred.
Drawings	£200 per month.

Required

Prepare a cash forecast for the business of Grant for the first six months of 19X6 that shows the cash balance at the end of each month.

14.9 Required

Use the information in Question 14.8 to prepare Grant's forecast trading and profit and loss account for the six months to 30 June 19X6 and his balance sheet at that date.

The fixed assets are to be depreciated at the rate of 20 per cent per annum on cost, and Grant calculates selling prices of goods by adding 50 per cent to their cost price.

Grant expects that the interest on the forecast overdraft will cost £300 and be paid in July.

14.10 Required

Use the information in Question and Solution 14.9 to prepare Grant's cash flow statement for the six months to 30 June 19X6.

14.11 Required

The balance sheet of Harris Ltd as at 30 November 1993 is shown below:

	£000		£000
Fixed assets	775	Share capital	800
Stock-in-trade	240	Reserves	318
Trade debtor	384	Trade creditors	297
Cash-at-bank	27	Accruals	11
	1,426		1,426

You are informed that:
(i) The firm's anticipated sales and purchases for the next six months are:

	£000	£000
December	410	205
January	290	224
February	364	236
March	392	249
April	440	273
May	484	293

(ii) Customers are allowed one month's credit and Harris Ltd take a similar period of credit from suppliers. (*You may assume that these terms and conditions are strictly adhered to.*)
(iii) Expense creditors will be paid during December.

(iv) Overheads for the next six months are estimated at £71,000 per month. This figure includes £14,000 depreciation and £43,000 in respect of wages and salaries. Payments will be made during the month in which the expense is incurred.

(v) The firm experts to purchase some new capital equipment during late May. The cost of the equipment will be £360,000 and be paid for during the months of purchase.

(vi) The accountant of Harris Ltd had negotiated a loan of £350,000 from the firm's bank to be paid during late May to cover the cost of new capital equipment.

(vii) The firm expects to sell its stock at a mark-up of 100 per cent.

Required

(a) Prepare a cash budget for Harris Ltd in respect of the six months ending 31 May 1994.   *(8 marks)*

(b) Advise the firm's accountant whether there is a need for a loan to cover the purchase of the new capital equipment.   *(3 marks)*

(c) Calculate Harris Ltd's net profit or net loss for the six months ending. 31 May 1994.   *(7 marks)*

(ICSA, December 1993)

14.12 Hilary Pringle plans to set up in business on 1 January 19X6 with a capital of £5,000 with which she will open a bank account for her business. Early in January she will buy fixtures and fittings for her shop estimated to cost £2,000, which she will pay in cash. Hilary expects to have to replace her fixtures and fittings in four years' time and will at that time donate her old ones to charity. She has already made arrangements for renting a shop from 1 January when she will be required to pay £1,500 rent for the six months to 30 June. Hilary estimates that her monthly expenses (wages, telephone, insurance, etc.) will average £400 per month and will be paid as incurred, and she realizes she will have to draw £300 per month for living expenses.

Hilary will sell some goods for cash, expected receipts £1,000 per month, but most of her sales will be on credit and are expected to be £2,000 in January rising by £1,000 per month thereafter. Credit customers will be expected to settle their accounts in the month following delivery, for example, sales in January will be paid for in February.

Hilary has arranged credit accounts with various suppliers who require her to pay two months after delivery. Purchases planned are £4,000 per month for the first three months. The customary gross profit/sales ratio in Hilary's type of business is 25 per cent.

Required

1. Produce a statement showing the forecast receipts, payments and balance of cash for each of the months January to March 19X6.

2. Produce a forecast profit and loss statement for that period and a balance sheet at 31 March 19X6.

(AAT, Numeracy and Accounting)

15
STANDARD COSTING AND BUDGETARY CONTROL

The objectives of this chapter are to

- identify the types of comparisons made in order to monitor the achievement of business objectives;
- identify, distinguish between and appreciate the main features of a system of budgetary control: namely, planning, forecasting, co-ordination and control;
- explain the advantages of a system of budgetary control;
- distinguish between budgets and forecasts;
- demonstrate the preparation of budgets for sales, purchases and cash;
- show how the results of individual budgets are summarized in a budgeted profit and loss account and budgeted balance sheet;
- outline the nature and purpose of a system of standard costing;
- explain the advantages of a system of standard costing;
- calculate the main variances for sales, materials and overheads;
- identify reasons for favourable and unfavourable variances and demonstrate possible inter-relationships between them; and
- familiarize students with the nature of the main overhead variances.

INTRODUCTION

A principal aim of business organizations is the maximization of profit within the constraints imposed by the need to ensure long-run financial stability. In other words, the aim is long-run rather than short-run profit maximization. It was noted in Chapter 13 that three types of comparisons might be made in order to monitor the achievement of these objectives – time series analysis; interfirm comparisons; and standards and budgets – and the use of the first two types of comparison has already been considered.

In this chapter we consider, for the first time, the use of standards and budgets to help ensure the most efficient use of available resources. Systems of standard costing and budgetary control are installed by management for this purpose and, unlike the other methods of performance appraisal, their utilization is confined to the internal user group. The *purpose* of the two systems is identical; their aim is to estimate what future achievements should be and thereby provide an objective yardstick against which actual performance can be measured. The difference is that budgetary control is concerned with aggregate costs and revenues at departmental or company level, whereas standard costing is concerned with the costs and revenues relating to individual goods and services.

BUDGETARY CONTROL

The main features of a system of budgetary control are as follows:

- *Planning* and *forecasting* levels of business activity.
- *Co-ordinating* different aspects of business activity so they work in harmony with one another.
- *Controlling* performance and costs.

The key words are therefore *planning, forecasting, co-ordinating* and *control*, and their combined purpose is to achieve maximum profitability consistent with long-run financial stability.

The advantages of a system of budgetary control may be summarized as follows:

- The company's business objectives are established, e.g. maximization of profit; maximization of market share; the provision of employment opportunities; survival; financial stability; and the supply of quality products. Some of these objectives are clearly complementary, but they may contain an element of conflict, e.g. preoccupation with survival may conflict with profit maximization – which must be resolved. The outcome of this difficult process is that the firm 'knows where it is going'.
- Targets for sales, production, etc., are identified, which are achievable assuming a reasonable level of efficiency. For example, it is no use assuming a level of sales that cannot be met in order to show a budgeted profit, which is, in reality, unlikely to be achieved.
- The activities of each department and individual are co-ordinated in order to ensure, for example, that there are sufficient skilled personnel to enable production targets to be met. The result is that the budgets are not simply a set of vague and unrelated hopes and wishes. They must cover the whole of the organization to ensure that all activity is geared towards achieving the budget objective. Co-ordination ensures that, provided each individual in charge of a budget centre (typically a department) fulfils his or her responsibilities, the organization as a whole moves in the right direction.
- The responsibilities of individuals are stated so that each employee knows what is expected from him or her. In particular, the budgetary process facilitates delegation of responsibilities to individuals in charge of specified areas of activity, called budget centres.
- Actual results are recorded and compared with budgets enabling the identification of deviations, both favourable and unfavourable. Management is then able to concentrate on areas which require corrective action to be taken. This is called 'management by exception'.

The main differences between budgets, considered here, and the forecasts, considered in the previous chapter, are as follows:

- A forecast is what is expected to happen assuming existing business conditions remain constant, e.g. advertising policy or geographical areas of operation remain unchanged.
- A budget sets out what is achievable following the introduction of changes designed to improve operating efficiency.

PREPARATION OF BUDGETS

A budget is a financial plan based on targeted future activity and is used to control that activity. It is possible to make a number of estimates of the financial outcome under different assumptions, and the one that best meets the firm's objectives and is within its capabilities is chosen.

The sales budget

This is the logical first stage in the planning process as the predicted volume of sales determines most of the other features of the organization, such as the amount of office accommodation required and the number of employees to be engaged. The sales manager must analyse the market in which the firm intends to operate and consider such questions as: the products to be sold; the geographical areas in which the product is to be sold; the potential size of the market; when the sales will take place; the price to be charged; and the number of units to be sold.

The sales budget (similarly all other budgets), once prepared, must be compared with the firm's resources to see it if can be achieved and whether it contributes towards the realization of an adequate level of profit. If not, consideration must be given to the effect of charging a higher price, and possibly reducing sales, or the effect of charging a lower price and increasing the level of activity. The impact on sales of increasing the level of advertising might also be considered.

Example 15.1

Paxton Ltd is a new company incorporated on 1 December 19X0. It is located in Bristol with sales agencies in the south west and in Wales. Forecasts have been made of sales levels under different assumptions and the following budgetary information has been agreed:

- Sales in the south west to amount to 200 units in March 19X1 and increase by 20 per cent in each of the next two months. The target level of sales for the month of May to then be repeated in each subsequent month.
- Sales in Wales to commence at 250 units in the month of February, remaining at that level each month until October. Sales in November and December and in January 19X2 to amount to twice the level previously achieved.
- The budgeted selling price is £50 per unit.

Required

The sales budget for Paxton Ltd for each of the months of 19X1.

Solution   Sales Budget for each of the months of 19X1

Month	Units sold			Price per unit £	Value £
	South west	Wales	Total		
January					
February		250	250	50	12,500
March	200	250	450	50	22,500
April	240	250	490	50	24,500
May	288	250	538	50	26,900
June	288	250	538	50	26,900
July	288	250	538	50	26,900
August	288	250	538	50	26,900
September	288	250	538	50	26,900
October	288	250	538	50	26,900
November	288	500	788	50	39,400
December	288	500	788	50	39,400
					299,700

The sales budget therefore sets out the monthly targets for managers responsible for each geographical location and gives the total sales value for inclusion in the trading account for the year (of course, trading accounts could be prepared more regularly for management if required, for example, on a monthly or quarterly basis).

The purchases (production) budget

All companies operating a system of budgetary control require a purchases budget; in the case of a manufacturing company, a production budget is also required. We concentrate on the preparation of a purchases budget for a trading organization, though similar principles would be applied for the purpose of preparing a production budget.

The essential requirement, when preparing the purchases budget, is to make sure that purchases are sufficient to ensure that goods are available for delivery to customers as and when required. The contents of the purchases budget therefore depends on

- the budgeted sales for the budget period; and
- planned increases or decreases in stock.

Example 15.2   Paxton Ltd (see Example 15.1) is to purchase and take delivery of 500 units of stock in December 19X0. The company's buyer will subsequently make purchases sufficient to meet budgeted sales for the forthcoming month. The budgeted purchase price is £30 per unit.

Required   The purchases budget for Paxton Ltd for each of the 13 months to December 19X1.

Purchases Budget for each of the 13 months to December 19X1   **Solution**

Month	Units sold total	Price per unit £	Value £
19X0			
December	500	30	15,000
19X1			
January	250	30	7,500
February	450	30	13,500
March	490	30	14,700
April	538	30	16,140
May	538	30	16,140
June	538	30	16,140
July	538	30	16,140
August	538	30	16,140
September	538	30	16,140
October	788	30	23,640
November	788	30	23,640
December	788	30	23,640
			218,460

Other expense budgets

There are separate budgets for costs incurred in respect of administration, selling and distributing a company's products. A specific manager should be given responsibility for each budget and the costs should be measured, monitored and controlled as carefully as purchases and production costs.

The cash budget

This shows the cash implications of each of the above budgets. However, it also reflects the impact of capital transactions, such as the purchase of fixed assets and the issue of shares and loans. The basic principles involved in the preparation of the cash budget are similar to those explained in Chapter 13 relating to cash forecasts. In particular, the impact of 'time lags' between sales and the receipt of cash and purchases and the payment of cash must be given effect.

The policy of Paxton Ltd (see Examples 15.1 and 15.2) is to allow two **Example 15.3** months' credit to customers and it has agreed one months' credit with its suppliers. The company will issue 100,000 shares of 50p each for cash, at par value, on 1 December 19X0. An annual rental of £5,000 will be paid, in advance, on 1 December, and fixed assets costing £30,000 paid for on 31 December 19X0. Operating expenses (including wages) will amount to £4,000 per month, commencing December 19X0, and these costs will be paid for in the month they are incurred.

A cash budget for the 13 months to December 19X1 showing the surplus or **Required** deficit at the end of each month.

Note
Ignore interest payable.

Solution

Cash Budget for the 13 months to 31 December 19X1

Month	Opening balance £	Share issue £	Sales £	Purchases £	Fixed assets £	Rent £	Other expenses £	Closing balance £
19X0								
December		50,000			30,000	5,000	4,000	11,000
19X1								
January	11,000			15,000			4,000	(8,000)
February	(8,000)			7,500			4,000	(19,500)
March	(19,500)			13,500			4,000	(37,000)
April	(37,000)		12,500	14,700			4,000	(43,200)
May	(43,200)		22,500	16,140			4,000	(40,840)
June	(40,840)		24,500	16,140			4,000	(36,480)
July	(36,480)		26,900	16,140			4,000	(29,720)
August	(29,720)		26,900	16,140			4,000	(22,960)
September	(22,960)		26,900	16,140			4,000	(16,200)
October	(16,200)		26,900	16,140			4,000	(9,440)
November	(9,440)		26,900	23,640			4,000	(10,180)
December	(10,180)		26,900	23,640		5,000	4,000	(15,920)

The following can be noticed:

* The two-months credit allowed to customers means that the sales made in November and December, amounting to £39,400 each month, will not be received until after the end of the present budget period, giving rise to closing debtors of £78,800.
* Similarly, purchases in the month of December amounting to £23,640 are not paid until January 19X1, and these will appear in the budgeted balance sheet at 31 December 19X1 as trade creditors.
* Cash inflows are budgeted to exceed outflows in the month of December 19X0, but the cash balance of £11,000 is soon converted into an overdraft due to the fact that there are no sales proceeds until the month of April. The budgeted maximum cash deficiency is £43,200 at the end of April and this then falls quite quickly up to the end of December. The budgeted overdraft then increases marginally due to the need to purchase additional stock to meet the budgeted increase in sales in Wales during the months of November and December 19X1 and January 19X2.

Readers should now attempt Questions 15.1 and 15.2 at the end of this chapter.

The master budget

When each budget has been finalized, their overall results can be brought together in a master budget for the organization as a whole. The master budget consists of a budgeted profit and loss account and budgeted balance sheet. It is the responsibility of management to review the contents of the master budget in order to assess whether the results appear satisfactory, particularly in terms of profitability and financial stability. If the results are unsatisfactory in any respect, action must be taken to achieve an improvement. This is the advantage of the budgeting exercise: problems can be identified in time for corrective action to be taken.

The fixed assets of Paxton Ltd (see Examples 15.1–15.3) which were pur- **Example 15.4**
chased on 31 December 19X0 are expected to have a useful life of six years
and a residual value of £3,000 at the end of that period.

(a) The budgeted profit and loss account for Paxton Ltd for the period to **Required**
    31 December 19X1 and the budgeted balance sheet of that date.
(b) Brief comments on the budgeted profitability and cash position.

(a) **Budgeted Trading and Profit and Loss Account for the period to 31** **Solution**
    December 19X1

	£		£
Sales (see Example 15.1)			299,700
Purchases (see Example 15.2)	218,460		
Less: Closing stock	38,640	W1	
Cost of goods sold			179,820
Gross profit			119,880
Rent	5,417	W2	
Depreciation	4,500	W3	
Other expenses	52,000		61,917
Net profit			57,963

Budgeted Balance Sheet at 31 December 19X1

	£		£
Fixed assets at cost			30,000
Less: Accumulated depreciation			4,500
			25,500
Current assets			
Stock	38,640		
Trade debtors (see Example 15.3)	78,800		
Prepaid rent	4,583	W4	
	122,023		
Current liabilities			
Trade creditors (see Example 15.3)	23,640		
Cash deficit (see Example 15.3)	15,920		
	39,560		
Net current assets			82,463
Total assets less current liabilities			107,963
Share capital			50,000
Net profit			57,963
			107,963

W1 £15,000 (base stock) + £23,640 (purchases to meet budgeted sales in January 19X2).
W2 £5,000 (payment December 19X0) + £5,000 × 1/12 (payment December 19X1).
W3 £30,000 (cost) − £3,000 (estimated residual value)/6.
W4 £5,000 × 11/12.

(b) The budgeted results are very encouraging and might well be even better in 19X2 due to the following: there will be no need to pay rent and expenses for a month in which no production takes place, as was the case in December 19X0; and sales are budgeted to continue in January 19X2 at a much higher level than in January 19X1.

There is a cash deficiency of £15,920 at the end of the year. The cash budget will have drawn to management's attention the need to arrange additional finance of approximately £45,000 on a short-term basis to meet the budgeted deficiency in the early months of 19X1. It would seem that a bank overdraft would be a suitable form of finance in the circumstances.

Summary

We now present the budget process in the form of a diagram (Figure 15.1). This reminds us that the organizational objectives are first decided upon by management and, on that basis, results are forecast for a future accounting period using a range of different assumptions. The outcomes are examined by management, which must take steps to review the expected results in the light of organizational objectives: these include the need to ensure that actions are fully co-ordinated and that the plans indicate an adequate level of profitability and financial stability. The plans are then formalized, as budgets, and managers responsible for activity at budget-centre level are informed of their responsibilities. These managers will have played a full part in the budgeting process and should, therefore, have confidence in the budget process and in the budgets being achievable. Actual results are then recorded in accordance with the budgetary framework in order to facilitate comparison. Differences between budget and actual are identified and reported to the appropriate level of management, who is expected to take corrective action. The information obtained also feeds into the future budgeting process and business objectives will be reviewed.

Readers should now attempt Question 15.3 at the end of this chapter.

STANDARD COSTING

A system of standard costing makes use of predetermined standard costs relating to each element of cost (labour, material and overhead) for each type of product manufactured or services supplied. The actual costs incurred are then compared with standard costs as work proceeds. The difference between actual and standard is termed the *variance* and this is analysed to help identify the reason for the variance so that inefficiencies may immedi-

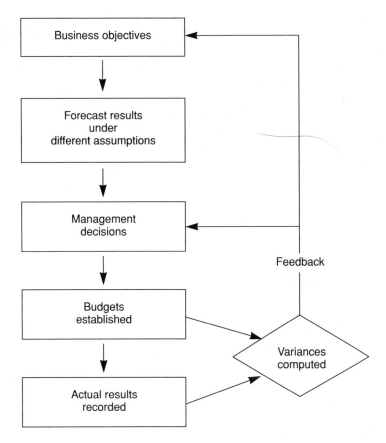

Figure 15.1   Management planning, decision-making and control

ately be brought to the attention of the responsible managers and corrective action taken.

We can therefore see that there are broad similarities between standard costing and budgetary control; the essential difference is that we are here concerned with controlling costs at the level of the individual or product rather than at the level of the department.

The first stage in the operation of a system of standard costing is to establish the standards. It may be necessary to employ work-study engineers to measure time taken on particular jobs and the materials used. It is possible to distinguish between ideal (or theoretical) standards that assume 100 per cent efficiency and expected (or attainable) standards given the conditions prevailing in a particular business organization. Ideal standards are almost certain not to be achievable and are likely to have a demotivating effect on personnel. For this reasons systems of standard costing are usually based on a reasonably ambitious but achievable level of efficiency. The advantages of a system of standard costing may be summarized as follows:

- The installation of a system of standard costing requires the company to review existing practices and this often results in substantial improvements being made.

- Standard costs are a more meaningful yardstick than the alternatives, which are to compare results with those of a previous year or a different company. For example, this year's results may be better than last year's but last year's results may have been abysmal, so the observed improvement, although welcome, does not indicate whether the firm has achieved its potential.
- Variances are quickly identified enabling corrective action to be taken before further losses are unnecessarily incurred.
- There is a saving in management time in that attention is focused on problem areas.
- The system identifies areas of achievement as well as difficulty, and draws management's attention to areas of success, which the company may be able to exploit more fully.
- The system promotes cost consciousness; individuals know that standards have been set and financial results of their work are under scrutiny.

CALCULATION OF VARIANCES

The broad operation of a system of variance analysis is illustrated in Figure 15.2. The overall variance is the difference between the actual profit and the budgeted profit for a particular produce line. The simple explanation for the overall variance is that revenue has been lower than expected and/or costs have been higher. These magnitudes are reflected, respectively, in the 'total sales variance' and the 'total cost variance'. These two variances may then be the subject of further analysis and the appropriate calculations are now considered.

Variances arise for two basic reasons:

- The actual volume of activity differs from the standard volume of activity giving rise to a volume variance.
- The actual price may differ from the standard price giving rise to a price variance.

The variances may be either favourable (F) or unfavourable (U) giving rise to three possible combinations:

- Both variances favourable.
- Both variances unfavourable.
- One variance favourable and one unfavourable.

Sales variances
The total sales variance may be analysed into the sales volume variance and the sales price variance as indicated in Figure 15.2. The calculations of the three variances are as follows:

Total sales variance = Actual sales proceeds – Standard sales proceeds

A positive figure, in the case of sales variances, indicates a favourable variance (actual revenue exceeds standard) and a negative figure an unfavourable variance.

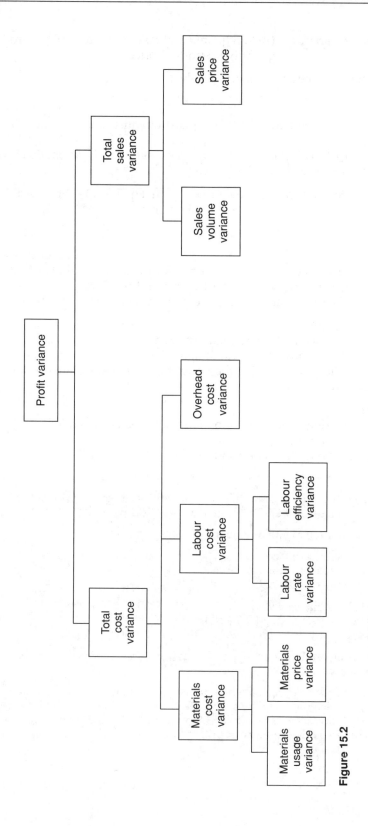

Figure 15.2

Sales volume variance = (Actual quantity × Standard price) − (Standard quantity × Standard price)

The calculation may be shown algebraically as

$$(AQ - SQ)\,SP$$

Where: AQ = actual quantity; SQ = standard quantity; and SP = standard price.

The effect of this calculation is to value any variation in actual quantity from standard quantity at standard price.

Sales price variance = (Actual price × Actual quantity) − (Standard price × Actual quantity)

$$(AP - SP)\,AQ$$

Where: AP = actual price; SP = standard price; and SQ = standard quantity.

The effect of this calculation is to identify, for the actual quantity of sales, the effect of any variation between actual price and standard price.

Reasons for the sales volume and price variances include the following:

Sales volume variance:
- Competition weaker/stronger than expected.
- Success/failure of advertising campaign.
- A rise or fall in prices causing the volume of sales to be higher or lower than expected.

Sales price variance:
- The need to reduce prices to respond to unforeseen competition.
- An unanticipated change in fashion.
- Unanticipated rise/fall in demand for product.

Example 15.5   The budgeted sales for the month of January are 500 units at a price of £250 per unit. Actual sales amounted to 480 items at £225 per unit.

Required   Calculations for the month of January:

(a) The total sales variance.
(b) The sales volume variance.
(c) The sales price variance.

Solution   (a) Total sales variance = (480 × £225) − (500 × £250) = £17,000 (U).
(b) Sales volume variance = (480 − 500) £250 = £5,000 (U).
(c) Sales price variance = (£225 − £250) 480 = £12,000 (U).

There has been an unfavourable total sales variance of £17,000 which has come about because

- the volume of sales has fallen 20 units below standard, producing an unfavourable volume variance of £5,000; and
- the units have been sold at £25 below standard price producing an unfavourable price variance of £12,000.

The nature and inter-relationship between the variances can be shown diagrammatically as in Figure 15.3. In this instance, the outer square on the graph represents the standard sales proceeds ($SQ \times SP$) whereas the inner square represents actual sales proceeds ($AQ \times AP$). The shaded area, in total, represents the total sales variance. It comprises two parts:

- The sales price variance (area A) representing the actual level of sales made at a price of £25 below standard.
- The sales volume variance (area B) represents the shortfall in sales, 20 units, valued at the standard price of £250 per unit.

It should be noted that, in practice, the above analysis of the total sales variance into volume and price is unlikely to exhaust the possibilities available. In particular, it is possible to calculate a sales mixture variance where a company deals in a range of products and the standards are based on an assumed ratio concerning the sales of particular items. If the ratio alters then this causes a total sales variance despite the fact that the sales price of each item and the overall sales volume may not have altered. For example, a company may plan to sell 10,000 units of A at £50 and 5,000 units of B at £10. If the sales prices remain unchanged but the quantities of sales achieved are reversed, this has an enormous impact on the total sales figure which can be pinpointed by calculating the sales mixture variance. This is beyond the scope of an introductory text, however, and is not considered further.

Total cost variance

Total cost variance = Actual cost – Standard cost
(for actual level of production)

A positive figure, in the case of cost variances, indicates an unfavourable variance (actual cost exceeds standard) and the negative figure a favourable variance.

Figure 15.3 The nature and relationships between variances

Materials variances

The materials cost variance arises because actual materials costs differ from standard and may be calculated as follows:

Materials cost variance = Actual materials cost – Standard materials cost (for actual level of production)

This may then be analysed into usage and price variances as follows:

Materials usage variance = (Actual quantity × Standard price) – (Standard quantity × Standard price)

$$(AQ - SQ)\, SP$$

Where: AQ = actual quantity; SQ standard quantity; and SP = standard price.

Materials price variance = (Actual price × Actual quantity) – (Standard price × Actual quantity)

$$(AP - SP)\, AQ$$

Where: AP = actual price; SP = standard price; and AQ = actual quantity.

Reasons for the materials usage and price variances include the following:

Materials usage variance:
- Careful/careless use of materials.
- The use of materials of a better or worse quality than expected.
- The use of defective materials.
- Pilfering.
- The use of the wrong type of material.
- The work being done by employees more skilled or less skilled than anticipated.

Materials price variance:
- The failure to obtain anticipated trade discounts.
- The level of inflation higher/lower than expected.
- Change in the rate of import duties.

Example 15.6   The standards for component No. 124–8 are as follows:

Price of raw material input – £5 per kilo.
Quantity of raw material input – 4 kilos per unit.

Actual production data for the month of February:

1,000 units of component No. 124–8 produced.
Price of material input – £6 per kilo.
Quantity of material used – 4,500 kilos.

Required   Calculations for the month of February:

(a) The materials cost variance.
(b) The materials usage variance.
(c) The materials price variance.

(a) Materials costs variance = $(4,500 \times £6) - (4,000 \times £5) = £7,000$ (U).   **Solution**
(b) Materials usage variance = $(4,500 - 4,000) £5 = £2,500$ (U).
(c) Materials price variance = $(£6 - £5) 4,500 = £4,500$ (U).

We can therefore see that all three variances are unfavourable. These are clearly matters that require management's attention. At this stage, however, the causes of the unfavourable variances are unknown. It is therefore necessary to conduct investigations with the relevant managers or supervisors, perhaps at shopfloor level, in order to obtain satisfactory explanations for these losses in order to enable corrective actions to be taken.

Labour variances

The labour cost variance arises because actual labour costs differ from standard and may be calculated as follows:

Labour cost variance = Actual labour cost – Standard labour cost
(for actual level of production)

The total variance may, again, be analysed into the quantity and price elements using, in this case, the terms 'efficiency' as a measure of the time taken to do the job, and 'rate' representing the amount paid for doing the job.

Labour efficiency variance = (Actual hours × Standard rate) –
(Standard hours × Standard rate)

$$(AH - SH) SR$$

Where: AH = actual hours; SH = standard hours; and SR = standard price.

Labour rate variance = (Actual rate × Actual hours) –
(Standard rate × Actual hours)

$$(AR - SR) AH$$

Where: AR = actual rate; SR = standard rate; and AH = actual hours.
Reasons for the labour efficiency variance include the following:

• Inadequate or improved training of employees.
• Dissatisfaction among the workforce or unexpected rise in morale.
• Poor working conditions, for example, inadequate ventilation.
• Machinery breakdowns.

Reasons for labour rate variance include the following:

• Employing the wrong grade of labour.
• An excessive amount of overtime worked.
• Wage increases higher/lower than anticipated due to effective/ineffective trade union action.

Example 15.7   The labour standards for component No. 124–8 are as follows:

Labour rate £20 per hour.
Hours of work – 2 hours per component.

Actual production data for the month of February:

1,000 units of component No. 124–8.
Labour rate paid – £21 per hour.
Hours worked – 1,950.

Required   Calculations for the month of February:

(a) The labour cost variance.
(b) The labour efficiency variance.
(c) The labour rate variance.

Solution   (a) Labour cost variance = (1,950 × £21) – (2,000 × £20) = £950 (U).
(b) Labour efficiency variance = (1,950 – 2,000) £20 = £1,000 (F).
(c) Labour rate variance = (£21 – £20) 1,950 = £1,950 (U).

It can therefore be seen that an unfavourable labour rate variance results from the fact that employees were paid £1 per hour more than expected. This unfavourable variance has been partially offset by the fact that the output was produced in 50 hours less than had been expected. One might speculate that the company has employed a higher grade of labour than anticipated to do the work, resulting in it being performed more efficiently than had been expected. These suspicions must, of course, be the subject of investigation.

Overhead variances

The overhead cost variance is the difference between the total standard and total actual overhead cost. It may be further analysed into the overhead expenditure (budget) variance and volume variance, and even further to take account of efficiency and changes in the length of a calendar month between one budget period and another. For the purpose of this introductory text we do not need to examine overhead variances in detail but simply note some of the reasons why they arise:

Expenditure (budget) variance   Particular items of overhead, e.g. rent, cost more than expected.

Volume variance   This covers factors, such as machine breakdowns, which cause the factory to be idle and the level of output to be less than anticipated.

Efficiency variance   This arises because of factors similar to those that account for the labour efficiency variance, e.g. machinery breakdowns.

Calendar variance   Differences in the length of budget periods, e.g. a 30-day month compared with a 31-day month.

The relationship between variances

We have considered each variance separately, but readers should be aware of the fact that business activity involves interaction between a range of different resource inputs and that factors which may have favourable effects in one direction may produce negative outcomes elsewhere.

It is therefore important for management to ensure that activities are fully co-ordinated and that actions are not taken that, although improving apparent performance in one area, may have unfavourable repercussions for the performance of a company as a whole. For example, the decision might be taken to engage a lower grade of labour than anticipated when setting the budget in order to reduce personnel costs and produce a favourable labour rate variance. The low-cost employees may, however, take much longer to do the job, producing an unfavourable labour efficiency variance, and may fail to process materials with sufficient care, resulting in an unfavourable materials usage variance. In a similar vein, the purchase of cheap materials (to produce a favourable materials price variance) may result in more materials being used (unfavourable materials usage variance) and more time being taken due to a high rejection rate (unfavourable labour efficiency variance).

Readers should now attempt Questions 15.4 and 15.5 at the end of this chapter.

Questions

15.1 The stock levels of Fife Ltd were often inadequate and as a consequence the ability to meet sales contracts was weakened. Production levels were found to be insufficient to replace stock that had been sold.

In addition the company has been using a bank overdraft facility which at 1 March 1992 was £6,000. The company has also 10,000 8 per cent debentures of £1 each which are due for redemption in three years' time.

As part of a general view of the company it was agreed that production should be more closely related to sales so a minimum stock level was agreed. It was further decided to compile both a production and a cash budget in an effort to control the business more effectively.

The details of the product cost of one unit are as follows:

	£
Materials	18
Labour	13
Variable overhead	9
Fixed overhead	6
	46

The following details are available at 1 March 1992 relating to the four months ending 30 June 1992:

1. The stock in hand is 120 units but this is to be increased to 150 units by equal steps over the next three months.
2. The sales in units were expected to be

February	March	April	May	June
180	180	190	170	230

3. The selling price per unit is £56. All sales are on a credit basis. One quarter of the selling price is receivable in the month of sale and the remainder in the month following. Goods are sold in the month they are produced.

4. Materials for production are purchased in the month before they are sold. One half of the price is paid in the month in which they are sold and the balance in the month following. Units purchased in February were 180.
5. Wages are paid in the month of occurrence.
6. Both fixed and variable expenses are paid on the basis of two fifths in the month of occurrence and three fifths in the month following.
7. Debenture interest is paid half yearly on 1 June and 1 December.
8. The following payments are also due:

		£
March	– Fixed assets	1,470
April	– Fixed assets	570
May	– Corporation tax	1,085

9. Bank interest on the overdraft is paid each month. The amount due is calculated at a rate of 10 per cent per annum on the balance at the beginning on the month.
10. Fife Ltd receives rent for premises it owns. The annual rent is £4,880 receivable quarterly on 1 April and subsequent dates.

Required

(a) A production budget in units and a cash budget for the four months March to June 1992.   *(15 marks)*
(b) State clearly what other steps the management should consider in order to improve the company's position.   *(10 marks)*

(AEB, Accounting, November 1992)

15.2 The balance sheet of Harris Ltd as at 30 November 1993 is shown below:

	£000		£000
Fixed assets	775	Share capital	800
Stock-in-trade	240	Reserves	318
Trade debtors	384	Trade creditors	297
Cash-at-bank	27	Accruals	11
	1,426		1,426

You are informed that:

(i) The firm's anticipated sales and purchases for the next six months are

	£000	£000
December	410	205
January	290	224
February	364	236
March	392	249
April	440	273
May	484	293

(ii) Customers are allowed one month's credit and Harris Ltd take a similar period of credit from suppliers. (*You may assume that these terms and conditions are strictly adhered to.*)
(iii) Expense creditors will be paid during December.
(iv) Overheads for the next six months are estimated at £71,000 per month. This figure includes £14,000 depreciation and £43,000 in respect of

wages and salaries. Payments will be made during the month in which the expense is incurred.

(v) The firm expects to purchase some new capital equipment during late May. The cost of the equipment will be £360,000 and be paid for during the month of purchase.

(vi) The accountant of Harris Ltd has negotiated a loan of £350,000 from the firm's bank to be paid during late May to cover the cost of new capital equipment.

(vii) The firm expects to sell its stock at a mark-up of 100 per cent.

Required

(a) Prepare a cash budget for Harris Ltd in respect of the six months ending 31 May 1994. *(8 marks)*

(b) Advise the firm's accountant whether there is a need for a loan to cover the purchase of the new capital equipment. *(3 marks)*

(c) Calculate Harris Ltd's net profit or net loss for the six months ending 31 May 1994. *(7 marks)*

(Total: 18 marks)

(ICSA, Introduction to Accounting, November 1992)

15.3 The following information is available from the books of Abbington Ltd for the financial year ended 31 October 1993:

Trading and Profit and Loss Account for the year ended 31 October 1993

	£000		£000
Cost of goods sold	910	Sales	1,300
Gross profit	390		
	1,300		1,300
Administration costs	70	Gross profit	390
Selling and distribution costs	40		
Financial charges	10		
Depreciation of fixed assets	30		
Net profit	240		
	390		390

Balance Sheet as at 31 October 1993

	£000	£000	£000		£000	£000
Fixes assets				Issued capital		
at cost			1,100	50p ordinary shares,		
Less: aggregate				fully paid		400
depreciation			230	11% £1 preference		
				shares, fully paid		50
			870			
						450

			Share premium			200
			Retained earnings			700
Current assets			Current liabilities			
Stock		120	Trade creditors		100	
Trade debtors	100		Accrued expenses		20	120
Less: Provision for						
doubtful debts	10	90				
Balance at bank		390	600			
			1,470			1,470

The newly appointed managing director decided that in order to increase profits it is absolutely necessary to control costs. Thus he decided to introduce budgetary control.

The following forecast information is available for the year ending 31 October 1994:

1. The sales are forecast to increase to £1.6 million for the year.
2. A more efficient buying programme is expected to increase the gross profit/sales ratio to 32 per cent.
3. In order to finance further expansion as the recession recedes, a rights issue of one new ordinary share for each two shares currently held is to be made on 1 August 1994. It is expected that the issue will be fully subscribed and the issue will also be underwritten. The issue price is 65p per share, fully paid.
4. Despite inflationary pressures the managing director is determined to reduce costs. The forecast level of costs is: administration costs will be 5 per cent of forecast sales. Selling and distribution costs will be 3½ per cent of forecast sales. There will be no change in financial charges as compared to 1992–3.
5. Owing to the recession bad debts are expected to rise substantially and thus the provision for doubtful debts is to be increased to 15 per cent of trade debtors. Forecast trade debts as at 31 October 1994 are £150,000.
6. A general reserve will be created on 31 December 1994 of £300,000.
7. Land and buildings which cost £350,000 (nil depreciation as at 31 October 1993) are to be written down to £200,000 due to the falling prices in the property market.
8. Dividends during 1993–4 will be restricted to paying
   (i)   the preference dividend for the year; and
   (ii) a final ordinary dividend of 3p per share, but only on the shares issued before 1 August 1994.
   The dividends would be paid on 1 January 1995.
9. All fixed assets other than land and buildings will be depreciated at 10 per cent per annum based on the cost of assets held at the end of the financial year. There are to be no additions or disposals of fixed assets during 1993–4.
10. Other forecast balances as at 31 October 1994:

	£000
Expense creditors	17.00
Trade creditors	97.00
Stock	290.00
Balance at bank	760.50

Required

(a) A budgeted trading, profit and loss and appropriation account for the year
   ending 31 October 1994. *(18 marks)*
(b) A budgeted balance sheet as at 31 October 1994. *(16 marks)*
(c) Identify ways in which profits could be increased by making better use of
   forecast current assets. *(16 marks)*

(AEB, Accounting, November 1993)

15.4 Bragg Ltd manufactures a household product. The standard cost of this
article is

Direct material   3 kilogrammes at £1.25 per kilogramme
Direct labour   3 hours at £5.10 per hour

The company manufactures this product in batches of 50,000 units per
month and all production is completed by the end of the period.
   In June 1992 the actual results were

Direct materials   158,000 kilogrammes costing £189,600
Direct labour   156,000 hours costing £819,000

Prior to the compilation of the actual results some of the senior management
were asked to comment on the possible outcome of the comparison exercise
that would take place.
   The purchasing manager stated that he had obtained very good terms
from his suppliers and there should be a favourable price variance. The
personnel manager reported that no increase in wage rates had been agreed
so there should be no variance emerging in the wage rate calculation.
Finally, the production manager was of the opinion that the labour force was
efficient and the usage of materials would be improved.

Required

(a) Calculate the following variances:
   (i)   Total direct cost variance.
   (ii)   Direct material price and usage variances.
   (iii) Direct labour rate and efficiency variances. *(12 marks)*
(b) In light of the variances calculated in (a), comment on the managers'
   views. *(8 marks)*
(c) A report to the senior management team in respect of the advantages and
   disadvantages of standard costing. *(5 marks)*

(AEB, Accounting, November 1992)

15.5 Nester Ltd manufactures towing equipment and operates a standard costing system. A standard cost sheet for Model A94 is as follows:

Raw materials   3 kilos at £2 per kilo
Direct labour per model   1 hour at £4 per hour

The actual production of this model for the period 1 January to 31 March
1993 resulted in the following details:

Number of items produced   2,000
Quantity of material used   6,400 kilos
Purchase price of material   £2.20 per kilo
Labour hours worked   1,800 hours
Actual labour rate   £4.10 per hour

There was no defective output and all production was complete.

Required

(a) Calculate the material and labour variances for the production period 1 January 1993 to 31 March 1993.   *(12 marks)*

(b) Comment on the labour rate and efficiency variances calculated above.
                                                                        (6 marks)

(c) Define standard costing.   *(6 marks)*

(d) Describe how standard costing may be useful to management.   *(6 marks)*

(AEB, Accounting, November 1992)

APPENDIX:
SOLUTIONS TO QUESTIONS

Odd-numbered solutions appear here, as well as 6.2, 6.4 and 6.6. All other even-numbered solutions appear in the Solution Manual.

Question 2.1 Business transactions: 2, 3, 4. Personal transaction: 1. Part business/part personal transaction: 5.

Question 2.3

(a) **Balance Sheet of Roger's business, 1 September 19X3**

	£		£
Cash at bank	1,200	Capital	1,200

(b) **Balance Sheet of Roger's business, 2 September 19X3**

	£		£
Machine	750	Capital	1,200
Bank (£1,200 + £1,000)	2,200	Endridge Local Authority	1,000
		Creditors	750
	2,950		2,950

(c) **Balance Sheet of Roger's business, 3 September 19X3**

	£		£
Machines (£750 + £1,820)	2,570	Capital	1,200
Stock	420	Endridge Local Authority	1,000
		Creditors	750
		Bank overdraft	
		(£2,200–£1,820–£420)	40
	2,990		2,990

(d) **Balance Sheet of Roger's business, 4 September 19X3**

	£		£
Machines	2,570	Capital	1,200
Stock (£420 = £215)	635	Endridge Local Authority	1,000
		Creditors (£750 + £215)	965
		Bank overdraft	40
	3,205		3,205

Question 2.5

(a)   Balance Sheet of Daley at 31 December 19X1

	£		£
Business premises	9,000	Capital (balancing figure)	13,450
Stock	5,250	Loan from Weakly	3,000
Trade debtors	3,340	Trade creditors	2,890
Cash	1,750		
	19,340		19,340

(b)   Balance Sheet of Daley at:

	1 Jan	2 Jan	3 Jan	4 Jan	5 Jan	6 Jan	7 Jan
Sources of finance	£	£	£	£	£	£	£
Capital	13,450	13,450	13,450	13,450	13,450	13,450	13,450
Add: Profit					180	180	180
Less: Drawings							(100)
					13,630	13,630	13,530
Loan from Weakly	3,000	3,000	3,000	3,000	3,000	2,000	2,000
Trade creditors	3,390	3,390	2,720	2,980	2,980	2,980	2,980
	19,840	19,840	19,170	19,430	19,610	18,610	18,510
Assets							
Business premises	9,000	9,000	9,000	9,000	9,000	9,000	9,000
Typewriter	500	500	500	500	500	500	500
Stocks	5,250	5,250	5,250	5,510	5,160	5,160	5,060
Trade debtors	3,340	3,150	3,150	3,150	3,150	3,150	3,150
Cash	1,750	1,940	1,270	1,270	1,800	800	800
	19,840	19,840	19,170	19,430	19,610	18,610	18,510

Question 2.7

1. *Accountancy* This is a system for recording and reporting business transactions, in financial terms, to interested parties who use this information as the basis for decision-making and performance assessment.
2. *Entity concept* It is assumed, for accounting purposes, that the business entity has an existence separate and distinct from owners, managers and other individuals with whom it comes into contact during the course of its trading activities.
   The assumption requires business transactions to be separated from personal transactions and accounting statements to concentrate on the financial position of the firm and its relationship with outsiders.
3. *Balance sheets* This is a financial statement that shows, on the one hand, the sources from which a business has raised finance and, on the other, the ways in which those monetary resources are employed. The balance sheet sets out the financial position at a particular moment in time and has been colourfully described as an instantaneous financial photograph of a business.
4. *Realization concept* This assumes that profit is earned or realized when the sale takes place. The justification for this treatment is that a sale results in the replacement of stock by either cash or a legally enforceable debt due from the customer.
5. *Trade credit* This is the period of time that elapses between the dates goods are supplied and paid for.

6. *Trading cycle, credit transactions* This is a series of transactions that begins with the delivery of stock from suppliers. The stock is then sold and delivered to customers resulting in a profit being realized or a loss incurred. Next, cash is collected from customers and the cycle is completed by paying suppliers the amount due.

7. $C + L = A$ This formula expresses the balance sheet relationship between sources of finance and assets where

> C = Capital invested by the owners, including retained profits
> L = Liabilities
> A = Assets

The balance sheet must always balance because all assets appearing on the right-hand side of the balance sheet must be financed, and the various sources employed appear on the left.

8. *Owner's capital* This is the amount of the initial investment in the concern, to which is added any further injections of capital plus profit earned, and from which is deducted drawings made by the owner for personal use.

9. *Money measurement concept* Assets are reported in the balance sheet only if the benefit they provide can be measured or quantified, in money terms, with a reasonable degree of precision.

10. *Fixed assets* These are purchased and retained to help carry on the business. Fixed assets are not sold in the normal course of business and their disposal will usually occur only when they are worn out, e.g. machinery.

11. *Current assets* These are assets that are held for resale or conversion into cash, e.g. stock-in-trade and trade debtors.

12. *Current liabilities* These are debts payable within twelve months of the balance sheet date, e.g. trade creditors and a bank overdraft.

13. *Gross assets* These are the total assets belonging to a business entity and therefore include both fixed assets and current assets.

Question 2.9

Balance Sheet of C. Forest at 31 December 19X3

	£	£		£	£
Fixed assets			Opening capital		52,380
Leasehold premises	25,000		Add: Profit		12,600
Plant and machinery	26,500		Less: Drawings		(10,950)
		51,500			54,030
			Loan repayable 19X9		9,000
Current assets			*Current liabilities*		
Stock-in-trade	14,200		Loan repayable 19X4	2,500	
Trade debtors	14,100		Trade creditors	10,600	
Cash-in-hand	270	28,570	Bank overdraft	3,940	17,040
		80,070			80,070

Question 3.1

(a) Gross assets, £6,700. Net assets, £6,500 (gross assets £6,700 – liabilities £200). Working capital, £4,500 (current assets £4,700 – current liabilities £200).

(b)

Trans.	Profit	Net assets	Gross assets	Working capital
1	NIL	NIL	NIL	NIL
2	NIL	Increase, £500	Increase, £500	Increase, £500
3	Decrease, £100	Decrease, £100	Decrease, £100	Decrease, £100
4	NIL	Decrease, £50	Decrease, £50	Decrease, £50
5	NIL	NIL	Increase, £150	NIL
6	NIL	NIL	NIL	Decrease, £700

Question 3.3

(a) Calculation of capital

Statement of assets, liabilities and capital at 31 December

	19X3		19X4	
	£	£	£	£
Gross assets				
Fixed assets		9,000		12,144 W1
Stocks		2,650		3,710
Trade debtors		5,200		5,600
Bank balance		—		50
		16,850		21,504
Less: Liabilities				
Trade creditors	1,710		1,210	
Bank overdraft	360	2,070	—	1,210
Capital		14,780		20,294

	£
Calculation of profit	
Closing capital	20,294
Less: Opening capital	14,780
Increase in capital	5,514
Add: Drawings	8,100 W2
Less: Capital introduced	(600)
Profit	13,014

Workings

W1   £9,000 + £3,144 = £12,144
W2   (£150 × 52) + £300 = £8,100

(b) **Balance Sheet at 31 December 19X4**

	£	£		£	£
Fixed assets		12,144	Opening capital		14,780
			Add: Net profit		13,014
			Additional capital		
			investment		600
					28,394

	£	£			£	£
Current assets						
Stocks	3,710		Less: Drawings – cash		7,800	
Trade debtors	5,600		stock		300	8,100
Bank balance	50	9,360				
						20,294
			Current liabilities			
			Trade creditors			1,210
		21,504				21,504

Question 4.1

(a) Balance Sheet at 31 December 19X4

	£	£		£
Fixed assets			Capital (A–L)	3,190
Furniture and fittings at			*Current liabilities*	
cost less depreciation		400	Trade creditors	1,630
Current assets				
Stock	2,040			
Debtors	1,900			
Bank	480	4,420		
		4,820		4,820

(b) Trading and Profit and Loss Account of Stoll for 19X5

		£	£	
Sales			32,004	W2
Less:	Purchases	25,100	W1	
	Add: Opening stock	2,040		
	Less: Closing stock	(1,848)		
	Cost of goods sold		25,292	
Gross profit			6,712	
Less:	General expenses	2,524		
	Rent	300		
	Depreciation	40	2,864	
Net profit			3,848	

Workings

Convert cash flows to flows of goods.

		£
W1 Purchases:	Payments to suppliers	24,800
	Less: Opening creditors	(1,630)
	Add: Closing creditors	1,930
		25,100

		£
W2 Sales:	Received from debtors	31,560
	Less: Opening debtors	(1,900)
	Add: Closing debtors	2,344
		32,004

Balance Sheet of Stoll at 31 December 19X5

	£	£
Fixed assets		
Furniture at cost less depreciation		360
Current assets		
Stock	1,848	
Debtors	2,344	
Bank	816	
	5,008	
Less: Current liabilities		
Trade creditors	1,930	
Working capital		3,078
		3,438
Financed by:		
Opening capital		3,190
Add: Net profit		3,848
Less: Drawings		(3,600)
		3,438

Question 4.3

(a) **Balance Sheet of Stondon at 31 December 19X3**

	£	£		£	£
Fixed assets			Capital (A–L)		9,947
Furniture and fittings		800	*Current liabilities*		
			Trade creditors	3,586	
Motor van at cost			Bank overdraft	782	4,368
less depreciation		2,500			
		3,300			
Current assets					
Stock	6,891				
Trade debtors	4,124	11,015			
		14,315			14,315

(b)

	£
Capital at 31 December 19X3	9,947
Less: Capital at 31 December 19X2	7,940
Increase in capital	2,007
Add: Drawings	12,840
	14,847
Less: Capital introduced	4,200
Net profit for 19X3	10,647

(c) **Trading and Profit and Loss Account for 19X3**

	£		£	
Sales (25,067 × 4)			100,268	(4)
Less: Purchases (by difference)	76,708	(8)		
Add: Opening stock	5,384	(7)		
Less: Closing stock	(6,891)	(6)		
Cost of goods sold			75,201	(5)
Gross profit			25,067	(3)
Less: Running expenses			14,420	(2)
Net profit			10,647	(1)

Note
The numbers in brackets indicate the order in which the trading and profit and loss account is reconstructed.

Question 4.5

(a) **Bar Trading Account for 19X8**

	£			£
Opening stock	8,200		Sales	107,600
Add: Purchases	81,248	W2		
Less: Closing stock	(11,936)			
Costs of goods sold	77,512			
Gross profit	30,088			
	107,600			107,600

(b) **Income and Expenditure Account for 19X8**

	£			£
Rent	2,800		Bar profit	30,088
Rates	2,000		Subscriptions	12,400
General expenses	5,448	W3	Interest	4,160
Depreciation	3,040	W4		
Salaries	16,840			
Surplus	16,520			
	46,648			46,648

(c) **Balance Sheet at 31 December 19X8**

	£	£		£	£
Fixed assets			Accumulated fund		96,840 W1
Furniture		30,400	Add: Surplus		16,520
Less: Depreciation		3,040			
					113,360
		27,360			
			Current liabilities		
Current assets			Creditors: Supplies	4,568	
Investments	75,200		Expenses	248	
Stocks	11,936				
Bank	3,680				4,816
		90,816			
		118,176			118,176

Workings

W1 **Balance Sheet at 1 January 19X8**

	£			£
Furniture	30,400	Accumulated fund (A–L)		96,840
Investments	49,200	Creditors: Supplies		4,080
Stocks	8,200	Expenses		160
Bank	13,280			
	101,080			101,080

W2 Purchases	£
Payments for purchases	80,760
Less: Opening creditors	(4,080)
Add: Closing creditors	4,568
	81,248

W3 General expenses	£
Payments for general expenses	5,360
Less: Opening creditors	(160)
Add: Closing creditors	248
	5,448

W4 Depreciation
£30,400 × 10% = £3,040.

Question 4.7

(a) Income and Expenditure Account year to 31 May 1993

	£	£	
Bar and social functions profit		13,350	W1
Yacht-racing competitions surplus		12,100	W2
Hire of boats surplus	6,200		W3
Training school receipts	20,500		
Wages for training and boat hire	(15,000)		
Depreciation: Club boats and yachts	(20,500)		
Paint and trim shop	(5,000)		
Deficit on training school and boat hire		(13,800)	
Subscriptions		198,100	W4
		209,750	
General expenses*	22,000		
Depreciation: Freehold premises*	20,000		
Boat yard and launch facilities*	4,000		
Fixtures and fittings*	3,000		
Donations*	817		W5
Boat sunk less salvage value*	18,000	67,817	
Surplus		141,933	

(b) Balance Sheet as at 31 May 1993

	£
Fixed assets	
Paint and trim shop (£50,000 – £5,000)	45,000
Freehold premises (£400,000 – £20,000)	380,000
Boat yard and launch facilities (£80,000 – £4,000)	76,000
Fixtures and fittings (£30,000 – £3,000)	27,000
Boats and yachts (£410,000 W6 – £20,500)	389,500
	917,500
Current assets	
Bar stocks	28,500
Subscriptions in arrears	3,500
Cash	285,900 W7
	317,900
Current liabilities	
Subscriptions in advance	7,900
Creditors	9,650
Donations	817
	18,367
Net current assets	299,533
	1,217,033

Financed by:
Accumulated fund	1,045,100 W8
Boat willed to club	30,000
Surplus	141,933
	1,217,033

Workings

W1 Bar and social profit	£		£
Takings	£	80,000	
Purchases	51,200 W9		
Stock:1 June 1992	31,000		
3 May 1993	(28,500)		
Cost of sales		(53,700)	
Wages (W10)		(12,950)	
		13,350	

W2 Yacht-racing competitions	
Takings	30,800
Outgoings	18,700
	12,100

W3 Hire of boats	
Takings	28,600
Repairs (W11)	(22,400)
	6,200

W4 Subscriptions		
Received		200,900
In advance:	1 June 1992	5,600
	31 May 1993	(7,900)
In arrears:	1 June 1992	(4,000)
	31 May 1993	3,500
		198,100

W5 Donation	
19,600 × ⅙ × 25%	817

W6 Boats and yachts		
Balance:	1 June 1992	350,000
Boat lost		(20,000)
Boat willed to club		30,000
Purchases		50,000
		410,000

W7 Balance at bank	
Balance: 1 June 1992	110,700
Receipts	362,800
Payments	(187,600)
	285,900

W8 Accumulated fund	
Paint and trim shop	50,000
Freehold premises	400,000
Boat yard and launch facilities	80,000
Fixtures and fittings	30,000
Club-owned boats and yachts	350,000
Subscriptions in arrears	4,000
Balance at bank	110,700
Bar stocks	31,000
	1,055,700
Less: Subscriptions in advance	(5,600)
Bar creditors	(5,000)
	1,045,100

W9 Bar purchases	
Payments	50,100
Balance: 1 June 1992	(5,000)
31 May 1993	6,100
	51,200

W10 Bar wages	
Payments	12,600
Balance: 31 May 1993	350
	12,950

W11 Repairs	
Payments	19,200
Balance: 31 May 1993	3,200
	22,400

Note
* These expenses cannot be identified with particular activities.

(c) There was a healthy cash balance at the beginning of the year of £110,700. The club has generated a substantial surplus during the year, and relatively modest expenditure on fixed assets has meant that the cash balance has increased substantially to £285,900. The financial position is extremely strong and, unless there are plans for substantial investment, consideration should be given to a possible reduction of charges to members for various facilities.

Question 5.1

Cash Account

January		£	January		£
1	Capital introduced	5,000	2	Van	4,000
1–31	Cash sales	2,250	3	Rent	100
1–31	Debtors	450	1–31	Creditors	2,500
			15	Drawings	110
			30	Insurance	120
			31	Balance c/d	870
		7,700			7,700
February					
1	Balance b/d	870			

Question 5.3

Double column cash book

	Cash £	Bank £		Cash £	Bank £
Capital		10,000	Premises		8,000
Loan	5,000		Equipment		2,750
Cash		750	Van	4,000	
Sales	5,500		Bank	750	
Cash		4,250	Purchases	1,000	3,000
			Wages	100	
			Drawings	150	
			Rates		250
			Bank	4,250	
			Balance c/d	250	1,000
	10,500	15,000		10,500	15,000
Balance b/d	250	1,000			

Question 5.5

Petty Cash Account

	1985		£		1985 Oct.		Total £	Wages £	Postage £	Stationery £	Purchase ledger £
1985 Oct.	1	Balance b/d	3.75		4	Wages	11.60	11.60			
	1	Bank	46.25		5	Postage	3.94		3.94		
					8	Stationery	4.09			4.09	
					11	Postage	2.00		2.00		
					18	Wages	12.93	12.93			
					21	F. Smith – creditor	3.42				3.42
					24	Stationery	4.66			4.66	
					28	Postage	3.80		3.80		
							46.44	24.53	9.74	8.75	3.42
					31	Balance c/d	3.56				
			50.00				50.00				
Nov.	1	Balance b/d	3.56								
	1	Bank	46.44								

Question 5.7

(a) Cash Book

March 1993	£	March 1993	£
		Balance b/d	6,076
Undercast	600	Bank charges	48
Correction (154–145)	9	Dividend cheque	340
		Standing order	110
Balance c/d	6,150	Dishonoured cheque	185
	6,759		6,759

Bank Reconciliation

	£
Overdraft on statement	(2,129)
Outstanding lodgement	1,550
Outstanding cheques	(4,920)
Standing order (120×3)	(360)
Credit transfer	(291)
Balance in cash book	(6,150)

(b) It is necessary to prepare a bank reconciliation to identify:

- items in the cash book that are not on the bank statement, which should comprise only outstanding lodgements and cheques. The lodgements should be traced to the following bank statement, and any undue delay investigated; outstanding cheques should be monitored and followed up as the date when they expire approaches; and
- items on the bank statement that are not in the cash book. Where such items are found to be correct, they should be entered in the cash book. Any that do not relate to the company should be reported to the bank as errors to be corrected.

By enabling these checks to be carried out, the bank reconciliation provides proof that the company's record of its bank transactions is correct and also identifies any errors made by the bank. It aids the internal control of the company as the day-to-day running of the cash book can be delegated and then checked by management by using the reconciliation statement.

Question 6.1

	Debit £	Credit £
Capital		8,500
Current liabilities		4,600
Plant and machinery	4,500	
Stock	2,700	
Debtors	5,200	
Cash	700	
	13,100	13,100

Question 6.2

Sales day book (SDB)

Customer	£
Vision	7,000
Sister	4,000
Batty	2,700
Flat	200
Broke	300
	14,200

Purchases day book (PDB)

Supplier	Total	Goods for resale	Motor expenses	Office expenses
	£	£	£	£
Tele	3,000	3,000		
Trany	2,000	2,000		
Valve	2,400	2,400		
Garage	100		100	
Paper	50			50
	7,550	7,400	100	50

Returns inwards day book (RIDB)

Customer	£
Vision	300
Batty	200
	500

Returns outwards day book (RODB)

Supplier	£
Trany	100
Valve	150
	250

Cash book (CB) receipts (debit)

Detail	Discount	Cash	Debtors	Sundry
	£	£	£	£
Balance b/d		700		
Vision	50	6,350	6,350	
Sister	40	3,500	3,500	
Batty	25	2,600	2,600	
Scrap		100		100
	115	13,250	12,450	100

Cash book (CB) payments (credit)

Detail	Discount	Cash	Creditors	Wages	Motor expenses	Sundry
	£	£	£	£	£	£
Tele	55	2,950	2,950			
Trany	35	1,950	1,950			
Valve	20	2,200	2,200			
Plantmax		1,000				1,000
Wages		1,500		1,500		
Accom.		600				600
Supplies		250				250
Garage		300			300	
	110	10,750	7,100	1,500	300	1,850
Balance c/d		2,500				
		13,250				

Question 6.3

Capital

	£			£
			Journal	8,500

Purchase Ledger Control Account

		£			£
January	RODB	250	January	Journal	4,600
	CB Discounts	110		PDB	7,550
	CB Cash	7,100			
	Balance c/d	4,690			
		12,150			12,150

Plant and Machinery

		£			£
January	Journal	4,500	January	Balance c/d	5,500
	CB	1,000			
		5,500			5,500

Stock

		£		£
January	Journal	2,700		

Sales Ledger Control Account

		£			£
January	Journal	5,200	January	RIDB	500
	SDB	14,200		CB Discounts	115
				CB Cash	12,450
				Balance c/d	6,335
		19,400			19,400

Sales

		£			£
January	RIDB	500	January	SDB	14,200
	Balance c/d	13,700			
		14,200			14,200

Purchases

		£			£
January	PDB	7,400	January	RODB	250
				Balance c/d	7,150
		7,400			7,400

Motor Expenses

		£			£
January	PDB	100	January	Balance c/d	400
	CB	300			
		400			400

Office Expenses

		£			£
January	PDB	50	January	Balance c/d	300
	CB	250			
		300			300

Discounts Allowed

		£		£
January	CB	115		

Discount Received

	£			£
		January	CB	110

Sale of Fixed Assets

		£		£
January	CB	100		

Wages

		£		£
January	CB	1,500		

Rent

		£		£
January	CB	600		

Question 6.4

Sales Ledger

Vision

		£			£
January	Balance b/d	2,500	January	RIDB	300
	SDB	7,000		CB Discounts	50
				CB Cash	6,350
				Balance c/d	2,800
		9,500			9,500

Sister

		£			£
January	Balance b/d	1,500	January	CB Discounts	40
	SDB	4,000		CB Cash	3,500
				Balance c/d	1,960
		5,500			5,500

Batty

		£			£
January	Balance b/d	1,200	January	RIDB	200
	SDB	2,700		CB Discounts	25
				CB Cash	2,600
				Balance c/d	1,075
		3,900			3,900

Flat

		£		£
January	SDB	200		

Broke

		£		£
January	SDB	300		

Purchases ledger

Tele

		£			£
January	CB Discounts	55	January	Balance b/d	2,300
	CB Cash	2,950		PDB	3,000
	Balance c/d	2,295			
		5,300			5,300

Trany

		£			£
January	RODB	100	January	Balance b/d	1,000
	CB Discount	35		PDB	2,000
	CB Cash	1,950			
	Balance c/d	915			
		3,000			3,000

Valve

		£			£
January	RODB	150	January	Balance c/d	1,300
	CB Discount	20		PDB	2,400
	CB Cash	2,200			
	Balance c/d	1,330			
		3,700			3,700

Garage

	£			£
		January	PDB	100

Paper

	£			£
		January	PDB	50

Question 6.5

Sales Ledger

	£
Vision	2,800
Sister	1,960
Batty	1,075
Flat	200
Broke	300
As per control account	6,335

Purchase ledger

	£
Tele	2,295
Trany	915
Valve	1,330
Garage	100
Paper	50
As per control account	4,690

Question 6.6

	Debit £	Credit £
Cash	2,500	
Capital		8,500
Creditors		4,690
Plant and machinery	5,500	
Stock	2,700	
Debtors	6,335	
Sales		13,700
Purchases	7,150	
Motor expenses	400	
Office expenses	300	
Discounts allowed	115	
Discounts received		110
Wages	1,500	
Rent	600	
Sale of fixed asset		100
	27,100	27,100

Question 6.7

(a) (i) Real accounts represent assets, or items of property other than claims against external persons. Balances on real accounts are, in normal circumstances, assets, for example, when motor vehicles, furniture or plant and machinery are purchased, real accounts under those headings are debited.

  (ii) Personal accounts are those which show the relationship of the business with other persons or firms. A debit balance on a personal account is an asset and represents the right to receive money in the future. A credit balance is a liability.

  (iii) Nominal accounts are used to record items of income and expense. Debit balances are expenses and credit balances are income.

(b) (i) Fixed asset at cost £10,000 – real account.
  (ii) Wages £700 – nominal account.
  (iii) Discounts received £1,400 – nominal account.
  (iv) Balance due from Double Ltd £1,500 – personal account.

Question 6.9

Sales Ledger Control Account

19X4		£	19X4		£
1 October	Balance b/d	102,300	1 October	Balance b/d	340
	Sales	630,800		Cash	498,660
				Returns	2,700
				Discounts	
				purchase ledger	11,790
				Contras	5,200
				Bad Debts	3,950
19X5			19X5		
30 September	Balance c/d	510	30 September	Balance c/d	210,970
		733,610			733,610

Note
Items 4, 6 and 8 do not belong in the sales ledger control account.

Question 6.11

(a) Creditors Ledger Control Account

	£		£
Discounts r/d	3,608	Balance: 1 December 1989	45,870
Cash and cheques paid	231,570	Purchases	249,560
Sales ledger set-offs	818		
Returns outwards	4,564		
Balance: 30 November 1990	54,870		
	295,430		295,430

(b)

(i) Corrected Creditors Ledger Control Account

Item		£
	Balance: 30 November 1990	54,870
2	Invoice omitted	1,850
3	Credit note	(870)
4	Petty cash payments	(625)
		55,225

(ii) Corrected total on the individual creditors accounts

Item		£
	Given total	51,120
1	Invoice omitted	1,125
2	Invoice omitted	1,850
3	Credit note	(870)
5	Undercast	2,000
		55,225

Question 6.13

Transaction	Original document	Book of original entry	Double entry
Purchase of goods on credit	Purchase invoice Goods received note	Purchases day book	As part of total: Debit purchases Credit creditors
Goods returned by credit customer	Credit note	Returns inwards day book	As part of total: Debit sales Credit debtors
Petty cash payment	Petty cash voucher supported by receipts	Petty cash book	The entry in the petty cash book is the credit; the debit is to the entertainment account
Credit card sales	Card voucher and invoice for card charges	Cash book	Debit cash book; credit sales On subsequent receipt of invoice for card charges to support direct debit: Debit charges Credit cash book
Recovery of bad debt	Cheque received	Cash book journal	Reinstate the debt: Debit debtors Credit bad debts Record receipt: Debit cash Credit debtors

Question 7.1

(a)

Item	Location	Comment
Sales	Trading account	Revenue
Returns inwards	Trading account	Reduces the value of sales
Stock 1 January	Trading account	Charged against sales
Returns outwards	Trading account	Reduces purchases
Purchases	Trading account	Expense
Capital	Balance sheet	Liability to ownership
Cash at bank	Balance sheet	Asset
Debtors	Balance sheet	Asset
Creditors	Balance sheet	Liability
Premises	Balance sheet	Asset
Wages	Profit and loss account	Expense
Discounts received	Profit and loss account	Sundry revenue
Rent and rates	Profit and loss account	Expense
Delivery costs	Profit and loss account	Expense
Cash withdrawn	Balance sheet	Reduces capital
Heat and light	Profit and loss account	Expense
Sundry expenses	Profit and loss account	Expense

(b) **Trading and Profit and Loss Account for the year 31 December 19X4**

	£	£
Sales		130,000
Less: Returns inwards		250
		129,750
Opening stock	15,000	
Purchases	80,000	
Less: Returns outwards	(150)	
Closing stock	(17,750)	
Cost of goods sold		77,100
Gross profit		52,650
Discounts received		300
		52,950
Wages	17,300	
Rent and rates	3,000	
Delivery	2,750	
Heat and light	3,500	
Sundry expenses	2,750	
		29,300
Net profit		23,650

Balance Sheet at 31 December 19X4

	£	£		£
Premises		8,000	Capital, 1 January	27,600
Stock	17,750		Profit for year	23,650
Debtors	15,400			51,250
Cash	3,100		Drawings	(12,000)
		36,250	Capital, 31 December	39,250
			Creditors	5,000
		44,250		44,250

Question 7.3

Trading and Profit and Loss Account for the year to 30 June 19X7

	£	£
Sales		108,920
Opening stock	9,470	
Purchases	72,190	
Closing stock	(9,960)	
Cost of goods sold		71,700
		37,220

	£	£
Gross profit		
Depreciation	3,000	
Rent	1,000	
Wages	14,330	
Other costs	4,590	
		22,920
Net profit		14,300

Balance Sheet at 30 June 19X7

	£	£
Fixed assets		
At cost		35,000
Less: Accumulated depreciation		
(12,500 + 3,000)		15,500
		19,500
Current assets		
Stock	9,960	
Debtors	7,350	
Cash	1,710	
	19,020	
Current liabilities		
Creditors	6,220	
		12,800
		32,300
Capital		
At 1 July 19X6		30,350
Profit		14,300
		44,650
Drawings		(12,350)
		32,300

Question 7.5

Insurance Account

19X8		£	19X8		£
1 January	Balance b/d	450	31 December	Balance c/d	510
June	Cash	1,020		Profit and loss	
				account	960
		1,470			1,470

Rates Account

19X8		£	19X8		£
1 January	Balance b/d	290	31 December	Balance c/d	390
March	Cash	780		Profit and loss	
September	Cash	780		account	1,460
		1,850			1,850

Gas Account

19X8		£	19X8		£
March	Cash	850	1 January	Balance b/d	600
June	Cash	840	31 December	Profit and loss	
September	Cash	610		account	3,340
December	Cash	960			
31 December	Balance c/d	680			
		3,940			3,940

Electricity Account

19X8		£	19X8		£
February	Cash	900	1 January	Balance b/d	300
May	Cash	820	31 December	Profit and loss	
August	Cash	690		account	3,050
November	Cash	550			
31 December	Balance c/d	390			
		3,350			3,350

Question 7.7

Trading and Profit and Loss Account for the year to 31 December 19X6

	£	£
Sales		234,481
Stock 1 January	32,193	
Purchases	164,770	
	196,963	
Less: Goods taken as drawings	(1,250)	
Stock 31 December	(34,671)	
Cost of goods sold		161,042
Gross profit		73,439
Profit on sale of van		500
		73,939
Rent and rates (3,000 – 300)	2,700	
General expenses	7,263	
Wages (26,649 + 271)	26,920	
Bed debts (693 + 104)	797	
Depreciation	7,000	44,680
Net profit		29,259

Balance Sheet at 31 December 19X6

	£	£	£
Fixed assets			
Freehold land and buildings			114,000
Motor vans at cost			
(37,500 − 2,500 + 1,500)		36,500	
Less: Depreciation			
(15,450 + 7,000 − 1,500)		20,950	
			15,550
			129,550
Current assets			
Stock		34,671	
Debtors	20,911		
Less: Provision for doubtful debts			
(876 + 104)	980		
		19,931	
Prepaid rent and rates		300	
Cash		32,728	
		87,630	
Less: Current liabilities			
Creditors	13,006		
Accrued wages	271		
		13,277	
Working capital			74,353
			203,903
Capital			
At 1 January			193,894
Profit for 19X6			29,259
			223,153
Less: Drawings: Cash		18,000	
Stock		1,250	
			19,250
			203,903

Question 7.9

(i) Bad Debts Account

	£		£
Trade debtors	1,340	Profit and loss account	1,340

(ii) Provision for Bad Debts Account

	£		£
Balance c/d	3,233	Balance b/d	2,570
		Profit and loss account	663 (W1)
	3,233		3,233

W1 (£88,000 debtors – £1,340 bad debts) × 5% = £3,233
$\quad$ £3,233 – £2,570 = £663

(iii) Asset Disposals Account

	£		£
Motor vehicles at cost	15,000	Motor vehicle depreciation	12,000
Profit and loss account	1,500	Cash	4,500
	16,500		16,500

(iv) Provision for depreciation – land and buildings

	£		£
Balance c/d	17,600	Balance b/d	16,000
		Profit and loss account	1,600 (W2)
	17,600		17,600

W2 £80,000 × 2% = £1,600

(v) Provision for depreciation – fixtures and fittings

	£		£
Balance c/d	55,000	Balance b/d	44,000
		Profit and loss account	11,000 (W3)
	55,000		55,000

W3 (£88,000 cost – £44,000 depreciation) × 25%

(vi) Provision for depreciation – motor vehicle

	£		£
Disposal account	12,000	Balance b/d	27,000
Balance c/d	21,000	Profit and loss account	6,000 (W4)
	33,000		33,000

W4 (45,000 cost – 15,000 disposal) × 20%

Question 8.1

(a) There are two main tests:

(i) Expenditure that enhances the ability of the firm to earn profits is capital, whereas expenditure designed merely to maintain the existing level of operation is revenue.

(ii) Capital expenditure is incurred on the purchase of assets that are expected to possess a useful life that extends over a number of accounting periods; moreover, it is not intended to sell these assets in the normal course of business. Revenue expenditure is incurred in acquiring goods and services that are consumed in a short space of time. A correct allocation is important, because otherwise profit and asset values are wrongly reported. For example, the misallocation of capital to revenue causes both profit and gross assets to be understated.

(b) (i)   *Revenue* This is a normal repair to make good wear and tear.
   (ii) *Capital* Hourly capacity is increased.
   (iii) *Capital* This is part of the cost of acquiring the new asset.
   (iv) *Capital* This increases the firm's productive capacity.
   (v)   *Capital* This expenditure is needed to make the plant ready for use.

Question 8.3

(a)

	(i) Straight line £	(ii) Diminishing balance £	(iii) Units of output £
Year 1	7,000	15,400	5,600
Year 2	7,000	6,930	7,000
Year 3	7,000	3,119	7,700
Year 4	7,000	1,403	7,700
	28,000	26,852	28,000

Workings

Straight line = 28,000/4 = £7,000 per annum (full year).
Diminishing balance = 55% charge applied to net book value at the beginning of the year.
Unit of output = £28,000/200,000 = 14p per hour

(b) **Minilab Account**

		£			£
1.1.X1	Cost	28,000	30.6.X3	Asset disposals account	28,000

Provision for depreciation

		£			£
30.6.X3	Asset disposals account	17,500	1.1.X3	Opening balance	14,000
			30.6.X3	Depreciation account	3,500
		17,500			17,500

Asset Disposals Account

		£			£
30.6.X3	Minilab account	28,000	30.6.X3	Provision for depreciation	17,500
			30.6.X3	Cash	10,000
			30.6.X3	Loss on sale	500
		28,000			28,000

Question 8.5 The fundamental rule is that stock should be valued at the *lower* of cost and net realizable value, taking each item or groups of similar items separately.
    Valuation of stock calculated as follows:

Product	Cost	NRV	Lower of cost and NRV
A	2,400	2,760	2,400
B	1,290	740	740
C	3,680	750	750
D	2,950	4,760	2,950
E	6,280	9,730	6,280
Value of stock			13,120

Question 8.7 *Perpetual inventory* Stock records are written up on a regular basis to record receipts and issues of stock and the quantity on hand after each transaction. Sometimes the records are also maintained in terms of values and, where this is done, values for total issues (cost of goods sold) and closing stock are readily available under this system. Where values are not recorded, the cost of goods sold is obtained as the balancing item (see below).
    Periodic stock-take Stocks are physically counted and valued at the end of each accounting period. The figure for cost of goods sold is the balancing item obtained by applying the formula:

$$\text{Opening stock} + \text{Purchases} - \text{Closing stock} = \text{Cost of goods sold}$$

Question 8.9

(a) **AVCO basis – stock card**

		Receipts			Issues			Balance		
		Units	Price £	Total £	Units	Price £	Total	Units	Price £	Total £
1	Jan.	50	165	8,250				50	165	8,250
10	Jan.	200	143	28,600				250	147.40	36,850
31	Jan.				180	147.40	26,532	70	147.40	10,718
1	Feb.	120	170	20,400				190	161.67	30,718
28	Feb.				120	161.67	19,401	70	161.67	11,317
2	March	220	210	46,200				290	198.33	57,517
31	March				250	198.33	49,583	40	198.33	7,934
		590		103,450	550		95,516	40		7,934

FIFO basis
Receipts, 590
Issues, 550
Balance: 40 units
Balance of stock valued at most recent prices
Stocks: £210 × 40 = £8,400

(b) Trading Account, January–March 1993

		FIFO £	LIFO £
Sales:	£175 × 180	31,500	
	£215 × 120	25,800	
	£230 × 250	57,500	
		114,800	114,800
Purchases		103,450	103,450
Closing stock		8,400	7,934
Cost of goods sold		95,050	95,516
Gross profit		19,750	19,284

(c) The basic rule is that stocks should be valued at the lower of cost and net realizable value. This rule is designed to ensure compliance with the prudence concept which requires that

- profits should not be recognized until they are realized; and
- provision should be made for all foreseeable losses.

For the purpose of applying the rule, the comparison between cost and net realizable value should be made in respect of individual items of stock or groups of similar items. This is to ensure that full provision is made for foreseeable losses.

Stocks must be valued for the purpose of the published accounts on the total cost basis, including any overhead costs incurred in bringing the stock into its present condition and location. This complies with the accruals concept by ensuring that the full cost of an item of stock is matched with the related revenue when the sales take place.

Companies may use FIFO, AVCO or certain other acceptable methods to match stock purchases with stock sales. Whichever method is selected should be applied consistently to ensure comparability of results from one accounting period to the next. It can be seen from the above example that, in circumstances where prices are rising, the use of FIFO will result in a higher stock valuation and a higher figure for gross profit.

Question 8.11 Examples are as follows:

(a) Insurance premiums received before the period covered by the insurance; rents received before the rental period.
(b) Cash sales of goods; sale of goods on credit where the cash is collected in the same accounting period.
(c) Collection of customers' accounts in the period following the sale; receipt of interest after the period to which it relates.
(d) Prepayment of insurance premiums or subscription fees.
(e) Payments for office salaries and telephone charges in the period in which they are used (debit entry is to an expense account).
(f) Payment of suppliers' accounts outstanding at the year end; payment for rent accrued at the year end.

Question 8.13

(a) (i)   *Dual aspect* This means the financial effect of each transaction undertaken by a business must be entered in the books twice: a debit entry to record items such as the acquisition of an asset, an expense incurred, a revenue reduced or a loan repaid; and a credit entry to record a liability incurred, a revenue received, an expense reduced or an asset reduced.

(ii) *Consistency* The consistency concept requires businesses to use the same valuation methods each year when preparing accounting statements. The need for the consistency concept arises because there is available a variety of different ways of valuing particular assets and liabilities.

(iii) *Prudence* The prudence concept (sometimes also called the concept of conservatism) requires the accountant to make full provision for all expected losses and not to anticipate revenues until they are realized. The justification for the accruals concept is that the risks inherent in overstatement (for example, overstating profit) are much greater than result from an understatement.

(iv) *Matching/accruals* The accountant measures profit for a period of time, such as a year, by comparing or 'matching' revenue and expenditure identified with that time period. For this purpose, revenue is assumed to be realized when a sale takes place while costs are matched against revenue when the benefit of the expenditure is received rather than when the cash payment is made.

(v)   *Going concern* This assumes that the business is a permanent venture and will not be wound up in the foreseeable future. This means that the accountant can assume that the business will remain in existence long enough to enable the recovery of the initial investment, and that liquidation values can be ignored.

(b) (i)   *Dual aspect* An example would be the sale of goods on credit for £2,000. The debit entry would be to 'trade debtors' and shown as a current asset in the balance sheet; the credit entry would be to 'sales' and included in the profit and loss account.

(ii) *Consistency* In the case of stock, alternative methods include first in first out (FIFO), last in first out (LIFO), and the weighted average cost method (AVCO). Once the method of stock valuation has been selected, it should be adopted in subsequent years.

(iii) *Prudence* A company may have made a sale on credit which is recognized in the manner indicated under (i). If it becomes apparent that the debtor is unlikely to repay the amount owing, provision has to be made for this foreseeable loss. The amount involved is written off in the profit and loss account, and the balance of trade debtors is reduced by a corresponding amount.

(iv) *Matching/accruals* A company may have purchased a fixed asset for £30,000 which it expects to last for four years and then have residual value of £2,000. In these circumstances the total amount to be written off is £28,000 and, applying the straight-line method, £7,000 must be matched against revenue arising over each of the four years.

(v)   *Going concern* The resale value of the fixed asset referred to under (iv) may fall to, say, £15,000 immediately following acquisition. This change in market price is considered to be irrelevant as there is no intention to resell the asset. Provided the company remains in existence for four years, it is perfectly legitimate to ignore the decline in the resale value of the fixed asset and, instead, depreciate the asset at the rate of £7,000 per annum.

Question 9.1

Appropriation Account

		£	£			£	£
Salaries:	Jack	10,000		Profit			42,000
	Jill	7,500		Interest on drawings:			
	Jane	5,000		Jack		600	
		———		Jill		450	
			22,500	Jane		400	
Interest on capital:						——	
Jack		3,600					1,450
Jill (W1)		2,700					
Jane		4,800					
		———					
			11,100				
Residue:	Jack	3,940					
	Jill	3,940					
	Jane	1,970					
		———					
			9,850				
			———				———
			43,450				43,450
			———				———

Workings

W1 12% × 20,000 (opening capital) + 12% × 5,000 × .5 (capital introduced halfway through the year) = 2,700.

Question 9.3

Current Accounts

	Ice	Cube		Ice	Cube
	£	£		£	£
Drawings:			Balance b/d	30,000	20,000
Cash	12,500	14,000	Share of profit	22,500	22,500
Car disposal a/c	1,500				
Transfer to capital					
account	20,000	10,000			
Balance c/d	18,500	18,500			
	———	———		———	———
	52,500	42,500		52,500	42,500
	———	———		———	———

Capital Accounts

	Ice	Cube		Ice	Cube
	£	£		£	£
Balance c/d	70,000	70,000	Balance b/d	50,000	60,000
			Transfer from		
			current account	20,000	10,000
	———	———		———	———
	70,000	70,000		70,000	70,000
	———	———		———	———

Question 9.5

(a) Realization Account

	£		£
Freehold land and property	80,000	Mars capital account:	
Equipment	9,000	Property	120,000
Motor car	3,000	Equipment	11,000
Stock	24,000	Stock	26,000
Debtors	6,500	Debtors	6,100
Cash – expenses	1,500	Total assets acquired	163,100
Profit on realization		Saturn capital account:	
Jupiter	21,000	Car	2,900
Mars	10,500		
Saturn	10,500		
	166,000		166,000

(b) Bank Account

	£		£
Mars capital account	90,000	Balance b/d	6,400
		Realization expenses	1,500
		Creditors	4,100
		Capital accounts:	
		Saturn	32,600
		Mars	45,400
	90,000		90,000

(c) Capital Account

	Jupiter £	Mars £	Saturn £		Jupiter £	Mars £	Saturn £
Realization account		163,100	2,900	Balance b/d	55,000	32,000	25,000
				Realization account	21,000	10,500	10,500
Mars	30,600			Jupiter		30,600	
Cash	45,400		32,600	Cash		90,000	
	76,000	163,100	35,500		76,000	163,100	35,500

(d) Balance Sheet at 1 July 1984

	£	£
Fixed assets		
Freehold land and premises		120,000
Equipment		11,000
		131,000
Current assets		
Stock	26,000	
Debtors	6,100	
		32,100
		163,100
Less:		
Loan from Jupiter	30,600	
Bank loan	90,000	
		120,600
		42,500
Financed by:		
Capital account – Mars		42,500

The above balance sheet shows that the balance on the capital account of Mars represents his personal investment in the business; a substantial part of the firm's assets are financed by funds from outside sources.

Question 9.7

Trading and Profit and Loss Account for the year to 31 March 19X3

	£	£
Sales		150,000
Opening stock	30,000	
Purchases	110,000	
Goods lost	(700)	
Stock drawings	(340)	
Closing stock	(40,000)	
Cost of goods sold		98,960
Gross profit		51,040
Depreciation	1,500	
Wages (14,500 + 500)	15,000	
Rent (5,000 – 1,000)	4,000	
Expenses	3,000	
Heat and light	1,200	
Delivery	5,300	
		30,000
Net trading profit		21,040

	£	£
Appropriation:		
Interest on drawings:		
Bean		200
Stalk		300
		21,540
Salaries:		
Bean	2,000	
Stalk	4,000	
		6,000
		15,540
Interest:		
Bean	1,500	
Stalk	500	
		2,000
		13,540
Residue:		
Bean	6,770	
Stalk	6,770	
		13,540

Balance Sheet at 31 March 19X3

	£	£	£
Fixed assets			6,000
Less: Depreciation			1,500
			4,500
Current assets:			
Stock		40,000	
Debtors		14,000	
Debtor for goods lost		700	
Prepaid rent		1,000	
Cash		4,500	
		60,200	
Current liabilities:			
Creditors	11,500		
Accrued wages	500		
		12,000	
Working capital			48,200
			52,700

	£	£	£
	Bean	*Stalk*	
Capital	30,000	10,000	40,000
Current accounts:			
Balance 1 April 19X2	3,000	5,000	
Interest on drawings	(200)	(300)	
Drawings: Cash	(7,000)	(9,000)	
Stock	(340)	—	
Interest on capital	1,500	500	
Salaries	2,000	4,000	
Share of residue	6,770	6,770	
	5,730	6,970	12,700
			52,700

Question 10.1

(a) Profit and Loss Account

	19X0	*19X1*
	£000	*£000*
Gross profit	2,930	3,605
Less: Administration expenses	1,620	1,809
Selling costs	520	572
Distribution costs	140	164
Depreciation costs	250	300
	2,530	2,845
Net profit	400	760
Less: Proposed dividend	100	200
Transfer to general reserve	—	·500
	100	700
Retained profit for the year	300	60
Add: Retained profit at 1 January	290	590
Retained profit at 31 December	590	650

Balance Sheet at 31 December

	19X0		*19X1*	
	£000	*£000*	*£000*	*£000*
Plant and machinery at cost		1,840		2,650
Less: Depreciation		520		820
		1,320		1,830

Current assets:	£000	£000	£000	£000
Stock	724		771	
Debtors	570		524	
Bank	92		305	
	1,386		1,600	
Current liabilities:				
Creditors	416		480	
Dividend	100		200	
	516		680	
Working capital		870		920
		2,190		2,750
Financed by:				
Share capital		1,600		1,600
General reserve		—		500
Profit and loss account		590		650
		2,190		2,750

(b) The revised accounts show that the *retained* profit is much lower in 19X1, but the *net* profit earned is almost twice as high as in 19X0. The draft accounts do not distinguish between *charges* against profit and *appropriations* of profit, and the revised accounts show that the lower retained profit is principally due to the large transfer to general reserve that was not made in the previous year. The fact that profits have substantially increased fully justifies the directors' decision to increase the dividend to £200,000. A further point that should be considered is whether there is sufficient cash available to finance the proposed distribution. However, there is £305,000 in the bank account and this suggests that the company will have no difficulty in meeting the dividend payment when it falls due.

Question 10.3

(a) Accounting bases is the term used, in SSAP 2, to describe the various methods that have been developed for valuing assets and liabilities. For example, the alternative bases available to account for the decline in value of fixed assets include reducing balance basis, straight-line and the units of service method.

Accounting policies is the term used to describe the particular accounting bases adopted by a company for the purpose of valuing assets and liabilities when preparing the accounts. The policies adopted must be described by the company in its report. The accounting policies used by a company must be consistent with the following four fundamental accounting concepts:

(i)   *The going concern concept*, which assumes that the company will continue in business for the foreseeable future. The main significance of this assumption is that the liquidation values of fixed assets can be ignored and it is instead assumed that the company will remain in business long enough to enable the resources tied up in fixed assets to be fully recovered.

(ii) *The accruals concept* requires revenues and expenses to be reported in the periodic profit and loss account as they are earned and incurred rather than when the amounts of cash are received and paid.

(iii) *The consistency concept* requires the company to employ the same accounting policy for valuing a particular asset in each consecutive accounting period. The purpose of this is to enable comparisons to be made.

(iv) *The concept of prudence* stipulates that a company should not take credit for profits before they are earned but should make provision for all foreseeable losses.

An accounting policy such as the reducing balance basis conforms to each of the four fundamental concepts. It spreads the cost of the fixed asset, over a number of accounting periods, on the assumption that the company will continue indefinitely as a going concern. It allocates the cost of the fixed asset less residual value between accounting procedures based on benefits received. This achieves compliance with both the accruals concept and the consistency concept. Compliance with the prudence concept is also assured because, by the time the asset is written off, all foreseeable losses are provided for.

(b) Compliance with the requirements of SSAP 2 goes a long way towards ensuring that the published accounts show a true and fair view. There are, however, other matters that require attention in the case of a limited company. It is necessary for the directors to take steps to ensure that there is compliance with the Companies Act 1985 and the many other SSAPs and *FRSs* issued by the accounting profession. In the case of quoted companies, there are further stock exchange rules that have to be satisfied, for example, the obligation to publish interim accounting statements. These regulations are useful because they ensure an adequate level of disclosure, comparability between accounting periods and comparability between one company and another.

It is, of course, important for the directors to ensure that their company's accounts portray a true and fair view, because a reputation for openness and frankness is likely to make it easier to raise the finance needed to carry on business operations. At the same time, it is necessary to guard against the possibility of the directors manipulating the accounts in order to make the company appear a more attractive proposition than is justified by the underlying commercial performance. It is for this reason that the Companies Act makes provision for appointment of independent auditors to report whether the accounts prepared and presented to the shareholders and filed with the Registrar of Companies portray a true and fair view.

Question 10.5 The purpose of the bonus issue is to give formal acknowledgement to the fact that profits, retained by the directors in previous years, have been permanently invested in business assets and no longer remain available for distribution. At 31 March 19X6 the company has cash available of £268,000, of which £75,000 is required to finance the proposed dividend, and £120,000 is needed to pay for the plant recently purchased. This leaves a modest balance to meet operating expenses. It is therefore clear that the company has no surplus cash resources, and it was therefore perfectly reasonable to capitalize the bulk of the retained profits. It is possible to argue that a smaller bonus issue might have been made some years earlier, but certain formalities are involved and it is not a process management will wish to undertake on a regular basis.

Question 10.7

(a) **Profit and Loss Appropriation Account year to 31 December 1992**

	£000	£000
Net trading profit		350
Less: Preference dividend	44	
Ordinary dividend	75	
Transfer to general reserves	200	319
Retained profit for the year		31
Retained earnings at 1 Jan. 1992		444 W1
Retained earnings at 31 Dec. 1992		475

(b) **Balance Sheet as at 31 December 1992**

	£000	£000
Fixed assets		2,300
Investment in: Yalsat plc		825 W2
Oviedo plc		320
		3,445
Current assets	1,705 W3	
Current liabilities	625 W4	
Net current assets		1,080
		4,525
Ordinary shares		1,500
Convertible stock		250
11 % preference shares		400
Share premium account		1,100
General reserve		800
Retained earnings		475
		4,525

W1 £750,000 – [£350,000 (profit for year) – £44,000 (preferred dividend paid)].
W2 £700,000 + £125,000.
W3 £1,900,000 – [£125,000 (W5) + £70,000 (W6)].
W4 £550,000 + £75,000.
W5 50,000 × £2.50 = £125,000.

	£
W6 Shares acquired valued at	320,000
Less: Convertible stock	250,000
	70,000

(c) Where a company exerts effective control over the affairs of another company –
such as will be the case where it owns more than 50 per cent of the voting share
capital of the other company – the first company is called the 'holding company'
and the second company is called the 'subsidiary'.

Both Yelstet and Oviedo appear to be subsidiaries because Lander owns more
than 50 per cent of the ordinary share capital in each case, i.e. 57.1 per cent for Yelstet and 53.3 per cent for Oviedo.

Yelstet (400,000/700,000) × 100 = 57.1%.
Oviedo 320,000/(400,000 + 200,000) = 53.3%.

(d) Prior to the share issues, Lander owned 50 per cent of the share capital of Yelstet and none of the shares in Oviedo. The result of the share acquisitions is that Lander now has voting control and will be in a position to appoint directors to the board of each company and control their financial and operating policies.

It is difficult to be precise concerning the advantages accruing to Lander due to the fact that we are not told what products they deal in. If all three companies are in the same line of business, there will be the possibility of benefiting from economies of scale and dividing up the potential market, which includes the European Community, between the three companies in the most efficient manner. It may alternatively be the case that the acquisition will enable Lander to safeguard sources of supply or consumer outlets as a result of vertical integration.

Question 11.1

Manufacturing, Trading and Profit and Loss Account for the year to 31 March 19X6

		£	£	£
Raw materials:	Opening stock		12,000	
	Purchases		40,000	
			52,000	
	Closing stock		(14,000)	
	Consumed		38,000	
Production wages			30,000	
			68,000	
Depreciation			7,000	
Rent			4,800	
Light, heat and power			9,000	
Overheads			17,500	
			106,300	
Work-in-progress	at 1 April X5		2,000	
			108,300	
	at 31 March X6		(7,000)	
Manufacturing cost of goods completed			101,300	
Manufacturing profit (15% of total cost)			15,195	
Transfer to trading account			116,495	
Sales				208,000
Finished goods:	Stock at 1 April X5		11,500	
	Transfers		116,495	
			127,995	
	Stock at 31 March X6		(13,800)	
				114,195

	£	£	£
Gross profit on trading			93,805
Manufacturing profit			15,195
			———
Carried forward			109,000
Administration expenses:			
Rent	1,600		
Light, heat and power	3,000		
Expenses	7,500		
Salaries	15,000		
Hire of equipment	7,000		
Postage and telephone	5,350		
	———		
		39,450	
Finance costs:			
Bank charges	1,250		
Loan interest	3,000		
	———		
		4,250	
Delivery costs:			
Van hire	2,000		
Wages	7,000		
Petrol, etc.	1,000		
	———		
		10,000	
Adjustment for unrealized profit (W1)		300	
		———	
			54,000
			———
Net profit			55,000
			———

Balance Sheet at 31 March 19X6

	£	£	£
Fixed assets at cost			70,000
Less: Accumulated depreciation			21,000
			———
			49,000
Current assets			
Stocks: Raw materials		14,000	
Work-in-progress		7,000	
Finished goods (W1)		12,000	
		———	
		33,000	
Debtors		20,000	
		———	
		53,000	
Current liabilities			
Overdraft	10,000		
Creditors	5,000		
	———		
		15,000	
		———	
Working capital			38,000
			———
			87,000
			———

	£	£	£
Financed by:			
Capital at 1 April 19X5			50,000
Profit for year			55,000
			105,000
Less: Drawings			48,000
Capital at 31 March 19X6			57,000
Loan			30,000
			87,000

W1   The transfer price of stock is 115 per cent of its cost. To convert it to cost, it must be multiplied by 100/115, i.e.

$$£13,800 \times 100/115 = £12,000$$

The unrealized profit in closing stock is £13,800 – £12,000 = £1,800.
The required adjustment to the provision is £1,800 – £1,500 (opening balance) = £300

Question 11.3

Hire Purchase Trading and Profit and Loss Account for 19X5

	£	£
Cash received		33,600
Cost of sales:		
VCs (250 × 96)	24,000	
EPs (200 × 144)	28,800	
	52,800	
Less: Stock held by HP debtors (W1)	33,600	
		19,200
Gross profit		14,400
Expenses (1,980 + 460)	2,440	
Bank interest	1,086	
		3,526
Net profit		10,874

Balance Sheet 31 December 19X5

	£			£
Stock with HP debtors	33,600	(W1)	Capital at start	10,000
Stocks held			Add profit	10,874
VCs	4,800			
EPs	7,200	12,000		20,874
			Less: Drawings	3,500
				17,374

		£	
Current liabilities			
VCs	4,800		
Expenses	460		
Bank overdraft	22,966	28,226	

45,600	45,600

Workings

W1   Stock with HP debtors   *Vacuum cleaners*   *Electric polishers*

			Vacuum cleaners	Electric polishers
C	= Cost of goods sold	=	24,000	28,800
S	= Total selling price	= $250 \times 168 =$	42,000	$200 \times 252 =$ 50,400
	Cash collected		21,000	12,600
I	= Instalments due in future accounting periods		21,000	37,800
V	= Stock out on HP =			

$$\frac{I}{S} \times C = \quad \frac{21,000}{42,000} \times 24,000 = \underline{12,000} \qquad \frac{37,800}{50,400} \times 28,800 = \underline{21,600}$$

	Total
Vacuum cleaners	12,000
Electric polishers	21,600
	£33,600

Question 11.5

(a) **Bank Account**

	£		£
Capital	50,000	Purchases (W2)	72,664
Sales (W1)	86,019	Expenses (W3)	12,976
Sellup's debtors	2,740	Purchase of business	40,000
		Paid to Sellup	2,610
		Closing balance	10,509
	138,759		138,759

(b) Trading and Profit and Loss Account 19X3

	£	£
Sales		92,968
Cost of sales		71,034
Gross profit		21,934
Expenses	13,168	
Depreciation	395	
		13,563
Net profit		8,371

Balance Sheet at 31 December 19X3

	£	£	£
Fixed assets			
Freehold land and buildings			22,100
Motor vans		1,975	
Less: Depreciation		395	
			1,580
Goodwill (W4)			6,933
			30,613
Current assets			
Stock		15,594	
Debtors		6,949	
Bank		10,509	
		33,052	
Current liabilities			
Purchases	4,972		
Expenses	192		
Sellup (2,740–2,610)	130		
		5,294	
Working capital			27,758
			58,371
Financed by:			
Capital			
Balance at 1 January			50,000
Profit			8,371
			58,371

Workings

W1 Cash from sales	£	W2 Cash to suppliers	£
Sales	92,968	Cost of sales	71,034
Less: Closing debtors	6,949	Plus: Closing stock	15,594
		Less: Opening stock	(8,992)
	86,019		
		Purchases	77,636
		Less: Closing creditors	4,972
			72,664

W3 Cash for expenses	£
Cost of expenses	13,168
Less: Closing creditor	192
	12,976

W4 Goodwill	£	£
Purchase price		40,000
Assets taken over:		
Freehold land	22,100	
Motor van	1,975	
Stock	8,992	
		33,067
		6,933

Question 11.7

	£
Sales (W1)	137,000
Gross profit (25% × 137,000)	34,250
Cost of goods sold	102,750
Opening stock	66,000
Purchases (W2)	64,800
Closing stock (balancing figure)	(28,050)
	102,750
Theoretical closing stock	28,050
Undamaged stock	18,000
Stock lost	10,050

Workings

W1 Sales	£	W2 Purchases for resale	£
Cash from debtors	97,000	Cash paid	68,000
Discounts allowed	1,000	Discounts received	400
Closing debtors	57,000	Closing creditors	39,000
Opening debtors	(54,000)	Opening creditors	(42,000)
Cash sales	36,000	Drawings	(600)
	137,000		64,800

Question 11.9

List of errors:

1. The cash sales of £235 should be entered as

$$\text{Sales } 235 \times 100/117.5 = 200$$
$$\text{VAT } 235 \times 17.5/117.5 = 35$$

2. The cheque for £60 paid to A. Young represents 90 per cent of the value of the invoice. Therefore, the discount is $60 \times 10/90 = £6.67$.
3. The cash received from A. Berry is 90 per cent of £450 = £405. £405 should be entered in the bank column.
4. The cash sales of £470 should be entered as

$$\text{Sales } 470 \times 100/117.5 = 400$$
$$\text{VAT } 470 \times 17.5/117.5 = 70$$

5. The cheque for £171 received from E. Ferguson has been wrongly entered as £117.
6. The bank charges of £45 have been entered as a receipt; they should appear in the bank column on the payments side of the account. (Note that the bank refers to the charges as a debit as, from the bank's point of view, it reduces the amount of money in Crowther's account.)
7. The discount columns are wrongly headed. Discounts allowed should be on the debit side (left) and discounts received on the credit side (right).
8. The discount and VAT columns should not be balanced; the totals should be posted to accounts in the nominal ledger.
9. Crowther must ensure that the amounts recorded in the nominal ledger in respect of sales and costs are *net* of VAT. For example, the telephone bill should be recorded as a cost of £86 and recoverable VAT of £16. It is not clear that the method of writing up the cash book will achieve this.

Question 12.1

A useful starting-point when answering this type of question is to prepare a work-sheet which shows the differences between the closing and opening balance sheet and lists them according to whether they represent an inflow or outflow of cash. For this question, the worksheet appears as follows:

Worksheet

	19X1 £	19X1 £	19X2 £	19X2 £	Differences Inflow £	Differences Outflow £
Fixed assets						
Plant at cost	52,000		70,000			18,000
Less: Depreciation	16,500	35,500	22,700	47,300	6,200	
Transport at cost	10,000		10,000			
Less: Depreciation	3,600	6,400	4,800	5,200	1,200	
		41,900		52,500		
Current assets:						
Stocks	10,200		12,600			2,400
Debtors	8,300		13,700			5,400
Bank	4,900		—		4,900	
	23,400		26,300			

	£	£	£	£	£	£
Less: Current liabilities						
Trade creditors	5,100		5,800		700	
Bank overdraft	—		1,300		1,300	
	5,100		7,100			
Working capital		18,300		19,200		
		60,200		71,700		
Financed by:						
Share capital		50,000		54,000	4,000	
Profit and loss account		10,200		17,700	7,500	
		60,200		71,700	25,800	25,800

Cash Flow Statement for 19X2

	£
Net cash flow from operating activities (Note 1)	7,800
Returns on investment and servicing of finance	—
Taxation	—
Investing activities	(18,000)
Financing	4,000
Increase (decrease) in cash	(6,200)

Note 1
Net cash flow from operating activities

Profit	7,500
Depreciation	7,400
Increase in stock	(2,400)
Increase in debtors	(5,400)
Increase in creditors	700
	7,800

Question 12.3

Cash Flow Statement for the year to 31 March 19X1

	£	£
Net cash flow from operating activities (Note 1)		284,200
Returns on investment and servicing of finance		(50,000)
Taxation		—
Investing activities:		
Sale of plant and equipment	169,500	
Purchase of property	(50,000)	
Purchase of plant and equipment	(528,600)	
		(409,100)
Financing:		
Issue of debentures		100,000
Increase (decrease) in cash		(74,900)

Note 1
Net cash flow from operating activities

Profit	191,300	(W1)
Depreciation	295,600	(W1)
Loss on sale of fixed asset	33,000	(W2)
Increase in stock	(281,200)	
Increase in debtors	17,800	
Increase in creditors	27,700	
	284,200	

Workings
W1

	Plant £	Depreciation £	Profit £
Net increase (worksheet)	138,600	108,100	31,300
Add: Sale of plant	390,000	187,500 *	
Proposed dividend			60,000
Bonus issue			100,000†
Gross changes	528,600	295,600	191,300

Notes
* Accumulated depreciation £187,500 = Cost, £390,000 – Book value, £202,500.
† The bonus issue is a book entry and does not result in a flow of funds. It must therefore be added back to profit so that cash generated from operations is stated correctly and so that the increase in share capital does *not* appear as a source of funds.
W2 Loss on sale, £33,000 = £202,500 (Book value of plant sold) – £169,500 (Sales proceeds).

Question 12.5

(a) **Reconciliation of operating profit to net cash inflow from operating activities**

	£000
Operating profit	1,363
Depreciation of fixed assets	152
Amortization of goodwill	34
Sale of tangible fixed assets	(29)
Increase in stocks	(572)
Increase in debtors	(342)
Increase in trade creditors	44
	650

(b) **Cash Flow Statement**

	£000	£000
Net cash flows from operating activities		650
Returns on investment and servicing of finance		
Interest paid	180	
Dividend paid	219	
Net cash flow from returns on investment and servicing of finance		(399)
Taxation		
Mainstream corporation tax		(255)
Tax paid		
Investing activities		
Payments to acquire tangible fixed assets	1,314	
Acquisition of brands	300	
Receipts from sale of tangible fixed assets	(131)	
Net cash outflow from investing activities		(1,483)
Net cash flow before financing		(1,487)
Financing		
Issue of shares	1,733	
Redemption of debentures and other loans	(102)	
Net cash flow from financing		1,631
Increase in cash		144

(c)

	£000	
Cash from sales	5,864	(W1)
Purchase of raw materials and consumables	(3,460)	(W2)
Staff costs	(609)	
Other operating charges	(1,145)	(W3)
Cash flow	650	

Workings (£000)

W1 Cash from sales:
6,206 (profit and loss) – 1,690 (closing debtors) + 1,348 (opening debtors).

W2 Purchase of raw materials and consumables:
2,932 (profit and loss) – 351 (closing creditors) + 307 (opening creditors) – 2,261 (opening stock) + 2,833 (closing stock).

W3 Other operating charges:
1,150 (profit and loss) – 34 (amortization of goodwill) + 29 (profit on sale of fixed assets).

- The purpose of the cash flow statement is to highlight the significant components of cash flow, while a standardized format facilitates comparison of cash flow performance with other businesses.
- The reconciliation shows that the bulk of cash from operations has been used to finance an increased investment in stock and debtors.

- A further £399,000 has been absorbed in paying out cash returns on share and loan capital.
- Approximately the remainder of the cash flow from operations has been used to pay the previous year's mainstream corporation tax charge.
- The company has made a substantial investment in new fixed assets and in the acquisition of brands. This has produced a net cash outflow before financing of £1,487,000.
- The company has funded the net cash outflow by making a large issue of shares which has been sufficient to cover that outflow and also enabled the cash balance to increase by £144,000.

Question 13.1

(a) Gross profit margin
$$\frac{54,000}{180,000} \times 100 = 30\%$$

Net profit as a % of sales
$$\frac{15,000}{180,000} \times 100 = 8.3\%$$

Return on capital employed
$$\frac{15,000}{150,000} \times 100 = 10\%$$

(b) An increase in the ROCE to 12.5 per cent would require additional profit of £150,000 × 2.5% = £3,750. The gross profit margin is 30 per cent and an additional turnover of £3,750 × (100 ÷ 30) = £12,500 would produce the required increase in net profit.

Question 13.3

(a)

	19X1			19X2		
Return on capital employed	$\frac{200}{700}$	x 100	28.6%	$\frac{250}{720}$	x 100	34.7%
Working capital			200			170
Working capital ratio	$\frac{300}{100}$	: 1	3:1	$\frac{350}{180}$	: 1	1.9:1
Liquidity ratio	$\frac{125 + 25}{100}$	: 1	1.5:1	$\frac{150}{180}$	: 1	0.8:1

Workings

Balance Sheet, 31 December

		19X1		19X2	
		£000	£000	£000	£000
Fixed assets			500		550
Current assets:	Stock	150		200	
	Trade debtors	125		150	
	Cash at bank	25		—	
		300		350	
Less: Current liabilities:	Trade creditors	80		100	
	Proposed dividend	20		60	
	Overdraft	—		20	
		100		180	
Working capital			200		170
Shareholders' equity (capital employed)			700		720

Profit and Loss Account

		19X1		19X2	
Sales			2,000		3,000
Less:	Cost of sales	1,000		1,450	
	Overhead costs	800	1,800	1,300	2,750
Net Profit			200		250

(b) Lock Ltd earned a high rate of return on the shareholders' investment during 19X1, which has been improved on during 19X2. The balance sheet, at 31 December 19X1, shows a strong financial position with the working capital and liquidity ratios each at a high level for a wholesale trading company. There has been a significant decline in the solvency position during the year. The ratios suggest that the company will find it difficult to meet its debts as they fall due for payment. The proposal to pay a final dividend three times last year's level may need to be reconsidered.

Question 13.5

(a) **Trading and Profit and Loss Accounts for 19X5**

		Metalmax		Precision Products	
		£000	£000	£000	£000
Sales			800		950
Less:	Variable cost of sales	640		760	
	Depreciation	54		54	
Cost of sales			694		814
Gross profit			106		136
Less:	Administration expenses	30		30	
	Selling expenses	45	75	60	90
Net profit			31		46

Balance Sheets at 31 December 19X5

	Metalmax		Precision Products	
	£000	£000	£000	£000
Plant and machinery at cost		360		360
Less: Depreciation		164		164
		196		196
Current assets				
Stocks and work-in-progress	120		200	
Other current assets	120		200	
	240		400	
Less: Current liabilities	120		320	
Working capital		120		80
		316		276
Share capital		200		200
Reserves		116		76
		316		276

(b)

Accounting ratios	Metalmax	Precision Products
Gross profit margin	13.3%	14.3%
Net profit percentage	3.9%	4.8%
Return on total capital employed	7.1%	7.7%
Return on owners' equity	9.8%	16.7%
Working capital ratio	2:1	1.25:1
Liquidity ratio	1:1	0.6:1

Metalmax is the more solvent whereas Precision Products is the more profitable.

Variable cost of sales is 80 per cent in the case of both companies. Precision Products produces the higher gross profit margin because, on the basis of an identical investment in fixed assets, it produces a significantly higher level of sales. The selling expenses of Precision Products are much higher, perhaps due to the fact that they advertise their products more heavily and distribute them more widely. However, the company retains its advantage and achieves the higher net profit margin. The rates of return on both versions of capital employed are higher at Precision Products. The difference is substantial in the case of return on owners' equity. This is because a large proportion of Precision Products' current assets are funded out of the 'free' finance provided by trade creditors. The consequence of this, however, is that Precision Products' solvency position, at the end of 19X5, is extremely weak. Metalmax, with a working capital ratio and liquidity ratio in line with conventional 'norms', is in a sound financial condition.

Question 13.7

(a) Cash Flow Statement for 19X8

	£000	£000
Net cash flow from operating activities (Note 1)		(10)
Returns on investment and servicing of finance		
Interest received	20	
Dividends paid (W1)	(400)	
Net cash flow		(380)
Investing activities		
Payments to buy fixed assets	(410)	
Receipts from sale of fixed assets	130	
		(280)
Net cash outflow before financing		(670)
Financing		
Issuing of shares (500 + 200)	700	
Long-term loan	300	
		1,000
Increase in deposits at bank		330

Note 1
Reconciliation of operating profit to net cash inflow from operating activities:

	£000
Operating profit	700
Depreciation charge	350
Increase in stocks	(1,220)
Increase in debtors	(40)
Increase in trade creditors	200
	(10)

(b)

Accounting ratios	19X7	19X8
Working capital	2:1	3.1:1
Liquidity	1:1	1.2:1

The financial position at the end of 19X7 appears satisfactory when judged on the basis of relevant accounting ratios. The liquidity ratio is 1:1 and the working capital ratio is 2:1, both of which are about right for an engineering firm. At the end of 19X1, the working capital appears to be too high and the company is verging on excess liquidity.

The statement of funds show that the company both raised and generated long-term funds significantly in excess of present business requirements. Funds generated from operations more than cover the dividend and plant acquisition, yet the company has issued shares, raised a loan and benefited from the sale of investments. A great deal of the surplus finance is tied up in stocks; a non-income producing asset. The company's system of stock control should be examined to check whether it is being operated efficiently.

The effect of financial developments during 19X8 is a very strong financial position at the end of the year, but there is some doubt whether available resources are being effectively employed. Perhaps additional resources have been raised to finance *future* expansion, but there is no indication that this is the case.

Question 13.9

(a)

			1991	1992
Creditor days:	Cost of goods sold		60	67
	Opening stock		(11)	(9)
	Closing stock		9	12
	Purchases		58	70
	Creditors		12	12
			$(12/58) \times 365$ = 76 days	$(12/70) \times 365$ = 63 days
Debt equity ratio:	Debt		45	90
	Equity		108	158
	Ratio		$45/108 = 42\%$	$90/158 = 57\%$
Debtor days:	Sales		100	110
	Debtors		24	18
			$(24/100) \times 365$ = 88 days	$(18/110) \times 365$ = 60 days
EPS:	Profit after tax		7	6
	Shares in issue		120	180
	Ratio		$7/120 = 5.8p$	$6/180 = 3.3p$
Interest cover:	Interest		5	9
	Profit before interest		15	17
	Cover		$15/5 = 3$ times	$17/9 = 1.9$ times
Liquid ratio:	Debtors		24	18
	Creditors		12	12
	Overdraft		5	6
	Dividend due		6	6
	Tax payable		3	2
			26	26
	Ratio		$24/26 = 1:0.92$	$18/26 = 1:0.69$
Operating profit % of sales:		Sales	100	110
		Operating profit	15	17
		Ratio	$15/100 = 15.0\%$	$17/110 = 15.4\%$
Return on equity:	Profit after tax		7	6
	Equity		108	158
	Ratio		$7/108 = 6.5\%$	$6/158 = 3.8\%$

		1991	1992
Sales % of capital employed:			
	Sales	100	110
	Capital employed		
	(Fixed assets + working capital)	153	248
	Ratio	100/153 = 65%	110/248 = 44%
Stock turnover:	Closing stock	9	12
	Cost of goods sold	60	67
	Rate of turnover	60/9 = 6.7 times	67/12 = 5.6 times

(b)

(i)   The shareholders are interested in how well their investment is performing and so would be interested in the *earnings per share ratio* and the *return on equity*. In general, they would look for as high a figure as possible for both EPS and return on equity, preferably as part of a rising trend.

(ii) Management should aim to maximize sales per £ invested, which is monitored by the ratio of *sales as a percentage of capital employed*. Once sales are made, as much profit should be sought from each £ of sales as possible, and so management should monitor the ratio of *operating profit as a percentage of sales*.

(iii) Suppliers of stock on credit want to be sure that they will be paid; once they are sure of this, the next consideration is to be paid as quickly as possible. The *liquidity ratio* indicates the likelihood of being paid, while the *creditor days* shows on average how long they have to wait.

(iv) Debenture holders want to be sure that the company can meet the interest, and this is shown by the *interest cover*. Companies that are highly geared are riskier than those which have low gearing, and so a second ratio of interest to the debenture holders is the *gearing ratio*.

Question 14.1

Rock Ltd – forecast results for additional sales

	(i)		(ii)		(iii)	
Proposal						
Additional sales (in units)	25,000	50,000	25,000	50,000	25,000	50,000
Process X						
Materials	5,000	10,000				
Wages	7,500	15,000	80p x	80p x		
Depreciation	12,000	12,000	25,000	50,000		
Rent	8,000	8,000				
To process Y	32,500	45,000	20,000	40,000		
					180p x	180p x
Process Y					25,000	50,000
Materials	2,500	5,000	2,500	5,000		
Wages	10,000	20,000	10,000	20,000		
Depreciation	12,000	12,000	12,000	12,000		
Rent	8,000	8,000	8,000	8,000		
Cost of production	65,000	90,000	52,500	85,000	45,000	90,000
General expenses	2,000	4,000	2,000	4,000	2,000	4,000
Net profit (loss)	(17,000)	6,000	(4,500)	11,000	3,000	6,000
Sales	50,000	100,000	50,000	100,000	50,000	100,000

Question 14.3

(a) Overhead Analysis Sheet

Type of expenses	Basis of apportionment	Total £	Dept. XX £	Dept. YY £	Stores £
Rent and rates	Floor area	81,000	26,129	19,597	35,274
Power	Cubic capacity	23,200	6,725	4,833	11,642
Heat and light	Cubic capacity	11,740	3,403	2,446	5,891
Salaries and wages	No. of employees	196,300	139,373	33,371	23,556
Ins. and deprec'n					
Buildings	Floor area	14,850	4,790	3,593	6,467
Machinery	Value	28,750	5,500	21,000	2,250
Office equipment	Floor area	5,000	1,613	1,210	2,177
Misc. expenses	Equally	2,190	730	730	730
		363,030	188,263	86,780	87,987
Salaries and wages		337,240	128,640	64,185	144,415
Misc. expenses		24,860	12,210	6,875	5,775
Recharge	Share requisition		119,088	119,089	(238,177)
		725,130	448,201	276,929	

(b) Overhead recovery rate:

Dept XX: £448, 201/121,620 (labour hours) = £3.69 per labour hour
Dept YY: = £276, 929/46,000 (machine hours) = £6.02 per machine hour

(c)

	XX	YY
Labour hours per unit 121,620/162,160	0.75	
Machine hours per unit 46,000/322,000		0.143
Units	162,160	322,000
	£	£
Direct wages	891,880	144,900
Direct material	2,043,216	5,924,800
Direct cost	2,935,096	6,069,700
Direct cost per unit	18.10	18.85
Overhead cost per unit		
£3.69 × 0.75	2.77	
£6.02 × 0.143		0.86
Other costs and profit	1.80	1.80
Selling price	22.67	21.51

Question 14.5

Workings

	Output = 0	Output = 100,000
19X4		
Revenue	0	£500,000
Variable cost	0	£300,000
Fixed cost	£100,000	£100,000
Total cost	£100,000	£400,000
19X5		
Revenue	0	£450,000
Variable cost	0	£200,000
Fixed cost	£180,000	£180,000
Total cost	£180,000	£380,000

£000

Revenue 19X4
Revenue 19X5
Total cost 19X4
Total cost 19X5

Fixed cost 19X5

Fixed cost 19X4

Units (000)

Break-
even
point
19X4

Break-
even
point
19X5

Question 14.7 (£000)

(a) Payback period: Zero 1.75 years
                       Nemo 2.75 years

(b) Average annual profit: Zero (140 – 80)/4   = 15
                             Nemo (160 – 90)/4 = 17.5
    Average capital employed: Zero 80/2   = 40
                               Nemo 90/2   = 45
    ROCE: Zero 15/40   = 37.5%
            Nemo 17.5/45 = 38.9%

(c)

	20% discount factor	Project Zero Cash flow	Project Zero Present value	Project Nemo Cash flow	Project Nemo Present value
Year 1	0.833	50	41.65	30	24.99
2	0.694	40	27.76	30	20.82
3	0.579	30	17.37	40	23.16
4	0.482	20	9.64	60	28.92
			96.42		97.89
Less: Initial investment			80.00		90.00
NPV			16.42		7.89

(d) Profitability index: Zero 96.42/80   = 1.21
                          Nemo 97.89/90 = 1.09

(e) Zero has a better payback period, NPV and profitability index, while Nemo gives a better return on capital employed. These results are consistent with the fact that Nemo's cash flow increases towards the end of its life, and these flows are given less weight by the former methods of appraisal. Zero appears to be the better investment.

Question 14.9

Forecast Trading and Profit and Loss Account

	£	£
Sales (W2)		72,000
Less: Cost of goods sold (W3)		48,000
Gross profit		24,000
Expenses (W1)	4,800	
Loan interest (.5 × 8,000 × 10%)	400	
Overdraft interest	300	
Depreciation (.5 × 20,000 × 20%)	2,000	
		7,500
Net profit		16,500

Forecast Balance Sheet

	£	£
Fixed assets		
Cost		20,000
Less: Depreciation		2,000
		18,000
Current assets		
Stock (W3)	8,000	
Debtors (May + June sales)	24,000	
Cash (W1)	1,600	
	33,600	
Current liabilities		
Trade creditors (June purchases)	8,000	
Accrued interest	300	
	8,300	
Working capital		25,300
		43,300

	£	£
Capital		
Capital introduced		20,000
Profit		16,500
		36,500
Less: Drawings (W1)		1,200
Closing capital		35,300
Loan		8,000
		43,300

Workings

W1 Forecast cash account produced by adding across the individual columns in the solution in Question 11.7.

Cash Account

	£		£
Capital	20,000	Plant	20,000
Loan	8,000	Creditors	48,000
Debtors	48,000	Expenses	4,800
		Drawings	1,200
		Loan interest	400
		Balance c/d	1,600
	76,000		76,000

W2 Sales can be calculated in two alternative ways:

(a) Sales = Cash from debtors + Closing debtors*
    = £48,000 (W1) + £24,000 (May + June sales) = £72,000

or

(b) £12,000 (monthly sales) × 6 (number of months) = £72,000

W3 Cost of goods sold
Purchases can be calculated in two alternative ways:

(a) Purchases = Payments to creditors + closing creditors*
               = £48,000 (W1) + £8,000 (June purchases) = £56,000

or

(b) £16,000 (January purchases) + (5 × £8,000) = £56,000

$$\text{Cost of goods sold} = \text{Purchases} - \text{Closing stock*}$$
$$= £56,000 - £8,000† = £48,000$$

Note
* As this is the first period of trading, there are no opening debtors, creditors or stocks.
†

	7y£
Purchases	56,000
Less: Cost of goods sold:	
$\frac{100}{150} \times £72,000$ (sales)	48,000
Closing stock	8,000

Question 14.11

(a) Cash flow forecast for the six months to 31 May 1994

	Dec. £000	Jan. £000	Feb. £000	March £000	April £000	May £000
Cash in						
Sales	384	410	290	364	392	440
Loan						350
	384	410	290	364	392	790
Cash out						
Creditors	297	205	224	236	249	273
Accruals	11					
Wages and salaries	43	43	43	43	43	43
Overheads	14	14	14	14	14	14
Equipment						360
	365	262	281	293	306	690
Summary						
Opening balance	27	46	194	203	274	360
Cash in	384	410	290	364	392	790
Less: Cash out	(365)	(262)	(281)	(293)	(306)	(690)
Closing balance	46	194	203	274	360	460

(b) The company's bank balance, if the loan is not raised, will be £460,000 – £350,000 = £110,000. This is a very healthy balance and so, unless the company has other anticipated commitments, the loan is not required.

(c) Profit and Loss Account for the six months to 31 May 1994

	£000
Sales	2,380
Less: Cost of sales (2,380/2)	1,190
Gross profit	1,190
Overheads (71 × 6)	426
Net profit	764

Question 15.1

(a) Production Budget, March–June 1992

	Units
March	190
April	200
May	180
June	230

Cash Budget, March–June 1992

	March £	April £	May £	June £
Sales: Cash	2,520	2,660	2,380	3,220
Credit	7,560	7,560	7,980	7,140
	10,080	10,220	10,360	10,360
Opening balance	6,000	6,000	6,640	6,060
Materials: Cash	1,710	1,800	1,620	2,070
Credit	1,620	1,710	1,800	1,620
Wages	2,470	2,600	2,340	2,990
Fixed and variable:				
2/5	1,140	1,200	1,080	1,380
3/5	1,620	1,710	1,800	1,620
Debenture interest				400
Fixed assets		1,470	570	
Corporation tax			1,085	
Rent		1,220		
Bank interest	50	50	55	51
	16,080	16,860	16,420	16,191
Closing balance	6,000	6,640	6,060	5,831

(b) Possible ways of reducing the bank overdraft are as follows:

- Reduce the amount of credit allowed to customers. Over £7,000 is owed throughout the four-month period and if customers could be persuaded to pay immediately without any adverse effect on the level of sales, the overdraft could be repaid.
- Arrange a longer period of credit from suppliers. If all suppliers allowed one month's credit, creditors outstanding would increase by approximately £1,800 and the bank overdraft reduced by an equivalent amount.
- Similar considerations apply in the case of fixed and variable expenses, which would reduce the overdraft by approximately a further £1,200.
- Make arrangements to purchase fixed assets on hire purchase rather than for cash. In this case the overdraft would be reduced by £2,040, less any HP instalments paid in the four-month period.

Question 15.3

(a) **Budgeted Trading Profit and Loss Account and Appropriation Account year to 31 October 1994**

	£000	£000
Sales		1,600
Cost of goods sold (68%)		1,088
Gross profit (32%)		512
Administration costs (5%)		80
Selling and distribution costs (3.5%)		56
Bad debts (£150,000 × 15%) − £10,000		12.5
Depreciation £150,000 + (£750,000 × 10%)		225
Financial charges		10
		383.5
Net profit		128.5
Dividends: Ordinary 3p × 800,000	24	
Preference	5.5	29.5
Retained profit for year		99
Retained profit brought forward		700
		799
Transfer to general reserve		300
Retained profit carried forward		499

(b) **Budgeted Balance Sheet as at 31 October 1994**

	£000	£000
Land and buildings at valuation		200
Other fixed assets at cost	750	
Less: Aggregate depreciation	305	445
		645
Current assets		
Stock		290
Trade debtors		150
Less: Provision		22.5
Balance at bank		127.5
		760.5
		1,178

	£000	£000
Current liabilities		
Trade creditors		97
Expense creditors		17
		114
Net current assets		1,064
		1,709
Ordinary share capital		600
11% preference shares		50
Share premium £200,000 + (15p × 400,000)		260
General reserve		300
Retained profit		499
		1,709

(c) The most noticeable feature of the forecast current assets is the massive balance of cash at bank, which amounts to £760,500. This seems substantially in excess of operating requirements and could be utilized to improve profitability in the following ways:

- Repay the 11 per cent preference shares and avoid the preference dividend of £5,500 per annum.
- Explore remunerative ways of investing surplus cash available. Possibilities include the acquisition of income-producing securities or shares in another company.

There has also been a significant increase in stocks and debtors and steps should be taken to see whether these can be reduced generating further cash available for investment.

Question 15.5

(a)

Material cost variance =		
(£2.20 × 6,400) – (£2 × 6,000 [W1]) =	2,080	(U)
Material usage variance =		
(6,400 – 6,000 [W1]) £2	800	(U)
Material price variance =		
(£2.20 – £2) 6,400	1,280	(U)

W1 3 kilos × 2,000

Labour cost variance =		
(4.10 × 1,800) – (£4 × 2,000)	620	(F)
Labour efficiency variance =		
(1,800 – 2,000) £4	800	(F)
Labour rate variance =		
(£4.10 – £4) 1,800	180	(U)

(b) The labour rate variance is favourable and possible reasons include

- employing the wrong (lower) grade of labour; and
- wage increases lower than anticipated due to ineffective trade union action.

The labour efficiency variance is unfavourable and possible reasons include

- inadequate training of employees;
- dissatisfaction among the workforce; and
- poor working conditions, for example inadequate ventilation.

(c) A system of standard costing makes use of predetermined standard costs relating to each element of cost (labour, material and overhead) for each type of product manufactured or services supplied. The actual costs incurred are then compared with standard costs as work proceeds. The difference between actual and standard is termed the *variance* and these are analysed to help identify the reason for the variance so that inefficiencies may immediately be brought to the attention of the responsible managers and corrective action taken.

(d) A system of standard costing is useful to management for the following reasons:

- The installation of a system of standard costing requires the company to review existing practices and this often results in substantial improvements being made.
- Standard costs are a more meaningful yardstick than the alternatives, which are to compare results with those of a previous year or a different company.
- Variances are quickly identified enabling corrective action to be taken before further losses are unnecessarily incurred.
- There is a saving in management time in that attention is focused on problem areas.
- The system identifies areas of achievement as well as difficulty, and draws management's attention to areas of success which the company may be able to exploit more fully.
- The system promotes cost consciousness; individuals know that standards have been set and financial results of their work are under scrutiny.

INDEX